KIERKEGAARD

AND THE SELF

BEFORE GOD

INDIANA SERIES IN THE PHILOSOPHY OF RELIGION
Merold Westphal, editor

KIERKEGAARD

AND THE SELF

BEFORE GOD

Anatomy of the Abyss

SIMON D. PODMORE

INDIANA UNIVERSITY PRESS

Bloomington and Indianapolis

This book is a publication of

Indiana University Press
601 North Morton Street
Bloomington, Indiana 47404-3797 USA

www.iupress.indiana.edu

Telephone orders	800-842-6796
Fax orders	812-855-7931
Orders by e-mail	iuporder@indiana.edu

∞ The paper used in this publication meets the minimum requirements of
the American National Standard for Information Sciences—Permanence of Paper
for Printed Library Materials, ANSI Z39.48-1992.

Manufactured in the United States of America

LIBRARY OF CONGRESS CATALOGING-IN-PUBLICATION DATA

Podmore, Simon D., [date]
    Kierkegaard and the self before God : anatomy of the abyss / Simon D. Podmore.
    p.   cm. — (Indiana series in the philosophy of religion)
    Includes bibliographical references and index.
    ISBN 978-0-253-35586-7 (cloth : alk. paper) — ISBN 978-0-253-22282-4
(pbk. : alk. paper) 1. Kierkegaard, Søren, 1813–1855. 2. Self—Religious aspects—
Christianity. I. Title.
    B4378.S4P63 2011
    230'.044092—dc22   2010024964

1 2 3 4 5 16 15 14 13 12 11

TO KEITH, EDITH, AND JONATHAN

One must obtain forgiveness for every essay in theology. In all senses.

—JEAN-LUC MARION, *God Without Being*

The joy in the thought that before God a man is always in the wrong.

—SØREN KIERKEGAARD, *Gospel of Sufferings*

CONTENTS

PREFACE

> *. . . but what madness, when he who himself has lost the eternal wants to heal him who is at the extremity of sickness unto death.*
>
> —*Works of Love*

I wish to begin by confessing that this project commenced under the belief that the meaning of Kierkegaard's "infinite, radical, qualitative difference" (*uendelig svælgende qualitativ Foskjel*) between humanity and God was essentially *sin*. Mercifully, it concluded with the conviction that the true meaning of the infinite qualitative difference between God and humanity is expressed through *forgiveness*. The former approach would result in a theological madness: a "loss of the eternal"—to adopt Kierkegaard's warning—in which the abyss itself threatens to become all-consuming. This trajectory would further corroborate the suspicion, shared by many philosophers and theologians, that Kierkegaard provides a detailed cartography of the abyss without showing any exit from it. My initial suspicion that Kierkegaard's God was ultimately a God of despair was itself merely an echo of the discomfort that many readers of his work have felt before. Such a misgiving has found one of its most influential expressions in Karl Barth's warning that those who remain within Kierkegaard's schema have been consumed by it: Kierkegaard's "infinite qualitative difference between God and man, with all its consequences, has eaten itself right into them."[1]

This Barthian sense of ambivalence toward the melancholy Dane has never been far away during this project. That said, it is notable that this oft-repeated legend for Kierkegaard—"the melancholy Dane"—represents a perception that only sees half the face, as it were, of one of modern theology and philosophy's most insightful exponents of the *triumph of faith over despair*. The phrase itself derives from P. T. Forsyth's 1910 book, *The Work of Christ*, and Forsyth's full expression is "the great and melancholy Dane in whom Hamlet was mastered by Christ."[2] Unfortunately, as with much relating to Kierkegaard, the darker aspect has prevailed and the second part of Forsyth's "dialectic," which redeems Kierkegaard from the melancholy of the first, fades, unheeded, into obscurity.

Despite frequently acting the apologist for Kierkegaard, it cannot be denied that one must first enter into the darkness of the abyss in his writings before one can discover the light of forgiveness that shines through them. It just so happens that on first glance at Kierkegaard's corpus, a certain darkness glimmers more brightly than the divine light he seeks. Reading his dramatic evocations of melancholy and despair in particular, it can be tempting to echo William Blake's assessment of Milton's *Paradise Lost*: "The reason Milton wrote in fetters when he wrote of Angels & God, and at liberty when of Devils & Hell, is because he was a true Poet, and of the Devil's party without knowing it."[3] But this would be a great injustice to Kierkegaard, in whom the Romantic impulse toward demonic heroism is recognized as a hubristic despair which—as Forsyth himself recognized—must be mastered by the grace of divine forgiveness. It is because he intimately knew the bitter waters of religious melancholy that Kierkegaard is so adept at evoking the unconditional love of God without subsequently undermining the human pathos of despair. What he endured spiritually—admittedly, partly because of his "crazy upbringing" and partly due to unhealthy self-mortification—would have consigned many to the nihilism of a final despair. But Kierkegaard was able to derive hope by showing in his writings how despair (Dn. *Fortvivelse*) is born from doubt (*tvivl*), and therefore how its spell can be broken by faith in forgiveness and the love of God.

By making the transition from a reading of the "infinite qualitative difference" as *sin* to a reading of the infinite qualitative difference as *forgiveness,* the process of research, reflection, and writing has in one significant regard reflected the *metanoia* of the "self before God" that I have sought to elucidate in Kierkegaard's writings. The endeavor to exist as a self before God— *coram Deo,* according to Martin Luther's earlier formulation—begins with an initial sense of abyssal estrangement: the consciousness of an impasse that separates humanity from divinity. The difference between self and God— and therefore the source of the self's estrangement from knowledge of its own true self—is firstly sensed as an irreconcilable chasm whose darkness is inhabited by despair. The God before whom one strives to stand initially appears to be an onerous and dark infinity; and in the infinite space that separates the self from God (and thus from itself) lies what appears to be an unfathomable and vertiginous abyss of sin and alienation. What is more, the gaze of the self cannot, of its own willing, penetrate this abyss. But the longer one remains with the abyss the more one's eyes become accustomed to its darkness and the more one may begin to discern a *beyond* to the fear and trembling of apparent divine abandonment. There is a mystery in this abyss, and the great *mysterium* of the abyss is divine forgiveness. The self's own self-searching gaze is lost in the swarming darkness of the abyss; and so the self must see itself *through the gaze of the Other*: it becomes known to itself relationally, through the forgiving gaze of the divine.

But this theological reading of the "self before God" requires a preliminary disclaimer: this work is not a straightforward attempt to determine definitively what Kierkegaard's personal conception of the self was. Such an endeavor is inevitably subverted to some extent by Kierkegaard himself—by the "indirect communication" of his authorship, by his hiding the secret heart of Søren Kierkegaard among the various alter egos of his creation. Therefore, as regards his pseudonymity (or polynymity), I generally heed what Kierkegaard in 1846 declared to be "my wish, my prayer": he asks others to cite "the respective pseudonymous author's name, not mine."[4]

So I seek to explore and develop a contemporary theological reading of the theme of the "self before God" as defined by way of the category of "infinite qualitative difference" in Kierkegaard's writings, without forcing this reading directly into Kierkegaard's "hand." Consistent with the perspective of a personal journey toward self-knowledge, the "hiddenness" of Kierkegaard forces the reader to confront their own hiddenness. Hence Kierkegaard frequently encourages his reader to read his works aloud to themselves, so as to efface the authority of the author and discover a personal address to one's own hidden self that is contained within the act of reading. While this has proven amenable to poststructuralist receptions,[5] it should also be noted that there are theological and pastoral motives and precedents for such an approach. The hidden and the revealed reside at the heart of all theological endeavor. The central tenet of the hiddenness of God disrupts human attempts to possess certain knowledge of God-in-Godself, turning us instead toward an anthropocentric reflection on knowing God in relation to ourselves. This implies not only the subjectivity of faith, but also the subjectivity of reading. As Kierkegaard himself noted in 1851's aptly titled *For Self-Examination,* perhaps the most potent disruption of objective reading and the subsequent existential assertion of *metanoia* is exemplified by the moment of self-recognition—"the transition to the subjective" (FSE, 38)—that David realized in his confrontation with the prophet Nathan: "Thou art the man!" (2 Samuel 12:7).

But once again, this is not a work about reading Kierkegaard; nor a work about how Kierkegaard should be read. It is a work that proposes a reading of Kierkegaard which, by exploring the relation between two hitherto underexamined themes in his writings, seeks to construct a theological account of the "self before God" that passes through the problems of despair, anxiety, melancholy, the "death of God," and the "death of self." But this work does not seek to evade the charge that the search for "the self" is often a dubious, vain, or narcissistic enterprise, destined to suffer from its own futility and hubris. On the contrary, it is my contention that Kierkegaard's writings contain some of the most valuable and insightful expressions of *abortive attempts at self-knowledge* in modern Western theology, philosophy, and literature. Kierkegaard's writings *transcribe* the failure of the modern self, and *identify* this failure to transmute primal anxiety into faithful religious selfhood as despair in its various guises. Situated firmly within the milieu of modernity, the idiom that Kierkegaard expresses is that of selfhood or the "self." However, as Kierkegaard's (consciously anachronistic) rehabilitation of older religious notions such as *desperatio, praesumptio, Anfechtung,* etc., demonstrates, modern humanity may still be in need of a physician of the *soul.* Although often expressed in modern forms of inauthenticity which are recognizable to even the most bourgeois reader, Kierkegaard is adept at penetrating the heart of the enigma of self-knowledge—an enigma that has recurred in various forms since the earliest Christian writings. In this regard, for example, Kierkegaard observes that the classical *acedia* ("carelessness") of the desert monastic anticipates and shares some of the pathos that is found in the *ennui* of modern aesthetes.

In one sense, Kierkegaard's works could be read as developing an *apophatic* or negative theological anthropology in which the failure of self-knowledge is evoked in order to unveil a *cataphatic,* or positive, truth of selfhood that cannot be attained by merely natural means. It is only through the mystery of the self's relation "before God" that the self can come to know itself. The self is revealed to itself in relation before God: the self learns to see itself through the eyes of God, not as an object of divine wrath, but as forgiven and accepted—a recipient of the divine gift of freedom and selfhood expressed through the "impossible" gift of the forgiveness of sins. And yet, in the endeavor to stand before God, the self is explicitly confronted by the fear and trembling of the infinite qualitative difference between humanity and divinity. It is at this point that the self must come to recognize its despair and, by acknowledging its own sinfulness, accept the "impossible" gift of forgiveness through which the self can become itself, and become free, *before God.*

It is this point that marks what is arguably Kierkegaard's most important contribution to theological anthropology. For all his illustrations of fallen, hubristic selfhood, despair, and self-deception, Kierkegaard conspicuously refuses to eliminate the modern idiom of selfhood—even though he is not averse to undermining many of its conceits, along with numerous other philosophical and theological categories of modernity. Nor does Kierkegaard reverse the modern quest for selfhood into a mystical negation or oceanic absorption of the self in God. God remains the Other—albeit, this work argues, the *Holy* Other that is revealed in forgiveness, rather than the *Wholly* Other that is primarily discerned through the consciousness of sin and despair. Despite the numerous dangers of self-delusion, Kierkegaard's writings leave the reader with the impression that it is not necessarily a mere modern hubris to wish to become a self, to earnestly strive to heed the old oracle: "Know thyself." In fact, it is a divine gift, an obligation of eternity and anxious freedom, to become oneself. The essential difference between the modern self and the "self before God" is that the self before God must behold itself in the divine "mirror of the Word" (JP 4:3902 / Pap. X⁴ A 412) rather than through the self-regarding gaze of a Narcissus. The error of non-relational modes of self-knowledge lies in the solipsistic or even demonic attempt to take hold of and define oneself through the sheer exertion of self-will. In Kierkegaard's works, God calls for the individual to become a relational self, a self that expresses its own God-given freedom; a self, or an "I," that is capable of loving God, the Absolute "Thou," in return. As such, Kierkegaard does not simply excoriate the self as a manifestation of hubristic will-to-power or as a modern conceit or philosophical construct. Instead he retains the idiom of the self as a means of expressing the modern Western form of the human drive for self-understanding, and rearticulates it, via the Christian narrative of sin and forgiveness, in its authentic theological relation *before God.*

It is perplexing why Kierkegaard's category of the "before God" has remained so under-examined, though some indication as to why this is so can be found in the under-recognized depths of its resemblance to Luther's notion of the individual *coram Deo.* Following the decline of the dialectical theologies of the early twentieth century—with their emphasis upon such Kierkegaardian-Lutheran themes as the infinite qualitative difference between man as sinner and God as Wholly Other—there has been conspicuous reserve concerning Kierkegaard's influence by Luther.⁶ Indeed, an avowedly "contemporary application" of Kierkegaard's thought has explicitly announced a desire to "loosen the thread of Kierkegaard's Lutheran straitjacket."⁷ This polemic may seem strange given M. Jamie Ferreira's recent observation that "the more general question of Kierkegaard's relation both to Luther's thought and to the Lutheranism of his day is an important one and awaits comprehensive treatment."⁸ There are notable exceptions to the recent lack of recognition given to Lutheran themes in Kierkegaard, and I know of several doctoral theses recently written or being written around this subject. But the present work is not one of those that is principally concerned with Kierkegaard's admittedly often highly ambivalent relation to Luther.⁹ This work does, however, give prominence to the recognition of the Lutheran resonances in Kierkegaard's notion of "before God" and the "spiritual trial"

(Dn. *Anfægtelse*)[10] evoked by the infinite qualitative difference in particular. In this reading, it is Kierkegaard's overarching and similarly under-examined notion of the "infinite qualitative difference" that I take as the hermeneutical key to unlocking the apparent impasse of the self before God. In this way, I address the questions: how the self can be known in *relation* to a divine other who is infinitely qualitatively *different* from itself? And how can one stand *before* God when there is an infinite abyss *between* self and the divine? In attempting to resolve these central questions, I argue that the true expression of the infinite qualitative difference is found, not in the self's initial sense of sin and estrangement, but in the Holy *mysterium* of forgiveness. And as such, I maintain that the key to understanding this (implicitly Lutheran) transition from the consciousness of sin to the acceptance of forgiveness is also the key to the abyss.[11]

Kierkegaard's writings provide an outline of a theological anthropology of the self before God; but it is a vision that requires better contemporary elucidation than would be provided by a retrospective of Luther. As such, I read Kierkegaard's works in relation to a broader Judeo-Christian theological tradition that describes a disruption and healing of personhood via a theology of sin and forgiveness and which, in turn, establishes itself upon the otherness and holiness of God. This notion of "otherness" through "holiness" evokes another category which is of great importance to this present study: Rudolf Otto's theological category of the numinous. For reasons that will be examined in chapter 4, the affiliation of Otto and Kierkegaard may seem surprising and lacking in precedents. However, through the course of this work, I hope to demonstrate how Otto's sense of the numinous as *mysterium tremendum et fascinans* and the self-abnegation of "creature-feeling" can supplement and articulate, along explicitly theological lines, a Kierkegaardian vision of the infinite qualitative difference and the self before God.

As outlined below, the central elements of melancholy, anxiety, despair, and spiritual trial also emerge from particular traditions and cultural milieus in Western philosophy and theology—particularly the historically contingent sense of religious loss and divine hiddenness. It is not my aim to universalize this narrow and harrowing path to faith via despair, but rather hopefully to illuminate a particular dark journey of the self to God, narrated by way of the theological terms of sin and forgiveness. The spirit of the Talmudic dictum, "We do not see things as they are; we see them as we are," holds particularly true in relation to the abyss of objective uncertainty in which, according to Kierkegaard's aphorism, faith swims out over 70,000 fathoms. This is also the abyss in which there is a hidden joy: in which the gaze of the self seeks to penetrate the darkness and behold itself within the mirror of God.

The theme of Kierkegaard's infinite qualitative difference between humanity and God—in both its negative and positive connotations—is employed throughout as the prime hermeneutical key through which to explore a Kierkegaardian vision of the self before God. Both the "infinite qualitative difference" and the "self before God" remain fundamental but under-examined themes in Kierkegaard's thought—themes that have not, as yet, received comprehensive treatment. It is this deficit that the present work aims to go some way toward rectifying.

In the present work, a perennial question of the relation between knowledge of self and knowledge of God is explored expressly via the evocative and often equivocal motif of "the abyss." Within these pages, "the abyss" in question is taken as evoking, in general terms, the post/modern crises of self-knowledge and divine knowledge in Western philosophy and theology, while referring, in specific terms, to Kierkegaard's category of the infinite qualitative difference between humanity and God. The abyss thus provides an evocative and fertile metaphor for the epistemological and existential struggle of the self before God. As such, the often disorientating metaphor of the abyss is frequently used as a stand-in for ineffability: it designates an area of preliminary unknowing, of darkness and opacity. But more than that, the metaphor of the abyss denotes the existential and psychological anxiety evoked by the loss of grounding, by separation and estrangement from a distant Absolute that lies beyond its shores.

Beneath the expansive banner of Kierkegaard's infinite qualitative difference lie other thematic expressions of the divine-human difference that are central to Kierkegaard's notion of the journey to selfhood: namely melancholy, anxiety, despair, and the frequently overlooked notion of spiritual trial (Dn. *Anfægtelse*).[12] These themes facilitate an anthropocentric consideration of the consciousness of sin and express the external and internal rupture that sin causes for the task of becoming a self. Through consideration of these overlapping themes, I explore how selfhood is not only problematized by the consciousness of sin, but also by the difficulty in accepting the "impossible possibility" of divine forgiveness. As the work proceeds, it is the emerging theme of forgiveness and its relation to the consciousness of sin that becomes the key to the abyss and the gift of the self before God.

The emergence of divine forgiveness as a means of saving the self from despair inevitably conveys something decisive about the loving nature of God as perceived from the human side of the God-relationship. As such, I explore the proposition that the Wholly Otherness of God is best expressed through a theology of the forgiveness of sins, rather than being articulated solely by way of self-accusation and the consciousness of sin. Essentially, the former perspective (forgiveness) delivers the self from the potential *mysterium horrendum* of the latter perspective (sin, despair). In this sense, I question the assumption that the "Wholly Other" is appropriate as a final designation for God in Kierkegaard's writings. By moving from the despairing consciousness of sin to the acceptance of the *Holy* otherness of forgiveness, we come toward a more theologically "apposite" reflection of the infinite qualitative difference than sin and the Wholly Other can provide. When the name of the "Wholly Other" is applied to God solely from the perspective of sin, we risk being left with the remote God of despair rather than the intimate God of faith. Forgiveness is thus viewed as the means by which the estrangement of the infinite qualitative difference between self and God is reconciled and transformed into the relational possibility of the self before God. The consciousness of sin is, in this schema, a vital step on the road to faith. However, when despair of/over sin occludes the divine light of forgiveness, the self remains trapped in its "inclosing reserve" and God remains identified as the Wholly Other before whose wrathful gaze none can stand. True repentance and reconciliation of the abyss is discovered in faith's acceptance of forgiveness, since the acceptance of forgiveness recognizes how morbid self-accusation can itself signify a final narcissistic grasp at the self—an attempt to "know thyself" internally through the consciousness of sin rather than through the relational endeavor to become a self before God.

SCOPE

Engaging with the themes of the self before God and the infinite qualitative difference, this work is based upon Kierkegaard's authorship as a whole, although greater attention is inevitably given to more avowedly religious works and works in which the theme of selfhood is more explicit. As such, *The Sickness unto Death* from the crucial biographical period of 1848–1849 is undoubtedly the most significant single text for the argument.[13] However, I have endeavored to trace the central themes throughout Kierkegaard's authorship, and hopefully I have been sufficiently vigilant against the temptation to homogenize Kierkegaard's works via these themes. Nonetheless, I have found Kierkegaard's writings—signed, pseudonymous, editorial, and personal—to be strikingly consistent with regard to the categories of the infinite qualitative difference and the self "before God." As with the notions of anxiety and despair in particular, Kierkegaard appears to have attempted to remain fairly consistent with these terms throughout his authorship. This commitment to "consistency" is evidenced by instances of cross-referencing between pseud-onyms with regard to important themes and concepts.[14] However, this is not to say that Kierkegaard's works provide a finished or comprehensively sys-tematic theology of the self before God. This is neither Kierkegaard's method nor his aim. Viewed as a whole, Kierkegaard's works are frequently too frag-mentary, poetic, or ironic to provide a theology that does not require further explication and consolidation. Nonetheless, his works provide a wealth of thematic inspiration, tone, and insight into the psychology of faith which can be successfully applied to contemporary theological anthropology. It is in lieu of any single comprehensive work by Kierkegaard or his interpreters on the notions of "before God" and the "infinite qualitative difference" that the present work aims to articulate a Kierkegaardian theological anthropology of the self before God.

Rather than being a straightforward interpretation of Kierkegaard, how-ever, this book is intended to be an original theological development that employs Kierkegaard's works in order to introduce and explore the theme of the self before God in relation to a theology of the forgiveness of sins and the *Holy* otherness of God. As well as drawing out these themes in Kierke-gaard's writings, the vision of the self presented herein is supplemented, but hopefully not distorted, by being placed in dialogue with the theological and philosophical contributions to the question of the self-God relation from such relevant figures as Augustine, Luther, John of the Cross, Hegel, Feuer-bach, Barth, Otto, Levinas, and Derrida. In particular, I have sought to give a broader and more thorough theological grounding to this Kierkegaardian vision of the self before God through reading and applying the insights of Rudolf Otto's notion of the numinous and the reflections on various forms of spiritual anxiety, melancholy, and despair in Christian mysticism and the Lutheran notion of spiritual trial (Gn. *Anfechtung*). As such, in addition to exploring themes in Kierkegaard's writings, this work also contains extended treatments of such figures as Augustine, Luther, and Otto on the relation between self-knowledge and knowledge of God. Some of the thinkers that Kierkegaard is placed alongside are here examined in this context or in such detail for the first time in English-language Kierkegaard research. As such, it is also hoped that this book will stimulate further debate on the continuing relevance of its themes.

The themes of the work are further elucidated through imaginative theo-logical reflection on particularly resonant biblical motifs such as the revela-tion at the burning bush (Exodus 3), Jacob wrestling with the stranger (Gen-esis 32), Isaiah's vision of the throne of God (Isaiah 6), and Christ's passion at Gethsemane (Matthew 26 and parallels). These motifs are read as allegories for the themes of knowing God (Exodus 3), the struggle for recognition between self and God (Genesis 32), the numinous (Isaiah 6), and spiritual trial (Genesis 32; Isaiah 6; Matthew 26).

I have also sought to describe the wider historical developments of the themes of selfhood and religious melancholy in Western thought. By doing so, I hope to indicate the historical contexts of contemporary debates and how these ongoing debates reflect and continue aporias that derive from a long and expressive genealogy. Accessing major themes in modern and contemporary philosophy and theology—illustrating these themes through biblical, cultural, and literary motifs—I hope to identify analogies to key debates that predate the modern era. As such, I relate modern debates on melancholy, anxiety, and despair to previous theological treatments of *acedia, Anfechtung,* and *desperatio.* Such an approach is, I suggest, consistent with Kierkegaard's own method of approaching the modern manifestation of despair and selfhood from within an established theological tradition of sin and salvation. This approach is particularly evident in Kierkegaard's own attempts to rehabilitate—via the "older and better devotional literature" (JP 4:4384 / Pap. XI² A 132)—the spiritual pathos of spiritual trial within the "spiritless" ambience of modernity. Indeed, the very idiom "before God" derives from the Lutheran endeavor to exist *coram Deo,* and Kierkegaard's adjunct of the term "self" signifies an attempt to rehabilitate older theological truths without undermining orthodox biblical Christianity (as he perceived Hegelianism to be doing), while at the same time speaking within and critiquing the lexicon of modernity.

CLARIFICATIONS: KNOWLEDGE OF SELF AND GOD

Although, in Kierkegaardian terms, the self can only become "transparent" to itself in relation *before God,* it should be maintained that the human self is not a straightforward analogue of the divine "self." In fact, Kierkegaard is emphatic here: "There is only One who completely knows himself, who in himself knows what he himself is—that is God. And he also knows what each human being in himself is, because he is that only by being before God."[15] God alone knows what God is and who each individual truly is. The self-knowledge of every individual is therefore only attainable before God; but knowing oneself before God is not tantamount to "knowing what God is in Godself."[16] From the perspective of the infinite qualitative difference, any anthropomorphic projection of self-knowledge into the metaphysical or divine realm would fail to amount to knowledge of Godself. God-in-Godself remains unknown and inaccessible to metaphysical reasoning alone. The infinite qualitative difference does not separate us from nothing, or from an infinitized/

divinized version of the self; it separates the self from the Holy Other. As such, in the course of this work I invoke Otto's notion of the numinous in order to further assert the *objective* reality and *otherness* of God, which the self must nonetheless come to terms with through the *subjective* and relational activity of becoming itself *before God*. In fact, from this perspective, it is the prior reality of God's otherness that actually forms the basis for the suspension of human ontotheological[17] claims about God. The otherness of God thus provides the basis for a theological distinction between *anthropomorphism* (the attribution of human characteristics to God) and *anthropocentrism* (a relational understanding of God within the limits of human perspective—as opposed to metaphysical interpretations of God-in-Godself). The infinite qualitative difference denies the possibility of anthropomorphic projection of a prior notion of the self onto "God." By denying the possibility of detached metaphysical speculation concerning God-in-Godself, it also asserts that our limited knowledge of God is anthropocentric: that is, known in relation to our (God-given, or *theocentric*) selves.

ORGANIZATION

Chapter 1 broaches our "anatomy of the abyss" by introducing the central hermeneutical theme of the infinite qualitative difference as it appears at various points throughout the course of Kierkegaard's authorship. It outlines the centrality of this divine-human *alterity* to Kierkegaard's descriptions of the self's relation to God, while also describing how the motif of "the abyss" (Dn. *Dyb / Afgrund*) in Kierkegaard's writings is employed to evoke depth, distance, and groundlessness, as well as pointing toward its evocative relation to the integral themes of the self, the Wholly Other, guilt, repentance, dizziness, nothingness, anxiety, despair, melancholy, and spiritual trial (*Anfægtelse*). This introductory chapter concludes by outlining the central principle of this work that the true meaning of Kierkegaard's "infinite qualitative difference" for the "self before God" is to be found *initially* through the consciousness of sin, but *ultimately* through the divine possibility of forgiveness.

Chapter 2 initially outlines a Kierkegaardian reading of "despair" as the failure of isolated modern self-authentication and eternity's primal obligation upon the individual to become a self "before God." This vision is placed in relation to a reading of the modern turn toward the "know thyself" and its arguably inevitable collapse into the postmodern "death of the self." The relation between the "death of the self" and the "death of God" is hence considered in critical relation to Kierkegaard's insistence upon the infinite qualitative difference between humanity and divinity: a difference that disrupts the possibility of both anthropocentric projection and ontological deductions concerning knowledge of God-in-Godself. In considering God in Kierkegaard's writings as initially Wholly Other, comparison is made with Jacques Derrida's influential reading of the wholly other as referring to the alterity of *every other*—a reading which is itself critiqued via Rudolf Otto's theological view of the Wholly Other as *mysterium tremendum et fascinans*. In doing so, I further explicate the central argument that the difference of sin is most appositely understood as "estrangement" between self and God; and that "forgiveness" expresses the transfigured and authentic meaning of the infinite qualitative abyss between humanity and God.

In chapter 3 the theme of melancholy, which has emerged in chapter 2, is elucidated as an existential response to the difference/distance between self and God and the characteristically modern turn inward in Kierkegaard's thought. The Kierkegaardian impulse toward a specifically *religious* melancholy is then traced and illustrated through the antecedent monastic notion of *acedia* ("carelessness") to the secularized boredom, or *ennui,* of the modern aesthete. By way of an anatomy of melancholy in Kierkegaard's writings, this chapter ultimately proposes a narrative progression of self-knowledge from the "aesthetic" to the "religious" which directs melancholy's disillusionment toward a curative awakening of religious longing within the self (articulated as the metamorphosis of *Ånd:* spirit). This melancholy is epitomized conceptually by the ambivalent desire to behold the face of God, though to see God means death—an anxiety which is acutely and lyrically expressed in Augustine and John of the Cross.

The elemental theme of melancholy, which chapter 3 discerned as a symptom of self-alienation and the modern loss of God, is further developed in chapter 4 with more explicit reference to the self's longing to stand before a God who appears—at least initially—as "Wholly Other" to itself. Here a religious melancholy is primarily characterized by a rise in the restless and antagonistic longing of "spirit"—a religious longing which the self is unable to consummate for itself. Ultimately I question the extent to which a theology of the Wholly Other (as epitomized by Rudolf Otto) effectively expresses a historically contingent response of a modern *horror vacui* (in this context the "empty space" created by a loss of the sacred) to the melancholy consciousness of a *deus otiosus* ("withdrawn god"). Ultimately, I argue that the Wholly Other, as read in both Kierkegaard and Otto, rather creates the space in which the gift of the self can be realized—albeit a self which, in fear and trembling, enters into an initially anxious struggle with the *mysterium tremendum*.

In chapter 5 we turn to the symbolic motif at the heart of our anatomy of the abyss, considering the image of Jacob's striving with the stranger

(Genesis 32) as an allegory for the anxiety and spiritual trial that is evoked by the endeavor to know oneself before God. As well as illustrating such anxiety, however, this allegory evokes the reconciliation of the self by gesturing toward the reception of the divine gift of a God who, by a giving of Godself in the relational tangibility of divine-human struggle, negates Wholly Otherness while also creating the relational space for the self to become itself *before God*. It is through Kierkegaard's notions of spiritual trial (*Anfægtelse:* a Danish cognate of the German *Anfechtung*) and the stigmatic motif of the "thorn in the flesh" that I proceed to discuss certain vertiginous descriptions of the anxiety of the God-relationship, the dangerous intoxication of the "imagination," and the analogy of the Kantian sublime—a category which, in the context of the self before God, I contend is more appropriately supplanted by Otto's theological category of the "numinous."

As the self's journey to know itself before God becomes increasingly "intensified," chapter 6 progresses to a more specific anatomy of Kierkegaard's decisive and under-examined dialectic of spiritual trial and its critical relation to the Lutheran tradition of *Anfechtung*. The essential difference between Kierkegaard and Luther at this point transpires in Kierkegaard's decision to situate the tension of spiritual trial between the self and God, rather than self and the devil. Both thinkers are, however, united in looking to the trial of Christ's God-forsakenness as exemplary for the individual's struggle with *Anfechtung*. It is here, when forgiveness and the love of God are themselves cast into doubt (*Tvivl*), that the struggle of prayer emerges as the means for the self to transcend the despair (*Fortvivlese*) over human *impossibility* through the leap of faith into divine *possibility:* namely, faith in the thought that for God all things are possible.

Chapter 7 constitutes both a reprise and a conclusion of the work's narrative vision of the self before God. In order to further illustrate and elucidate the theological anthropology explored in this study, I condense and focus the previous anatomization of the self's relation "before God" through an examination of the optical motif which suffuses the work. From this ocular perspective, the struggle of the self before God is appraised through a hermeneutic of "the gaze": the "gaze of the abyss" by which the self beholds the chasm of infinite difference; the internalized "gaze of despair" by which the self, in "offence" against its consciousness of sin and the apparent *impossibility* of forgiveness, severs itself from any relation to the other; and ultimately the downcast gaze which, in humility, manages to behold God—whom "none may see and live"—through the "eyes of faith" by which the self comes to accept the divine *possibility* of forgiveness. It is this final sense of the gaze that penetrates the darkness of the abyss and which allows the self to behold itself, reflected through the "divine mirror," as a forgiven and relational self becoming "transparent" (*gjennemsigtigt*: "see-through") to itself in freedom before God. The infinite qualitative difference is therefore defined in the preliminary terms of the consciousness of sin, and in ultimate terms, as the *mysterium* of the divine *possibility* of forgiveness. Finally, the chapter concludes with an exploration of how the self before God entails the Kierkegaardian paradox of "inverse resemblance" between the human self and God. This conclusion offers a transfigured reinterpretation of the motto which begins the first chapter of this work: "Precisely because there is the absolute difference between God and man, man expresses himself most perfectly when he absolutely expresses the difference" (CUP, 412).

The final chapter of the work is a reflection in which the ultimate meaning of the infinite qualitative difference as "forgiveness"—which constitutes the emerging central argument of this work—is employed as a lens through which to view the relation between being forgiven by God and the *im/possibility* of forgiving "the other." In this concluding exploration, the key notion of the "impossible possibility" of divine forgiveness is read as a model for the "suspension" of offence by which the self remains open to the possibility of forgiving the "unforgivable." This finally gives rise to the more expansive question of what it might mean for the self to "forgive God" in the struggle of faith. It is with this final, yet open and provocative question mark, that the work concludes.

ACKNOWLEDGMENTS

I was fortunate to have the wonderful guidance of Dr. Murray Rae, who managed to pull me out of the more abyssal moments of my research and writing and remains an inspiration to me. During my time at King's College the Research Institute in Systematic Theology was thriving under the leadership of the esteemed Prof. Colin Gunton. The passing of this great British theologian in May 2003 had an enormous impact on all of his colleagues and students, among whom I number myself.

I have been blessed by many great teachers in my life, the first among whom was David Harbertson who was an incredible embodiment of theological and philosophical education. As an undergraduate in theology at the University of St. Andrews, I became particularly indebted to Prof. Daphne Hampson and Prof. Alan Torrance, whose friendship and guidance I am proud to have to this day. The colorful world of Kierkegaard studies has afforded me many great friends, mentors, and colleagues. In particular I would like to thank Prof. Hugh Pyper, Prof. George Pattison, Dr. Leo Stan, The Søren Kierkegaard Society of the United Kingdom, and the late Roger Poole (1939–2003).

Much of the work for this book has been supported by visiting scholarships and a research fellowship at the Howard V. and Edna H. Hong Kierkegaard Library, St. Olaf College. I am grateful for the warmth and generosity of Prof. Howard Hong (1912–2010) and Edna Hong (1913–2007). All who pass through the Kierkegaard Library will also understand the extent of the gratitude that I extend to Prof. Gordon Marino and Cynthia Lund. I would also like to thank my colleagues and students at New College, University of Edinburgh, where I had the pleasure of being a Teaching Fellow in 2009–2010. I would like to thank Dee Mortensen and the series editor, Prof. Merold Westphal, along with the anonymous reviewers of this book at Indiana University Press for their encouragement and insight. Indiana University Press currently publish many of the finest works in the contemporary interface between philosophy and religion, and I am proud to have my own work in such company. David L. Dusenbury also did a superb job in copyediting the typescript. I am grateful for his significant literary and philosophical talent. Any awkward sentences that persist are due to my own stubbornness rather than any oversight by him.

Finally, I would like to thank the following, for reasons that go beyond what can be disclosed in this space: Katie Townend, Prof. Alex Marr, James Rankine, and, never to be forgotten, Sarah Walton.

ABBREVIATIONS

For works by Søren Kierkegaard
*(with pseudonyms and original Danish publication dates where relevant;
see bibliography for full details)*

AN   *Armed Neutrality and An Open Letter* [Posthumous 1880]

BA   *The Book on Adler* [Posthumous 1872]

CA   *The Concept of Anxiety* (Vigilius Haufniensis) [1844]

CD   *Christian Discourses, The Crisis and A Crisis in the Life of an
          Actress* [1848]

CI   *The Concept of Irony: With Constant Reference to Socrates*
          [Dissertation 1841]

CUP   *Concluding Unscientific Postscript* (Johannes Climacus) [1846]

E/O I–II *Either/Or*, 2 vols. ("A" and Judge William; ed. Victor Eremita)
          [1843]

EUD   *Eighteen Upbuilding Discourses* [1843–1844]

FSE   *For Self-Examination* [1851]

FT   *Fear and Trembling* (Johannes de Silentio) [1843]

JP   *Søren Kierkegaard's Journals and Papers*, 7 vols. (Followed by
          volume number and entry number: e.g., JP 2:1383. References
          to Alexander Dru's translation, *The Journals of Søren Kierkeg-
          aard—A Selection*, cite his pagination following his name.)

LW   *The Moment and Late Writings* [Articles published 1854–1855]

Pap.	*Papirer* (Followed by reference to volume, section, and number in standard Danish edition: e.g., Pap. X¹ A 59.)
PC	*Practice in Christianity* (Anti-Climacus; ed. Søren Kierkegaard) [1850]
PF	*Philosophical Fragments* (Johannes Climacus) [1844].
PV	*The Point of View for My Work as an Author* [Posthumous 1859]
R	*Repetition* (Constantin Constantius) [1843]
SLW	*Stages on Life's Way* (Judge William and Frater Taciturnus; published by Hilarius Bookbinder) [1845]
SUD	*The Sickness unto Death* (Anti-Climacus; ed. Søren Kierkegaard) [1849]
TA	*Two Ages: The Age of Revolution and The Present Age (A Literary Review)* [1846]
UDVS	*Upbuilding Discourses in Various Spirits* [1847]
WA	*Without Authority* [1849–1851]
WL	*Works of Love* [1847]

For other languages

Dn.	Danish
Gn.	German
Gr.	Greek
Heb.	Hebrew
Lat.	Latin

KIERKEGAARD

AND THE SELF

BEFORE GOD

ONE

Introduction

Anatomy of the Abyss

Precisely because there is the absolute difference between God and man, man expresses himself most perfectly when he absolutely expresses the difference.

—*Concluding Unscientific Postscript*

This striking assertion, from the pen of Kierkegaard and the perspective of Johannes Climacus, could be claimed as the sacred motto for the "anatomy of the abyss" that will follow in this work. Human nature, Johannes Climacus (and elsewhere Kierkegaard) claims, is most legitimately expressed through an absolute expression of our difference from the divine. In other words, it is by expressing its difference from God—this infinite qualitative abyss—that humanity will come to its most legitimate self-knowledge. As such, it is by way of an anatomy of this difference, or this abyss, that humanity will come to a deeper understanding of its own nature. But is this to say that self-knowledge is attained by expressing one's difference as nothing else but one's separation from God: as *sin*? Is it by expressing one's own sinfulness, one's utter darkness in contrast to the unequivocal light of the divine, that one comes to authentic self-knowledge? Are we then only known to ourselves as we express our irremediable *unholiness* before the Holy? Does humanity therefore only come to know itself truly through "fear and trembling," through melancholy and despair? How can one's nature be expressed via absolute difference? And how can one then come to know oneself in relation before the God who is Wholly Other? Such questions decisively shape and motivate the present exploration of the self before God.

In this work, I maintain that the Kierkegaardian notion of the self before God has its origins and expression in the infinite qualitative abyss between God and humanity and, as such, the answer to the foregoing questions resides in an exploration of the abyss as it pertains, not only to the *alterity* of human sinfulness, but also to the *mysterium* of divine forgiveness. Ultimately, this work will argue that it is the paradox of an "impossible" forgiveness which holds the key to the paradox that one will express one's own nature most adequately when one expresses this difference absolutely. However, prior to this "absurd" endeavor to unlock one paradox by another, it is necessary to introduce and outline one of the most enduring and under-examined themes in Kierkegaard's writings, and the hermeneutical key to this vision of the self before God—namely, the "infinite qualitative difference" between humanity and God.

Any attempt to explore Kierkegaard's writings in search of a theological anthropology will find itself on the edge of an abyss, and it is this Kierkegaardian motif of the "infinite qualitative difference" which I shall initially broach in its various permutations throughout Kierkegaard's works. The abyss which one inevitably gazes upon in Kierkegaard's writings cannot simply be subsumed under nothingness; it is not fundamentally a void, though at times it may resemble one and may at all times threaten to become one. This abyss may be spoken of as nothingness, as an absence; but it also designates a discernible, albeit infinite, space between humanity and God. For how could one anatomize nothingness? And, for that matter, why an *anatomy*? All anatomy involves a dissection (from the Gr. *anatome:* "dissection"), and dissection requires a cutting-apart (from the Lat. *dissecare:* "to cut into pieces"); hence the *severance* of the abyss is implied in its very anatomization—the infinite severance between God and humanity. This anatomy requires that one speak not only of divinity and humanity, but of the severance between them: divinity and humanity on two sides (as it were) of a chasm. But this anatomy of a "spacious nothingness" (to echo Augustine) is no detached science. Inescapably, it is a *self-examination* involving the "*autopsy* of faith" (PF, 70).

Although there is no unified concept of "the abyss" in Kierkegaard's writings, its image is one that Kierkegaard and his pseudonyms persistently evoke with stylistic flourish and existential pathos. The pseudonymous author of *Repetition* for example, Constantine Constantius, writes of "the abyss of anxiety" (R, 155)—a dictum which recalls the vertigo of anxiety's gaze into the abyss in Vigilius Haufniensis's *Concept of Anxiety:* "Anxiety may be compared with dizziness. He whose eye happens to look down into the yawning abyss [*svælgende Dyb*] becomes dizzy" (CA, 61).[1]

Despite this vertiginous horror, however, one who is "educated by anxiety" discovers what Haufniensis calls "Anxiety as Saving through Faith." Such a person, though they may sink in the abyss, in turn emerges "from the depth of the abyss [*Afgrundens Dyb*] lighter than all the troublesome and terrible things in life" (CA, 158). It is not the abyss that is dreadful in itself; more precisely it is in the *relation* of the individual to the abyss that anxiety is located. The dizziness of anxiety is essentially derived from the subject's *gaze* into the abyss. "But what is the reason [*Grunden:* 'the ground'] for this? It is as much in his own eye as in the abyss [*Afgrunden:* 'without-ground'], for suppose he had not looked down" (CA, 61).

As the above references to *The Concept of Anxiety* demonstrate, the English word "abyss" translates both the Danish *Dyb* and also the more horrifying *Afgrund* (literally "without-ground") in Kierkegaard's writings. While *Dyb* often denotes empty space or depth, *Afgrund* evokes the intangible and paradoxical presence of something exceeding mere "emptiness" (*Tomhed*). As such, "abyss" can refer not only to spatial separation but also to that which is *dramatically* groundless, bottomless, fathomless, inscrutable (*uudgrundelige*)—hence Johannes Climacus's invocation of the word when describing, in *Philosophical Fragments,* how "humanly speaking, consequences built upon a paradox are built upon the abyss [*Afgrund*]" (PF, 98). One may thus be tempted to suggest that *Afgrund* is employed to denote "groundlessness," while *Dyb* denotes "distance" or "severance." In the Christian discourse titled "The Joy of It: That One Suffers Only Once But Is Victorious Eternally," Kierkegaard explains how "just as there was a chasmic abyss [*svælgende Dyb*] between that rich man in hell and Lazarus in Abraham's bosom, so also there is a chasmic difference [*svælgende Forskjel*] between suffering and sin" (CD, 102–103). Yet when a more psychological phenomenon is to be described, the abyss is invoked as something horrifyingly "without-ground" (*Afgrund*). Hence, when implying the vanity of the maxim, "Let us eat and drink, because tomorrow we shall die" (1 Corinthians 15:32), Kierkegaard detects: "This very remark echoes with the anxiety about the next day, the day of annihilation, the anxiety that insanely is supposed to signify joy although it is a shriek from the abyss [*Afgrunden*]" ("The Care of Self-Torment," CD, 77). The *Afgrund* thus designates not only the vacuity and implicit despair of decadent or hedonistic indulgence, but also its inherent anxiety of non-being.

However, one must be careful not to infer too firm a distinction from what is also the poetic-rhetorical choice of a highly stylized author—hence Haufniensis's emphatic combination of both terms in evoking "the depth of the abyss" (*Afgrundens Dyb*) (CA, 158).[2] Kierkegaard writes in his discourse on "The Care of Loftiness": "The eminent pagan with his care belongs in the abyss [*Afgrund*]; he actually is not lofty but in the abyss [*Afgrund*]" (CD, 58). And yet this image is also developed spatially, according to a sense of untraversable distance: "Over this abyss [*Afgrund*] [of paganism] no bird could fly; it would have to perish on the way" (CD, 59). One may recall the elegiac lament of Kierkegaard's aesthete A when describing the abyss of his boredom in *Either/Or:* "My soul is like the Dead Sea, over which no bird is able to fly; when it has come midway, it sinks down, exhausted, to death and destruction" (E/O I, 37). Indeed it is the image of the sea—deep, dark, and boundless—that perhaps provides the consummate motif for the anxious abyss of existence. "Just as the shipwrecked person who saved himself by means of a plank and now, tossed by the waves and hovering over the abyss [*Afgrunden*] between life and death, strains his eyes for land, so indeed should a person be concerned about his salvation" ("We Are Closer to Salvation Now—Than When We Became Believers," CD, 220). Here one cannot help but invoke the abyss resounding in the evocative horror of what Kierkegaard identifies as "one of my favourite phrases, which is attributed to another author [viz. Frater Taciturnus]" (BA, 107–108):[3] that is, to be out over 70,000 fathoms of water in faith's struggle with inexorable objective uncertainty. And indeed, the abyss (*Dyb*) commonly refers to "the deep."

Kierkegaard's favored phrase encapsulates the anxious dual-nature of the human condition: "man is a synthesis of the temporal and of the eternal, every moment out upon '70,000 fathoms'" (JP 5:5792 / Pap. VI B 18). More specifically for Johannes Climacus, the phrase signifies "the martyrdom of believing against the understanding, the mortal danger of lying out on 70,000 fathoms of water, and only there finding God" (CUP 1:232). This suffering, which is the essential expression of the God-relationship, "is, to recall Frater Taciturnus's words, the 70,000 fathoms of water upon whose depths the religious person is continually" (CUP 1:288). It is Frater Taciturnus's "Letter to the Reader" in *Stages on Life's Way* that devises the term which so pleases Kierkegaard and his other pseudonymous conspirators: "Spiritual existence, especially the religious, is not easy; the believer continually lies out on the deep [*Dybet*], has 70,000 fathoms of water beneath him" (SLW, 444). And yet, despite this anxious abyss (*Dyb*), hovering over the deep (*Dybet*), repentance is itself an infinite opening of *possibility* in the religious life which is the pathway to salvation, "for repentance has specifically created a boundless space [*uendelig Plads*], and as a consequence the religious contradiction: simultaneously to be out on 70,000 fathoms of water and yet be joyful" (SLW, 477).

The "boundless space" of repentance (which, as will be explored later on, helps to clear an opening for the decisive "impossible possibility" of divine forgiveness) begins to convey the sense in which sin induces a profound severance between humanity and God—a rupture that also affects a related internal fracture within the self. Fundamentally, in the task of becoming a self before God, the decisive abyss that faces theological anthropology throughout the Kierkegaardian oeuvre is the insurmountable difference/distance between humanity and God which is initially diagnosed as *sin*. The god whom Johannes Climacus describes in *Philosophical Fragments* is decisively "absolutely different" (*absolut forskjelligt*) (PF, 46) from any person who may wish to relate to it. "What, then, is the difference?" Johannes ponders. "Indeed, what else but sin, since the difference, the absolute difference, must have been caused by the individual himself" (PF, 47). While Johannes Climacus is fond of reminding us that between God and humanity "there is an absolute difference" (CUP, 412), it is also an insistence he has in common with his "higher" namesake Anti-Climacus: "God and man are two qualities separated by an infinite qualitative difference [*uendelig Qualitets-Forskjel*]" (SUD, 126). Furthermore, at the risk of ostensibly homogenizing Kierkegaard's authorship according to this "qualitative difference," it must be emphasized that this idea is not exclusive to the Climacean works. For example, in *The Book on Adler* Kierkegaard asserts with his own hand how "between God and a human being there is an eternal essential qualitative difference [*evig væsentlig qualitativ Forskjel*]" (BA, 181). The difference is one which also presents itself in Kierkegaard's *Discourses*: for instance, "The Gospel of Sufferings" relates how the Christian knows that, as far as suffering is concerned, between God and every person there is "an eternal difference" (*evig Forskjel*) (UDVS, 287). This difference is described, variously, as "absolute" (*absolut*), "eternal" (*evig*), "essential" (*væsentlig*), "qualitative" (*qualitativ*), and "infinite" (*uendelig*). While each word in itself is far from synonymous with the others, there is a case to be made that these substitutions and embellishments represent stylistic permutations more than crucial deviations from the central idea of the abyss. This is not to say that Johannes Climacus's understanding of the "absolute difference" is identical with Anti-Climacus's understanding of the "infinite qualitative difference" (indeed, I intimate that the understanding of the former is not resolved to the same depth as the latter concerning the expression of the infinite qualitative difference through the forgiveness of sins).[4]

However, to infer too much from the choice of one word over another is the constant temptation of the non-native speaker—a particular danger in the case of so poetic and stylistic a writer as Kierkegaard. So, for instance, there is an insistent string of these words in Kierkegaard's *Journals* when describing "the law of the relations between God and man in the God-relationship": "There is an infinite, radical, qualitative difference [*uendelig svælgende qualitativ Foskjel*] between God and man" (JP 2:1383 / Pap. X¹ A 59). Added here is an instance of another deeply evocative adjective for this difference: "radical" (*svælgende*). The translation as "radical" does not fully convey the evocation of this word which, one might say, is decidedly abyssal. As the Danish word *slugt*—which denotes a "gorge"—is close to the verb *sluge*, "to swallow," so too can *svælg* denote "abyss" in a manner close to the verb *svælge*—also a verb for "swallowing." Hence, it might be more apt to talk about "an infinite, swallowing/yawning, qualitative difference" which threatens to devour the self. The benefit of suggesting this image is that it prompts the very anxiety of annihilation that is inherent to relating to a Wholly Other and concomitantly to oneself across such a yawning abyss (*et svælgende dyb*)—as is translated in the above reference from *The Concept of Anxiety*: "He whose eye happens to look down into the yawning abyss [*svælgende Dyb*] becomes dizzy" (CA, 61). Anti-Climacus also summons just this image when he writes in *The Sickness unto Death* of how: "As sinner, man is separated from God by the most chasmic qualitative abyss [*Qvalitetens meest svælgende Dyb*]" (SUD, 122).

In attempting to define one's existence *before God* one must come to terms with the abyssal distance which separates humanity from divinity. Any attempt to bring together those between whom there is such an abyss will inspire a vertigo of the understanding: "We warn the person who stands on a ship which ploughs ahead with the speed of the storm that he should not look into the waves, for he will become dizzy; thus does the comparison between the infinite and the finite make a man dizzy" (WL, 180).[5] It is across such a seemingly impassable abyss of sin that one must come to relate to God. It is not in attempting to possess myself, or to speculate upon God, that I become known as a self; it is first of all through coming to terms with the infinite difference—that is, the apprehension of the abyss itself as the consciousness of sin: "the yawning abyss [*svælgende Dyb*] is *here* where Christianity posits man's cognition as defective on account of sin, which is rectified in Christianity" (JP 3:3245 / Pap. I A 94).

But one must be careful not to become lost in looking down, for one will become dizzy; or, appropriating Friedrich Nietzsche's celebrated warning, "when you gaze long into an abyss, the abyss gazes also into you."[6] And yet, to a point, this is what Kierkegaard proposes *must be done* with much fear and trembling and spiritual trial. Nietzsche's philosophical anthropology itself evokes the abyss when he writes: "Man is a rope, tied between beast and overman [*Übermensch*]—a rope over an abyss [*Abgrund*: again, literally 'without-ground']."[7] The existential difference, according to Hoberman, is that "Nietzsche situates man over the abyss, while Kierkegaard situates the abyss within man."[8] This is true in relation to the internal vertigo of Kierkegaardian anxiety; but where the God-relation is concerned, Kierkegaard also inscribes the individual *over* "70,000 fathoms" of a deep that separates them from God, namely sin: an internal abyss which nevertheless severs one from an *other*. Authentic self-consciousness is contingent upon consciousness of God, or self before God; but this is itself only initiated through the consciousness of sin—the gaze of the abyss. But our gaze into the abyss, during which the abyss also penetrates the eye that looks into it, may become an entrapment of *self-reflection* that loses sight of the other (God) whom the abyss severs us from. Such abyssal guilt may come to signify "the demonic": what Vigilius Haufniensis calls "anxiety about the good" which is self-incarcerated in an "inclosing reserve" (*Indesluttethed*) (CA, 123). The task then is to break guilt out of its anxious self-communion with the abyss. But this hypnotic introversion is not easily ruptured, since: "Guilt has for the eye of the spirit the fascinating power of the serpent's glance" (CA, 103). Therefore the internal contemplation of the abyss of sin itself, the gaze of guilt, becomes a narcissistic dizziness. "The continuity that inclosing reserve has can best be compared with the dizziness a spinning top must have, which constantly revolves upon its own pivot" (CA, 130). One might call this the dizziness of the internal abyss—it is, in one sense, we ourselves who own this abyss between self and God since we are the cause of it, though, inevitably, the abyss will come to own us when the consciousness of sin becomes all-consuming. Anxiety (*Angst*) is therefore both vertiginous and claustrophobic or narrow (*trang*).

But more of anxiety in due course. Suffice it to say for now that the anxiety of this self-oriented "inclosing reserve" (*Indesluttethed*) must ultimately deliver its gaze toward the (Holy) other. Sin must be understood authentically, not through guilt's introspective and serpentine self-fascination, but *relationally* as the distance that separates the sinner from God. Only through such a relational understanding of sin can one come to accept a relational understanding of *forgiveness* that transfigures the meaning of the infinite qualitative difference between humanity and God.

And still, the central paradox—or unsurpassable chasm—is such that the self must become known to itself in relation to that which is infinitely differentiated from it. It is in this sense that Johannes Climacus initially calls the god, simply, "the Unknown." This anxious and despairing task is one of becoming an authentic self before a God whose absolute otherness apparently defies any such relation. Yet how can I know myself in relation to that which is wholly unknowable? "[I]f a human being is to come to know something about the unknown (the god) [*det Ubekjendte (Guden)*], he must first come to know that it is different from him, absolutely different from him" (PF, 46). Yet, as Johannes Climacus ponders, how can one come to know anything about this God since "the understanding cannot even think the absolutely different" (PF, 45)?

Here is the abyss of an apparently unassailable *alterity* and alienation which this theological anthropology must confront if it wishes to define itself before a God who is understood, at least initially, as Wholly Other: "At this point we seem to stand at a paradox," Johannes Climacus rightly insists. "Just to come to know that the god is the different, man needs the god and then comes to know that the god is infinitely different from him" (PF, 46). In other words, the *alterity* of the absolutely different is not something I can come to know of myself, even though I myself as sinner am apparently the cause of this abyss of absolute difference. Consequently, the consciousness of sin, which is also the consciousness of human-divine *alterity* conceived as alienation, cannot come by way of introspection, but only through the gift of God. And it is in the consciousness of sin via divine revelation, rather than introspection, that the self receives also the gift of forgiveness: the hand that reaches out across the impassable abyss. As Kierkegaard decisively formulates "the law of the relations between God and man in the God-relationship":

DIVISIO
There is an infinite, radical, qualitative difference between God and man.
This means, or the expression for this is: the human person achieves absolutely nothing; it is God who gives everything; it is he who brings about a person's faith, etc.
This is grace, and this is Christianity's major premise. (JP 2:1383 / Pap. X^1 A 59)

However, the challenge which will be explored is the danger that the consciousness of the infinite qualitative difference is always at risk of transmuting into a dreadful yawning abyss: an irremediable darkness into which one's gaze may fall continually. Unremitting contemplation of the abyss of sin may itself induce the very despair that Kierkegaard's writings strive to alleviate. Standing before God, the Wholly Other against Whom one had previously been defended by the distance of the abyss, may seem more like losing oneself in crushing annihilation than becoming oneself in loving relation to one's Creator and Redeemer. This is reflected by the crucial warning in Kierkegaard's "SUBDIVISIO" to the above "DIVISIO": "If the *Divisio* is everything, then God is so infinitely sublime [*uendelig ophøiet*] that there is no intrinsic or actual relationship between God and the individual human being" (JP 2:1383 / Pap. X^1 A 59). As this work will contend, therefore, when the infinite qualitative abyss is understood only in part or is received in "offence," then God may appear so Wholly Other, so "absolutely different," so "infinitely sublime" as to seem irremediably and essentially a God of despair.

The abyss (*Dyb*) describes our severance and distance from God; but it is also, I suggest, an abyss (*Afgrund*) into which one can fall, in which one loses any ground (*grund*) on which one might stand before God. In the endeavor of the God-relationship, God can become so dreadful, so "infinitely sublime" to the mind's eye that, adopting Rudolf Otto's theological idiom, the awe of the *mysterium tremendum et fascinans* plunges into the awfulness of the *mysterium horrendum*.[9] The danger is that God becomes so dreadfully and irreconcilably Other to the self that one is swallowed up by the horror of this infinite qualitative abyss. God becomes the God of a fantastic despair that cannot reconcile itself to the *mysterium* of divine forgiveness: God is thought of as irrevocably, absolutely, and Solely Other. The gaze into the infinite abyss of sin has thus become an intoxication in which standing as a self before God is thought of primarily in terms of the abyss itself. This fatal abyss is a form of what Anti-Climacus calls "the second severance" (SUD, 109).

It is this edge that the present work reaches in its concluding chapter. The question of the self before God is a question of receiving the revelation of the infinite qualitative difference between self as sinner and God as the Wholly Other in such a way as to come to terms with the healing grace of *forgiveness*—the divine gift by which one becomes a self in *relation* rather than annihilation. Such a task involves theological anthropology in a painstaking anatomy of the abyss: not simply in terms of a doctrine of sin and forgiveness, but also a mutual interrogation of and by the infinite abyss which separates the sinner from God and which holds the paradoxical secret of our forgiveness. It is here that the gaze of the abyss hopes to see with "the eyes of faith": the gaze by which the self begins to envision itself through the eyes of God as healed and forgiven, as called to realize the gift of its selfhood—that is, to become itself before God. However, before the self can behold itself in this divine mirror, it must first recognize its solipsistic disintegration—its failure to know itself according to its own powers, and consequently a need to orient self-knowledge in relation to a divine *other*. It is this initial dissolution of the egocentric self, diagnosed in Kierkegaardian terms by way of an anatomy of despair, that allows the anatomy of the abyss to which the next chapter turns. There, I will explore how the recognition of one's hidden despair (sin) becomes the dialectical key to becoming a (forgiven) self before the Holy Other God.

TWO

The Inner Abyss

KIERKEGAARD AND THE SELF-FASCINATION OF MODERNITY

Not, I'll not, carrion comfort, Despair, not feast on thee;
Not untwist—slack they may be—these last strands of man.
—GERARD MANLEY HOPKINS, *"Carrion Comfort"*

. . . despair has inflamed something that cannot burn or be burned in the self.
—*The Sickness unto Death*

Kierkegaard's anatomization of the despair and redemption of the self, as it is unveiled *before God,* is a composition of both negative and positive attitudes toward the modern passion for self-knowledge. Kierkegaard, as a distinctively modern thinker, makes an impassioned plea on behalf of the struggle for authentic selfhood; yet, in also operating as a rigorous critique of modernity, Kierkegaard's works incisively transcribe the inevitable failure of the modern self. This should be taken in response to what David Gouwens identifies as the common erroneous tendency by which "Kierkegaard is charged with being the primary creator of a modern myth of the self as the 'solitary individual,' unmoored from history or tradition, a permutation of the Cartesian ego or the self-creating individual Romanticism, a myth that many see in need of radical deconstruction."[1] In fact, as will be argued in this chapter, Kierkegaard exacts his own method for deconstructing the modern figure of self that he is accused of valorizing. A more sensitive reading clearly discloses that Kierke-gaard's corpus essentially "dramatizes the decomposition of the modern self."[2] Moreover, there is such anxiety and uncertainty inherent to Kierkegaard's "genesis of the self" that, as George Pattison observes, "the origin of the self and its fall virtually coincide."[3] If Kierkegaard's anatomy of the self can, on the other hand, be called nihilistic rather than Cartesian then it is so only in the sense that it seeks to authentically "demolish the ground which has become false, turning the being of the self into a question mark"—to appropriate Kyoto School philosopher Nishitani Keiji's words.[4] "To disclose the nihility at the ground of the self is to live in sincerity, and within such sincerity the self becomes truly itself."[5] But Kierkegaard's anxious dialectic of selfhood also proposes a redemptive answer to the question mark of the self. Beyond the mere dramatization of this degeneration, Kierkegaard's writings seek to tempt the reader toward undergoing what his pseudonym Johannes Climacus succinctly calls "the *autopsy* of faith" (PF, 70) in 1844. It is in this dissection by faith that the self is able to see itself (Gr. *autos:* self; *optos:* seen)—though it must see itself initially through the anatomy of its own disintegration.

Hence, it would not be wholly inappropriate to designate a Kierkegaardian anatomy of selfhood—at least initially—as characteristically negative, or *apophatic.* Kierkegaard ultimately "has no anthropology that may be taught by him and adopted by his disciples."[6] This is because the person for Kierkegaard is not considered conceptually, but as existing individually through anxiety, choice, subjectivity, freedom, inwardness, and finally through faith. It is this psychological and literary fascination with the lived disruption of selfhood which causes Kierkegaard to contemplate the very real experience of the dissolution of the self as his anthropological starting point. The abyssal process of the un-grounding of the self-reflective self signifies the deconstruction of its inauthenticity. *Authentically,* the self can only finally come to see itself through the eyes of an other. The failure and putrefaction of the self which wills to be itself—described as a burrowing fire of despair—sanctifies the ground for the refined self to become itself *before God* in the transfiguration of faith. Dramatizing the failure of the hubristic impulse of modern self-knowing subjectivity, Kierkegaard prompts the modern individual toward the recognition that, as Augustine of Hippo had discovered in his *Confessions* more than fourteen hundred years previously, authentic consciousness of self is inextricable from one's mindfulness of God. And yet, in terms increasingly radicalized by the *Zeitgeist* of modernity, mindfulness of God involves an apparently inviolable consciousness of our infinite qualitative difference from the very God one is called to stand before. As such, this severance ensures that theology and anthropology, though entering into an ultimately indissoluble union, cannot undergo an identity crisis in the Feuerbachian sense.

SOLITUDE AND OTHERNESS

In primitive terms, it appears that the elementary sense of "self" emerges through the sense of separation from the other. A notion of severance pervades modern Western reflection on the ego, beginning in the earliest stages of human life. According to the developmental psychology that arose in the twentieth century (and was perhaps adumbrated in the infancy meditation in the *Confessions*), the infant suffers from a traumatic primal severance of its symbiotic relation with the mother, and it is through this loss and separation that it must now come to terms with the isolating difference between "Me" and "not-Me." This desire for internally authenticating the "I" thereby remains continually endangered by the intrusion of "the other" into its fragile world. For Hegel's philosophy (whose influence dominated the tone of theology and philosophy in Kierkegaard's Denmark), as will be examined further in chapter 5, a similar trauma is expressed in the way in which self-consciousness is inherently threatened by "this otherness of itself."[7] Generally speaking, from the perspective of such a tenuous and fearful ego, it becomes inevitable that when I am entangled in the world of "objects" and "others," the grasp upon my self is loosened. In the most focused study of the self in Kierkegaard's authorship, *The Sickness unto Death*, the pseudonymous Anti-Climacus aptly describes such a fear of self-diffusion in the modern terms of the bourgeois inauthenticity of "the crowd":

> Surrounded by hordes of men, absorbed in all sorts of secular matters, more and more shrewd about the ways of the world—such a person forgets himself, forgets his name divinely understood, does not dare to believe in himself, finds it too hazardous to be himself and far easier and safer to be like the others, to become a copy, a number, a mass man. (SUD, 33–34)

As such, in order to guard against the unwanted dilution of subjectivity, the "self" frequently initiates its search for itself in seclusion from the objects and others that it mistrusts. The widely regarded initiator of modern philosophy, René Descartes, opened his epoch-defining *Meditations* (1641) in solitude—and it is, after all, Descartes who is frequently admonished as the proto-Enlightenment thinker who, through questioning the existence of that which is separate from the self, "gave man, the subject, an ontological warrant for his nascent obsession with himself."[8] It is in the emerging Cartesian ego, averring that "I think therefore I am," where—as Paul Tillich alleges—"Man becomes pure consciousness, a naked epistemological subject; the world (including man's psychosomatic being) becomes an object of scientific inquiry and technical management."[9] Such a passion for separation—and therefore an implicit mistrust of the adulterating effects of the other—recurs throughout Western philosophy's search for self-knowledge. Solitude was also the impulse toward inner self-knowledge found in the *Essays* (1580) of Michel de Montaigne; but inevitably, as philosopher Charles Taylor explains, Montaigne could not transubstantiate his solitude into self-certainty, for "when he sat down to write and turned to himself, he experienced a terrifying inner instability."[10]

Ultimately, as discovered again and again in the history of Western philosophy, theology, and literature, the self is mystified as it grasps after itself, as it enters inside its own labyrinth of introspection. It is in the loneliness of reflection that the "I" becomes most conscious of the elusive hiddenness of the self. It is in entering into itself that the I can only further tighten and entangle the inner Gordian knot it seeks to resolve. Reflecting this perennial frustration of Western culture, Albert Camus confesses in his 1942 essay on suicide, *The Myth of Sisyphus*, "For ever I shall be a mystery to myself." As I struggle to take hold of my self, "it is nothing but water slipping through my fingers."[11]

A culture of obsessive and ineffectual introspection in Western philosophy and literature has contributed to a gathering cloud of post/modern suspicion regarding the integrity of the "self." Unlike the "soul" which had been ontologically and religiously assured, the "self" seems only to subsist as it is perceived—though it appears, paradoxically, to be unable to survive this process of self-perception. Furthermore, it appears that this contrived modern "self" is ultimately the elitist and privileged reserve of the reflective, aristocratic, and luxurious master—whereas any mere slave could be in possession of an "immortal soul." Kierkegaard's works, on the contrary, assert the shared summoning of "eternity" in every self and in doing so implore that *each individual*, as equal before God, learn to become a "self" through an anxious obligation to the eternal gift of freedom. I argue that by doing so Kierkegaard indicted the delusions of self-mastery inherent in reflective introspection, in deference to a relational self conceived as the struggle for existence of every human being *before God*. But becoming a self before God, Kierkegaard warns, is an anxious struggle beset on all sides by the possibility of inauthentic self-willing. Every human being is mutually allied under "the sickness unto death" (despair) and in consequence suffers an unconscious need of salvation from this universal dis-ease of isolated selfhood. In this sense, pseudonym Anti-Climacus in *The Sickness unto Death* scrutinized the phenomenon of despair, in its conscious and unconscious forms, and discerned in it something reminiscent of the ancient Socratic proof, via intractable inner suffering, for the universal immortality of the soul:

> Socrates demonstrated the immortality of the soul from the fact that sickness of the soul (sin) does not consume it as sickness of the body consumes the body. Thus, the eternal in a person can be demonstrated by the fact that despair cannot consume his self . . . If there were nothing eternal in a man, he could not despair at all; if despair could consume his self, then there would be no despair at all. (SUD, 20–21)[12]

A "cold fire" of despair ignites in the self and, by its "impotent self-consuming," affirms the indestructible but anguished presence of the eternal (SUD, 18). The torture of the self's inability to be itself and the impossibility in knowing itself paradoxically asserts the inviolable reality of the unrealized self. Yet, since this "self" is not yet a self (before God), its existence is felt as despair: "the sickness unto death, this tormenting contradiction, this sickness of the self, perpetually to be dying, to die and yet not die, to die death" (SUD, 18). The self is therefore in the grip of a dilemma. The fact that the self—sick unto death—is unable to realize its own death testifies to the tormenting eternity of the self. But, insofar as the self does not authentically will to become itself before God, despair is experienced as a kind of enduring, internal hell-fire: despair cannot "consume the eternal, the self at the root of despair, whose worm does not die and whose fire is not quenched [Mark 9:48]" (SUD, 18).

Here the self is victim to an omnivorous despair whose fire cannot devour the soul. Though a person despairing in this sickness unto death longs to be rid of the self, longs to die, "wants to tear his self away from the power that established it" (SUD, 20), such decisive self-slaughter, as the final severance from eternity, is not possible for the self. All despair is, at root, "to will to be rid of oneself" (SUD, 20). But this is a revolt against eternity, and therefore against oneself, which eternity in us will not tolerate. Even if one wishes to evade despair by refusing to become conscious of it, by refusing to become conscious of the self, then eternity will reveal one's despair to oneself and "nail him to himself" so that he cannot escape himself (SUD, 21). The self as crucified to itself by despair is indeed an evocative image for the anguished obligation of eternity. The self bears the hidden wounds of this stigma of eternity. Melancholy, anxiety, and despair manifest the invisible and secret agitations of the self's distress at its failure to possess itself. By struggling to become a self, one experiences the opposition of the eternal that wishes one to become oneself—what shall subsequently be explored under the rubric of the anxious "over-againstness" (Gn. *Anfechtung* / Dn. *Anfægtelse*) of eternity's claim upon the self. This despair is eternity's obligation upon the self; but it is also the birth-pain of the metamorphosis of "spirit" (Dn. *Ånd*). As such, despair is the mark of a double-edged sword, both a gift and an obligation: "Eternity is obliged to do this, because to have a self, to be a self, is the greatest concession, an infinite concession, given to man, but it is also eternity's claim upon him" (SUD, 21).

Repentance—the repentance of inauthentic self-willing—is ultimately the narrow path toward the alleviation of despair promised by the forgiveness of sins. "Despair Is Sin," and therefore as eternity reveals despair to oneself so one "has to learn what sin is by a revelation from God" (SUD, 95).[13] It is penitence alone that quenches the flames of despair. As Kierkegaard himself observes in his *Journals:* "Sin in a man is like the Greek fire which is not extinguished with water—but in this case only with tears" (JP 4:4008 / Pap. VI A 30).[14] But talk of this metamorphosis through repentance and forgiveness would be premature. Anti-Climacus's assertion that "next to God there is nothing as eternal as a self" (SUD, 53) is, at first glance, also vulnerable to the deconstruction of the myth of modern selfhood. However, a Kierkegaardian anatomization of the disintegration of the self in despair—and its consequent relational reconstruction before God—proposes a religiously existentialist account of the "death of the self": a religious narrative which revolves around an emerging trust in the self's "self"-denying relation to the eternal.[15] As such, before the repentant metamorphosis of spirit can take hold, the self must fully realize the despair of the modern self to which it is crucified. There must be a death of the self preceding the metamorphosis or resurrection of the self "before God."

A GENEALOGY OF THE SELF:
FROM "KNOW THYSELF" TO THE "DEATH OF THE SELF"

Paganism required: Know yourself. Christianity declares: No, that is provisional —know yourself—and look at yourself in the mirror of the Word in order to know yourself properly. No true self knowledge without God knowledge or before God. To stand before the mirror means to stand before God.

—KIERKEGAARD's *Journals*

This entry from his *Journals* (JP 4:3902 / Pap. X⁴ A 412) provides a succinct expression of Kierkegaard's approach toward a critique of solitary self-reflection by way of a relational vision of self-knowledge "before God." But Kierkegaard is conspicuously not alone in Western thought in bearing witness to the impossibility and consequent disintegration of the modern self. The observations that Kierkegaard made concerning the delusional tendencies which underlie the modern figure of the self have subsequently been surpassed by radical proclamations of the "death of the self" in the twentieth century. Rather than being a primal authentic truth, "Man" is, as Michel Foucault famously identifies in his 1966 study *The Order of Things,* "only a recent invention, a figure not yet two centuries old . . . and he will disappear again as soon as that knowledge has discovered a new form."[16] Despite the Delphic charge to "know thyself" (Gr. *gnōthi seatoun*), according to which Socrates was praised and to which Kierkegaard refers, it is considered naïve by Foucault to align modern anthropological investigation with such a primitive history. Evidently, even Kierkegaard is—at the beginning of his authorship at least—culpable of believing that Socrates originated the notion of self-hood. As Kierkegaard declares in his 1841 dissertation *The Concept of Irony: With Constant Reference to Socrates,* "The phrase 'know thyself' means: separate yourself from the other. Precisely because this self did not exist prior to Socrates" (CI, 177). However, this allegedly Socratic self represents the sense of the specifically introspective "self" known in isolated differentiation from "the other." Socrates, as Kierkegaard saw him, "isolated" and "abandoned" the individual of his own time with his dialectical method. And yet it is *modernity* that translates the Delphic oracle's recommendation for self-knowledge into inwardness and agency.[17] It is essentially in modernity that the solipsistic "self" has become itself: hence Kierkegaard's observation that it was nevertheless "reserved for a later age [i.e., the modern age] to go deeply into this self-knowledge" (CI, 178).[18]

Plato himself wrote of the "absurd phrase" of self-mastery in reference to the ordering of the higher and lower parts of the soul[19]—a centering which Charles Taylor describes as a precondition for interiorization. However, while it was necessary to its development, Platonic centering is not identifiable with modern interiorization: "it took a further step to bring it [modern selfhood] about."[20] In modernity "know thyself" becomes the motto for a task of solitary self-reflection. "In the Socratic view," writes Kierkegaard's pseudonym Johannes Climacus, "every human being is himself the midpoint, and the whole world focuses only on him because his self-knowledge is God-knowledge" (PF, 11). Anthropology and theology are thus so aligned in Socratic thought that, according to David Willows, this thought concludes itself with the "conviction that the epistemologist is divine."[21] Crucially, the "self" as a distinct object which is amenable to scrutiny emerges with the evolution of anthropology from theology. The "self" had been conceived as an object for God—albeit one that is anxious to be so; now in modernity it becomes increasingly an object for itself. The "self" is both subject and object: an absurd tension which, as Plato had already warned, this "self" is unable to sustain.

However, prior to the modern severance of anthropology and theology, it was—according to Charles Taylor—not Plato but "Augustine who introduced the inwardness of radical reflexivity and bequeathed it to the Western tradition of thought."[22] Indeed, postmodern theologian Mark C. Taylor suggests that, while initial murmurings of Western subjectivity can be detected in Paul's epistles, the now obsolete "epoch of selfhood" was effectively inaugurated by Augustine's *Confessions* in the fourth century and wrecked upon Hegel's *Phenomenology of Spirit* in the nineteenth.[23] However, philosopher Richard Sorabji disputes Charles Taylor's notion that "we have to wait for Augustine to find the idea of an inner self where God resides."[24] In his recent survey, *Emotion and Peace of Mind: From Stoic Agitation to Christian Temptation,*

Sorabji specifically highlights Augustine's avowed debt to Neo-Platonism. The impulse toward an inward discovery of God in Augustine, Sorabji argues, echoes the writings of Plotinus as well as Paul. This can be seen in Plotinus's brief autobiographical account of his journey inward, in which he recalls: "I become at one with the Divine, and I establish myself in it."[25]

And yet Augustine went beyond Plotinus in postulating a decisive distance, or estrangement, between God and the soul—a distance not simply derived from embodiment but from enslaving *concupiscence*: the doctrine of sin. As Charles Taylor describes it: "The soul is present to itself, and yet it can utterly fail to know itself."[26] Augustine is also here following the Pauline tradition of early Christianity which confesses an anxious "I" that is sabotaged and split by the alienating and insidious presence of sin: "For I do not do the good I want, but the evil I do not want is what I do. Now if I do what I do not want, it is no longer I that do it, but sin which dwells within me" (Romans 7:19–20). Sin is present like a disease within the "self" (a sickness unto death): sin is in some sense alien to the "I," and yet is an ineradicable aspect of its existence. Sin devours being from within, creating a schizoid "I" that is torn between will and desire, good and evil. This is an "I" at war with itself, a tension between the lower and the higher which Augustine felt so acutely and which Paul expressed so vehemently: "For the desires of the flesh are against the Spirit, and the desires of the Spirit are against the flesh; for these are opposed to each other, to prevent you from doing what you would" (Galatians 5:17).

Furthermore, perhaps the most decisive innovation established in Augustinian selfhood is not the melancholy frustration of introspection, nor the inner raging between "flesh" and "spirit," but the actual formation of the self's narrative. While *Enneads* IV 8 (1, 1–11) represents the only truly autobiographical account in Plotinus, what is a rarity for Plotinus and an occasional impassioned vignette in Paul becomes for Augustine a highly charged, diverse, yet subtle narrative structure in the *Confessions*. By ostensibly inventing the literary form of the autobiography, Augustine indulges in a narrative that "at once *tells* of a self and *constructs* the self it tells of. . . . We might say, 'no self, no autobiography' . . . we might also say, and for the same reason, 'no autobiography, no self.'"[27] In other words, the self cannot be abstracted from the activity of its own narration: "this continuous 'I' who writes the autobiography is also constructed by the autobiography it writes."[28] Hence, one might say that it is through confessional narrative transcription that the self attempts to become the object of its own self-reflection in relation to its Creator. The self becomes articulated in terms of the narrative of its journey to God and to itself—a journey that reconciles its goals in one decisive eschatological destination. In Augustine one reads the narrative not only of inward self-seeking, but also of the realization of the potential for personal failure through self-enclosure; and finally the subsequent breaking-open of subjectivity in relation to God. Salvation and selfhood are intertwined, as Jean-François Lyotard observes in his posthumous work, *The Confession of Augustine:* "Augustine confesses his God and confesses himself not because he is converted: he becomes converted or tries to become converted while making confession."[29]

Time and again, it is seemingly at the very moment when the "self" attempts to attain an all-too-certain grasp on itself that, like water falling through one's fingers, the notion of selfhood undergoes its most fatal crisis. This irony is epitomized by the legacy of Descartes's *cogito ergo sum* which, despite Descartes's professed epistemological dependence upon God, ultimately constructs an autonomous ego dependent first and foremost upon its own isolated introspection. In contrast to Augustinian dependence upon a divine other, Charles Taylor explains, "for Descartes the whole of the reflexive turn is to achieve a quite self-sufficient certainty."[30] Furthermore, "this new conception of inwardness, an inwardness of self-sufficiency, of autonomous powers of ordering by reason, *also* prepared the ground for modern unbelief."[31] This keystone for the "death of God" and consequent "death of self"—an implication unforeseen by Descartes—was formed by a severance of anthropology from theology and "the other," and also to some degree by a reliance upon a subject-object paradigm which internalized the solipsism of the *cogito ergo sum.* The modern Cartesian "self" strives to sustain itself as both the subject and the object of its own self-knowledge—though introspection inevitably vanquishes itself by the intensity of this very tension it has created.

The Cartesian "self" becomes so irrecoverably dependent upon this subject-object structure that, according to the diagnosis in radical theologian Don Cupitt's *The Time Being,* "The duality between subject and object goes, and the self therefore disappears."[32] The "inner self," as Cupitt sees it, was previously regulated by an "outer-inner dualism" to the extent of establishing a personal metaphysical dualism of public/private, appearance/reality internalized within each individual.[33] Cupitt therefore urges the collapse of what he detects as an archaic Pauline metaphysical dualism in deference to emphasizing the contemporary primacy of the "immanence" and "appearance" of the person: "A person has become merely a personality, a mask, an improvised role. Nowadays we are all parts, not soul."[34] Disavowed of the arcane metaphysical heritage of the soul, Cupitt's progressive diagnosis seems to sit within the perspective in which, as Lyotard explains in his influential 1979 book *The Postmodern Condition:* "A *self* does not amount to much, but no self is an island; each exists in a fabric of relations that is now more complex and mobile than ever before."[35]

As shall become more explicit, however, Kierkegaard himself prefigures this whole multifarious impulse of the self toward disintegration by identifying the myth of the autonomous self as riddled with unrealized anxiety, unconscious despair, sublimated desires, and the unrecognized relations of antagonism, rebellion, and dependence upon the human and the divine other. Fundamentally the paradigm shift is from the internal grasp at "being" to the openness of a relational "becoming" whose horizon is infinitely receding. Inevitably, as Tillich explains in his 1952 reflection on the anxiety of the modern human condition, *The Courage To Be:* "A self which has become a matter of calculation and management has ceased to be a self. It has become a thing. You must participate in a self in order to know what it is. But by participating you change it."[36] In the light of recent assertions about the "self," one must ask whether any form of the idea of selfhood can survive the "death of the self." Initially it must be recognized that it is predominantly the modern "self" as a Cartesian *res cogitans* ("thinking substance," in contradistinction to the external world as "extended substance": *res extensa*) that has been indicted in deference to an increasingly relational and "de-centered self."[37] Following this indictment, Charles Taylor thus concedes that universal, metaphysical, or ontological descriptions of selfhood are no longer revealing: "this word ['self'] now describes an area of questioning. It designates the kind of being of which this question of identity can be asked."[38] But can the "self," in any form, endure its own dissolution? "Can a self be itself and know that the act by which it is known 'disowns' it? . . . If the self cannot be focused and cannot be centered, it is only this 'cannot.'"[39] In other words, does the post/modern "self" merely trace the melancholy impossibility of self-possession: an elegiac question mark inscribed over an inner abyss of absence?

THE ENIGMA OF DESPAIR

Following this dissolution of the self-knowing "self," selfhood in post/modernity has come to designate a domain of questioning more than an endpoint for anthropological inquiry. In this sense, however, I suggest that an allegory for this post/modern question of the "self" can be read in the ancient myth of the Sphinx at Thebes, and its deadly enigma whose answer was "Man."[40] It is Oedipus who solves the Sphinx's murderous riddle, and yet it is Oedipus's tragedy to destroy himself by marrying his mother and killing his father because he did not know their—and therefore his own—true identity: "the one who knows what man is does not know who he is."[41] And so Oedipus destroys all that has been given to him—destroys himself because, though he knows "Man," he does not know "*this* man." Again, in Kierkegaardian terms, an irony is manifest in his failure to realize the moment of recognition—"the transition to the subjective" (FSE, 38)—as recognized by David in his rebuke by the prophet Nathan: "Thou art the man!" (2 Samuel 12:7). Oedipus himself is never free from the irony of the question. According to Hegel's reading in *Lectures on the Philosophy of Religion,* the content of the Sphinx's riddle is "the human being, the free self-knowing spirit."[42] Furthermore, in his lectures on *Aesthetics,* Hegel aptly expands on how the "explanation of the symbol [of the Sphinx] lies in the absolute meaning, in the spirit, just as the famous Greek inscription calls to man: Know thyself."[43] It is the translation of the Sphinx into Greek mythology which, for Hegel, signifies the transition from the obscurity of the Egyptian religion to the clarity of God known as Spirit (Gn. *Geist*) in Greek religion. And yet, in Michel Despland's more contemporary reading, the nemesis is upon Oedipus precisely because Oedipus solved the riddle without any appeal to the wisdom of the gods and consequently endeavored to become the equal of his father. Essentially, the nemesis of the riddle is unleashed because "Oedipus made himself *isotheos,* equal to god."[44] The retribution of the question is the indecipherable repetition of the question which is put to "man." To escape this, one must turn the riddle over, as Oedipus failed to do, to the Other. Or, as Dietrich Bonhoeffer aptly phrased it in *Act and Being,* "man is the question put to God, to which only God can give the answer."[45]

The enigma of selfhood resides in the fact that in attempting to answer to itself, the self must multiply and defer itself through the very act of perception or questioning: the resolution of the self lies in its irreconcilable future. "The self becomes always the future project of the perceiving self. . . . The self is a permanent fugitive, escaping itself into the future of unceasing self-reflection."[46] This task of "becoming oneself" situates its struggle in the gap between the "perceiving self" and the "future self." In this sense, one could describe selfhood as truly abyssal insofar as it is severed from itself and falling into "groundlessness." One might say that between the question and answer of the riddle a gap has opened up inside myself, and "I" have fallen into it. Here the enigma of selfhood delivers us over to doubting. It is within this abyss in the self that Anti-Climacus situates his anatomy of despair: "despair is an existential gap within oneself, the willful and errant doubling in one's personality, the failure to be oneself."[47] The cipher to this abyss can be discovered within the word itself: *Fortvivlelse* (despair). Whereas the English word "despair" (from the Old French *desperer,* French *désespoir*) literally means "without-hope," the Danish word *Fortvivlelse* has its root in the German *Verzweifeln. Fortvivlelse* and *Verzweifeln* share a common structure: the root of both words is the word for "doubt" (Dn. *tvivl* / Gn. *Zweifel*), while both prefixes denote intensification (Dn. *for-* / Gn. *ver-*); as such, then, *Fortvivlelse* and *Verzweifeln* literally mean "intensified doubt." However, Kierkegaard's use of the word suggests more than the cognitive activity of doubting (as his unfinished biography of the pseudonym *Johannes Climacus*, subtitled *A Life of Doubt*, attests to). As Gregory Beabout explains, "The movement from doubt to despair, from tvivl to fortvivlelse, is not made by a quantitative increase in one's cognitive powers. Rather, despair is an existential act."[48] While *Fortvivlele* is etymologically centered around "doubt" (*tvivl*), in its existential intensification—especially where doubt of oneself is concerned—it also inevitably encompasses the Anglo-French sense of despair as "hopelessness." In fact, as will be examined further on, the most fatal aspect of *Fortvivlelse* is precisely that it relinquishes all hope in the *possibility* of salvation.

However, it is in its relation to *tvivl* that *Fortvivlelse* connotes something which is lost in the translation of "despair." As the German *Zweifel* and the English "doubt" are both indicative of duplicity (*zwei* / double), so the Danish *tvivl*, though not as etymologically explicit, is also suggestive of the Danish *to* (two). Once the anatomy of despair in *The Sickness unto Death* is examined, the sense of doubling or splitting comes into prominence. The duplicity of the human being is diagnosed in the notoriously abstract and cryptic opening passage to part 1 of the work in which Anti-Climacus avers: "A human being is a synthesis of the infinite and the finite, of the temporal and the eternal, of freedom and necessity, in short a synthesis. A synthesis is a relation between two. Considered in this way, a human being is still not a self" (SUD, 13). The despair of the synthesized human being (who is not yet a self) could thus be compared with, while being qualitatively different from, dizziness or vertigo.[49] This formula has been expressed before, though in a more primal from, by Kierkegaard's pseudonym Vigilius Haufniensis in *The Concept of Anxiety*: "Man is a synthesis of the psychical and the physical; however, a synthesis is unthinkable if the two are not united in a third. This third is spirit [*Ånd*]" (CA, 43). But this relation of spirit is one of anxiety (*Angst*) (CA, 44), a relation which Haufniensis later tells us is always "sympathetic and antipathetic," an ambivalent serpentine dance of seduction and revulsion (CA, 103). According to Anti-Climacus, the human being, as a synthesis of two apparently contrary sets of principles, has not yet become a self. "Spirit is the self. But what is the self? The self is a relation that relates itself to itself or is the relation's relating itself to itself in the relation. The self is not the relation [the synthesis] but is the relation's relating itself to itself" (SUD, 13). The synthesis relates opposites, but it is only in the synthesis' relation *of itself to* itself—not only as a relation to the duality—that it becomes "the positive third, and this is the self" (SUD, 13).

But how does the relation relate to itself and not merely to its doubleness? A self "must either have established itself or have been established by another" (SUD, 13). The first option might read as the cartography of the modern self striving to authenticate itself in the space of its self-reflection. It is in the self established by another that a further movement of openness is posited in the relation to that other. If there is another then "this relation, the third, is yet again a relation and relates itself to that which established the entire relation" (SUD, 13). Conceived visually: in the first option, the gaze of the relation's relating to itself falls back upon itself in the form of self-reflection; in the second, the gaze returns through the eyes of the other and as such is a further relation to another. "The human self is such a derived, established relation, a relation that relates itself to itself and in relating itself to itself relates itself to another" (SUD, 13–14). Without this other, the gaze of the self is a sophisticated narcissism: nothing more than the mirror of subjectivity in paganism's "know thyself." In Christian terms, recalling Kierkegaard's formula, "that is provisional—know yourself—and look at yourself in the mirror of the Word in order to know yourself properly. No true self knowledge without God knowledge or before God. To stand before the mirror means to stand before God" (JP 4:3902 / Pap. X⁴ A 412). Or, in Anti-Climacus's words: "The formula that describes the state of the self when despair is completely rooted out is this: in relating itself to itself and in willing to be itself, the self rests transparently [gjennemsigtigt] in the power that established it" (SUD, 14).

The self is thus able to behold itself—to become "transparent" (gjennemsigtigt: "see-through") to itself—in relation to the establishing power of God. It is this unrealized ontological dependence that identifies the self-reflective gaze as a form of willing, in despair, "to be oneself": a form of willing which only exists because there is another authentic way to become oneself, and that is, in relation to the establishing power. "If a human self had established itself, then there could be only one form: not to will to be oneself, but there could not be the form: in despair to will to be oneself" (SUD, 14). From the first perspective, all willing to be oneself would be inherently authentic; only not willing to be oneself would constitute despair. However, the existence of this "second formula [i.e., 'in despair to will to be oneself'] is specifically the expression for the complete dependence of the relation (of the self), the expression for the inability of the self to arrive at or to be in equilibrium and rest by itself, but only, in relating itself to itself, by relating itself to that which has established the entire relation" (SUD, 14).

If this is to be read as an expression of the modern self-reflective self's inability to authenticate itself, then one must also acknowledge that, instead of merely advocating a postmodern erasure of the project of selfhood, Anti-Climacus is also attempting to resituate the self relationally *before God*. In this sense, the third which also reconciles the two expresses the possibility of grounding the self in the establishing power. Here is the ontological facet of despair as more than the *feeling* of despair: it becomes a misrelation. As a misrelation rather than mere emotion, despair can be something of which one remains essentially unconscious: it must be revealed by the other. Finally, when "despair is completely rooted out," then "in relating itself to itself and in willing to be itself, the self rests transparently in the power that established it" (SUD, 14). And yet this relation, which Anti-Climacus concludes is *faith*, is an activity of becoming rather than being. As shall become clearer, becoming "transparent" to oneself before God, to see oneself through the eyes of God—in the mirror of the Word—is a becoming whose being is ultimately eschatological. As such, selfhood—if one wishes to conceive it in this modern vocabulary—is in a sense a personal journey whose destination is always deferred rather than possessed.

Ultimately for Anti-Climacus, the self becomes itself in the heterogeneous relation "before God": the relation relates itself to itself, not in its own eyes or the reflective mirror of Narcissus, but through the eyes of God or the mirror of the Word. But if "God is dead," as modernity has variously celebrated or mourned or simply assumed, then surely the "self" is also abandoned to the impossibility of becoming transparent to itself, for it cannot do so alone. Without God, the self has only its melancholy failure to become itself on which to meditate. If God is dead, then there is no "will to be oneself" that is possible in despair; or else it is a nihilistic despair without resolution—and surely this itself is either a new form of despair or else the abolition of this despair along with the God of despair. Perhaps there is only "in despair not to will to be oneself" as some kind of "bad faith"—as atheistic existentialism may have understood it; or else this is no longer despair but only an acceptance of the "death of selfhood." In other words, perhaps the only real despair of post/modernity is "in despair to will to be oneself," insofar as it represents an inability to accept the irrevocable veracity of the "death of the self." It is to this contagious relation between the "death of God" and the "death of the self" that we now turn our attention.

Post Mortem Dei: A COMMON GRAVE FOR SELF AND GOD

The self is only the shadow which sin and error cast by stopping the light
of God, and I take this shadow for a being.

—SIMONE WEIL, *Gravity and Grace*

. . . one who has gazed into the empty mirror can never regard God or self as he
did before.

—MARK C. TAYLOR, *Deconstructing Theology*

To know oneself, Kierkegaard affirms, is to become transparent to oneself, to see oneself in the divine mirror. But in the purported lacuna that Taylor identifies in our epigraph as the now vacant mirror of God, the self can see only a fractured self-reflection where once it had seen itself reflected through the eyes of God. The modern self emerges into the new dawn of its autonomy: it defines itself without the God on whom it once depended; and so it kills the God for whom it had been an object of intolerable scrutiny. However, the necessary consequence of this disappearance of God "is the disappearance of the self that killed him. When the conceptual ground of self-interiority dies, the self-as-self interior must die as well."[50] Subsequently alone and unable to possess itself as the object of its own subjectivity, the "self" then dies, no longer able to transcend and repossess itself from a higher vantage point. The innovative possibilities of the "self-creating self" have transpired as melancholy impossibilities. After Nietzsche's annunciation of the "death of God" and the will-to-power, writes the existentialist theologian Ralph Harper, "there ought to have been a new dawn, new horizons, an open sea. Man ought to feel cheerful; his logic ought to be gay."[51] But the failures to produce compelling truths and the inability or unwillingness of most people to face the dizzying anxiety of their own alleged freedom to create themselves initiates the self into the terrible secret of its own annihilation. Unable to depend on anything beyond itself and incapable of sustaining its own vital creativity, the relatively recent phenomenon of the autonomous self faces its own dissolution: "the death of God finds its completion in the death of selfhood."[52]

Accordingly, as Tillich describes it in his postwar *The Courage To Be,* the death of God initiates "the crisis that comes when man no longer knows what it means to be human and becomes aware that he does not know this."[53] In the postmortem of God it transpires that whatever has killed God is contagious and relentless. Modern humanity is thrown into an abyss, not simply of the death of God, but of the disorientation and dissolution of its own self-understanding. Such an abyss threatens us with a deathly silence. As Jean-Luc Marion asks in his *God Without Being:* "To what silence are we summoned today? Death, preeminently, imposes silence; the emptiness of infinite spaces opposes its suffocating vacuity like an eternal silence; aphasia [a loss of speech associated with skeptical silence], desertlike, grows with its silence."[54] Does this silence, which for Marion "threatens modernity more than any other," convey a sense of *apophatic* honor for the ineffable,[55] or does it rather express "contempt, renunciation, the avowal of impotence," or even idolatry?[56] Much depends upon the nature of this deathly silence for the im/possibility of theology. Who or what is it that has become silent? While an ontological assertion may evade us, it can be said that the "death of God" does speak with some veracity about the death of a particular understanding of "God." Marion, along with many other contemporary thinkers, rightly identifies that the God who has died in the "death of God" is essentially an idol. This death should not cause us to become silent *about* the silence between us and God. Such silence is the work of the idol: "To remain silent does not suffice in order to escape idolatry, since preeminently, the characteristic of the idol is to remain silent, and hence to let men remain silent when they no longer have anything to say—not even blasphemies."[57] As such, even when it seems that God is silent, theology should, like Job himself, be prepared to speak even when all that remains in the moment is the protest of despair—even blasphemy itself.

Nietzsche succeeded at the end of the nineteenth century in articulating an hour of the "twilight of the idols"; but "the idol," as Marion explains, is that which "allows the divine to occur only in man's measure."[58] The idol is constructed on an apex of thought which thought has submitted to. God is here the projection of our own desire for transcendence—unrealizable because hypostasized as the heteronymous other who demands my incapacity. In this sense, Ludwig Feuerbach also assaulted the idol of the imagination. For Marion, however, "God" as *causa sui* is the idol.[59] As such, the so-called murder of God errs as much as it succeeds. It is iconoclasm which reaches its limit in becoming aware of itself as such. The death of God, as Marion astutely observes, "presupposes a determination of God that formulates him in a precise concept; it implies then, at first, a grasp of the divine that is limited and for that reason intelligible."[60] As such, Marion rightly wishes to add quotation marks to the God who is indicted in the death of God.[61] And furthermore, the inference is that one should supplement the word "self" with cautionary quotation marks, since this idol of the "self" bears a reciprocal and irresolvable relation to the idol of "God." As Mary-Jane Rubenstein appositely explains: "We have killed him [namely, 'God'] because we created him in the first place, because there was never any God to ground us *as ourselves*—only 'God,' which was nothing but the product of our thought. And so we are free . . . Except. Except we were the ones oppressing us; killing God, we've killed ourselves."[62]

THE DEATH OF THE IDOL AND THE DEATH OF THE EGO

. . . you may have killed God beneath the weight of all that you have said; but don't imagine that, with all that you are saying, you will make a man that will live longer than he.

—MICHEL FOUCAULT, *The Archaeology of Knowledge*

As indicated above, the key to this abyssal relation between the death of God and the death of the self can itself be traced in the writings of the great nineteenth-century prophet of deicide, Friedrich Nietzsche. It is pertinent to this relation to remember that in Nietzsche's mythology, at least in *Zarathustra,* the death of God begins with the *gaze* of God. One is looked upon by a "strange God, a voyeuristic God (recalling the Sartrean stare)."[63] It is the Ugliest Man who has murdered God because he could neither bear the intrusion of God's witness to his shame, nor shake his resentment of God's pity for him:

> But he *had to* die: he saw with eyes that saw everything; he saw man's depths and ultimate grounds, all his concealed disgrace and ugliness. His pity knew no shame: he crawled into my dirtiest nooks. This most curious, overobtrusive, overpitying one had to die. He always saw me: on such a witness I wanted to have revenge or not live myself. The god who saw everything, *even man*—this god had to die! Man cannot bear it that such a witness live.[64]

The despair of the Ugliest Man, a despair that descends into pathological deicide, results from a conception of "God" as "the dysfunctional projection of a persecution complex and a delirium of self-accusation. 'God' is only the hypostasis of a delirious bad conscience, magnified by the metaphysical dimension into a constant presence."[65] This "God" is indivisible from an inner universe of secret guilt that seeks to incarnate itself as the morbid externalization of self-indictment. In Freudian terms, the death of God may thus symbolize the attempt of the Ego to bring about the "death" of the Super-Ego. And so the death of "God" initiates the death of the "self"; just as the death of the Super-Ego spells the abandonment of the Ego to its own melancholy end. There is also an apparent narcissism of guilt that is discernible in this relation. Indeed, Nietzsche's Zarathustra also discerned: "This fellow [i.e., the Ugliest Man] too loved himself, even as he despised himself."[66] And as such, Haar writes: "God's murder, the hyperbole of aggression, is the desperate attempt by man, suffering from himself, to get rid of the cause of his suffering."[67] But the crucial misinterpretation here would be the belief that the "delirious bad conscience" is an infliction that comes from the Other, the Master. This "bad conscience" is, rather, ultimately self-interpretative: self-indictment is projected onto a transcendent and incontestable height.

Through the projection of this "God"-image, the "self" thus transforms itself into an object for an imagined other "subject." This God is essentially the heteronymous desire of the self to know itself as its own object except that, in this instance, the self that fails to *grasp* itself *projects* itself in a movement of alienation in which it experiences itself as an essentially guilty object. And yet, rebellion is inevitable insofar as this guilt itself becomes something alien. This insurrection is well illustrated in Camus's *Myth of Sisyphus,* in which a het-eronomous guilt incurs an absurd punishment that is irreconcilable with the condemned individual's inner sense of innocence: "an attempt is made to get him to admit his guilt. He feels innocent. To tell the truth, that is all he feels—his irreparable innocence."[68] By rebellion, man frees himself from "God," who was only ever his metaphysically established self-indictment at the impossi-bility of possessing himself. By the act of deicide, man realizes through defi-ant expression what Feuerbach had articulated in more dialectical terms: he becomes nothing more or less than the assassin of his own imagination. Iden-tifying sin as metaphysics, he atones for it with the sacrifice of heteronomy. The God who originated in the desire of the self to know itself is murdered in the rebellion of this self against its metaphysically self-established self-indict-ment. In other words, "God" is killed because heteronomy apparently prohib-its the autonomous realization of self-knowing. The irony is that the "death of God" entails, in turn, the death of the (unknowable) autonomous "self."

It is, as Tillich elucidates, precisely the implicit subject-object dialectic within the divine-human encounter that causes the "God of theological the-ism" to be killed:

> God as a subject makes me into an object which is nothing more than an object. He deprives me of my subjectivity because he is all-powerful and all-knowing. I revolt and try to make *him* into an object, but the revolt fails and becomes desperate. God appears as the invincible tyrant, the being in contrast with whom all other things are without freedom and subjectivity . . . This is the God Nietzsche said had to be killed because nobody can tolerate being made into a mere object of absolute knowledge and absolute control.[69]

In transcending this "God of theological theism," Tillich extols the "God above the God of theism" who encounters humanity beyond the subject-object structure.[70] Hence one may wish to assert, as Paul Ricoeur does in 1969's *The Religious Significance of Atheism,* that Nietzsche has only closed one possibil-ity: "that of an ontotheology culminating in a moral God who would be the principle and foundation for an ethics of prohibition and condemnation."[71] Furthermore, more recently Merold Westphal differentiates the tradition of metaphysics—a thread running from Anaximander to Nietzsche—from "the tradition that stretches from Augustine to Kierkegaard."[72] As such, West-phal—like Ricoeur, who regards the "school of suspicion" as a theological asset[73]—believes that Christian theology can appropriate much from the atheism of modernity by regarding its critiques of religion as empathic with biblical indictments of inauthentic religion and idolatry.[74] Valuing Nietzsche, Feuerbach, Heidegger et al., Westphal thus makes a plea "for a religiously motivated hermeneutics of suspicion."[75] Evidently, Westphal is far from being alone in recognizing and appreciating philosophy's iconoclastic critiques of (philosophy's) Unmoved Mover.

In 1977's *God as the Mystery of the World,* theologian Eberhard Jüngel contributes to this recent "destruction" of the God of classical theism, while also critiquing the presumptions of modern atheism itself. Eventually, the "metaphysically established God," Jüngel explains, seems to have been "destroyed by his own perfection."[76] This God of metaphysics is incarcerated in His own self-consummation. It is, furthermore, this God who has been rendered explicitly incoherent by the *passio* and suffering of modernity. In other words, the God of classical theism is dealt a fatal blow by His inability to respond to the modern human condition: this God's perfect *essence* is contradicted by human *existence.*[77] The transcendent metaphysical deity, Jüngel identifies, is traditionally elevated "over us"; death is seen as "under us." Jüngel thus observes that death and transcendence are mutually exclusive: "it would appear as if one has torn the being of God apart. The thought of God appears to have destroyed itself."[78] Yet the thought which has destroyed itself is the thought of "God" that has been variously identified by Tillich, Marion, Westphal et al. as an idol of onto-theology. But the question remains, can one justifiably eliminate onto-theology from the biblical conception of the God of Abraham, Isaac, and Jacob? In asserting that the God of the scripture is not reducible to human comprehension, but rather exceeds all efforts at metaphysical (i.e., onto-theological) determination, I shall consider this question relative to the allegory of the divine name given to Moses in the theophany of the burning bush. Through this event and its subsequent mis/interpretation, I suggest that the mysterious disclosure of the divine name holds a cipher of the onto-theological contamination of Christian theology, while also pointing beyond the "death of God" to a God who eludes our attempts to name and therefore possess the essence of God-in-Godself.

Anomia: RECEIVING THE HOLY NAME

Exodus 3 tells the enigmatic story of the call of Moses through the theophany of the burning bush—a theophany in which God reveals the esoteric divine name as *'ehyeh asher 'ehyeh* (Exodus 3:14): a name which is above all names. This self-concealing, as much as self-revealing, disclosure has been simplified by the common variant English translation, "I am that I am." It is this which radical theologian Thomas Altizer calls "a self-naming which is not only the beginning of divine or ultimate speech, but therein and thereby is the release and the embodiment of total actuality, an actuality which is itself the origin of a full and total releasement."[79] Yet, on a closer reading of the biblical text, is it perhaps an unwarranted import to talk about this self-naming in terms of the "embodiment of total actuality" or as "self-embodiment"?[80] The I AM THAT I AM of Exodus 3:14 should certainly not be read as some divine correlative of the Cartesian *cogito ergo sum*—a correlation with some bearing upon the cross-contamination between the death of God and the death of the self. Surely one is importing terms when one talks of God, as Mark C. Taylor does, as "the absolute self-identity that resounds in the 'I AM THAT I AM.'"[81]

Nevertheless, one cannot simply vilify recent thought for smuggling Greek ontology into a Hebraic enigma. As Alfred Jäger explicates:

> The famous passage 'I am that I am' (Ex. 3:14) has nothing to do with ontology. Instead, this mysterious self-identification expresses God's pledge of himself to the dangerous path to be followed by his people. The translation of this passage in the Septuagint, however, became the entrée for Greek metaphysics into the understanding of the biblical text *Egō eimi ho ōn.* . . . Already the Septuagint, however, translates the unintelligible predicates of God *ēl šaddai* ['God almighty': derived from the Hebrew *shaddad*, 'to destroy,' or perhaps 'God of the mountain'; possibly connected to the fertility or blessings of God] with *pantokratōr* [the Greek 'dynamic omnipotent'], through which Hellenistic apprehensions of power penetrated the biblical understanding of God.[82]

The Hebrew *'ehyeh asher 'ehyeh* is translated into the Latin as *ego sum qui sum*—a translation which has been described as anticipating "the Thomist understanding of God as the one being whose very being it is to be (*ipsum esse subsistens*)"[83]—even though, as Marion rightly maintains, the "Hebrew verb *hayah* does not suffice to introduce a concept of 'Being.'"[84] This has not prevented many from introducing and inscribing such a concept into a Hellenized Christian understanding which is discomforted by such irresolvable ontological ambiguity. "In more contemporary idiom," Richard Kearney writes in his recent *The God Who May Be*, "this verbal play [of the verb *hayah*] compels us to wonder if God is here reducing himself to a metaphysics of presence or rendering himself immune to it for good and all."[85]

Reading the original, it becomes ultimately questionable to what extent the *'ehyeh asher 'ehyeh* can appropriately be called a "self-naming" at all. For example, when related to the contemporaneous Egyptian belief in magical and secret divine names of power, Moses' request for the name (Heb. *Shem*) of God calls to mind his impending altercation with the Egyptian magicians.[86] In this sense, does the divine response signify a name that exceeds the esoteric understanding, or a complete evasion of the magical paradigm itself? Either way, the response suggests a divine refusal to submit to the possessive terms of objectified conceptualization. God exceeds that which can be named or comprehended in the name—as such, in Kabbalistic tradition, even mystical meditations upon the permutations of the sacred Tetragrammaton יהוה are inexhaustible—and yet at the same time God's name expresses the substantiality of a historical relation to the material suffering of the people of Israel.

In *The God Who May Be*, Kearney offered a helpful rendering of Exodus 3:14 as "'I am who may be'—that is, as the possibility to be, which obviates the extremes of being and non-being."[87] In reaction to the traditionally onto-theological reading, Kearney proposes an "*eschatological*" God interpreted primarily in terms of "possibility" (a notion which, as shall be demonstrated further, becomes central to our present perspective on the self before God).[88] While Kearney remains deliberately opaque about this eschatological possibility, his emphasis upon the freedom of God from the conceptual shackles of onto-theology is a pertinent contemporary response to the *aporia* of post-metaphysical theology rooted in the ancient text that narrates Moses' theophany. Likewise Marion, in his desire to speak of "God without being," decisively claims that "Being says nothing about God that God cannot immediately reject. Being, even and especially in Exod. 3:14, says nothing about God, or says nothing determining about him."[89] As such, Marion, in his own way, exhibits a resistance to conceptual restraints upon God that debilitate divine inventiveness or possibility. God always exceeds all efforts to possess God. God is, for Marion, thinkable "only under the figure of the unthinkable, but of an unthinkable that exceeds as much what we cannot think as what we can."[90]

The incomprehensibility of God, for Marion, forces us to erase "the idolatrous quotation marks" around "God" in favor of "the very God that no mark of knowledge can demarcate." In doing so, Marion substitutes the idolatrous "God" with the caution of the G⊗d who "crosses out our thought because he saturates it; better, he enters into our thought only in obliging it to criticize itself."[91] In other words—contrasted with the Jewish tradition of writing "G-d," which suggests absence or silence in the prohibition against speaking or writing the Holy Name—writing "G⊗d" conveys the erasure of our idolatrous thinking about God, thereby also transcending human designations concerning what is *im/possible* for God. G⊗d gives himself as a gift to be thought but under G⊗d's admonition of human thought. As such, in place of the "God" whom we struggle with for "being-for-itself," and ultimately put to death, we encounter the God of an impossible possibility who gives himself to be struggled with, as Jacob struggled at Peni'el (Genesis 32), yet who ultimately exceeds what I can grasp.

In exceeding as much what we cannot think as what we can think, God even surpasses our declarations of what is *impossible*. Kierkegaard will emphasize the significance of this for selfhood by way of God's prevailing over what humanity believes is impossible regarding the forgiveness of sins. It is this sense of divine possibility in excess of what we say is impossible—even for God— that is the secret to the paradox of the self's forgiveness before God and the theological expression of the infinite qualitative difference. Kierkegaard was himself somewhat mystified by the ineffable sublimity of the "I Am Who I Am": "This is an analogy to the metaphysical point that the highest principles for all thought cannot be proved but only tautologically paraphrased: introverted infinity . . . in this case, then, anything other than tautology would be rubbish" (JP 4:4898 / Pap. X⁴ A 480). But Kierkegaard does not seek salvation for the self in metaphysics or in the attempt to unravel this tautology of divine ontology. Instead, Kierkegaard is concerned anthropocentrically with the self's relation to the God who exceeds and even evades its comprehension concerning what is im/possible. This is the God whom the self is separated from by an infinite qualitative difference: an abyss that continually forces itself upon all understanding. In the light of this difference, one cannot speak of God as God is in Godself; but of humanity as it stands, like Moses, before the enigma of a God who says "I will be with you." And yet, given the sense of the death of God in post/modern culture, and the *aphasia* and *anomia* of despair that suffocates the hearts of many individuals, does this infinite abyss of unknowing now speak more irremediably of the absent God and the lonely self than ever before? In order to explore this question further, we now turn to Kierkegaard's own anatomy of this infinite qualitative difference between self and God.

KIERKEGAARD'S INFINITE QUALITATIVE DIFFERENCE AND THE DEATH OF GOD

While it was yet to acquire the nihilism or irony it would take on in the twentieth century, the expression "death of God" would have already been somewhat familiar to Kierkegaard in the nineteenth century. In a book that was to have a massive influence on the philosophy and theology of Kierkegaard's time, *The Phenomenology of Spirit*, Hegel had identified the relation between loss of "self" and loss of "God" in terms of the "unhappy consciousness." The unhappy consciousness, as it experiences "the conscious loss of itself and the alienation of its knowledge about itself," expresses its anguish in the "hard saying that 'God is dead.'"[92] This is the expression of an "infinite grief" existing historically as "the feeling that 'God Himself is dead,' upon which the religion of more recent times rests; the same feeling that Pascal expressed in, so to speak, empirical form: 'la nature est telle qu'elle *marque* partout un Dieu *perdu* et dans l'homme et hors de l'homme' [nature is such that it *signifies* everywhere a *lost* God both within and outside man: *Pensées*, 441]."[93] This hard saying, first adumbrated on the hill called Golgotha, was to become the dark saying which would preside over the horrors of the twentieth century. But for Hegel in the nineteenth, this utterance signifies God's overcoming of the self-alienation that is posited in the split between Father and Son. It is as Spirit (Gn. *Geist*) that God comes back to himself in universal self-consciousness.[94] God himself has died. But effectively, as Schöndorf explains: "One could expand on this sentence and say he has died unto himself. The pure selfless abstract substance is negated so that it can become self. As substance in opposition to and opposite the subject, God no longer exists."[95] In mediation with creation, God effectively ceases to exist as the Wholly Other of the alienated unhappy consciousness.

From the Hegelian perspective, which saturated nineteenth-century Danish thought, Kierkegaard's avowal of the infinite qualitative difference between God and humanity consigns him to just this primal melancholy estrangement of the unhappy consciousness.[96] In a sense, Kierkegaard's writings embrace and transfigure this condemnation.[97] By erroneously claiming to have reconciled estrangement, as Kierkegaard saw it, Hegelianism actually reenforces estrangement in its most unconscious form—hence Kierkegaard's writings ironically encourage the recognition of, or will to, despair as essentially constituting a *rise* in the true consciousness of Spirit (Dn. *Ånd*). Hegelianism, by negating this estrangement, has contributed to the death of God—an implication Kierkegaard sees particularly as it was manifest in the bourgeois apostasy of Danish state-Christianity in his day. In contrast to the Hegelian reconciliation of Creator and creation, Kierkegaard's insistence upon the infinite qualitative difference between God and humanity serves to compound and emphasize the abyssal consciousness of the otherness of God and the estrangement of humanity. As such, while Christ, who for Danish Hegelianism—particularly represented by Kierkegaard's former theological tutor, Hans Martensen (1808–1884)[98]—embodies the doctrine of mediation between the divine and the human, he is represented by the pseudonym Johannes Climacus as the paradox: the living contradiction between divinity and humanity.

Hegel's death of God, which proposes to overcome alienation through *Geist*'s becoming conscious of itself in history, implies the death of a God who is radically other to humanity—an otherness that Kierkegaard sees as an inviolable implication of human sinfulness.[99] It is, however, perhaps Kierkegaardian alienation more than Hegelian reconciliation which best describes the progression of late-nineteenth and early-twentieth-century European history. As intimated above, "God is dead" has become a dark saying, an expression of humanity's distance from God—whether in Nietzsche's forsaking of God or more recently in God's apparent forsaking of humanity in a century of genocide, world war, and new global slave trades. Of course, as Schöndorf observes, "Hegel probably did not count on the fact that the further history of the thought of the 'death of God' would lead rather in the direction of an unhappy consciousness instead of necessarily to a resurrection and reconciliation since to us today the night of the I=I seems more abysmal than we would sometimes like."[100]

For now, we must return to the nineteenth century and the anatomy of Kierkegaard's abyss. The notion of the infinite qualitative difference clearly opposed the Hegelian doctrine of *mediation,* but the phrase also evokes broader contemporary connotations. As well as dissenting against theologians' prostitution to the ideals of Danish Hegelianism, Kierkegaard also found himself in the midst of a definite theological crisis of historicity. Enlightenment philosopher and playwright Gotthold Ephraim Lessing famously identified in "On the Proof of Spirit and of Power" that between "the accidental truths of history" and the "necessary truths of reason" there lay a personally impassable "broad ugly ditch"[101]—a phrase with some implicit resonance to Kierkegaard's deliberately exaggerated chasm. Hegel had also confessed in his diary something of the modern suspicion toward the contemporary relevance of a historically founded religion: "In Swabia they say of something which had long since happened: it's so long ago that soon it won't be true anymore. Thus Christ died for our sins so long ago that soon it won't be true anymore."[102] This chasm deepened further in 1835, when David Friedrich Strauss published his *Life of Jesus,* stoking the fires of the infamous "Jesus of history" versus "Christ of faith" debate. Notably, Strauss's book— along with the 1841 publication of Feuerbach's *Essence of Christianity,* with its central claim that "the true sense of Theology is Anthropology"[103]—generated significant intellectual disquiet in Denmark. And this unease involved certain doctoral candidates being refused their examinations after betraying an affinity to such precarious ideas. Indeed, even Kierkegaard's theological and intellectual nemesis, Hans Martensen, felt obliged to moderate his Hegelianism for fear of being identified with such allegedly un-Christian views.[104]

Yet Kierkegaard, as Arbaugh observes, "remarks that the freethinkers are less muddled in interpreting Christianity, than its orthodox defenders, and that they are at least honest in calling it myth and poetry, while the latter betray their own scepticism in their lives."[105] In particular, Feuerbach (the "firebrook"), with his discernment that "atheism . . . is the secret of religion itself,"[106] ironically "can serve for Christians as a purifying fire [*Ild Bæk*]."[107] Although Kierkegaard's infinite qualitative difference between humanity and God can be read as reacting against the grain of Feuerbach's identification of theology and anthropology,[108] his own relation to the earnestness of Feuerbach's project is less reactionary than that of the general intellectual establishment at the time. While he is himself concerned not to be identified with Feuerbach et al., it is possible, Kierkegaard suggests, to receive "*ab hoste consilium*" (advice from the enemy), even from one who may be a "*malitieus dæmon*" (evil dai-mon) (JP VI: 6523 / Pap. X² A 162). Although they assessed the phenome-non of Christianity from distinct perspectives and with divergent motives, Kierkegaard sees in Feuerbach someone who is capable of slicing into religion and exposing the grain of illusion. The fundamental distinction between them resides in the fact that what Feuerbach identifies as the illusion of *Christianity* is identified by Kierkegaard as the insidious delusion of *Christendom*. As such, Feuerbach's critique of Christianity, despite its essential qualitative conflation, can be translated as an "attack upon Christendom" which itself serves as a reminder of the need to insist upon the infinite qualitative difference between humanity and God. According to Kierkegaard, "Feuerbach is saying: No, wait a minute—if you are going to be allowed to go on living as you are living, then you also have to admit that you are not Christians . . . it is wrong of established Christendom to say that Feuerbach is attacking Christianity; it is not true, he is attacking the Christians by demonstrating that their lives do not correspond to the teachings of Christianity" (JP VI: 6523 / Pap. X² A 162). Consequently, as Arbaugh explains: "For Kierkegaard, for whom mere playing at Christianity is more spiritually dangerous than heresy or schism, and for whom hypocrisy is anathema, this exposé by Feuerbach came as welcome support from an unex-pected quarter."[109]

A similarly unexpected solidarity with Feuerbach's exposé of theology can be noted more recently in Karl Barth, who himself avowed a Kierkegaardian infinite qualitative difference. This may come as some surprise since, with his insistence upon the primacy of divine revelation in direct contradiction of Feuerbach's anthropocentrism, Barth apparently "represents the complete antithesis in religious thought to Ludwig Feuerbach."[110] As a theologian who was a contemporary of and greatly influenced by Barth, H. Richard Niebuhr succinctly states: "The great disagreement is that Feuerbach can so believe in man and Barth cannot; this is to no small extent the difference between the nineteenth century and the twentieth."[111] Despite this theological and his-torical chasm, Feuerbach embodies the dangers of taking anthropology as a starting point for religious thought. As a vilified embodiment of this orienta-tion, Feuerbach can serve as a corrective for the very thought he expounds—a corrective that may derive further intensity from the anthropological dis-figurations of the early twentieth century. Man is a starting point which it has become difficult to believe in. However, this should not obscure Barth's admiration for Feuerbach, whom Barth regarded as intensely occupied with the problem of theology—"although his love was an unhappy one."[112] In fact, commenting upon Feuerbach's words, Barth observes that "'theology long ago became anthropology,' ever since Protestantism itself, and especially Luther, emphatically shifted the interest from what God is in himself to what God is for man. Its course of development runs uninterruptedly in such a direction that man more and more renounces God and addresses himself."[113] It is in Lutheranism's anthropocentrism itself that Christianity finds its path toward the internal monologue of theology's dissolution by anthropology. Feuerbach, Kierkegaard, and Barth are in some agreement that where anthropocentrism eclipses the otherness of God, the absolute difference between God and humanity has been compromised within Protestantism itself. As such, in testifying to the Protestant transition toward reflection upon the self, they all share the open secret of the dissolution of Christianity into modernity— caused by a betrayal that has occurred from within.[114]

While this tendency has been discerned by all of them, Kierkegaard and Barth are emphatic that the movement that Feuerbach embraces must ultimately be resisted in the strongest terms. Hence the apparently mutual prominence of the infinite qualitative difference between humanity and God as Wholly Other, in Barth and Kierkegaard. Nevertheless it was, Barth confesses, only around 1919 that Kierkegaard made a profound entry into his thought "at the critical juncture between the first and second editions of my *Commentary on Romans,* and from that time onwards he appeared in an important role in my literary utterances."[115] Of all Barth's writings, Kierkegaard resonates most prominently through the invocations of "the Moment"[116] and "the individual"[117] throughout *Der Römerbrief.* Greater than these, however, is a discernment of the Kierkegaardian abyss, as Barth reveals in his preface to the second edition of that work: "If I have a 'system,' it is limited to a recognition of what Kierkegaard called the 'infinite qualitative distinction' between time and eternity, and to my regarding this as possessing negative as well as positive significance."[118] The revelation of this Kierkegaardian abyss is clearly an important moment in the initiation into faith: "In Jesus the communion of God begins with a rebuff, with the exposure of a vast chasm, with the clear revelation of a great stumbling-block."[119]

However, while Barth proceeds here to identify this stumbling block as the Kierkegaardian offence of the infinite qualitative difference, it also begins to become clear that although Barth may begin with the Kierkegaardian abyss he is reticent to conclude with it. Barth describes himself as graduating decisively from what he called the "school of Kierkegaard." In his address in Copenhagen on 19 April 1963, upon receiving the Sonning Prize for outstanding contributions to European culture, Barth takes the opportunity to account for his relation to "the Danish Lutheran." In this retrospective, the Dane who had embodied the spirit of authentic Christianity's critique of an apostate modern Christendom came to be seen as implicated in the very excesses of anthropocentrism that he intended to vilify. Barth increasingly sensed the uneasy absence of congregation and church in Kierkegaard's thought, and thereby developed a deep suspicion of the "holy individualism" (*Heils-individualismus*)[120] in which Kierkegaard apparently protracted the Lutheran renunciation of theology's "God in himself" in deference to the monologue of anthropology's self-address. Ultimately Barth concluded that he could not attack "man-centred Christianity as such, from a Kierkegaardian basis, because he himself had not attacked, but rather fortified it immensely."[121] Kierkegaard became nothing more or less than "a teacher into whose school every theologian must go once. Woe to him who has missed it! So long as he does not remain in or return to it!"[122] Barth warns how those who have failed to graduate from Kierkegaard's school are captivated by his abyss; it is as if his "infinite qualitative difference between God and man, with all its consequences, has eaten itself right into them."[123] Accordingly, Barth moderated the infinite qualitative difference in his own writings to the extent that, as Søe observes, it would be too stringent to claim that Barth's doctrine is taken directly from Kierkegaard since it "is demonstrably influenced both by Platonism and neo-Kantianism."[124]

Just as Niebuhr had historically distanced Barth from Feuerbach, so Barth's last word on the matter should perhaps be his summary that "Kierkegaard was bound more closely to the nineteenth century than we at the time wanted to believe."[125] This stands as some reproach to the so-called Kierkegaard Renaissance in the Neo-Orthodox, existential, and dialectical theologies of the twentieth century which appear to suggest that, on the contrary, "Kierkegaard was, somehow, born before his time, a prophet of the crises of the twentieth century, particularly with regard to the mutual alienation of Church and State, the advent of what was called 'mass society' and the consequent sense of isolation of the individual."[126] Finally Barth sees that, as a weapon against the malaise of the twentieth century, Kierkegaard cannot be fully transplanted from the battleground of the nineteenth. Bearing in mind Kierkegaard's relation to the cultural aporias of his time—Hegel, Feuerbach, Strauss et al.—is it therefore misleading to assert that "Kierkegaard belonged more to the twentieth century than to the nineteenth"?[127] Is it not rather more accurate to declare that theologians who appropriate such thought simply "deliver a nineteenth-century answer to a twentieth-century dilemma"?[128]

Historically and culturally speaking, the death of God evidently comes to express something subtly different in scope and meaning for Hegel, Kierkegaard, Nietzsche, and many others throughout the twentieth and into the twenty-first centuries. "Though anticipated in Hegel's speculative philosophy and Kierkegaard's attack on Christendom and proclaimed by Nietzsche's madman," Mark C. Taylor claims, "the death of God is not concretely actualized until the emergence of the twentieth-century industrial state."[129] But prior to this emergence, Hegel's "hard saying" also resounded with a

Feuerbachian accent: "the identification of divine and human natures means that God is human nature objectified; man's full appropriation of his own nature becomes the death of God."[130] Man becomes his own object in the correlation of theology and anthropology, and the Wholly Other vanishes. Once exposed as an illusion, "God" is marked for destruction.[131] Yet despite this apparently atheistic crisis in theology and philosophy, and prior to Nietzsche's iconoclasm and the twentieth century postmortem of "God," Kierkegaard had already asserted an infinite qualitative difference between God and the "thought of God." Kierkegaard was emphatic in his 1848 *Christian Discourses* that "one cannot kill God; on the other hand, as is said, one certainly can kill the thought of Him" (CD, 66). As such, Kierkegaard's preservation of the infinite qualitative difference categorically seeks to defend the excessive anthropocentric emphasis in theology from the Feuerbachian collapse of theology into anthropology that Barth discerned within Lutheranism.

While Feuerbach radically identified theology and anthropology, Kierkegaard repeatedly and defiantly asserted the infinite qualitative difference between humanity and divinity. And yet, seeing the self's implicit dependence upon God, Kierkegaard warned: "To slay God is the most dreadful suicide [*Selvmord*]; utterly to forget God is a human being's deepest fall [*dybeste Fald*]—a beast cannot fall that deep" (CD, 67). For Kierkegaard, the self is dependent upon God to the extent that presumptuously to "kill the thought of God" would be tantamount to obliterating the self. In this sense, he anticipated that the death of God was an announcement of the suicidal death of self. Once God has been killed, invigorated by the magnitude of his deed: *homo hominis deus,* man is the god of man. However, inevitably unable to sustain himself on his throne, this corrupts into the ignominy of *homo hominis lupus,* man is a wolf to man.[132]

Yet does the infinite qualitative difference successfully immunize the thought of God against contamination by the hard saying of the death of God? Or does Kierkegaard instead inadvertently testify to its inescapable veracity? According to theologian Gabriel Vahanian's 1961 study *The Death of God,* Kierkegaard's infinite qualitative difference and Nietzsche's death of God lead to the same conclusion. Both are resistant to immanentism; both imply that "no ladder leads from man to God . . . that there is no identity of substance between man and God, and, accordingly, that the problem of human existence is independent of the problem of God."[133] Though of course Kierkegaard strove precisely to return the problem of human existence to the problem of God, it can be argued that Kierkegaard fails to defy the cultural implications of the death of God, and even that he implicates himself at the heart of the lacuna. "For Kierkegaard, Christianity is dead," Vahanian alleges, "so dead that Kierkegaard would not call himself a Christian."[134]

Yet this assumption seems to base itself on a conflation of Christianity and Christendom, in Kierkegaard's thought—two ideas between which there is a qualitative difference. "Christendom is," according to Kierkegaard's late polemical attack on the bourgeois Danish church, "the decay of Christianity" ("The Fatherland," February 1855; LW, 41). In fact, as Kierkegaard states explicitly in the posthumous *Armed Neutrality:* "I believe it is an overstatement to say that Christianity in our time has been completely abolished. No, Christianity is still present and in its truth, but as a *teaching,* as *doctrine.* What has been abolished and forgotten, however (and this can be said without exaggeration), is *existing as a Christian*" (AN, 34). Kierkegaard detected a more insidious and covert atheism in the inauthentic theater of the bourgeois Danish church. In a culture where being born a Christian was synonymous with being born a Dane, Kierkegaard strove to reintroduce Christianity into Christendom, not through the reimagining of doctrine (as liberal and Hegelian theology had done), but by reenergizing the radical tension of subjectivity that is inherent to becoming a Christian. Furthermore, Kierkegaard's reluctance in identifying himself as a Christian was not due so much to the decay of Christianity, as the rigorous height at which he esteemed its authentic expression. His position was one to which he attached this military phrase, "armed neutrality": "Naturally, it cannot mean that I want to leave undecided the question of whether or not I myself am a Christian, am pursuing it, fighting for it, praying about it, and hoping before God that I am that. What I have wanted to *prevent* and want to prevent now is any sort of impression that I am a Christian to any extraordinary degree, a remarkable kind of Christian" (AN, 33).

It has been retrospectively surmised that Kierkegaard's own insistence upon the radical otherness of God prompted an existential style of modern theology that emerged partly in response to the capitulation of Christendom, but was also founded "more deeply in response to the advent of a reality that was wholly divorced from the world of faith, or, as Kierkegaard saw, a reality that was created by the negation of faith."[135] Altizer therefore alleges that "Kierkegaard knew the death of God only as an objective reality; indeed, it was 'objectivity' that was created by the death of God. . . . But in Kierkegaard's time the death of God had not yet become a subjective reality."[136] For Kierkegaard, the inner life of faith as subjectivity consolidated itself against a nineteenth-century culture of a heightening and spreading divine absence (if we can speak this way) which was increasingly bearing anxious witness to the shifts in evolutionary theory, scientific discovery, historical criticism, urban life, and economics. Although facing extinction in the world, it was still possible for God to take refuge in the hearts of individuals. It is an inner life that derived dialectical tension from an understanding of God as Wholly Other: a faith that rehabilitates and testifies to the classic opposition of God to the world. It is precisely this archaic enmity that Christendom had forgotten, thereby losing sight of an existential tension that Kierkegaard sought to rehabilitate in his polemic against the Danish church: "God is indeed a human being's most appalling enemy, your mortal enemy," Kierkegaard reminded his reader in an article in "The Moment," shortly before his own death, "he wants you to die, die unto the world; he hates specifically that in which you naturally have your life, to which you cling with all your zest for life" ("The Moment" no. 5, 27 July 1855; LW, 177).

According to Altizer's reading, however, while "faith as subjectivity" was feasible in Kierkegaard's time, it can no longer be deemed credible in the later twentieth-century climate of the full accomplishment of God's death. Tracing a similar trajectory, as Alasdair MacIntyre explains, much of the vitalizing tension of subjectivity has been dispelled as the self-consciously polemical atheism of the nineteenth and early twentieth century has increasingly deferred to the figure of "the secularized unbeliever, who sees no point in actually denying the existence of God because he never saw any point in affirming it in the first place."[137] As such, much of the dialectical fire of "faith as subjectivity" is extinguished as, in Altizer's terms, the death of God becomes increasingly a *subjective* as well as objective reality in twentieth-century Western Europe. The grief of the death of God has passed through culture to faith and finally infiltrated the inner heart of subjectivity. Consequently, Christendom *has* actually been demystified—though not quite as Kierkegaard would have envisaged. This separation of Christianity from "world" occurs more from the culminated process of secularization that Kierkegaard discerned to be emerging than from the kind of dialectical awakening from this process of decline that he himself sought to provoke. The secularism that in Kierkegaard's day was not conscious of itself as such, today sees little reason to question itself. But what becomes of Christianity now that Christendom has been abolished in the very secularism Kierkegaard urged it to resist? Perhaps surprisingly, as Harvey Cox has astutely observed in 1965's *The Secular City*, "the process of secularization in Europe has alleviated Kierkegaard's problem. . . . More and more, 'being a Christian' is a conscious choice rather than a matter of birth or inertia. The change can hardly be viewed as unfortunate."[138] In other words, secularization evacuates Christianity to the cultural periphery where, at least in its more Kierkegaardian formation, it is most indigenous and incisive. Perhaps the twist in the tale is that Kierkegaard has been revealed to be a certain kind of ironic prophet. Christendom has died, and so Christianity lives on in the crucible of "otherness" from which it first emerged.

While the "otherness" of Christianity alleviates to some extent Kierkegaard's problem of "becoming a Christian in Christendom," the subjective
tension of the choice of "becoming a Christian in the world," of the dilemma
between spirit and spiritlessness, still persists for the human subject since:
"Every creature feels best in its own element, can really live only there. The
fish cannot live in the air, the bird cannot live in the water—and for spirit
to have to live in an environment devoid of spirit means to die, agonizingly
to die slowly so that death is a blessed relief" ("This Must Be Said; So Let It
Be Said," 11 April 1855; LW, 78). The imagery employed here in an 1855 article is reminiscent of pseudonym Johannes Climacus's descriptions of spiritual trial (Dn. *Anfægtelse*) in 1846's *Concluding Unscientific Postscript*. In this
account, the infinite qualitative difference is perceived with such horror that
the person before God is like a fish trapped on dry land or a bird in a cage
(CUP, 483–484). Such a violent depiction of traditional Lutheran spirituality as *Anfechtung* typifies what Cupitt, in 1980's *Taking Leave of God,* has
subsequently admonished as the "spiritually crushing *over-againstness*"[139] of
the Wholly Other God which for many constitutes sufficient reason to also
embrace the death of God as *subjectivity.* In other words, if faith as subjectivity demands that the self must be captured, annihilated, or tortured by the
numinous fire of spirit, then who—in their right mind—would wish to venture to stand before such a dreadful God?

However, I shall ultimately contend that this spiritually crushing view of
God as Wholly Other should not finally be taken for the God who is spoken of in Kierkegaard's writings. In fact, Kierkegaard's writings, while taking
the reader to the very brink of this abyss, precisely recoil from the vision
of God as "infinitely sublime" (Dn. *uendelig ophøiet*)—recalling the earlier
important "SUBDIVISIO" of the God-relationship—and turn instead to the
impossible possibility of the divine look of love. To gaze into the abyss is
a gesture toward gazing through the abyss (which separates us from God,
but is *not* God) in order to meet in faith the forgiving gaze of the Holy One
of grace. Nevertheless, this present work seeks not to evade but to engage
with the understandable allegation that to be in a Kierkegaardian relation to
God inevitably means to become an irremediably unhappy consciousness,
alienated from the world no less than from the Wholly Other God. In this
vein, Jean-Paul Sartre described Kierkegaard as the "martyr of interiority"[140]
who, "whatever he did, acted within the limits of what Hegel had called the
unhappy consciousness."[141] Indeed, Kierkegaard's writings do apparently give
the reader many opportunities for concluding that faith as subjectivity entails
nothing but an alienating and archaic "fear of the Lord." Such, according to
Friedman, is the exalted subjectivity of Abraham as a "knight of faith" in
1843's controversial *Fear and Trembling*—someone who by forsaking creation

in order to follow the voice of the Wholly Other that commands him to sacrifice his son Isaac, also "bears witness to the 'death of God'":

> Kierkegaard's "knight of faith" must choose *between* God and creation. He
> rejects society and culture for the lonely relationship of the "Single One"
> to God, thereby losing any check on the reality of the voice that addresses
> him. In its very affirmation of faith, as a result, Kierkegaard's concept of the
> "knight of faith" is a consequence and an expression of the "death of God": it
> entails the loss of faith in the universal order and in the society that purports
> to be founded on it; the rejection of creation—the world and society—as an
> obstacle to the relationship with God; and the paradoxical "leap of faith" that
> is necessary to attain any sort of contact with God.[142]

Such is the vision of an arcane Kierkegaardian subjectivity which also
alarmed Martin Buber—what he influentially decried as Kierkegaard's "religious doctrine of loneliness."[143] The authentic God-relation, Buber counters,
must not demand the self-alienation of the Single One through subjectivity's
renunciation of the other: "Creation is not a hurdle on the road to God, it
is the road itself."[144] But to read the Abraham of Kierkegaard's pseudonym
Johannes de Silentio as Hegel's unhappy consciousness is to overlook the
exceptional singularity of Abraham in *Fear and Trembling*. The immensity
of Abraham's ordeal (Dn. *Prøvelse*) depends upon his esteem for the ethical
universal. Furthermore, if the universal *was* irrevocably renounced by the
God-relationship then Abraham would *never* have returned to it. The point
in *Fear and Trembling* is that God's command to sacrifice Isaac is a *suspension* of the ethical and not its irreversible annihilation. Abraham experiences a "repetition" in which the universal order is not subjected to nihilism,
but rather is restored and transfigured through its own suspension: "By faith
Abraham did not renounce Isaac, but by faith Abraham received Isaac" (FT,
49). Abraham returns to creation. If God is *irremediably* Wholly Other, then
one is irrevocably consigned to the unhappy consciousness: a permanently
alienated fugitive, even, from the consummation of the God-relationship.
The unhappy consciousness is a perpetual longing after what is absent. Here
we are returned to the abyss in which faith can be nothing but despair. But,
de Silentio implores, "actually it is not faith but the most remote possibility
of faith that faintly sees its object on the most distant horizon but is separated from it by a chasmal abyss in which doubt plays its tricks" (FT, 20). The
irremediably estranged faith of the unhappy consciousness is surely implicitly impeached by Silentio's pronouncement that "Abraham had faith, and
had faith for this life. . . . Abraham's faith was not of this sort" (FT, 20).[145]

And yet there is undeniably something that resembles unhappy consciousness in this faith—something redolent of the religious melancholy that will be discussed in the next chapter. Abraham, for the moment, does walk a higher path—though he does not for this reason disdain the universal in his passion for the estrangement of pursuing the absolute. The knight of faith "knows that it is beautiful to be born as the single individual who has home in the universal. . . . But he also knows that up higher there winds a lonesome trail, steep and narrow; he knows it is dreadful to be born solitary outside the universal, to walk without meeting one single traveller" (FT, 75–76). There is another reason why the knight of faith must take a path that winds solitary, narrow, steep, and otherwise than the universal. This reason is that this is where God can be found, not because God has chosen transcendence, but because God has allowed Godself to be evacuated. It is in this sense that Emmanuel Levinas calls Kierkegaard's God a "persecuted truth,"[146] a God who is exiled by the thought which renders the divine incommensurable with human reason. From this inverse perspective, the otherness of God proceeds from the evacuation of God from the world. It is therefore only by receiving the call of God as the hidden other, the crucified paradox, that humanity is called to salvation.[147] As such, the culture of the death of God is itself responsible for this God appearing as other than the world, because the world regards a living God—a God who asks such things of faith—to be anathema.

As such, God calls the knight of faith out of the universal and into what Sylviane Agacinski perceptively identifies as an *aparté*—an *aside* with God: "The relation to God is a *secret* link. . . . The relation to God that takes place in silence and darkness is *the most difficult attachment*."[148] And one senses that, in order to awaken the spirit of subjectivity from the stupor that hangs over Christendom, Kierkegaard and his pseudonymous conspirators would have it no other way than *difficult*. But this secrecy of faith is not first of all hermetic, mystical, or occult. It is not a secret for all but the initiate, because it is a secret openly offered to every "single one." It is the secret of the Wholly Other and also of the Holy One. The God who emerges from the tomb *post mortem Dei* must to an extent appear in secret, because the world will not believe in the resurrection of the one whom it has named among the dead. This is "offence," about which more will be said later. It is also the grief of God, since it is a *wounded* revelation that is called a paradox: a paradox that is consigned to the peripheries of human existence. It is this that informs the authentic meaning of calling God the Wholly Other.

THE WHOLLY OTHER: *Alterity* AND ESTRANGEMENT

In *The Gift of Death*, Derrida employs the *secrecy* of the Abrahamic God-relationship as an entry point for what has since become a highly prominent consideration of the wholly other in relation to Kierkegaard's *Fear and Trembling*: "Abraham himself is in secret, cut off both from man and from God."[149] Here Derrida reproduces something apparently similar to the Hegelian alienation of the Hebraic consciousness: what he calls "the still Jewish experience of a secret, hidden, separate, absent, or mysterious God, the one who decides, without revealing his reasons, to demand of Abraham that most cruel, impossible, and untenable gesture: to offer his son Isaac as a sacrifice. All that goes on in secret. God keeps silent about his reasons."[150] Derrida commences his discussion of *Fear and Trembling* with some reflections upon what he calls the "*Mysterium tremendum*. A frightful mystery, a secret to make you tremble."[151] Derrida apparently describes the *mysterium tremendum* in initially voyeuristic terms: the shudder of the one who is looked at yet "doesn't see what is looking at me."[152] His contemplation of the trembling before the *mysterium tremendum* is expressed in language that would not be out of place in a discussion of spiritual trial (Gn. *Anfechtung*): "We fear and tremble because we are already in the hands of God . . . and under the gaze of [the] God . . . we don't see and whose will we cannot know."[153]

These invocations of the *mysterium tremendum* are reminiscent of Otto's influential consideration of the numinous as *mysterium tremendum et fascinans* in his 1917 work, *Das Heilige*. Yet little of Otto's *fascinans* is apparent as Derrida reveals his essential concern to be the secret (*le secret*) as "*mysterium tremendum*: the terrifying mystery, the dread, the fear and trembling of the Christian before the sacrificial gift," which he had earlier considered in relation to Jan Patočka's *Heretical Essays on the Philosophy of History*.[154] Yet Derrida's invocation once again recalls Otto's category of the *mysterium tremendum* insofar as Derrida's consideration proceeds to the "wholly other" (*tout autre*)—a term Otto also applies to the *mysterium* as *das Ganz andere*. Derrida's attention, though, is not so much upon the numinous in its *fascinans* character as on the notion of the secrecy implicit in *alterity* itself. As such, the *mysterium* is here closer to what Otto identifies as the "purely natural" than the "religious sense." As Otto distinguishes:

> Taken, indeed, in its purely natural sense, "mysterium" would first mean
> merely a secret or a mystery in the sense of that which is alien to us, uncom-
> prehended and unexplained. . . . Taken in the religious sense, that which
> is "mysterious" is—to give it perhaps the most striking expression—the
> "wholly other" [*das Ganz andere*]. . . . That which is beyond the sphere of the
> usual, the intelligible and the familiar, which therefore falls quite outside the
> limits of the "canny," and is contrasted with it, filling the mind with blank
> wonder and astonishment.[155]

Derrida makes no explicit reference to Otto; however, by applying Otto's distinction between natural and religious senses of *mysterium,* I think one can begin to discern more clearly between a Derridean and Kierkegaardian sense of the Wholly Other. If one reads Derrida as concerned with something closer to what Otto describes as the "natural" than the "religious" sense of the secret or *mysterium,* then one begins to gather an idea of how Derrida eventually dissolves the absolute from his reading of *Fear and Trembling.*

Although Derrida does at least initially speak of God as the absolute, it is telling that, for Derrida, God as *"wholly other"* (*tout autre*) resides in his secrecy, or rather in his withholding: "if he were to speak to us all the time without any secrets, he wouldn't be the other, we would share a type of homogeneity."[156] If God revealed all his secrets, God would cease to be God (as wholly other): something that one might say is implicit in the secret concealing of the divine name. However, Derrida gradually reveals a hidden "homogeneity" between God's "otherness" and the "otherness of every other." Insofar as I bind myself exclusively in duty to "the other," Derrida explains, I am implicitly forsaking my duty to the infinite number of others to whom I am not binding myself (even insofar as my gift to one denies the other).[157] "I can respond only to the one (or to the One), that is, to the other, by sacrificing the other to that one."[158]

It is the homogeneity of secrecy in Derrida's account which deliberately disturbs the Kierkegaardian understanding in which the absolute alone is Wholly Other and calls Abraham into a secret relation that is like no other: what one might call the "religious sense" of the *mysterium.* In other words, as each is a secret to the other then, as Derrida often repeats: "every other (one) is every (bit) other" (*tout autre est tout autre*).[159] Each of us retains an inaccessible *alterity:* our inviolable secret. Therefore Derrida suggests that:

> God, as the wholly other, is to be found everywhere there is something of the wholly other. And since each of us, everyone else, each other is infinitely other in its absolute singularity, inaccessible, solitary, transcendent, non-manifest, non-present to my ego . . . then what can be said about Abraham's relation to God can be said about my relation without relation to *every other (one) as every (bit) other* [*tout autre comme tout autre*], in particular to my neighbour or my loved one who are as inaccessible to me, as secret and transcendent as Jahweh. Every other (in the sense of each other) is every bit other (absolutely other).[160]

The Kierkegaardian infinite qualitative difference is ultimately reduced to (human) *alterity.* Every "other" is "wholly other." The ramifications are as John Caputo describes: "The name of God, of the biblical God of Abraham and Isaac, need not be God for us; it is enough for 'God' to be the name of the absolutely other . . . God's mind is wholly other to Abraham, as is the mind of every other, my friends and my family, who are as transcendent to me as Yahweh."[161] From the Kierkegaardian perspective, God is Wholly Other for me, a stranger to myself as I also become a stranger to myself, due to *sin*. In the Derridean linguistic orientation, as Caputo describes, "saying 'God is wholly other' is a textual operation, a work of hyperbolic excess, that depends upon its textual, contextual base, a piece of hymnal, holy excess."[162] Once captivated in this web of linguistic play, the confession of God as "wholly other" becomes "*stricto sensu*, impossible. To say the least, God would then be wholly other than whatever is being said by saying that God is wholly other, wholly other even than God."[163] In other words, the "wholly other" multiplies itself by differentiation from even its own assertion of itself. It becomes the linguistic deferral of meaning in the name of an irreducible *alterity*. One might be forgiven for thinking that this entwines us in the linguistic web of a negative theology—though one in which, as such, the name of "God" is even subordinated to the "name" of the "wholly other."[164]

In the light of this appropriation, the infinite qualitative difference—which for Johannes Climacus is sin—becomes merely an expression of *alterity*. As Westphal explains, for Johannes Climacus, "apart from sin God is not wholly other. God becomes wholly other only when the self-estrangement of fault renders God a stranger."[165] The Kierkegaardian infinite qualitative difference is not simply the *alterity* that is shared between every other, but the qualitative *estrangement* of sin. God has become a stranger and not merely an other like every other. The difference is not only a "qualitative difference" (*qualitativ Forskjel*), but a "chasmic abyss" (*svælgende Dyb*) that should be characterized as "absolute" (*absolut*), "eternal" (*evig*), "essential" (*væsentlig*), and "infinite" (*uendelig*). It is a difference—an abyss—that induces anxiety, despair, fear, and trembling. Westphal therefore describes the individual's apprehension of the infinite qualitative difference as a form of "ontological xenophobia" (the fear of estranged being). This dreadful *estrangement* can be overcome by the *faith* that reconciles humanity and God in "the courage to meet one who has become a stranger."[166]

However, in this work I emphasize that faith does not negate the human-divine difference entirely—as if one were to become identical with God in the act of believing. "Difference is a sin—or rather: the sin is to differ," Sylviane Agacinski describes; "man is guilty of difference."[167] But one could be misled into thinking that the *only* difference between God and humanity is *sin*. Westphal seems to imply this when he says that "apart from sin God is not wholly other." But if one reads God as "Wholly Other" as the name one uses for God as the (un-named) *stranger*, then one can say that, once God is no longer a stranger, God can then be called by another name (albeit a name that also remains open to revision): a name that retains *alterity*, yet which reflects the overcoming of the estrangement of sin. Faith ultimately preserves *alterity*, both human and divine, in the face-to-face relation of becoming a self *before God*. Apart from sin, God is not *Wholly* Other—that is a *stranger*—but God is still *Other* than myself. For example, God as a stranger, as an unknown, confronts the reader of Genesis 32—as Jacob wrestles with the stranger who will not disclose his name. One might call this God the Wholly Other because this name describes our relation to God; at this point, one also has *no other name* for the stranger. But by even revealing Godself to be Wholly Other, there is some negation of this absolute estrangement. In the form of the stranger of Genesis 32, God is no longer inaccessible as the Wholly Other, but gives of Godself in the concession of the struggle. God preserves the life of Jacob who has not only seen God face-to-face and lived, but has been blessed with the divine gift of a new name, and a new self-knowledge (Genesis 32:28–30). The faceless stranger who always lives in the infinite distance of the absolute is not the same as the stranger who crosses the chasmic abyss in order to emerge face-to-face.

It is God who reveals the infinite distance, as Johannes Climacus explains, but this very revelation is also the beginning of reconciling the difference that revelation impresses upon the individual. One may call this God "the unknown" (*det Ubekjendte*), as the pagans referred to the divine,[168] and thus one "must *first* come to know that it is different from him [the god], absolutely different from him" (PF, 46; my emphasis). But the "absolutely different" (*absolut forskjelligt*), like the Wholly Other, is not the last name for God. One might call it an anthropocentrically derived name for God since sin, "the absolute difference, must have been caused by the individual himself" (PF, 47). As such, the absolutely different, the Wholly Other, are names for God primarily through the consciousness of estrangement or sin. But sin cannot be the resting point for our talking of God. As Anti-Climacus explains in one of the most significant expressions of the infinite qualitative difference in Kierkegaard's writings:

> Sin is the one and only predication about a human being that in no way, either *via negationis* [by denial] or *via eminentiæ* [by idealization], can be stated of God. To say of God (in the same sense as saying that he is not finite and consequently, *via negationis,* that he is infinite) that he is not a sinner is blasphemy. (SUD, 122)

The consciousness of sin, the "infinite qualitative difference," informs us anthropocentrically about our estrangement from God. One speaks of God as Wholly Other than oneself—though it is Godself who has revealed this difference to the individual. This recalls the spirit of anthropocentrism expressed in Buber's *I and Thou*: "Of course we speak only of what God is in his relation to man."[169] Buber is right: we can do no other. However, this is not to say that it is we who have fathomed the relation just because it is we who come to explicate it anthropocentrically. God as Wholly Other does not therefore solidify the self as the inevitable starting point for consciousness of God. For Kierkegaard, such a self has no such internal solidity apart from God. What matters is the new name given *by* God, which describes who Jacob is *before* God—*Yisraèl*, "struggling with God." This does not reveal who God is in Godself—the stranger refuses to reveal his own name to Jacob—but it reveals who Jacob is in relation to God. And it also says something about God anthropocentrically: God is one who has struggled with Jacob, but did not destroy him. What God is in relation to humanity (Wholly Other, absolute difference, etc.) has been revealed by God; but if one rests with these names then there is a risk of closing oneself off from a deeper revelation of the infinite qualitative difference. The abyss has not been understood until it is made known how it has been crossed, just as the infinite difference can only be revealed through a revelation which begins to overcome the very distance it inscribes.

As the name of the Wholly Other arises in the consciousness of sin, so in the consciousness of the forgiveness of sins does another name suggest itself. Just as human sin predicates nothing of God, so God's response to sin demonstrates something which cannot be predicated of humanity. Continuing the above vital passage in *The Sickness unto Death,* Anti-Climacus asserts that while God is so infinitely unlike me in my sinfulness, I am so infinitely unlike God in the forgiving of sins:

> As sinner, man is separated from God by the most chasmic qualitative abyss.
> In turn, of course, God is separated from man by the same chasmic qualitative abyss when he forgives sins. If by some kind of reverse adjustment the divine could be shifted over to the human, there is one way in which man could never in all eternity come to be like God: in forgiving sins. (SUD, 122)

Here is what I take to be a correlative to the earlier considered DIVISIO/SUBDIVISIO in Kierkegaard's *Journals*: sin is the infinite abyss that separates me from God; forgiveness is the same abyss viewed from the other side, as it were. The abyss can be more faithfully anatomized once both sides of the severance are made known—though we begin from the only side of the severance on which we find ourselves.

But we do not stand at the edge of the world, as it were, staring into an endless abyss. Beyond the abyss of sin lies the unknown who knows us and can yet become known to us, as it makes us known to ourselves. I shall suggest, therefore, that "Wholly Other" cannot be the last name for God, though it is an appropriate beginning for a theology of the self before God. It is at the edge, facing the abyss, that the self must begin. And yet there is always the danger of remaining there, of sliding into the abyss in which the Wholly Other becomes "so infinitely sublime" (*uendelig ophøiet*) that the God-relationship appears to call for nothing but an intractable melancholy, despair, and the deepest anxiety. It is the knife-edge between despair and faith which requires, and is required by, the present work. Yet the infinite chasmic abyss must be revealed to the self, and so there must be a time in which one is not mistaken, *humanly speaking*, in calling God the "Wholly Other."

Throughout Kierkegaard's writings God is spoken of as "absolutely different" (*absolut forskjelligt*), but also more vaguely, Johannes Climacus refers to "the Unknown." The Lutheran theologian Martin J. Heinecken in his 1956 *The Moment Before God* has described the general notion of the Unknown in a passage which, without making explicit reference to Johannes Climacus, is ostensibly reminiscent: "The unknown, which is really other than anything known, must come to man and disclose himself in such a way that this self-disclosure itself grants the condition and itself opens the eyes and illumines the understanding."[170] Interestingly, Heinecken the Kierkegaard scholar proceeds to identify what is commonly referred to as "the Unknown," not with Kierkegaard, but with Otto's *mysterium tremendum*.[171] It is further enticing to note that the description of God in Kierkegaard's writings as "completely other" (Dn. *ganske Andet*) finds an apparent parallel in Otto's naming of God as "the Wholly Other" (Gn. *das Ganz Andere*) who is also "*alienum*."[172] Yet, pursuing such terminological coincidences and affinities briefly, it is particularly Otto's naming of "the Holy" (Gn. *Das Heilige*) which echoes the name for God in Kierkegaard's devotional writings as "the Holy One" (Dn. *den Hellige*) (cf. UDVS, 285)—a name that suggests that "the Unknown" and the "Wholly Other" are not final appellations within the God-relationship.

Adapting these designations, I shall suggest that it would be more appropriate to speak of the Kierkegaardian self before God in terms, not of the Wholly Other, but rather the *Holy* Other—a name which is itself open to effacement. Yet the *Holy* Other, instead of negating the Wholly Other, actually encompasses and surpasses it in resonance insofar as the word "Holy" (deriving from the Old English *hálig*) encompasses "Whole" (from the Old English *hál*, meaning "healthy"). Furthermore, while denoting "completely," "Holy" also implies *alterity*. That which is Holy is relationally *other*: according to Otto's schema, it is set apart from the profane in relation to God.[173] Despite recent attempts to conceive Wholly Other in terms of sheer *alterity*, I suggest that God as Wholly Other rather implies the infinite qualitative difference of divine-human estrangement. Yet when the self, becoming itself before God, perceives itself through the eyes of God as forgiven, the Wholly Other reveals itself as the *Holy* Other: the God who loves, suffers, and graciously creates the gift of selfhood. In other words, God as Wholly Other results from and is asserted by sin and the consciousness of sin. God as Holy Other is that which overcomes the estrangement of the "infinite qualitative difference" of sin and reveals a forgiveness which invites the self to a communion predicated upon heterogeneity. It announces: "Be holy as I am Holy" (Leviticus 11:44).[174]

However, this is not to say that human-divine *alterity* is annihilated in sacred "oneness." God's overcoming of the infinite qualitative difference does not represent mystical or ontological fusion, but an overcoming of *estrangement*.[175] In order to become transparent to oneself before God, the self must be willing, as Westphal indicates, to meet the God "who has become a stranger." The *Holy* Other, as such, is still the Other, and as Other—as *mysterium*—will always elude the self's possession, identification, or ultimate naming of God-in-Godself. And just as God remains the Other, so Kierkegaard's writings are interested in how one becomes oneself before God, *coram Deo,* in the dreadful and loving epiphany of the face-to-face. This abyssal heterogeneity, as I shall propose, may take the self through the dark night of melancholy, anxiety, spiritual trial, and despair. And it is in the depths of this night that the self discovers its annihilation and transmutation—the triumph of divine *forgiveness* over *impossibility*: the impossibility of knowing oneself, ingrained in the impossibility of knowing God, entangled in the impossibility of overcoming the infinite abyss of sin. The strenuous impossibility of the task is the *metanoia* which prepares the self to see itself from the other side of a seemingly abyssal and endless night—through the forgiving eyes of the *Holy* Other. And so the self must *initially* come to terms with the grief and estrangement of its Unhappy Consciousness: its sense of mourning and melancholy over the impossibility of knowing a God and a self that continues to elude the consummation of the understanding. And yet, proceeding in a minor key, I argue that this melancholy, like despair, can be dialectically understood as a potentially soteriological symptom of the presence of the lost eternal and hence a latent desire for divine communion within the as yet unreconciled self.

The only legitimate tears are those cried over oneself. Praised be the one who can say: Myself—that is the only object I have found worthy enough— or wretched enough—to cry over.

—KIERKEGAARD'S *Journals*

THREE

The Abyss of Melancholy

I was flung down into the abyss of melancholy . . .

—KIERKEGAARD'S *Journals*

As explored in the previous chapter, the call of the eternal resonates with both a presence and an absence within the self. The self is destined to become itself before God; but, through the call of the eternal, it also knows that it is not yet a self, not yet spirit. Furthermore, the self knows that between itself and God—and hence between itself and its self—there lies an infinite qualitative abyss of unknowing. This is despair, which is bound to the will to be, or not to be, oneself. But there is also the presentiment melancholy (Gr. *melancholiā*)[1] of the self which feels the presence and the absence, the loneliness and grief of the abyss between self and self, self and God. This melancholy has not yet willed itself into despair (as will become clearer later), but instead wanders listlessly under the dark cloud of its own deficit and longing. Melancholy, in this relation, thus signifies a "self" in mourning for itself, or for God: in essence, the nascent "self" mourns the loss of something that it nevertheless feels a trace of within itself. Its task is ultimately to realize its longing for the divine other in whom alone the self will receive true knowledge of itself.

Throughout the previous chapter it became apparent that the emergence of selfhood in modernity occurs in constant relation to a backdrop of loss. The human subject consolidates its loss of metaphysical ground through withdrawal into introspection—a self-reflection collapsing into its own abyss (Dn. *Afgrund*). Man, Foucault therefore wagers, is destined to be "erased, like a face drawn in sand at the edge of the sea."[2] The notion is that while the melancholy of modernity originates in the apparent loss of God, its consummation is manifest in the apparent loss of self. The melancholy of the absence of God is both a symptom and a cause of the modern turn toward a selfhood that inevitably comes to see itself as unobtainable. As the sociologist Harvie Ferguson writes in his excellent study of Kierkegaard's religious psychology, *Melancholy and the Critique of Modernity:* "Melancholy sets in motion, through the deepening self-awareness implied in the failure of distraction to cure us of unhappiness, the specifically modern longing for authentic selfhood."[3] But this is a longing which the disillusion of melancholy alone is destined to be unable to fulfill. As such, I shall suggest that melancholy plays an important instructive role, for Kierkegaard particularly, in the rise of self-consciousness; and also, at the same time, in inscribing the failure to authenticate the very self which promises the alleviation of melancholy. Melancholy is therefore essentially an expression of the infinite qualitative difference between self and God. In directing its longing toward the divine, therefore, a religious melancholy can have a significant dialectical role to perform in the self's struggle to become itself before God.

KIERKEGAARD AND THE ANATOMY OF MODERN MELANCHOLY: FROM *Acedia* TO THE ABYSS OF BOREDOM

La mélancholie, toujours inséparable du sentiment du beau.

—CHARLES BAUDELAIRE

How wonderfully melancholy and religion can blend together.

—KIERKEGAARD'S *Journals*

Kierkegaard reads as one of modernity's greatest anatomists of melancholy, but no less as one of the most virile and ironic critics of melancholic modernity. Kierkegaard stands among the most expressive modern exponents of a Christian tradition that evokes a long and vitalizing historical affinity between the search for religious truth and the aspirational disillusion of "the traditional *tristitia,* the melancholy world-view of the *homo religiosus.*"[4] Fictional and yet profoundly personal, Kierkegaard's writings anatomize an inner tension between the aesthetic and the religious that reveals a dialectical melancholy within the modern self. Kierkegaard's propensity for dramatic lyrical confessions has itself consistently attracted morbid and salacious speculation about the secret suffering which, invoking the suffering of St. Paul, he provocatively names his "thorn in the flesh." The pathology of Kierkegaard's neurotic religiosity (a pathology that is secondary to the concerns of the present study) has been traced variously to such—sometimes speculative—hidden sources as manic-depression, psychosis, sexual anxiety, syphilis,[5] epilepsy,[6] or even Kierkegaard's alleged hunchback.[7] Although Kierkegaard never devoted a conceptual publication to melancholy as such, as he did for instance with anxiety and despair, his writing frequently exhibits insightful autobiographical application of the tradition of melancholy: "What in a certain sense is called 'spleen' and what the mystics knew by the designation 'the arid moments,' the Middle Ages knew as *acedia*" (JP 1:739 / Pap. II A 484). It is to this *tristitia* that Kierkegaard relates his father's brooding temperament, invoking "A *quiet despair*" (JP 1:740 / Pap. II A 485).[8] Under this phrase Kierkegaard recounts a genealogy of hereditary melancholy: a father laboring under a secret burden and a silent confidant, his son Søren, "upon whom the whole of that melancholy descended in inheritance" (*Journals*, ed. Dru 600 / Pap.VII A 126).[9]

By relating his most intimate acquaintance with melancholy to the religious notion of *acedia* ("carelessness," also related to being grieved: *acedieris*),[10] Kierkegaard alludes to the fundamental realization that melancholy can constitute a sickness of *spirit* as well as the mind. In this diagnosis, Kierkegaard consciously evokes a Christian genealogy of melancholy which endures from the early monastic and mystical traditions, through the cloisters of the Middle Ages, and, through Kierkegaard's own descriptions, into the secularized boredom of the modern urban aesthete. According to the classical rhetoric of *acedia*, it is at the height of the midday sun that the "noonday devil" induces apathy in the ascetic, tempting him away from the struggle (spiritual trial) of the religious vocation by seductive thoughts of comfort and shelter. This notion of *acedia* was traditionally identified with the deadly sin of sloth—a dreadful obstacle on the path of spiritual self-refinement. In this arid moment, the sun burns in its zenith and the shadows fall at their shortest: "A cold shadow falls over the hermit's soul even as the burning sun stands directly above him in the sky. The soul becomes both actually and metaphorically opaque, impenetrable to the activating radiance which was the nurturing medium of human physical and spiritual wellbeing."[11]

In spite of its significance to the development of religious approaches to melancholy, *acedia*, as Kierkegaard recognized, is scarcely mentioned as a modern malady—an omission that, according to E. W. Trueman Dicken's study of the mysticism of John of the Cross and Teresa of Jesus, implies "a disquieting comment on the superficiality of our spiritual education."[12] Despite this acknowledged decline in focus, it has been suggested by the psychiatrist and pioneer in pastoral counseling Frank Lake, in his *Clinical Theology*, that "under the term 'akedia' or 'accidie' clinical theologians of the past thought and wrote a great deal about what we now call depression."[13] However, it would be misleading to assert that the spiritual notion of *acedia* is a malady that is always synonymous with melancholy itself. Due to its voluntary and sinful quality, the indictment of *acedia* in monastic life is often stricter in tone than more sympathetic treatments of melancholy itself. Counter-Reformation mystic and Carmelite friar John of the Cross, for example, regarded those of "melancholy temperament" (*mal humor*) as "objects of the deepest pity" even when their affliction lends itself to terrible delusions of demonic interaction.[14]

To succumb to *acedia* is to capitulate under the temptation to withdraw from the higher life of the soul, preferring instead to satiate the careless desires of the flesh. In subtle contrast to melancholy, *acedia* was considered within the crucible of temptation rather than debilitating illness. According to John of the Cross, the melancholic who suffered under Satan's thrall required physiological, as well as spiritual, restoration.[15] Such physical nurture was itself a consideration of what John saw as the "natural accidie" of sleeplessness or dyspepsia; but it was "spiritual sloth" (*acidia espiritual*) which most grievously threatened "the way of perfection."[16] While a degree of disillusion with the vanity of the world is a requisite melancholy for the monastic *homo religiosus,* this virtue of detachment, or the freedom of *apatheia,* must not infect the whole of spiritual existence itself. When this occurs then inertia and "aridity" contaminates prayer—a dryness of the soul in which devotional activities become burdensome and even abhorrent.

Since the late medieval period, however, an increasing identification of *acedia* with the sin of sloth in Christian theology signifies a more material and increasingly naturalized rendering of a malaise which was earlier understood within the spiritual crucible of ascetic self-refinement. Such a transition inevitably associates *acedia* as much with laziness as with religious disillusion. For Michael Raposa in *Boredom and the Religious Imagination,* this fixation upon one particular outward manifestation of an inner condition constitutes "an impoverishment of the earlier conception."[17] The radical dangers of *acidia espiritual* give way to the discomforts of "natural accidie." In this vein, for example, Lake quotes from a reference to the "wise words" of the modern Russian Orthodox ascetic, Father Seraphim (1759–1833):

The counsel he gave to nuns in the convent he supervised is recorded.

"He commanded us to fear above all things, and to flee as we should from fire, the chief of sins, accidie." "There is no worse sin, my mother, and nothing more terrifying or destructive, than the sin of accidie!" said Father Seraphim.[18]

Yet, while *acedia* is identified as "the chief of sins," Father Seraphim encouraged his nuns to observe distinctly pragmatic preventatives such as ensuring that "one always sleeps with bread under the pillow in case one awakes hungry and is visited with sorrow."[19] This tendency toward materiality and tangibility is, however, present as early as the fourth-century monk Evagrius of Pontus (ca. 345–399) who, in numbering *acedia* among the "bad thoughts," illustrates his point with the example of a monk struggling against inane distractions in the tedious exertion of studying his book in solitude.[20] Evagrius, as Richard Sorabji observes, was well aware that *acedia* often verges on "idleness" (Gr.

argia) and in time "the concept and even the name of sloth came to replace that of depression."[21]

In the seventh century, Pope Gregory the Great, translating the "eight bad thoughts" (Gr. *logismoi*) of Evagrius into the "seven cardinal sins" (Lat. *principalia vitia*), decisively supplanted *acedia* with *tristitia*.[22] But a further reason for this lapse in modern consideration of *acedia*, and the naturalization of the concept, is surely that, as part of the vocabulary of ascetic literature, its decline in the lexicon of faith is related to the decline of the monastic way of life. As such, in Robert Burton's virtually canonical seventeenth-century compendium, *The Anatomy of Melancholy*, *acedia* is referred to more imprecisely as the "idleness" that reaches beyond the exclusively monastic setting—a cause of melancholy conceived outside of the ascetic rigors of the monastery as "an appendix to nobility."[23] Here one approaches a sense of the more modern perception of *acedia* as a spiritually indifferent and increasingly secularized malaise: a boredom that is encountered not within the cloister but in the modern city. In *Melancholy and Society*, sociologist Wolf Lepenies correctly points out that Kierkegaard himself "provided a surprisingly spatially related conclusion to his views on boredom." Boredom, in Kierkegaard's world, inextricably encompasses "the sociological aspect."[24] In Kierkegaard's time this boredom was the melancholy which accompanies the modern figure of the languid and urbane *flâneur*, typified by Kierkegaard's depiction of the seducer, whom Steven Shakespeare describes as "the romantic poet, the ironist, the gentleman of leisure—roles made possible by cultural and social economic upheavals which had left their mark on the nascent bourgeoisie of the Danish capital."[25] Ironically, these two apparently inverse lifestyles of asceticism and excess are thus both susceptible to a similar inner fate: just as excessive fasting, solitude, and meditation in the monastic life could lead to idleness, so too can the *flâneur*'s life of leisure, recreation, and even excess succumb to a deep boredom. Both directions risk the descent into "spiritlessness" that Kierkegaard warned would lead the self away from its true self-becoming before God.

Essentially, it is when the condition persists "to the extent that the individual makes no effort to alleviate it"[26] that *acedia* becomes drained of its spiritual dimension. But the danger *acedia* poses to the life of the soul is an ancient admonition which has fallen on stony ground of late. In fact, in modernity, the fashionable boredom of the gentleman of leisure, the aristocrat, or the aesthete becomes something to be cultivated by the self-conscious urbanite. But this affectation, it should be noted, long preceded the geographical and historical milieu of Kierkegaard's Copenhagen. Aristotle had already remarked a relation between genius and melancholy,[27] and in the France of Montaigne's day, for example, it could be said that "Tristesse suggested noble sensitiveness; melancholy suggested genius—no wonder so many thought they were marked by it. No affectation was so widely cherished."[28] In nineteenth-century Paris, the poet and contemporary to Kierkegaard, Charles Baudelaire, similarly praised the scornful decadence of one who "does not speak to other people except to insult them": "Dandyism is a setting sun; like a diminishing star, it is proud, without warmth and full of melancholy."[29]

According to Ferguson's genealogy of the malaise, it is primarily through the form of *boredom* "that melancholy makes its way into the modern world."[30] Indeed, in the writing of his melancholy aesthete A in 1843's *Either/ Or,* Kierkegaard furnishes us with an outstanding case study of modern boredom and its contribution to the emaciation of the modern self:

> I do not feel like doing anything. I don't feel like riding—the motion is too powerful;
> I don't feel like walking—it is too tiring. I don't feel like lying down, for either I would have to stay down, and I don't feel like doing that, or I would have to get up again, and I don't feel like doing that, either.
> *Summa Summarum:* I don't feel like doing anything. (E/O I, 20)

To lie in bed all day is a solitary pleasure for the leisurely melancholic. As Burton's *Anatomy of Melancholy* observes: "A most incomparable delight it is so to melancholize, and build castles in the air."[31] But for Kierkegaard's A, boredom—drained of the delights of idleness—eventually comes to contaminate itself. Indolence (Lat. *in-dolens:* "without-griefs") succumbs to the restlessness of mind and body; existence no longer accommodates languid repose. One is delivered over to the abyss: "Boredom, extinction," as Vigilius Haufniensis aptly contemplates in *The Concept of Anxiety,* "is precisely a continuity in nothingness" (CA, 133).

Essentially, whereas *acedia* had indirectly signified the call toward the devotional life, the boredom of the modern subject no longer regarded religious discipline as its cure. On the contrary, modern boredom induces the ulterior and contrary impulse, as Vigilius Haufniensis warns: *"The demonic is the contentless, the boring"* (CA, 132). Such a modern realization is echoed once again by Baudelaire's confession, as his own melancholy leads him into a desert of apathy, away from the gaze of the divine:

> Thus, far from the sight of God, he leads me,
> Panting and crushed by fatigue, into the midst
> Of the plains of Boredom [*ennui*], extensive and deserted . . .[32]

Boredom, disdaining the remedies of spirit, seeks increasingly more exotic distractions and sinks further into decadence rather than devoting itself to devotional practice. Yet as Kierkegaard's A laments: "Wine no longer cheers my heart; a little of it makes me sad—much depressed. . . . In vain do I seek to abandon myself in joy's infinitude; it cannot lift me, or, rather, I cannot lift myself" (E/O I, 41). In the "boundless sea of joy," A is not sustained but sinks like one plunging into an abyss. And so boredom gives birth to despair: "Boredom is the shadow of doubt—a doubt that can grow and grow until one despairs of one's life."[33] Even a life sustained by perennial intoxication will succumb to the infection of inertia.[34] And so the influence of boredom reveals an abyss in which the vertiginous eye can fix upon nothing. Boredom disdains the religious, and yet comes to nothingness within the aesthetic. It delivers the self over to the deadly brink of an irremediable nihilism of despair, as A himself confesses: "Boredom rests upon the nothing that interlaces existence; its dizziness infinite, like that which comes from looking down into a bottomless abyss" (E/O I, 291).

KIERKEGAARD AS ANATOMIST OF MELANCHOLY: THE AESTHETIC AND THE RELIGIOUS

Yet is there hope for deliverance from this abyss within the religious? Despite the abyssal nihilistic tendencies of boredom, it has been suggested in Raposa's *Boredom and the Religious Imagination* that boredom "can serve as midwife for the birth of religious knowledge, it is the pallid half-darkness that sometimes lingers just before the dawning of religious insight."[35] For Kierkegaard, this deliverance from boredom's nothingness involves realizing and accepting that only God can truly unburden melancholy from the gravity and vertigo of the abyss. As the foregoing discussion of *acedia* and boredom suggests, one may thus wish to differentiate between melancholy in what Kierkegaard refers to as the aesthetic and religious spheres of existence. However, before formalizing any such distinction, it should be noted that Kierkegaard himself makes no formal differentiation between an *aesthetic melancholy* and a *religious melancholy*. Despite this, in *The Phenomenology of Moods in Kierkegaard*, Vincent A. McCarthy "loosely" ventures such a distinction corresponding to the uses of the Danish words *Tungsind* and *Melancholi* in *Either/Or*—a work he suggests can be understood as "the 'missing treatise' on melancholy in Kierkegaard's authorship."[36] McCarthy suggests that both words, commonly translated by the single English word "melancholy," signify two degrees of the one mood: "*Melancholi* being lighter, having a certain sweetness and the associations of passivity which the word also has in English; *Tungsind* being deeper, heavier, more intense, closer to brooding, and with an element of reflection present to it."[37]

McCarthy is not alone in discerning a difference between these words. As Mark Taylor explains: "Melancholi is more light-hearted and attractive, while Tungsind is a darker mood that involves brooding preoccupation."[38] But McCarthy makes more than a merely stylistic distinction between these terms. In contrast to an aesthetic *Melancholi,* McCarthy argues, *Tungsind* "is a reflective and more critical melancholy,"[39] and as such is suggestive of a religious melancholy. Yet the distinction appears to still be blurred. As Taylor also notes: "The aesthetic stage on life's way ends in what Kierkegaard calls 'melancholy' [*Tungsind*]."[40] For Taylor, *Tungsind* is the climax of the aesthetic, rather than the religious life. Yet for McCarthy, *Tungsind* implies the evolution of aesthetic *Melancholi* from "the first moment of melancholy" into "the second moment" of the religious. Religious melancholy's dependence upon aesthetic melancholy is understood in terms of *Tungsind's* critical disillusionment with "the first moment" of *Melancholi,* through which it claims to have moved beyond the aesthetic. Therefore McCarthy describes religious melancholy as "the melancholy of a subject become reflective in the wake of the failure of all finite objects to satisfy an unquenchable longing."[41]

Yet the distinction appears too fluid to generate an interpretative consensus. For instance, McCarthy's notion of *Tungsind* as an "intensified" *Melancholi* has been convincingly critiqued by Abrahim Khan. According to Khan, there is insufficient evidence supporting an emphatic, radical distinction between the two terms. The material "leads to an equally plausible hypothesis that 'Tungsind' is a stylistically elegant variation of 'Melancholi."[42] Thus Khan emphatically rejects any assertion that *Melancholi* is the longing of aesthetes, poets, and Romantics while *Tungsind* represents a more profound development. Instead, *Melancholi* is a kind of irony, while *Tungsind* is allied to desire and imagination.[43] While maintaining a difference between the two, Khan is most anxious to avoid the trap of intensifying one at the expense of the other: "there is a definite difference," he asserts, "but it seems to be more a difference in kind rather than degree."[44]

The translation of the Danish word *Tungsind* is also somewhat contentious. McCarthy translates *Tungsind* specifically as "heavy-spirited,"[45] and *Tung-* straightforwardly means "heavy" here, but Khan claims that the *-sind* more loosely denotes "mind/spirit."[46] Rendering *sind* precisely as "spirit" implicitly suggests a religious, not to mention Hegelian, appurtenance. If, on the contrary, *sind* is read as "mind" or "temperament" then a different emphasis is conveyed, without necessarily implying an awakening of "spirit" (Dn. *Ånd*). As such, McCarthy acknowledges that "spirit" is already "gestating" in *Melancholi*.[47] Furthermore, before enforcing too technically over-determined a reading of the word, it would be wise to note T. H. Crox-hall's observation that *Tungsind* "is a very common word, often used to describe the character of Jutlanders, of whom Kierkegaard's father was one. *Tungsind* means brooding rumination, ceaseless introspection, perpetual cogitation, lack of decision, and listlessness, rather than just 'listlessness.'"[48] As such, it is not necessarily an expedient trait. The suggestion that *Tungsind* denotes an awakening of spirit to the religious would also seem to conflict with Anti-Climacus's words in *Practice in Christianity*: "Christianity is not at all closer to heavy-mindedness [*Tungsind*] than to light-mindedness; they are both equally worldliness, equally far away, and both have just as much need of conversion" (PC, 154). As such, then, *Tungsind* is not necessarily closer to the religious than a "light-mindedness" (and "light-spiritedness" would not sound correct here). This idea is again present in Kierkegaard's 1847 upbuilding discourse on "The Gospel of Sufferings," where the question of bearing the burden of forgiveness of sins is discussed. To bear sins with "heavy-mindedness" is to refuse forgiveness for that which one believes is too heavy a burden to be displaced; to bear sins with "light-mindedness" is to take the forgiveness of sins too lightly—as if forgiveness itself is to be eas-ily forgotten. "Every extreme, of heavy-mindedness or of light-mindedness [*Tungsindeghedens eller Letsinddighedens*], is promptly a sign that faith is not really present" (UDVS, 246).[49]

Without subscribing to a formal identification of religious melancholy with *Tungsind* and aesthetic melancholy with *Melancholi*, however, it is still possible to affirm that there are points in Kierkegaard where a melancholy directed toward the religious can be differentiated from a melancholy that orients itself exclusively around the aesthetic. It is ultimately through the reli-gious that melancholy is sublimated into a desire for that which is missing in relation to the self: namely the God-relation. Once melancholy becomes conscious of a religious longing, it can become transfigured by that long-ing of spirit and remain restless until it finds fulfillment in relation to God. But, as explored below, melancholy may first have to become intensified—namely, become despair—before this metamorphosis of spirit can occur. This breaking through of the negative energy of melancholy toward a longing for the God-relationship (the self before God) can be more clearly elucidated by way of a further examination of the sketches of melancholy found within Kierkegaard's authorship.

There is a difference between melancholy [*Tungsind*] and melancholy [*Tungsind*]. There is a melancholy that for poets, artists, thinkers is the crisis and with women can be an erotic crisis. Thus the melancholy of my character [Quidam] is the crisis prior to the religious. ("Epistle to the Reader," SLW, 429–430)

Before God, Kierkegaard ultimately extols, the mystery of the self will become resolved and, in this transparency, no secret of melancholy will remain concealed from the divine mirror. But if one refuses to become transparent to oneself before God, then melancholy's apparent lightness of being—the lightness by which one seemingly dances across the abyss—risks the loss of self through the nihilistic perpetuation of self-abstraction. This danger is illustrated by a perturbing thought experiment that is set out in a journal entry from 1849:

> Question: Whether It Would Be Psychologically Correct, whether It Is Even Psychologically Conceivable.
>
> A basically melancholic individual who otherwise had never been tormented or tempted by the thought of suicide.
>
> He takes a walk one day in a beautiful wooded area. It has just been raining; everything smells fresh and fragrant; it occurs to him that he never or only rarely had felt so indescribably, so ineffably good.
>
> As he walks along the thought comes to him *en passant:* what if you took your life—and he does it.
>
> Here there is no pre-meditation about such a step, no sequence of events or violent agitation. The thought comes to him something like this: see, there is a delightful little flower; he commits the deed in about the same state of mind as that in which one bends down and picks a little flower; therefore death in this case would be a kind of well-being carried to a higher power.
>
> Is such a thing conceivable? (JP 3:2692 / Pap. X^1 A 642)

Traditionally, melancholy has been metaphorically associated with weight and heaviness, but here is an instance of what Kierkegaard calls "an extreme example of being loosely attached to life" (JP 3:2692 / Pap. X^1 A 642). The veil of the "self" becomes insubstantial, a virtually translucent, dreamlike veneer between oneself and the world: "Melancholy's point of contact with insanity is, as in so many other respects, that one himself becomes an object. What is peculiar and unusual is the most idyllic objectivity, idyllically to mistake oneself for a little flower" (JP 3:2692 / Pap. X^1 A 642). This "insanity" denotes the loss of self enacted through mistaking the self for a mere trivial object.[50] Like Narcissus, metamorphosed into an object by his own self-reflection, the melancholy individual in Kierkegaard's vignette is transformed into a flower. He has misplaced himself, as it were, and either believes himself to be a flower, or else picks a flower unaware that, in doing so, he has plucked himself out of existence.

Such a moment, bringing in its wake a loss of the self, is a moment of solitude. And, as Kierkegaard recognized, it is in such solitude that melancholy's embrace is at its most potent and seductive. Before "the others," however, the melancholy aesthete is always adept at dissembling the secret of his melancholy—a hermetic masquerade revealed in "Quidam's Diary" in *Stages on Life's Way:* "I am able at any time of the day to divest myself of my melancholy or, more correctly, put on my disguise, because melancholy simply waits for me until I am alone. If there is anyone present, no matter who it is, I am never entirely who I am" ("Guilty/Not Guilty?" SLW, 196). Once again, it is only in solitude that melancholy can unveil itself and seduce the fragile self. It is here that melancholy, unrelieved by distraction, meditates within itself. "Just as a woman who is unhappy at home spends a lot of time looking out the window, so the soul of the melancholy person keeps on the lookout for diversions. Another form of melancholy is the kind which keeps its eyes shut in order to have darkness all around" (JP 3:2688 / Pap. VIII^1 A 239). This self-beguiling and erotic brooding can be discerned further in Quidam's poetic sighs: "Then shall I have peace, for the person who melancholically recollects is also blessed and soothed and is as happy as the weeping willow when it is swayed by the evening Breeze" (SLW, 266). Melancholy becomes, as Kierkegaard aptly phrases it, the melancholic person's "one intimate confidante." Within the confines of the aesthetic, this inner relationship betrays the internalized eroticism of an unrecognized or dreamlike narcissism: "she beckons to me, calls me aside, even though physically I remain on the spot. It is the most faithful mistress I have known—no wonder, then, that I must be prepared to follow at any moment" (JP 5:5496 / Pap. III A 114).[51] In this poetic evocation, melancholy appears in the guise of an other within the self, an other who beckons me aside and leads me into the enchanted secret places of myself—even though she is, like all others, merely a veiled and un-owned aspect of my own self. As such, as Ronald Grimsely aptly describes, "melancholy itself may be a subtle form of enjoyment and reveal the complacent egoism of a man who refuses to abandon a secret form of self-indulgence."[52] Such aesthetic melancholy, through the solitude of self-communion, thereby risks the dissolution of the self, disassociating self-identity from its authentic relation before God.

Refuting its seduction by melancholy's self-enclosure, however, the self must therefore come to recognize the disillusion inherent to melancholy as a double-sided passion that can inspire the longing to become itself before God, to become spirit. As Kierkegaard's B (Judge William) prescribes to the melancholic aesthete A in *Either/Or*: "the persons whose souls do not know this melancholy are those whose souls have no presentiment of a metamorphosis" (E/O II, 190). But this melancholy must not remain locked up in internalized self-infatuation; instead it must be directed toward the earnest heterogeneous transformation of the self before the Wholly Other. A laments how "Life for me has become a bitter drink, and yet it must be taken in drops, slowly, counting" (E/O I, 26). And yet, admonishing A's affectation, Judge William shows a critical awareness of how such lyricism can conceal a fashionable pretence that obscures the potential gravity of melancholy: "In our day, it has become somewhat prestigious to be melancholy . . . but only through his own fault does a person become melancholy" (E/O II, 185). Poetic embellishment and distraction thus constitute commonly sought evasions of a brooding energy of spirit which, according to the Kierkegaardian anatomy, struggles latently within melancholy's disillusionment. When spirit refuses "the satiation of pleasure" that intoxication offers to it, then it "masses within . . . like a dark cloud . . . and it becomes an anxiety that does not cease even in the moment of enjoyment" (E/O II, 186). Just as in *The Concept of Anxiety* Vigilius Haufniensis prescribed that one must "renounce anxiety without anxiety" (CA, 117), so one must finally conquer melancholy with a renunciation of melancholy's erotic self-fascination or distraction. Hence Judge William encourages A to recognize his melancholy as a form of hidden (unconscious) despair:

> You see, my young friend, this life is despair if you conceal this from others, you cannot conceal it from yourself that it is despair. And yet in another sense this life is not despair. You are too light-minded [*letsindig*] to despair, and you are too heavy-minded [*tungsindig*] not to come in contact with despair. (E/O II, 205)

Melancholy, therefore, may function as a presentiment of despair for A which, by remaining in erotic communion with itself, can also signify an evasion of conscious despair (the admission of need for the eternal). As such, by following Judge William's counsel to "choose despair" (E/O II, 211), A would consciously and freely submit to the *possibility* of a spiritual metamorphosis. As will become progressively apparent, the confession of despair, even the hopeless despair over the apparent *impossibility* of reconciliation between God and self (i.e., forgiveness), is the entry point for divine *possibility*. Within its gloomy shade, melancholy bears the presentiment of its own resurrection; for "Only the spirit can eliminate it, for it inheres in the spirit" (E/O II, 190).[53] And yet, as the following section will take up, the longing struggle of spirit's relation to the Wholly Other is far from simple: the struggle to become a self directly before God is itself harrowed by its own persistent danger of falling back down into a deeper abyss.

THE LONGINGS OF SPIRIT

I must dare to believe that I can be saved by Christ from the power of melancholy in which I have lived.

—KIERKEGAARD'S Journals

The previous section concluded with the notion that the persistence of melancholy within the self should be recognized as an inexhaustible yet apparently unfulfilled longing of spirit that can become central to the struggle to become a self before God. "Spirit [*Ånd*] is restlessness," as Kierkegaard declares in his *Journals*. "Christianity is the most profound restlessness of existence—so it is in the New Testament" (JP 4:4361 / Pap. XI² A 317). However, this restlessness is perpetuated by the melancholic realization that the mere recognition of spirit's restless longing is necessary but not in itself sufficient to fulfill a longing for the eternal that seems to remain continually and frustratingly defied. Spirit represents the self's inner longing for God— the transfigured form of the self—but, Kierkegaard contends, spirit (*Ånd*) must strive in the inner and outer environment of modern "spiritlessness" (*Åndløsheden*): it must confront the melancholy consciousness of the infinite qualitative difference between the human and the divine. Furthermore, this restless agitation does not resolve itself in a fluent transmutation of the individual into spirit, since spirit struggles within an internal world divided against itself. "Flesh and blood or the sensate—and spirit are opposites," Kierkegaard writes echoing the dualism of Paul. "From what do flesh and blood shrink from most of all? From dying. Consequently spirit is to will to die, to die to the world" (JP 4:4354 / Pap. XI¹ A 558). Spirit is thus the expression of the inner death (spiritual trial) to an old way of being; as well as the transubstantiation of the self into a new way of becoming *before God*. However, just as flesh and blood resist transubstantiation into their own opposite, so spirit's tension is manifest through a form of struggle between the individual and the divine. In terms designed to provoke a realization of this radical tension, Kierkegaard thus claims that "God is indeed a human being's most appalling enemy, your mortal enemy. Indeed, he wants you to die, die unto the world" ("The Moment," No. 5, 27 July 1855; LW, 177).

By this uncompromising and polemical expression, the later Kierkegaard strives to reinvigorate the perennial tension of the infinite qualitative difference that confronts the singular endeavor to exist as an individual before God: a tension that modern bourgeois Christendom has become perilously insensate toward. Such restlessness and antagonism, for Kierkegaard, characterizes the melancholy love relationship between two qualities so infinitely different as humanity and divinity. In this sense, religious melancholy can be understood as the restless inner longing for a God who remains beyond its grasp. Unlike the *melancholia* that mourns the lost object of the past,[54] this melancholy of spirit is the wound of a longing that has not yet attained to itself, not yet reached a God who it believes waits in its soteriological future, in eternity. In this sense, although melancholy mourns the distance between self and God, it still retains a hope—albeit a hope born from disillusionment—that the presence of this longing is itself evidence that reconciliation between self and God remains a divine *possibility*. It is to this religious longing that Ferguson alludes when he claims that melancholy "is a sign that we have not been abandoned by God."[55] Yet as Kierkegaard knew only too well, melancholy's persistent lack of fulfillment may also indicate that one has not yet entirely left behind the dreaming of the aesthetic. In its melancholy the "self" longs for God—but this melancholy may itself darken or embellish the (fantasized) vision of that which it longs for. Furthermore, unable to attain to the object of its desire, melancholy can fall into resentment, or the conviction that melancholy is itself the only possible relation to God that is available to the self. Consider, for example, the elaborate divine-human antagonism described by Kierkegaard's melancholic A in *Either/Or*.

> But there is yet another demonstration of the existence of God that has hitherto been overlooked. It is introduced by a servant in Aristophanes' *The Knights*, 32–35 (Demosthenes and Nicias conversing):
> DEMOSTHENES: Stat-at-ues is it? What, do you really think that there *are* gods?
> NICIAS: I know it.
> DEMOSTHENES: Know it! How?
> NICIAS: I'm such a wretched god-detested chap.
> DEMOSTHENES: Well urged indeed. (E/O I, 37)

At the close of our previous section, Judge William counseled A to "choose despair" in order to deliver his melancholy over to God. But here A provides an ironic "proof for the existence of God" deriving from an unjust sense of divine persecution. In this reference from Aristophanes' 424 BCE comedy, Nicias complains to Demosthenes (both of whom were prominent Athenian generals) that he feels unduly persecuted and hated by the gods, even though he tries to please them. Despite the satirical tone of *The Knights*, A's invocation of this argument alludes to a melancholic persecution complex which finds further expression in his dramatized confession: "I feel as a chessman must feel when the opponent says of it: That piece cannot be moved" (E/O I, 22). Here A articulates the familiar immobility of melancholy; yet, in contrast to the sterile inertia of *acedia*, A defines his anxious paralysis as, at least in a certain sense, "before God": that is, in relation to the power of an unseen and unknown Wholly Other.

Religious melancholy can indeed represent the stirring of spirit's longing, but it is a longing that does not necessarily have its gratification transpire in the very arousal of its need. In fact, the arousal of religious melancholy may further traumatize the effort to know oneself before God. In the agitation of spirit there is a decisive and irrevocable incitement of opposition: the adversity between God and humanity, between spirit and spiritlessness. There is, however, a sense in which the erotic tension of religious longing is indefinitely preserved, or suspended, in this denial of consummation. Yet it is this very denial which asserts that authentic faith is not the self-gratification of religious need, but a long arduous transmutation of flesh into spirit whose soteriological fulfillment is ultimately eschatological. The individual must first learn that to long for God and to possess God are not identical. The self must be prepared to become itself before a God who remains Other. Therefore, the melancholy of spirit is not the repossession, internalization, or reinstatement of a lost object; rather it is the future-oriented striving for a relational self-becoming before God that radicalizes the internal and external existence of the here and now. The melancholy of spirit represents both a longing to overcome and a lament over the existence of the abyss: the infinite qualitative difference between humanity and God.

In accord with this, the notion of religious melancholy in Kierkegaard's writings has been aptly described by Vincent McCarthy as ultimately expressing a "longing for the Beloved, not as the young and the romantics understood it but rather as did the Christian mystics."[56] In this sense, Kierkegaard rearticulates for modern Christendom a spiritual-erotic element in the soul's longing for the divine that has a long historical association with the concept of melancholy.[57] For example, Robert Burton, who was the first to identify a distinctive category of "Religious Melancholy," notably recognizes it as a variety of "love-melancholy" in a discussion that commences with a consideration of the allure and enticement of divine beauty. While a similar interaction of seduction and frustrated longing seems to affiliate love-melancholy and the religious, the Beloved of religious melancholy implies an essentially unobtainable vision that overwhelms the desirous gaze of any prospective lover. As Burton's *Anatomy of Melancholy* identifies, this frustration of desire has its biblical precedent and exemplar in the theophany of Exodus 33, since Moses, "when he desired to see God in His glory, was answered that he might not endure it, no man could see His face and live."[58]

Albeit with a Neoplatonic heritage of metaphysical longing at work in his biblical appropriation, it is Augustine who perhaps most appositely defines the restless desire for God in his *Confessions:* "Hide not Thy face from me. Even if I die, let me see Thy face lest I die."[59] The paradoxical tension of religious melancholy is here epitomized by Augustine: the absence of the face of the Beloved means an arid, living death; the theophany of the face promises annihilation of the self. The Beloved, and consequently the kingdom of the Beloved, must remain ultimately absent to the melancholic soul.[60] "Where, beyond Heaven and earth, could I go that there my God might come to me—he who said, 'I fill heaven and earth'?"[61] Or as Augustine describes further, "Thou didst lift me up, that I might see that there was something to be seen, though I was not fit to see it."[62] Just as when Moses desired to behold the divine glory (Heb. *kavod*) he was permitted only to see the back of God ("And I will take away mine hand, and thou shalt see my back parts [Lat. *posteriora dei*]: but my face shall not be seen": Ex. 33:23), so analogously is the Augustinian ecstasy qualified by a bittersweet disclosure of God's inaccessibility to the unworthy soul, and it therefore also implies a concealment or an abyss between self and divine.

Once again, McCarthy is therefore apt to describe religious melancholy as "the moment of crisis when the separation of the finite from the Infinite reaches a point of unendurable severity."[63] However, while the self longs to transcend this unendurable separation of the finite and the infinite, it cannot escape the fact that the gravity and distance of the infinite qualitative difference continually reasserts itself. The resulting grief is now perhaps deeper than the initial sense of estrangement between self and God, since this grief now knows the subsequent loss of the divine Beloved that the self has fleetingly glimpsed. This religious melancholy expresses a grief not only at the self's estrangement from God by virtue of the infinite qualitative difference, but also that the soul's desire for the divine Beloved is not sufficient in itself to overcome this abyss between the human and the divine. As such, this frustrated longing creates a "metaphysical wound" which is incessantly inflamed by its own aspiration for divine healing: as McCarthy describes it, this desire is "a wound which is never entirely healed (thus the enduring melancholy in the religious man)."[64] This pattern of disillusionment and longing that characterizes religious melancholy in Kierkegaard is, as McCarthy acknowledges,[65] foreshadowed by the writings of the medieval Christian mystics. Among others, this specific diagnosis of melancholy as a "metaphysical wound" is particularly reminiscent of the evocative depiction of the aspirant soul as "a living wound of desire" in the works of John of the Cross.[66] As John describes in "Living Flame of Love," the love for God constitutes "a living flame, within the soul, [and] it is ever sending forth its arrow-wounds, like most tender sparks of delicate love."[67] But this living flame wounds the lover since the Beloved God remains perpetually hidden (*escondido*)[68] from the lover's gaze. In her frustration, the soul proclaims her melancholy longing to God with all the eroticized vigor of an unconsummated love:

> her love's anxiety, reproaching Him for His absence, the more so because, being wounded by her love, for the which she has abandoned all things, yea even herself, she has still to suffer the absence of her Beloved and is not yet loosed from her mortal flesh that she may be able to have fruition of Him in the glory of eternity.[69]

This anxious inability to attain consummation of or release from the ceaseless longing after divinity has hence been described by Eugene A. Maio as an "Eros-induced suffering."[70] It is in the desert of this absence that, as John of the Cross warns, the soul may descend into a further spiritual *acedia* (*acidia espiritual*): a desiccated exhaustion in which even prayer refuses to yield its savour.[71] In this sense, the infinite qualitative difference between self and God means that the absence of the Beloved is so woundingly evident to the soul that even the lover's impassioned pronouncements of desire appear to be in vain. Even prayer seems to be lost in the abyss. As John of the Cross's contemporary and fellow reformer, Teresa of Jesus (i.e., Avila), explores in her remarkable spiritual autobiography *The Mansion of the Interior Castle*, prayer—the voice of longing between the soul and God—can itself succumb to this "aridity." As the distance between the soul and God seems vast and impenetrable, feebleness and boredom vitiate prayer life and the soul falls victim to "the pain of privation felt in arid prayer by contrast with the brief spells of union it has known. To the soul which has experienced union, God seems at all other times hopelessly far removed from it."[72] As John of the Cross similarly describes it, one who has fallen from prayer becomes morose, "like a babe weaned from the breast, which he found so sweet."[73]

Despite operating within a distinctly Western mystical tradition, John of the Cross and Teresa of Jesus were both influenced by the rhetoric of the soul's frustrated desire for union with the divine as given expression by the late-fifth and early-sixth-century Eastern theologian Pseudo-Dionysius (tradition's Dionysius the Areopagite). Like Augustine, Pseudo-Dionysius was considerably influenced by Neoplatonism (Plotinus in particular), and like Augustine he aspired to behold the face of God—"but under the condition imposed by Exodus: 'no one may see me and live.'"[74] Denys Turner aptly describes this longing fraught with suffering in terms of the convergence of the Mosaic theophany in Exodus with the Platonic allegory of the cave

(*Republic* VII): "In both the Allegory and in Exodus, there is an ascent toward a brilliant light, a light so excessive as to cause pain, distress and darkness . . . even, as in Exodus, death, but not the darkness of the absence of light, rather of its excess."[75] To see God is to die; and yet *not* to see God is also death. There is a comparable fusion of the Mosaic and Platonic theophany in Augustine's plea, "*Even if I die,* let me see Thy face *lest I die.*" Augustine pleads like Moses for the presence of God: to see the face that he had previously refused to seek. Moses, who in his fear had first hidden his face from the theophany of the burning bush (Exodus 3:6), later desires to behold the glory of God—a desire that God refuses to consummate since none can see God's face and live (Exodus 33:21). Instead, as earlier noted, God permits Moses to see "my back parts; but my face shall not be seen" (Exodus 33:23).

Ensuing from this allegory of the hidden Face of God, it appears that the notion of religious melancholy is embedded within the impasse of a wounded longing and the apparent inviolability of the abyss between the self and God. Essential to the enduring pathos of this melancholy is its desire to transcend the infinite qualitative difference that keeps it from the divine, expressed in visual terms as the desire to "behold" God—an ambivalent desire that is complicated by the notion that no one may see God (the Wholly Other) and live. But to what extent is it possible for the self to attain to such a relation with a Wholly Other God—to stand before God—without experiencing its own annihilation or death? And to what extent is this melancholy notion of distance or "otherness" between God and the self symptomatic of a sense of divine absence or hiddenness within "the world" of modern "spiritlessness"? Proceeding to an examination of this melancholic aspect of the Wholly Other, the next chapter turns to the critical question of the meaning of the otherness between the self and God in light of the apparent loss of the Holy in secular modernity.

FOUR

The Melancholy Theophany

If a human being did not have an eternal consciousness, if underlying everything there were only a wild, fermenting power that writhing in dark passions produced everything, be it significant or insignificant, if a vast, never appeased emptiness [bundløs Tomhed] hid beneath everything, what would life be then but despair?

—Fear and Trembling

Indeed, what else would life be but despair if beneath existence there were nothing but a formless deep, if there were no God lying "beyond" that originary abyss? And yet, the previous chapter concluded with the notion that even the desire to behold this God is not entirely free from the melancholic feeling of an abyss between self and God. By referring to a "melancholy theophany" in this chapter, I hope to evoke and examine the sense in which the self before God is confronted by a theophany which, at the same time as it discloses itself to be the Beloved of spirit's longing, also (re)asserts the infinite qualitative difference, distance, or impasse between self and God. In this, I seek to explore how this melancholy *alterity* forces the self to come to terms with the heterogeneity of the divine—an encounter with what Otto calls the *mysterium tremendum et fascinans*. Through this exploration, I suggest that this divine otherness is not reducible to a subjective sense of human alienation, nor can it be vanquished by conquering existential estrangement; it is rather an integral and irrevocable element within the self's relation to God.

THE VANISHING THEOPHANY

Does he alone see God who sees God turn his face toward him, or does he not also see God who sees him turn his back, just as Moses continually saw nothing but the Lord's back?

—Eighteen Upbuilding Discourses

At first glance, Otto's emphasis on the numinous as Wholly Other in *The Idea of the Holy* is indicative of a tacit nostalgia for a religion of *ekstasis* (Gr.

ek-stasis: "to be or stand outside oneself"), a melancholy longing for a sacred reality that escapes the infinite qualitative abyss between the human and the divine. For one, Otto exalts Plato in particular for his pursuit of knowledge of God "by the 'ideograms' of myth, by 'enthusiasm' or inspiration, 'eros' or love, 'mania' or the divine frenzy."[1] Otto even describes and extols the element of fascination by which mystery "captivates and transports . . . with a strange ravishment, rising often enough to the pitch of dizzy intoxication," which is "the Dionysiac-element in the numen."[2] Yet after the soul's descent from the *ekstasis* of sacred union, melancholy still awaits. In relation to the numinous, melancholy thus expresses a nostalgia (from the Gr. *nostos:* "returning home" and *algos:* "pain") for the sacred intoxication of the *mysterium tremendum et fascinans* and the soul's grief over its subsequent resumption of "its 'profane', non-religious mood of everyday experience."[3] The otherness of this experience inevitably postulates the religious as Wholly Other than the mundane. "Mysticism continues to its extreme point this contrasting of the numinous object (the numen), as the 'wholly other', with ordinary experience."[4] However, the difficulty resides in the realization that once the soul has been quickened by glimpsing the sacred behind the veil of the world—a mundane, less-real world whose gravity yet pulls it back—the soul sinks even deeper into the shadow of melancholy and pain of thirst.

However, it is essential to understand that Otto's endeavor to restore the pathos of religion in modernity does not rest with the ecstatic element of mystical experience. In 1938's *The Kingdom of God and the Son of Man,* Otto reiterated the position he established previously in *The Idea of the Holy,* that "it is only through some such a dualistic opposition between the entire present world and the 'wholly other', divine world that religion comes into its own. This dualism is essential to higher religion, and without it the latter cannot exist."[5] By "higher religion," Otto alludes to the *prophetic* rather than the Platonic experience of the "other world." By emphasizing the prophetic notion of the wholly other "divine world" found in the Hebrew scriptures, Otto disputes the (Feuerbachian) suggestion that belief in a metaphysical beyond is merely an anthropocentrically projected attempt to transcend disillusion with the material world. Instead, as articulated in his essay on "The Prophet's Experience of God," Otto gives primacy to the reality of spirit in contrast to which the flesh derives its comparative infamy:

> it is not because a "natural" pessimism first led man to regard himself and all things of the world as flesh, that the idea of *ruach* arose as an imaginary compensating counterpart. Just the opposite is true. It is when the intimation of *ruach* has been awakened that all the things of this world sink into flesh.[6]

In other words, religion and mystery are primal; contrary to the Feuerbachian premise, the idea of the sacred as wholly other does not originate in an anthropomorphic attempt to transcend the profane. Furthermore, the beyond is not a dream that arises from my shapeless unconscious; instead, profanity is overshadowed by the genuine awakening of the sacred via a mysterious revelation of consummate reality. If this priority is accepted, then could it be said that some form of disillusion must indirectly *result* from the awakening of spirit—as opposed to a "natural" melancholy disillusionment that first *projects* a psychogenic sacred from which to transcend itself? Melancholy, from this perspective, is therefore the reaction of disillusionment to the unrealized reality of spirit, rather than spirit being the invention of melancholy's desire to transcend itself. As Otto asserts: "Flesh is the shadow of *ruach* and can only appear when the latter has first been experienced."[7]

From this perspective of the prior reality of spirit, melancholy can be regarded as a response to what Kierkegaard describes as the awakening of spirit: an awakening that casts a shadow over profane modern existence. This sacred priority that Otto emphasizes is also implicit in Kierkegaard's juxtaposition of spirit to spiritlessness. The Danish words themselves imply the priority of "spirit" (*Ånd*) over its absence, "spiritlessness" (*Åndløsheden*). By referring to an opposition and enmity between spirit and spiritlessness, Kierkegaard is not principally expressing a metaphysical dualism or mystical "otherwordliness," however. Rather, this opposition refers to a duality whose meaning is felt in the subjective tension of the infinite qualitative difference between humanity and divinity. As explored in this work in relation to the self, spirit is that which is given by God and which longs for relation with God: it marks the obligation of eternity that elicits spirit's desire to become a self in relationship before God. The consciousness of spiritlessness is consequently an activity of the dialectical awakening of spirit: negatively conceived in this instance as melancholy.

In this sense, it may be more authentic to say that it is this world of spirit*lessness* that is actually "wholly other" than the sacred, divine spirit that grounds it. From this perspective, the search for selfhood in Kierkegaard begins with a decisive sense of *lack* within the self: the self's estrangement from itself and from the divinity whom, through the perspective of its own alienation, the self calls "Wholly Other." It is to further examine the significance and meaning of this infamous and often misappropriated phrase, "Wholly Other," that our attention now returns. In the following, I explore how this designation evokes the melancholy of modernity's estrangement from the sacred and the self's estrangement, via the consciousness of sin, from self-knowledge and knowledge of God. Finally, at the close of this chapter I reiterate how the Wholly Other, while not the final name for God, actually expresses the opening or sacred space in which the divine gift of selfhood can come to be before God.

THE WHOLLY OTHER: *Mysterium Tremendum*

The first half of the twentieth century, in the response of dialectical theology and Neo-Orthodoxy (partially inspired by Kierkegaard) to what was regarded as liberal theology's blurring of the boundaries between the human and the divine, saw an emphatic reemphasis of the Lutheran sentiment of the Wholly Otherness of God. "Turning to God as the Wholly Other," as Joerg Rieger writes, "theology now uncovered a new source of power, challenging the modern self's position of control. Pointing to God's Otherness, these thinkers demonstrated the courage to face the open-endedness of the theological enterprise."[8] In particular, Rudolf Otto has been credited with introducing the phrase "Wholly Other" (*das Ganz Andere*) into modern theological and philosophical parlance,[9] although Otto himself may in turn have taken the term from philosopher Jakob Fries (1773–1843), whose notion of *Ahndung* ("presentiment" or "intuition"), which expressed a yearning for a "feeling of truth," gave Otto a grounding for his own feeling of the numinous.[10] Regardless of the ingenuity or etymology of the phrase, Otto undoubtedly "filled the term with a content much richer than did Fries, using it against any attempt to confine religion within the web of human reason."[11] Prior to the Second World War, Otto and Barth were perhaps the most prominent theological proponents of the Wholly Other—although this loose alliance was tempered by a mutual suspicion that each other had taken *das Ganz Andere* too far. While Otto displays his Kantian and Friesian interests, Barth's development of the idea is avowedly indebted to Kierkegaard's infinite qualitative difference (as discussed above in chapter 1). However, I suggest that there are many suggestive and under-examined resonances between Kierkegaard's and Otto's descriptions of the human-divine relation—especially pertaining to the various responses of the self to the presence of the Holy. As such, Merold Westphal for one has claimed that when Kierkegaard, as Anti-Climacus in *Practice in Christianity*, "speaks of the 'shudder which is the first experience of worship,' he is talking about what Otto calls the *tremendum*."[12] However, Otto does not source the Kierkegaardian corpus in his anthology of numinous descriptions. As Almond deduces, "Otto's use of it [the phrase 'Wholly Other'] has overtones of Kierkegaard also, but I have found no evidence that Otto was at all familiar with Kierkegaard's works."[13] In fact, as Gooch points out, Otto even refers derisively to Kierkegaard as a "hysteric."[14] This comment suggests a particularly acid dismissal of the sort of dialectical and existentialist theology that elicits Otto's critique that "Christ did not come to 'solve existential problems

(*Existenzprobleme*)' or to save skeptics from their doubts. . . . Whoever wants to get rid of world-*ängste* would do better to consult his physician."[15]

Having suffered derision from the young students of the then fashionable Barth and Bultmann,[16] Otto appears intent on trivializing these theological movements—even though Barth had responded favorably to the publication of *Das Heilige* in a letter to Eduard Thurneysen. But, as Lynn Poland astutely explains: "What Barth finds to praise in Otto's work is, unsurprisingly, what they have in common: the notion of a transcendent that is 'wholly other,' beyond reason, but also beyond all human labor, a source of value securely placed 'across the border' from a civilization perceived to be in crisis."[17] Yet, despite a common appreciation for Luther's esteem of the non-rational knowledge of God, Otto may have been reticent to be enlisted as an ally of Barth's doctrine of *das Ganz Andere*. On Otto's death in 1937, the English translator of *The Idea of the Holy*, John Harvey, writes in his obituary how Otto "always held that the doctrine of the school of Karl Barth with its unmitigated assertion of the *Ganz Andere*, the 'wholly otherness of God,' was a one-sided aberration."[18] In turn, Barth, by the time he published the first volume of his thirteen-volume *Church Dogmatics* in 1932, had apparently grown wary of identifying *das Heilige* of Otto with the "Holy One" of the Bible.[19]

From the evidence, it seems reasonable to suggest that Otto was relatively unfamiliar with Kierkegaard and disinclined, by virtue of Barthian associations with him, to delve any further. However, this should not cause one to overlook the possible affinities between their descriptions of the God-relationship. Essentially, despite the disparities, mistrusts, and even misunderstandings between them, it is still possible to regard Barth and Otto—and before them Kierkegaard—as important respondents to what each in his own way perceived as a modern malaise with regard to the radical distance between humanity and the divine. However, the expression "Wholly Other" takes on different forms in Kierkegaard and Otto, as appropriate to their own personal concerns. Whereas Kierkegaard's writings initially locate the infinite qualitative difference between God and humanity in the gulf of sin and forgiveness, Otto's naming of the Wholly Other is firstly a preliminary reaction to the presence of the (pre-moral) *mysterium*: "something which has no place in our scheme of reality but belongs to an infinitely different one, and which at the same time arouses an irrepressible interest in the mind."[20] This is not to say that Kierkegaard and Otto fundamentally diverge. Rather, this variance conveys a sense that Otto's prime concern is to reawaken the numinous in the disenchanted modern understanding, rather than prompt a subjective overcoming of existential estrangement.

However, it soon becomes apparent that a no less melancholy lament resounds in both the Kierkegaardian vision of alienated selfhood and what

Otto perceived as the prevailing devolution of the supernatural in modern life. In order to function as a "cure" for rupture, the numinous must be rehabilitated, not simply in existentialist subjectivity, but in a reawakened modern consciousness that is open to the Wholly Other appearance of the Holy. Kierkegaard, Otto, and Barth were all conscious that modern disillusionment was no longer inevitably inclined toward the religious as a means of resolving melancholy, since the religious has itself become a *cause* of disillusionment. Modern life on the whole is not conducive to the reception of the Holy, and so Otto discerned that humanity's recognition of the numinous was endangered and in drastic need of reawakening. "For Otto," as Gooch describes recently in his insightful *The Numinous and Modernity*, "the disillusioned (*entnaivisierte*) culture of the twentieth century is an obstacle to the recognition of the holy. . . . Thus, the numinous origin of religion invoked by Otto on the pages of *Das Heilige* is one that remains ultimately irretrievable for the modern religious subject."[21]

Otto diagnosed the condition of modernity essentially in terms of the evacuation of the supernatural from the prevailing intellectual worldview. As Gooch explains: "Within the order of natural scientific knowledge, this exclusion is reflected in the demystification (*Entgötterung*) of nature in the wake of Copernican astronomy and Newtonian physics, and in the transition from metaphysics to critical philosophy inaugurated by Kant."[22] By asserting God to be Wholly Other, Otto thus brings the prevailing worldview into deliberate collision with something that infinitely differentiates itself from it. Reawakening the numinous consciousness will not constitute immediate reconciliation with our deeper hidden selves, but it will elicit an abrasive and provocative encounter with Absolute Otherness—with the *mysterium*. As such, Otto seeks to evoke the uncanny complexion of the Holy as something mysterious and made newly exotic by treading the re-hallowed ground of "a wonderfully defamiliarized Bible."[23] By transcribing the *mysterium tremendum et fascinans*, Otto's reminder of the core of religion is expressed in a form that itself invokes an infinite qualitative difference between humanity and the Holy. As such, *Das Heilige* "inevitably reproduces the estrangement that it is intended to overcome."[24] In this sense, Gooch argues that this sense of estrangement is exacerbated by the detaching nature of scholarship that determines Otto's venture. However, by invoking uncanny depictions of the numinous, Otto also indirectly draws attention to the estrangement of the modern reader from such defamiliarized experiences. The hope is, therefore, that evoking the uncanny *mysterium tremendum* will also provoke in the modern individual the (exoticized) *fascinans*, the desire for the Holy.

This estrangement of the *mysterium tremendum et fascinans* is not simply an alienation that calls for existential or epistemological reconciliation. The processes of rationalization and demystification of religion have not served to refine and perfect, but rather to undermine the core of religion. "Religion will have its mysteries as mysteries intact," insists Otto. "A religious mystery is not something obscure for the time, capable, like the mysteries of chemistry, of ultimate solution; nor is it an 'arcanum,' mysterious only for the lower orders, the 'profane,' and convertible for the adepts into Gnosis."[25] The resolution of mystery does not cause religion to evolve but to *dissolve* from the center. Mystery—the heartbeat of religion—is preserved in inscrutability, in de-familiarity, as "an absolute *ineffable*."[26] Thus Otto's rehabilitation of an antiquated religious heritage of the numinous, in riposte to the characteristic impiety of the age, serves to reacquaint the modern reader with the mystery from which they have become estranged. In this sense, emphasis upon naturalism and immanence actually signifies an unconscious alienation from the true *mysterium* of the sacred. In other words, humanity must overcome its estrangement from estrangement. *Mysterium* is primal and irreducible within the *alterity* of the Holy. The individual must therefore become reacquainted with the *mysterium* of the numinous—surmounting the fear and rational mistrust of the unknowable other via a *fascinatio* for the Holy. This recalls, as a mutual meeting point for Otto and Kierkegaard, Westphal's plea for overcoming "ontological xenophobia, the fear of meeting a stranger, even if the stranger should be God."[27] And yet, the prevailing over or suspension of fear does not negate our estrangement. God is the sacred stranger. As such, one must ask the question as to whether the enigma, or paradox, of the divine Wholly Other does not deliver the self over, once again, to the irremediable abyss of melancholy.

THE WHOLLY OTHER: A DOCTRINE OF MELANCHOLY?

As theologian and sociologist Peter Berger begins his 1970 study, *A Rumor of Angels: Modern Society and the Rediscovery of the Supernatural*, "If commentators on the contemporary situation of religion agree about anything, it is that the supernatural has departed from the modern world. This departure may be stated in such dramatic formulations as 'God is dead' or 'the post-Christian era.' Or it may be undramatically assumed as a global and probably irreversible trend."[28] However, Berger proceeds in this important consideration to argue that the disappearance of the supernatural in modernity is only an "alleged demise" which—as subsequent decades have affirmed—requires further epistemological verification.

Berger's initial affiliation of the notion of the "supernatural" with Otto's interpretation of the Holy as "wholly other" highlights an important aspect of the twentieth-century reception of the sacred as an element of existence that is qualitatively different from the profane. Despite pervasive modern anxiety and a spreading spiritual vacuity in Western Europe at the time, Otto's attempt in *Das Heilige* to rehabilitate the Holy as *mysterium tremendum et fascinans* in the early twentieth century appeared to resonate with a latent human longing. In the ideological and material ruins of a Western world for which the absence of God gaped wide like the wound of postwar anxiety, it is understandable that the most amenable possibility for a recovery of the sacred seemed to be the God whose absence is incorporated, even explained or sanctified, in an understanding of the divine as Wholly Other. The unanticipated popularity of Otto's study upon publication suggested a possibility for rediscovering a sense for mystery and the sacred in an era of loss and divine abandonment. Otto rendered the Holy retrievable, though uncompromisingly and essentially mysterious, by exploiting a sense of distance between modernity and the primal experience of the sacred that aroused a submerged longing that is itself infinitely unconsummated in the ultimate preservation of the inscrutability of the *mysterium.*

But is this reception of Otto's thought—in resonance with a modern moral-religious deficit in the West—therefore historically contingent? In other words, despite Otto's rehabilitation of archaic and defamiliarized descriptions of the *mysterium tremendum et fascinans,* does the modern pathos of the numinous essentially take its force from an anachronism? Friedrich Feigel, for one, in his critical 1929 response *"Das Heilige": Kritische Abhandlung über Rudolf Ottos gleichnamiges Buch,* accounted for the success of *Das Heilige* precisely according to the historical contingency of a world war which he pointedly described as "the manifestation of *the un*holy." According to Feigel, "with the intensity and passion of the defeat, which received its vigor from the *horror vacui,* the emaciated soul of the German people turned toward the 'holy.'"[29] In other words, the Holy embodies the diversionary lure of the transcendent in the face of immanent despair. Otto thereby presents a sanctified feeling of the uncanny as a mysterious distraction from all-too-immanent human desolation. In essence, this otherworldly relief derived from a rediscovered form of mystified *ekstasis* which was evoked by what Gooch calls the "de-familiarized world of ecstatic religious transport."[30]

Yet, despite the conspicuous historical crisis of the time, Gooch's *The Numinous and Modernity* convincingly argues—with the benefit of a further seventy years of reception of *Das Heilige*—that Feigel's critique fails to account for the appeal of Otto's work beyond postwar Germany, both geographically and historically. Instead, Gooch reads *Das Heilige* as a continuation of Otto's prewar theological venture[31] and astutely describes the work as "the expression of a melancholic form of religious subjectivity."[32] "Melancholic" is not a reference to Otto's own melancholy temperament *per se,*[33] but to "the sense of loss of religious immediacy built into Otto's writing."[34] In this sense, Otto's work nourishes itself upon a melancholic longing implicit in a modern loss of the Holy which actually predates the First World War (such a loss can arguably be discerned in Kierkegaard's plea to his contemporaries in the mid-nineteenth century to realize the radical difference between spirit and spiritlessness). "Melancholy," as Gooch therefore describes, "is characterized by a sense of yearning for a state of being that has been irrevocably lost or remains otherwise unobtainable, and is conceived as 'wholly other' than, and therefore absent from, the present in which the melancholic subject is located."[35]

However, it may well be that this melancholy loss is itself irretrievably historical. As Kierkegaard sought to reawaken the tension of the infinite qualitative difference within the malaise of modern Danish Christendom, so Otto was himself a man of his time and deeply affected by the aporias of his age. An essential contemporary concern for Otto's thought was the evolutionary optimism of Darwinism and its implicit threat of rendering religion superfluous. Faith in natural science gave rise to the possibility of "the assumption that religion was simply a leftover from a more primitive stage of man's development."[36] Otto wished to assert that religion was primal, but not therefore primitive and dispensable. Instead, Otto emphasized the qualitative and inviolable otherness of the sacred in order to preserve its primacy at a time when it was under the greatest threat of being lost.[37] Otto's insistence upon God as Wholly Other, and the irreducible mystery of the uncanny, effectively preserves the Holy in a space that is independent of and impervious to anthropological and scientific appropriation or revaluation.[38] Like Kierkegaard's infinite qualitative difference, the significance of the uncanny (das Unheimliche: literally, "the un-homely") thwarts any violating, Feuerbachian conflation of theology and anthropology. Any transmutation of the gods into humans marks a fatal compromise, rather than a perfection, of the religious impulse as it dilutes the uncanny element that resides at the heart of this primal impulse. Hence Otto is consciously retrogressive in the majority of his assessment of the sacred, as is apparent in his evaluation of ancient religion. Otto significantly engages with the Greek philosophical poet Xenophanes' satirical, proto-Feuerbachian suggestion that "if the oxen could paint, they would paint their gods as oxen." For Otto, this position's implicit failure to account for the genealogy of religion endorses his own genealogy of religion as an expression of the uncanny, rather than of familiarity: "If the oxen strove to see their gods as oxen, humans would appear on the contrary to have had quite the opposite ambition, portraying their gods as half or whole cows, calves, horses, crocodiles, elephants, birds, fish, as marvellous hybrids, hermaphrodites and hideous beings, as weird confused forms."[39] This should of course not be taken as Otto commending fantasy or idolatry, but rather it expresses how Otto perceived the instinctive portrayal of primal religious imagination more honestly in the uncanny mutations of otherness than in the transmission and projection of a sublimated human form.

Awed by the sublime and numinous effects of the Sphinx at Gizeh, set "throbbing in the soul almost like a mechanical reflex,"[40] Otto thus perceived in this ancient dread-inducing monument a more authentic expression of religious feeling than in the more "refined" deities of Greek civilization. Hegel's historical perspective on the evolution of religion, on the contrary, appraised the Sphinx as exemplifying the progressive (anthropomorphic) transition from primitive Egyptian to classical Greek religion (as acknowledged in chapter 1, above). Hegel endorsed the Greek inheritance and reinterpretation of the Egyptian Sphinx from uncanny mystery to Oedipal anthropomorphism as an evolution of Spirit: "It is Greece that makes the transition to God being known as spirit inasmuch as it knows in him essentially the moment of humanity."[41] Through metamorphosis into the human figure, "what had remained enveloped in the darkness of an Egyptian night, sealed in the hermetic indecipherability of the hieroglyph, now steps forth into the clear light of day."[42]

However, Otto reads this domestication as a profound adulteration of religious intuition—a compromise of the uncanny principle in religion that initiated a discernible historical decline in religious vitality: "Where the goddesses and gods become all-too noble and all-too charming and all-too human-like, belief in them was not at its highpoint, as one would have to assume according to the doctrine of anthropomorphism."[43] This demystification signifies the decadence of religion under the apparently civilizing constraints of anthropomorphism. Thus, as a historian of the numinous, Otto defies Hegel's evolutionary historical religious optimism, since what Hegel regarded as "a pivotal moment in the evolution of religion is taken by Otto to be an indication of its waning influence as a vital force in Greek culture."[44] However, for Otto, this taming of disenchanted deities then reopens space for a renewed "re-appropriation of the strange and exotic deities of Egypt and the far East, in whom the presence of the Wholly Other was more palpable, and whose power of attraction was for that reason more compelling than the domesticated inhabitants of Olympus."[45]

However, despite finding resonance with a modern longing—and despite the assimilation of the term "numinous" into wider interdisciplinary lexicons—it would be misleading to suggest that Otto entirely succeeded in rehabilitating the awareness of the Holy within postwar milieus. Even the polemical reactions of the Neo-Orthodox era of theology to the postwar crisis constituted merely "an interruption rather than a reversal of the secularizing trend."[46] As Berger describes it, this "anthropology of desperation," which had made extensive use of Kierkegaard's categories of anxiety and despair, was soon subsumed by the secular optimism of the 1960s.[47] Thus Thomas Altizer, in his 1966 work *The Gospel of Christian Atheism,* while prescribing that Kierkegaardian *Angst* must be outgrown in keeping with an exorcism of the numinous, identifies the Wholly Otherness of God with the death of God:

> Only an alien or empty form of God could be wholly other than man and the world, for the God whose very reality and power crushes the spirit of man is a God who is estranged from his own identity as Redeemer . . . thus an impassable gulf appears between man and God at precisely that point when God ceases to exist and to act in his redemptive form.[48]

But is Altizer correct to suggest that the Wholly Other ultimately serves to enforce an unredemptive abyss within Godself, and consequently an impassable distance of alienation between God and humanity? Is this not also the God who must die in order for humanity to be free? In other words, must the Wholly Other itself be consigned to the destiny of a *deus otiosus*?

As acknowledged in chapter 1, Altizer is not alone in his indictment of the dreadful "over-againstness" of the numinous Wholly Other. For many twentieth-century figures such as Levinas, Derrida, and Cupitt, it is morally questionable whether the numinous, as a self-obscuring *tremendum,* should be taken for the authentic expression of the God-relationship. Furthermore, on closer scrutiny, it appears to many that the so-called numinous experience itself can be reinterpreted and reincorporated independently of any objective Wholly Other divine reality.[49] The result of this is that Otto's insistence upon the numinous as relating to something fundamentally "objective and outside the self"[50] is weakened once the experience of the *mysterium tremendum* is "accounted for independently of religious experience."[51] Otto's emphatically realist foundation for the "otherness of religious experience"[52] is compromised once it is asserted that the numinous need not have its foundation in an objective *divine* reality.[53] Otto would undoubtedly resist any such "naturalization" since his account of the "feeling of dependence that characterizes numinous experience differs radically from any natural feeling of dependence. It is a difference of quality, not quantity."[54] The wholly otherness of numinous experience that Otto describes is "as little as possible qualified by other forms of consciousness,"[55] and this implies a qualitative purity that has itself been cast into doubt. Furthermore, Otto's understanding of "creature feeling" (*Kreaturgefühl*) as a subjective response to the objective reality of the numinous may itself be dependent upon certain human contingencies which he has failed to recognize.[56]

Moreover, further anthropomorphic appropriations of the notion of the numinous appear to suggest that the awe of the *mysterium tremendum* may not be so Wholly Other after all. Recent historical horrors of genocide, terror, and war remain compelling testament to the terrible and demonic aspects of this *tremendum* within humanity itself—thereby suggesting that the notion of the numinous may indeed reveal more about anthropology than it does theology. As such, rather than trembling before the awfulness of the divine *mysterium*, we have come to be struck in our own self-abasement before our own *tremendum*. Thus in 1981 Jewish theologian Arthur A. Cohen writes identifying the Holocaust as

> the human *tremendum*, the enormity of an infinitized man, who no longer seems to fear death or, perhaps more to the point, fears it so completely, denies death so mightily, that the only patent of his refutation and denial is to build a mountain of corpses to the divinity of the dead, to placate death by the magic of endless murder.[57]

The *tremendum* of the Holocaust and other modern genocides thus forms a caesura, an unsurpassable abyss, which expresses evil in the figuration of the human demonic. Although humanity, in its freedom, is ultimately responsible for the *tremendum,* there is a dark point of contact between the dread and fascination of the divine and the demonic. The analogy of the human *tremendum* implies the latent possibility of the presence of evil in the divine *mysterium tremendum*. It is through numerous acts of mass terror that humanity comes closest to resembling a demonic image of the divine. The *tremendum* thus evokes "a dead volcano, terrifying in its aspect but silent, monstrous in its gaping, raw in the entrails, visible reminder of fire and magma, but now quiet, immovable presence, yawning over the lives of man."[58]

And what becomes of the Wholly Other in this trembling of anthropology before the death camps and killing fields and gulags, the brutal reminders of "a meaningless inversion of life to an orgiastic celebration of death"?[59] Are we severed from the conciliatory meaning of a Wholly Other reality? Can we only turn to the face of a wholly other whose appeal to me is, as Levinas stresses, "thou shalt not kill"?[60] Ultimately, the absurdity of death camps, as philosopher of religion Wessel Stoker suggests, *"has no interpretation in the metaphysical view of meaning."*[61] Perhaps modern genocides evoke not simply a human *tremendum* but also a deeply consolidated, melancholy apprehension of the absence of the Holy itself. Perhaps these possibilities do not exclude, but accord with one another. Is it the *absence* of the Holy in the presence of the *tremendum* that itself becomes the ineffable, inscrutable elicitation of horror? As Melissa Raphael observes: "Contemporary theology cannot, and perhaps should not, come to terms with the Holocaust and other twentieth-century enormities in which the numinous has evoked less the majesty of God than the mystery of his averted face."[62]

Despite the analogous language, however, our own self-defiled "creature consciousness" before the *tremendum* of human malice does not seem to equate to the self-abased "creature-consciousness" in which, for Otto, the "numen, overpoweringly experienced, becomes the all in all."[63] In the human *tremendum*, the numen no longer appears to reduce us to nothing since humanity experiences its own infernal demonic magnitude in place of the absent Holy. Yet Otto seems to have already acknowledged that the contemplation of man can analogously arouse "the numinous in its aspects of mystery, awfulness, majesty, augustness, and 'energy'; nay, even the aspect of fascination is dimly felt in it."[64] This is what Otto reads in his rendering of the song in Sophocles' *Antigone*: "Much there that is monstrous [*ungeheuer*]; but nought is more monstrous [*ungeheuer*] than man."[65] Otto affiliates "the monstrous" (*Ungeheuer*) with "the uncanny" (*Unheimliche*); but Harvey's English translation of *ungeheuer* as "weird" compromises the dreadful force of Otto's choice of word. More than being an expression of sheer wonder, the "monstrous" (*Ungeheuer*) denotes something "scary" (*geheuer*) and can also suggest immensity, dread, and atrocity (*Ungeheuerlichkeit*). As such, it seems to resemble something closer to what is meant by the monstrous sublimity that is reflected in the human *tremendum*.

In evoking the numinous awe of man before the dreadful depths of genocide—in attempting to become as a god, a destroyer of worlds—humanity gives demonic expression to an inherently atheistic desire. It should not be forgotten that the *tremendum* which debases humanity was itself created out of the impulse of certain men to impose their own demonic sublimity and potency upon those who were deemed to be (wholly) other. The human *tremendum* ultimately seeks to thereby negate the divine *mysterium tremendum et fascinans*. Where the human *tremendum* is concerned, there is no self-negation or humility before the absolute. Instead, there emerges a consequent self-annihilating dread before humanity's own monumental desire for a monstrous and demonic sublimity. In this, man not only attempts to become the *tremendum*: he becomes an unholy expression of the abyss itself.

And so, does this demonic human *tremendum* not suggest that we are now more than ever in need of the Holy, as it appears as Wholly Other? Or does the *tremendum* itself also analogously imply the violence of the undeniable demonic within God? The previous chapter ended with an outline of a melancholy spiritual striving of love, desire, and longing for God. But can the *mysterium tremendum* ultimately only satisfy a relationship of "fascination" and "dread" toward the God whose most apposite expression is as a numinous consuming fire? In her recent *Rudolf Otto and the Concept of Holiness*, Melissa Raphael, for one, has emphatically challenged the impersonal nature of the numinous in these terms:

> An "I/Thou" relationship with God of the type made famous by Martin Buber is utterly rejected by Otto as being absurdly importunate and deficient in reverence. If the seraphim of Isaiah 6 would not venture such an address, then, *a fortiori*, creatures must be screened off from direct personal confrontation with divine holiness lest they be annihilated.[66]

Is the alienating *alterity* of the Wholly Other therefore preeminently expressed in an annihilating fear and trembling before the *mysterium tremendum*? "It has its wild and demonic forms," as Otto himself warns, "and can sink to an almost grisly horror and shuddering."[67] In light of the manner in which the *alterity* of the Wholly Other can seem to be preserved by fear, more than fascination or mystery, it is understandable how, in Nietzschean terms, the fearful and trembling human object of the divine gaze revolts by reclaiming its subjectivity in an act of deicide. Repudiating the Wholly Other, Altizer further endorses this emancipation from the heteronymous "fear of the Lord": "Once God has ceased to exist in human experience as the omnipotent and numinous Lord, there perishes with him every moral imperative addressed to man from a beyond, and humanity ceases to be imprisoned by an obedience to an external will or authority."[68] Even Otto acknowledges that such "numinous dread" seems at times to resemble something akin to a "daemonic dread."[69] "When awe overwhelms reverence," as Raphael warns, "all that seems to remain is Kierkegaardian 'fear and trembling': submission to the intoxicating terror of absolute divine might."[70] Yet is this indictment a just reduction of Kierkegaard's perception of God? Is such an element indigenous to Kierkegaard's understanding of the Wholly Other and is this an adequate assessment of what Kierkegaard means by "fear and trembling"? Given Kierkegaard's emphasis upon the centrality of anxiety, despair, spiritual trial, and melancholy, one may be forgiven for thinking so. But in calling this extreme conception "intoxicating," Raphael has touched upon a decisive term employed by Kierkegaard as a word of dialectical caution and not as an endorsement.

I do not struggle with a faceless God . . .

—EMMANUEL LEVINAS, *Totality and Infinity*

At the end of *Fear and Trembling,* Johannes de Silentio concludes that God "sees in secret and recognizes distress and counts the tears and forgets nothing" (FT, 120). Here Derrida, in *The Gift of Death,* perceives a thinly veiled reference to Matthew 6: "thy Father which seeth in secret shall reward thee." This saying occurs three times in Matthew 6: in relation to almsgiving (v. 4), prayer (v. 6), and fasting (v. 18). While Derrida considers this in relation to economic justice,[71] he also significantly suggests that the hidden voyeurism of the *mysterium tremendum* is never far away: "God sees me, he looks into me in secret, but I don't see him, I don't see him looking at me, even though he looks at me while facing me and not, like an analyst, from behind my back."[72] God watches me in secret, but it is a secrecy which is declared: God discloses the fact that God is watching and it is this which induces trembling. But God does not become visible to me by my initiation into this secret. God does not come out of hiding because God is not, like the analyst, watching "behind my back." God remains invisible in the act of *looking me in the face.*

Such an omnipresent, undetectable voyeurism seemingly seeks to posit God as the Absolute Subject who transcends all the self's efforts to perceive Him as object. The secret—though announced—voyeurism of the *mysterium tremendum* captures the self in a narrowing anxiety that is conscious of being watched from nowhere and everywhere. This divine voyeur is put to death in the self's struggle to become a subject who is freed from an inaccessible mystery that captures me ineluctably as an object of scrutiny. Thus Derrida implores: "We should stop thinking about God as someone, over there, way up there, transcendent, and, what is more—into the bargain, precisely— capable, more than any satellite orbiting in space, of seeing into the most secret of interior places."[73] Similarly, Levinas's refusal to struggle with a heter- onomous and faceless *mysterium tremendum* allows him to respond ethically to the visible face of the Other: "The presence of the face coming from beyond the world, but committing me to human fraternity, does not overwhelm me as a numinous essence arousing fear and trembling."[74]

While Levinas denounces captivity by the "invisible meshes" of the numinous,[75] Kierkegaard's pseudonym Johannes Climacus in *Concluding Unscientific Postscript*—in bleak contrast to the "immorality of our age" "in which individuals grope as in a dream for a concept of God without feeling any terror in doing so" (CUP, 544)—evokes how the "absolute conception of God" inevitably cages one in on all sides:

But the bird in the cage, the fish on the beach, the invalid on his sickbed, and the prisoner in the narrowest prison cell are not as captive as the person who is captive in his conception of God, because, just as God is, the captivating conception is everywhere present and at every moment. (CUP, 484)

While it has been argued that the Wholly Other is in many ways a necessarily melancholy notion, here is a harrowing reminder that we have not entirely left behind the murky shores of melancholy's possible capitulation into insanity. Given the irremediable agitation before the terror of the divine, as Johannes Climacus observes, "no wonder then that the Jews assumed that the sight of God was death and the pagans that the God-relationship was the harbinger of madness!" (CUP, 484).[76] Likewise, pseudonym Judge William comments in *Stages on Life's Way* that "the person who saw God must die. This was only a figurative expression, [but] it is literal and true that one loses one's mind in the same way as the lover does when he sees the beloved and, which he also does, sees God" (SLW, 122). The consistency of this strand in Kierkegaard's work is enforced and given its most emphatic expression in the words of Anti-Climacus in *The Sickness unto Death*:

To exist before God may seem unendurable to a man because he cannot come back to himself, become himself. Such a fantasized religious person would say (to characterize him by means of some lines): "That a sparrow can live is comprehensible; it does not know that it exists before God. But to know that one exists before God, and then not instantly go mad or sink into nothingness!" (SUD, 32)

Kierkegaard begins here with someone to whom God seems so "infinitely sublime" that they are prevented from becoming a self before God—which is what God really desires. Yet it must not be overlooked how Anti-Climacus puts these words in the mouth of "a fantasized religious person." For this fantast, existing before God seems ontologically unendurable: madness or annihilation present themselves as the self's only possibilities. But, crucially for Anti-Climacus, this self has become "fantastic"[77] and therefore "leads a fantasized existence in abstract infinitizing or in abstract isolation, continually lacking its self, from which it moves further and further away" (SUD, 32).[78] Such a person cannot become themselves: and it is at this point that the melancholy fantast occludes Kierkegaard's notion that God desires *selves* because God desires to be *loved*. One cannot ever stand as a self in a relationship of love before a God who, by sheer numinous force, causes one to "go mad or sink into nothingness."

According to Anti-Climacus's warning, the religious individual can become "carried away" by a fantastic conception of what it means to exist before God, and it is this fantasy itself that must be tempered if one is to become oneself in free and intimate relation to the divine. The self "is the conscious synthesis of infinitude and finitude that relates itself to itself, whose task is to become itself, which can only be done through the relationship to God" (SUD, 29–30). Although the relationship to God must be worked out in fear and trembling—since for Anti-Climacus they "signify that we are in the process of becoming" (PC, 88)—one must be dialectically vigilant lest they "plunge one headlong into fantasy." Emphatically: "To become oneself is to become concrete. . . . Consequently, the progress of the becoming must be an infinite moving away from itself in the infinitizing of the self, and an infinite coming back to itself in the finitizing process" (SUD, 30). Although the "God-relationship is an infinitizing," it still retains the individual's relation to the finite. The danger is that "in fantasy this infinitizing can so sweep a man off his feet that his state is simply an intoxication" (SUD, 32).

This involves us in a dangerous dialectical process and pursuit. Although the common bourgeois conception of God has, according to Johannes and Anti-Climacus, lacked the authentic absolute difference and concomitant "terror threat," pushing one's understanding to the opposite extreme will likewise provoke an inauthentic and ultimately nihilistic fantasy. On the one hand, we have the anthropological myth of Feuerbachian projection which asserts that the otherness of God "is only illusion, only imagination,"[79] and on the other hand lies the danger of an anthropomorphic intoxication which fantasizes God as Wholly Other to the point of madness. An understanding of God as the Wholly Other, while evading Feuerbach's conflation, is still vulnerable to the fetishism of religious imagination. God's appearance as the forbidding and voyeuristic Father-projection may *appear* to be irreducibly Wholly Other in its transcendence, but in actuality it is not far from an unconscious anthropic projection—an illusion of the imagination and a potential sign that one has not left the melancholy aesthetic (recalling A's fantasized divine-persecution complex, considered toward the end of the previous chapter). While "fear and trembling" signify the authentic God relationship (an expression of the infinite qualitative difference), one must be vigilant against the embellishing tendencies of the fantastic toward a crude "daemonic dread." Even "fear of the Lord," as Otto warns, must be learned from God.[80] The true sense of numinous awe is found in the call of the Seraphim: "Holy, holy, holy!"[81]

But what then becomes of the self before God if it does not succumb to madness or annihilation? For Otto, as for Johannes Climacus with regard to the Unknown in *Philosophical Fragments:* "There cannot even be a searching for God unless He has previously made Himself felt."[82] And yet it is impossible to escape the sense that in Otto and Kierkegaard this God is "felt" initially in the alienated fear and trembling of the self before that which is Wholly Other. So for Otto the primal experience of the numinous is fear: the awe and dread of the *mysterium tremendum.* This is demonstrated in the early biblical depictions of the wrath of Yahweh, "like stored-up electricity, discharging itself upon any one who comes too near."[83] However, this numinous dread is not the only word on Holiness. Let it be emphasized that "fear of the Lord is the *beginning* of all wisdom: and the knowledge of the Holy One is understanding" (Proverbs 9:10). The second clause of this verse can be read as a fulfillment of the first. Despite the inherent primal fear of ontological extinction—despite the fact that one *imagines* that one will sink into nothingness before God—one is decisively *not* so annihilated. In other (imperfect) words, divine love is the truly Holy expression of divine omnipotence, as Kierkegaard expresses it in one of his *Christian Discourses* on the topic:

> It is said that God's omnipotence crushes a human being. But it is not so; no man is so much that God needs omnipotence to crush him, because for omnipotence he is nothing. It is God's love that even in the last moment manifests his love by making him to be something for it. ("'The Joy of it' That the Weaker You Become, the Stronger God Becomes in You," CD, 128)

Divine omnipotence, as Kierkegaard describes it, does not crush a person. Out of love, it allows the person to become something before God. Even in the belief that one may be annihilated, one indirectly affirms the "I" which fears its own annihilation.[84] Hence when Kierkegaard writes in *The Point of View for my Work as an Author* of the fear and trembling of God's Mastery over him which he sensed "when he let me perceive his omnipotence and my nothingness," he implicitly testifies to a residual "I" which *perceives* its own "nothingness" (PV, 74). As such, true omnipotence, intriguingly and apparently contradictorily, actually ensures human freedom. Human independence is the gift of divine omnipotence—just as the self is the gift and obligation of the eternal. Rightly considered, divine omnipotence does not necessitate the dependence of the human being, since, as Kierkegaard describes in one of the most remarkable entries in his *Journals:*

it also must contain the unique qualification of being able to withdraw itself again in a manifestation of omnipotence in such a way that precisely for this reason that which has been originated through omnipotence can be independent. . . . Only omnipotence can withdraw itself at the same time it gives itself away, and this relationship is the very independence of the receiver. God's omnipotence is therefore his goodness. For goodness means to give oneself away completely, but in such a way that by omnipotently taking oneself back one makes the recipient independent. . . . It is incomprehensible that omnipotence is not only able to create the most impressive of all things—the whole visible world—but is able to create the most fragile of all things—a being independent of that very omnipotence. (JP 2:1251 / Pap. VII[1] A 181)[85]

Despite the fear of annihilation, divine omnipotence does not crush a person, but instead withdraws through the concessive gift of independence in the freedom of the self. Hence, in Anti-Climacus's words, "to have a self, to be a self, is the greatest concession, an infinite concession, given to a man, because it is also eternity's claim upon him" (SUD, 21). The search for self-knowledge is thereby divinely validated; but this concession is also an obligation, and freedom thereby becomes anxious. But the concession of divine omnipotence expresses the desire for the individual to become potent as a self—as a subject capable of relation—since: "To be *spirit* is to be *I*. God desires to have *Is*, for God desires to be loved" (JP 4:4350 / Pap. XI[1] A 487). Understood from this perspective as an expression of omnipotence, love, and goodness, the initial understanding of God as Wholly Other creates the space in which the self becomes itself, not in isolation, but in the independence that freely relates back to God as Holy Other. In this sense, the self is not absorbed in the (numinous) divine. Rather, the reconciliation, or unification, between self and God occurs through the clarification of personal identity (the becoming transparent to oneself before God). As Kierkegaard describes once more in his *Journals:*

According to Christian doctrine man is not to merge in God through a pantheistic fading away or in the divine ocean through the blotting out of all individual characteristics, but in an intensified consciousness "a person must render account for every careless word he has uttered" [Matthew 12:36], and even though grace blots out sin, the union with God still takes place in the personality clarified through the whole process. (JP 4:3887 / Pap. II A 248)

Nevertheless, does Kierkegaard's circuitous affirmation of selfhood implicitly conflict with the self-depreciation which Otto sees as an authentic response to the *tremendum* of the numinous? After all, though "numinous experience has both subjective and objective aspects,"[86] it is not the human subject that is at the heart of Otto's writing.[87] In preference to the modern idiom of the self that Kierkegaard adopts and refines, Otto employs the more Schleiermachian language of "creature-consciousness" or "creature-feeling" as "the emotion of a creature, abased and overwhelmed by its own nothingness in contrast to that which is supreme above all creatures."[88] It is in Abraham's words of inter-cession for Sodom that Otto finds this attitude exemplified: "Behold now, I have taken upon me to speak unto the Lord, which am but dust and ashes" (Genesis 18:27).[89] When Otto describes the *tremendum* as *tremenda majestas* ("overpoweringness") he explains that, "in contrast to 'the overpowering' of which we are conscious as an object over against the self, there is a feeling of one's own abasement, of being but 'dust and ashes' and nothingness."[90] That is to say, there is an overshadowing of the self that defines one's self-estima-tion in relation to divine *majestas*. One becomes aware of oneself—as dust and ashes—through a confrontation with the *tremendum*, but this insight manifests itself, in mysticism for example, as "*self-depreciation . . . the estima-tion of the self, of the personal 'I,' as something not perfectly or essentially real, or even as mere nullity, a self-depreciation which comes to demand its own fulfilment in practice in rejecting the delusion of selfhood, and so makes for the annihilation of self*."[91] Indirectly, this experience implies a rise in authentic creature-consciousness insofar as it illuminates the "delusion of selfhood." However, this self-consciousness originates in the revelation from the Other, and thus it is not "merely a category of *self*-valuation, in the sense of self-depreciation."[92] In other words, self-consciousness in *self-depreciation* remains contingent upon the heterogeneity of divine revelation. One does not need to ascribe to a modern sense of "self" to identify some sense of self-consciousness implicit in this self-abasement *before God*. Self-consciousness in *response* to the primacy of divine revelation is not identical with asserting the primacy of the "self" as the starting point for speculation about God.[93] Indeed, both Kierkegaard and Otto are concerned with various expressions of the "delusion of selfhood" made visible to the individual through a rela-tional encounter with the divine. For both thinkers, therefore, the encounter with the Wholly Other actually reveals the *otherness of the self*—the unreal-ity and alienation of selfhood. While Otto is more involved with anatomiz-ing this primal encounter with the Holy (describing the nothingness of the self before the numinous), Kierkegaard is concerned with re-transcribing the modern project of selfhood within this relation (emphasizing the divine call to become a self before God).

Both Otto's creature-feeling in response to the numinous and Kierke-gaard's self before God are, therefore, irreducibly relational to the primary encounter with the divine. The self-negation that Kierkegaard writes of is frequently the annihilation of the delusion of a self-willed selfhood which is symptomatic of much of the despair of modernity. Yet, while Otto fixates upon the awe of the creature before the potency of the numinous, Kierkegaard is concerned with just how the "I" will respond to the consciousness of its self-delusion in the freedom that omnipotence has granted to it. In the fear of God's omnipotence it is as if something is "held back" by God in creating the space for the "I" to *experience itself* as nothingness. The fear of annihilation by holiness is sensed but never actualized: what emerges is actually a sense of freedom which generates its own anxiety. There is even a self-assertive hubris in the belief that one endures the whole weight of the divine omnipotence of the *mysterium tremendum.* Indeed it is for Kierkegaard testament to God's omnipotence that God is not one who "rises in his might to crush the refractory spirits," but instead

> sits quite still and sees everything, without altering a feature as if He did not exist . . . the infinitely powerful, the eternally unchangeable . . . He knows with Himself that He is eternally unchangeable. Anyone not eternally sure of Himself could not keep so still, but would rise up in strength. Only one who is eternally immutable can be in this manner so still.[94]

Nonetheless, there is a dreadful warning and threat to this freedom of the self. Kierkegaard's alliance of divine immutability with divine hiddenness seems to imply an eschatological deferral of intervention, even the deferral of divine wrath or vengeance: "Work out your own salvation in fear and trembling" (Philippians 2:12). Or, as Derrida writes: "We fear and tremble before the inaccessible secret of a God who decides for us although we remain responsible. . . . God is himself absent, hidden and silent, separate, secret, at the moment he has to be obeyed."[95] God may hide but one cannot hide from God, cannot escape God's hand in the end—even in death. Indeed, the fact that God does not annihilate the one who comes into God's presence actually preserves one in the inescapable fear and trembling of freedom and anxiety. As Kierkegaard notes in *Christian Discourses:* "Precisely because you are immortal, you will not be able to escape God, will not be able to mislay yourself in a grave and behave as if nothing has happened; and the criterion by which you will be judged is that you are immortal" ("There Will Be the Resurrection of the Dead, of the Righteous—and of the Unrighteous," CD, 207). This claim of eternity upon one also asserts itself in the apparent hostility between the self and God—a hostility that is not concluded in annihilation but is perpetuated in freedom and its shadow: anxiety. It is this aspect of existing before God that is described by the antagonism of spiritual trial (Gn. *Anfechtung*): the inescapable freedom; the anxiety of relating to God; the volatile striving of spirit and spiritlessness; the struggle with the Wholly Other. This is the heavy price that Kierkegaard values the God-relation at, and it is the content of this struggle between self and God that will be explored in the following chapter, under an illustrative consideration of the allegory of Jacob's struggle with the stranger.

> *with the demise of the "God of the philosophers," the other side of God, the shadow side, the enigmatic attacking stranger of night, has emerged to unsettle and struggle with man. Man, in turn, must contend with both his bereavement over the death of the comforting God and the onslaughts of this "negative" side of God.*
>
> —SUSAN HANDELMAN, IN *The Sin of the Book*

FIVE

The Allegory of Yisra'el

Everyone shall be remembered, but each was great in proportion to the greatness of that with which he strove. For he who strove with the world became great by overcoming the world, and he who strove with himself became great by overcoming himself, but he who strove with God became greater than all. So there was strife in the world, man against man, one against a thousand, but he who strove with God was greater than all.

—*Fear and Trembling*

THE STRUGGLE OF EXILE: THE UNHAPPY CONSCIOUSNESS

"The present age is the age of despair," Kierkegaard pronounces in his *Journals,* "the age of the wandering Jew (many reforming Jews)" (JP 1:737 / Pap. I A 181). According to Kierkegaard, it is the melancholic trope of Israel in exile, the Wandering Jew, that haunts the modern Western consciousness as a symbolic expression of its God-forsakenness, nihilism, and estrangement. The evocation of this sentiment resounds from the Adamic banishment from Eden, the homelessness of Cain, captivities in Egypt and later Babylon to the medieval legends and Romantic literary myths of the Jew who spurned Christ and was cursed to wander the earth as a fugitive until Judgment Day. "Even in pre-exilic times," as Susan Handelman explains, "the Jew is a wanderer and a nomad who finds his truth in wilderness and desert, who encounters the Other as absence and alienation, who struggles with God through language, dialogue, dispute, and questioning—from Abraham to Job."[1] But this is a narrative portrait of perennial exile that has elicited stern resistance. Proliferation of this particular depiction of the Hebraic consciousness obscures the fact that the image in question does not make its entrance until the occurrence of a typically modern change in scenery. Rather than being an inherent primal archetype, the counterargument claims that the figure of the Wandering Jew is an irreducibly historical, indeed often disastrously applied, emblem of a categorically *modern* estrangement:

Is it so difficult for the modern consciousness to admit that the idea of the divided self, of a spirit alienated from itself, is itself a recent artefact—that the image of the Jew as congenitally alien is not itself congenital but rather a historical contrivance, nourished conscientiously in the romantic notion of alienation by volunteer poets and philosophers of the nineteenth century? ... As Zionism was moved by the nationalism of that century, so the conception of the Jew as wanderer and alien was also nourished externally, by the same currents, at the same time; it is itself, in some good measure, alien.[2]

As such, the allegedly eternal narrative of Jewish wandering—from ancient Egypt to modern Europe—is motivated less by an innate Semitic anxiety than by extraneous historical and cultural exigencies. This is not to deny that there is a spirit of exile permeating Jewish thought—a spirit that is evident in the notion of the exile of the Shekinah which bears witness to the historical contingencies of diaspora.[3] Thus, Kierkegaard's own appropriation of the figure of the exilic Jew reveals him as a connoisseur of his intellectual milieu. For Kierkegaard, the folkloric image of the Wandering Jew becomes a melancholy type for the exile of spirit within the spiritlessness of modernity. Essentially, as George Pattison summarizes, "the Wandering Jew symbolizes for Kierkegaard the despair of the present age, a despair rooted in its separation from its substantial ground of religion and manifesting itself in both political reform movements and philosophical nihilism."[4] One might say, therefore, that the Wandering Jew of the nineteenth century is the illegitimate son of a tragic modern humanism. His wandering is, recalling Ralph Harper's phrase from 1967's *The Seventh Solitude*, a "metaphysical homelessness." His despair is, in Kierkegaardian terms, an eternal sickness unto death without hope of alleviation. "The Wandering Jew," Kierkegaard muses, "seems to have his prototype in the fig tree Christ commanded to wither away [Matthew 21:19]" (Pap. I C 65). According to this image, he is apparently forsaken by God because he has forsaken God. He is a melancholy descendent of Cain in the modern semblance of *l'étranger*: the wandering, lonely son of a *deus otiosus* who is spurned alike by men and gods.

In Kierkegaard's time, it is primarily the figure of Ahasuerus, a Romantic incarnation of the Wandering Jew, who leaves his mark on modern Western culture. Among numerous other literary appearances, as Pattison highlights in his *Kierkegaard, Religion and the Nineteenth-Century Crisis of Culture*, he is presented in nihilistic depiction as the protagonist of the aphoristic *Ahasverus* by Kierkegaard's influential university teacher, Poul Martin Møller, and features memorably in Percy Bysshe Shelley's philosophical poem "Queen Mab," answering the question of the existence of God with the affirmative yet demonic response—not unlike A's melancholy proof derived from divine persecution: "ay, an almighty God / And vengeful as almighty!"[5] The Romantic version of the legend thrives on the fantasy of an exilic curse of long life, as apparent in Anglo-Irish clergyman C. R. Maturin's 1820 novel, *Melmoth the Wanderer,* about a scholar who sells his soul to the devil for an extra century and a half of living. Melmoth is described by Mario Praz as "something of the Wandering Jew, something of the vampire."[6] But perhaps the most revealing modern treatment of this figure belongs to Kierkegaard's French contemporary Edgar Quinet (1803–1875), whose epic prose-poem *Ahasverus* has the protagonist, consigned to wander till the Judgment Day, eventually *outlive God* at the end of the world. In Quinet's symbolization of human history through the figure of the Wandering Jew, an estranged and alienated consciousness is ironically depicted as outlasting his own damnation by surviving the death of his judge. A particularly Romantic hubris is manifest in this effectively Nietzschean irony: man is existing under the living curse of a death sentence; but at least he has outlived the God who worsened his sufferings.

In reference to his own authorial venture, Kierkegaard, echoing the melancholy of Romanticism, mused in his *Journals* that his quasi-Mosaic mission might itself be prey to the curse

> that, like the Wandering Jew in a beautiful legend, I should lead the pilgrims to the promised land and not enter myself, that I should guide men to the truth of Christianity and that as my punishment for going astray in my younger days I myself would not enter in but would venture only to be an omen of an incomparable future. (JP 5:5795 / Pap. VI B 40:33)

The Wandering Jew is no doubt a morbidly beautiful allegory, and one that attests to the twined threads of the aesthetic and the religious that run through Kierkegaard's authorship; but some may also struggle to reconcile it to the Kierkegaard who appears to have discovered some significant deliverance through faith. But it is significant that Kierkegaard, in his darker moments, is willing to inscribe even himself under this icon of the modern condition of despair. As Pattison astutely relates: "Kierkegaard's concern with the Wandering Jew is not directed towards delineating the Other, the One-who-we-are-not, but as articulating a condition that belongs to the inner destiny of all who have drunk from the bitter waters of modernity."[7]

The motif of abject immortality is further reminiscent of a Romantic meditation by Kierkegaard's young aesthete in *Either/Or* under the title "The Unhappiest One."[8] The phrase recalls Hegel's numerous considerations of the "Unhappy Consciousness,"[9] but in Kierkegaard's poetic reflection the title refers to the mysterious adornment on a gravestone in England. A, in this address, considers the meaning of its legend in light of the apparently ironic supposition that the tomb itself is empty. Could it mean that there is no such person as The Unhappiest One? Or is this tombstone essentially a monument to a secret truth? "Then why the tomb was empty could be explained," he conjectures, "namely, to indicate that the unhappiest one was the one who could not die, could not slip down into a grave" (E/O I, 220). As such, The Unhappiest One is one who is consigned to wander perpetually in his longing to rest in the grave that cannot be his. This despair is paralleled by Anti-Climacus's survey in *The Sickness unto Death*, where "the torment of this despair is precisely this inability to die . . . to be sick unto death is to be unable to die" (SUD, 18). And so we are returned stylistically to the despair of the present age, the despair of the age of the Wandering Jew, of the perpetually barren fig tree: "the sickness unto death, this tormenting contradiction, this sickness of the self, perpetually to be dying, to die and yet not die, to die death" (SUD, 18).

Yet in "The Unhappiest One" of *Either/Or*, A also has Hegel's Unhappy Consciousness in his sights:

> In all of Hegel's systematic works there is one section that discusses the unhappy consciousness. One always comes to the reading of such investigations with an inner uneasiness and palpitation of the heart, with a fear that one will learn too much or too little. . . . Ah, happy is the one who has nothing more to do with the subject than to write a paragraph about it; even happier the one who can write the next. The unhappy one is the person who in one way or another has his ideal, the substance of his life, the plenitude of his consciousness, his essential nature, outside himself. The unhappy one is the person who is always absent from himself, never present to himself. (E/O I, 222)

And so Hegel, as A ironically claims, in his happy aptitude for writing systematically about the Unhappy Consciousness, reveals himself as immunized against the alienation he is attempting to inscribe. And so it is not actually to Hegel's enquiries that one must look for the Unhappiest One; it is not Hegel's happy depictions of Unhappy Consciousness that generate the anxiety in Kierkegaard's authorship. Rather, it is a singular biblical figure who elicits the greatest fear and trembling—and this is not Ahasuerus but another wandering Jew whom Johannes de Silentio eulogizes in 1843: "Venerable Father Abraham!" (FT, 23). Yet such is the alienation evoked by Abraham that, in reflection upon this estranged figure, Johannes confesses: "Thinking about Abraham . . . I am shattered" (FT, 33).

By confessing his inability to properly transcribe the figure of Abraham, Johannes thus evades the self-contradiction which A, in "The Unhappiest One," accuses Hegel of falling into in his systematic description of the

Unhappy Consciousness. And furthermore: for Hegel, the Hebraic consciousness is itself the epitome of the alienated Unhappy Consciousness,[10] and it is *Abraham* who typifies this above all others. According to Mark C. Taylor, both Hegel's and Silentio's considerations of Abraham are determined by a discernible horror. Hegel's approach evokes a "*horror* that arises from the encounter with the terrible tension of estrangement."[11] However, while Hegel systematically determines the melancholy restlessness of the Unhappy Consciousness, Silentio's horror approaches Abraham with an unspeakable "*horror religiosus*, as Israel approached Mount Sinai" (FT, 61)[12]—thereby, as Sylviane Agacinski observes, effectively replacing the sublimity of the Creator with the sublimity of Abraham.[13] To what extent, then, can Abraham, as the "knight of faith" rather than the "tragic hero" of despair (i.e., not a poetically constructed Ahasuerus), be regarded as the definitive symbol of the estrangement of the Unhappy Consciousness?

In many senses, Abraham stands as an iconic expression of the fear and trembling of the infinite qualitative difference between humanity and God. "Abraham is an eternal prototype [*Forbillede*] of the religious man," Kierkegaard notes in his *Journals*. "Just as he had to leave the land of his fathers for a strange land, so the religious man must willingly leave, that is, forsake a whole generation of his contemporaries even though he remains among them, but isolated, *alien* to them. To be an alien, to be in exile, is precisely the characteristic suffering of the religious man" (JP 4:4650 / Pap. X³ A 114). For Kierkegaard, this suffering—the suffering evoked by the struggle of spirit against spiritlessness—should be realized in modernity. Throughout his writings, Kierkegaard works out this estrangement in terms of an often isolationist polemic of authentic Christianity in tension with the apostasy of bourgeois Christendom. Negatively regarded, the otherness of Spirit implies precisely this estrangement from one's contemporaries. Nevertheless, by invoking Abraham as the forefather of an alienated faith, Kierkegaard is sounding surprisingly, indeed ironically, in harmony with Hegel. Abraham, as discussed by Hegel in his early theological writings, is an individual who struggles against an entire creation that he can encounter only as opposition:

> The whole world Abraham regarded as simply his opposite; if he did not take it to be a nullity, he looked on it as sustained by the God who was alien to it.
>
> Nothing in nature was supposed to have any part in God; everything was simply under God's mastery. Abraham, as the opposite of the whole world, could have no higher being than that of the other term in the opposition, and thus he likewise was supported by God. . . . Mastery was the only possible relationship in which Abraham could stand to the infinite world opposed

to him; but he was unable himself to make this mastery actual, and it therefore remained ceded to his Ideal [i.e., God].[14]

Hegel thus identifies Abraham, living in alienated opposition to the world and the other, as the personification of a Hebraic unhappy consciousness: "He was a stranger on earth, a stranger to the soil and to men alike."[15] It was only "through God alone that Abraham came into mediate relation with the world"[16]—a world that existed solely in opposition to him. This dreadful solitude situates Abraham as "opposed," by virtue of his (estranged) relation to the created order, also "to the wholly other God upon whom he was absolutely dependent."[17] As such, Abraham only discovers his God, his absolute, outside of himself. Abraham "is enthralled to a Lord who is so radically different from himself that he cannot understand him at all."[18] Consequently, his is an unhappy consciousness since it is "fundamentally an *unhappy consciousness* which projects onto a transcendental and always distant God the fundamental identity of certainty and truth, of the Concept and Being."[19]

Similarly, in *Fear and Trembling*, Johannes de Silentio acknowledges that creation is permeated with enmity—"Thus did they struggle in the world, man against man, one against thousands" (FT, 16)—and furthermore Abraham himself also comes into conflict with the God who, according to Hegel's depiction, was his only support. In Silentio's portrait, the image of Abraham on Mount Moriah, before God, with knife in hand ready to sacrifice Isaac, is a dreadful memorial to faith. Yet the terrible site of Mount Moriah is a monument to a greater conflict than the strife between a Hegelian Unhappy Consciousness and the estranged creation that opposes it. This faith derives its vigor from a higher struggle than the struggle between man and creation. It is the passion of Abrahamic faith—"the holy, pure, and humble expression for the divine madness that was admired by the pagans"[20]—which goes beyond and "disdains the terrifying battle with the raging elements and the forces of creation in order to contend with God" (FT, 23).

Although Hegel saw that God "subjugated the world to him, gave him as much of the world as he needed, and put him in security against the rest,"[21] Abraham, in Silentio's depiction, struggles with the God who is the actual *telos* of his faith and the origin of his promise to become the father of many nations. As Silentio formulates the paradox: "Abraham was God's chosen one, and it was the Lord who imposed the ordeal [*Prøvelse*]" (FT, 19). However, the resolution of this particular conflict is wrought in contradistinction to the mastery that determines Abraham's relation to creation: "Thus did they struggle on earth: there was one who conquered everything by his power, and there was one who conquered God by his powerlessness" (FT, 16). Just what is meant by saying that Abraham—who conspicuously "did not challenge heaven with his prayers" (FT, 22), as he had when God threatened the destruction of Sodom and Gomorrah (Genesis 18)—"overcomes" God by his silence?

The nature of this victory is dependent on the nature of the trial that Silentio is describing. Perhaps it is closer to the "overcoming" that Luther had earlier attributed to another "knight of faith." In his sermons on the story of the Canaanite woman (Matthew 15:22–28), Luther surmised that "she is no simpleton in matters of faith; she is rather a Knight of Faith who wins the victory over God himself."[22] Decisively, Abraham's faith in God—a faith which for Hegel estranges him from an ever-distant transcendence and afflicts him with unrealizable longing—is a faith which is actually manifest and expressed in immanence: "Abraham had faith, and had faith for this life," Silentio insists— and this is the key to his "repetition," his receiving back of Isaac. "In fact, if his faith had been only for a life to come, he certainly would have more readily discarded everything in order to rush out of a world to which he did not belong" (FT, 20). Such a faith founded upon the estrangement of eschatological deferral would surely see Abraham hurrying to give up Isaac, himself, everything without anxiety, in order to hasten to the alienation-transcending *ekstasis* of the other world. "But Abraham's faith was not of this sort, if there is such a faith at all, for actually it is not faith but the most remote possibility of faith that faintly sees its object on the most distant horizon but is separated from it by a chasmal abyss within which doubt plays its tricks" (FT, 20).

It is in this "chasmal abyss" that the Unhappy Consciousness endures the weight and wait of melancholy—an abyss in which "doubt plays its tricks." Yet the strangeness or mystery of the Wholly Other need not be a persistent source of paralyzing estrangement and horror. Indeed as shall be explored further, faith, according to Kierkegaard, is precisely the joyful and lived passion for the mystery of the absolute that can only, by definition, occur in the space of the apparent absence of God. Hence the paradoxical possibility of being out over 70,000 fathoms and yet finding joy. Essentially this enigmatic struggle is resolved in a victory won by the Knight of Faith who is "great by that power whose strength is powerlessness" (FT, 16).

But Abraham himself struggles with the God who, as Derrida—can one say evoking Hegelian estrangement?—puts it in *The Gift of Death*, "is absent, hidden and silent, separate, secret, at the moment he has to be obeyed."[23] Instead of wrestling face-to-face like Jacob in Genesis 32, Abraham struggles with a God who apparently vacates the scene at the decisive moment of revelation. It is in this apparent lacuna of divine absence that Abraham's silence strives with God. That is why his striving with God is the victory of an absurd, self-denying faith; that is why Abraham is "great by that wisdom whose secret is foolishness, great by that hope whose form is madness, great by that love that is hatred to oneself" (FT, 16–17). As Kierkegaard explains in his 1847 discourse on "The Gospel of Sufferings," it is definitive of faith that it exists in the absence of that which it believes in—"faith simply means: What I am seeking is not here, and for that very reason I believe it" (UDVS, 218).

But there are many other struggles with God to be considered, some more indicative of insurrection than of faith. Yet all these struggles point toward the same inviolable expression of the infinite qualitative difference between the human and the divine: the notion of tension or enmity between the self and God. It is to the negative and positive connotations of this enmity for the prospect of the self before God that our attention now turns.

THE PRIMAL ENMITY

If I let the human race create God, then there is no conflict between God and man; if I let man disappear in God, then there is no conflict, either.
—*The Concept of Irony*

This assertion—an implicit rebuke of both atheism's and paganism's neglect of the infinite qualitative difference—appears in Kierkegaard's first published monograph, his thesis *The Concept of Irony,* and expresses a sentiment that endures throughout his authorship, from beginning to bitter end. In his polemical writings toward the end of his life, Kierkegaard warns us that in a profound and unforgettable sense, "God is indeed a human being's most appalling enemy, your mortal enemy. Indeed, he wants you to die, die unto the world" ("The Moment," No. 5, 27 July 1855; LW, 177). The mortal tension between spirit and the spiritlessness of modernity is derived from the hidden truth, asserted in Kierkegaard's *Journals,* that "there is a life and death battle between God and man; God hates man just as man hates God" (JP 4:4711).

In this sentiment the French Jesuit theologian Henri de Lubac has detected a surprising affinity with the antagonism between humanity and God in the "antitheism" of Kierkegaard's French contemporary, Pierre-Joseph Proudhon. Proudhon invokes the definitive biblical image of divine-human antagonism when he observes in his *Philosophie de la misère* that humanity must forever strive against God "like Israel against Jehovah, until death."[24] For Proudhon, the allegory of Jacob's struggle is actually inverted to symbolize humanity's drive for emancipation from the heteronomy of the God of Providence.[25] It becomes the destiny of modern humanity to strive to wrest itself free from this oppressive divine stranger. And Proudhon is not the last modern thinker to re-appropriate this archaic biblical motif for his own times. It is an emblem which, through Roland Barthes's poststructuralist interpretation of Genesis 32:23–32 in "Wrestling with the Angel," even renders itself *post*modern.[26] The allegory also figures in Maurice Blanchot's virtually contemporary "Être Juif"

(Being Jewish). In Blanchot's view, Jacob's struggle with the stranger enacts a portrayal of all human confrontation with the human, as much as a divine "Other." In Blanchot's words, the encounter with the human Other is equally represented in this struggle, since the human Other is

> no less inaccessible, separate, and distant, than the Invisible Himself; [it] also confirms what is terrible about such a meeting whose outcome could only be agreement or death. Who sees God is in danger of dying. Who encounters the Other can relate himself to him by mortal violence or by the gift of the word.[27]

But is this, as in Derrida, the equation or reduction of the Wholly Other to a mutual human alterity? Again, is the struggle with God, the Wholly Other, qualitatively different from the self's encounter with the human other? Here it may be useful to think of Hegel's dialectical struggle with the other for self-consciousness in *Phenomenology of Spirit*. To see God is to die; "each seeks the death of the other."[28] Indeed this motif is pertinent to Kierkegaard's schema, as Levinas remarks in "Existence and Ethics": "In [Kierkegaardian] belief, existence is always trying to secure recognition for itself, just like consciousness in Hegel. It struggles for this recognition by seeking forgiveness and salvation."[29] But Kierkegaard identifies that in defiant unbelief, as well as belief, consciousness seeks recognition for itself ("in despair to will to be oneself," as Anti-Climacus identifies in *The Sickness unto Death*)—albeit in the struggle to free itself from the gaze of a God who declares that consciousness must recognize itself through the eyes of a Wholly Other. Could such an analogous struggle for a consciousness emancipated from the gaze of the Lord God be read in Hegel, as some have suggested?[30]

According to Hegel's dialectic of "Independence and Dependence of Self-Consciousness: Lordship and Bondage" in *Phenomenology of Spirit*, self-consciousness confronted by another self-consciousness strives to overcome what it perceives as the threat of "this otherness of itself."[31] But this perceived threat is reciprocal. A shared mutuality of self-consciousness threatens to disrupt the sovereign subjectivity of each "being-for-self." And so the conflict begins with a gaze: "They *recognize* themselves as *mutually recognizing* one another."[32] Hegel thus describes a struggle based upon a recognition of the reciprocity of the other: based on an antagonistic and recognized mutuality between the gaze of the self and the gaze of the other, and not what Derrida calls "this abyssal dissymmetry"[33] between the gaze of the *mysterium tremendum* (the Wholly Other) and one's own. The threat of annihilation is mutual, and not founded upon the ontological oppression of the individual by the absolute: "they prove themselves and each other through a life-and-death struggle."[34]

Yet it is through this struggle that the bondsman "has experienced the fear of death, the absolute Lord."[35] Hegel ostensibly evokes the God of the Old Testament when he declares "fear of the lord is indeed the beginning of wisdom."[36] But this is a struggle in which the initial threat of annihilation is mutual; in the struggle with God, the risk of annihilation is radically one-sided. The human-divine paradigm is a struggle that takes place over the abyss of an infinite qualitative difference. And yet how can such a struggle take place across an abyss? How can one struggle with someone infinitely different, someone elusively Other, without some concession of the absoluteness of this otherness?

This apparent impossibility can be expressed by a return to the motif of Jacob's night-struggle with his enigmatic antagonist. In Genesis 32, does Jacob not discern the face of God at Peni'el—the face that none may see and live? Jacob wrestles all night with a figure who refuses to reveal his name. And yet, after receiving the blessing of this stranger, Jacob declares: "I have seen God face to face and my life is preserved" (Genesis 32:30). Jacob was indeed blessed (Genesis 32:29) to have wrestled with God in the flesh, face-to-face, despite the threat of annihilation. Surely God as the Wholly Other cannot be grasped, and especially not in the scandalous tangibility of such a struggle, unless God has become incarnated in the divine giving of Godself to be struggled with. While the threat of annihilation is not reciprocal, one sees a God who, by taking in some enigmatic way the form of a man, actually partakes to a degree in this human mutuality. The possibility of the struggle relies, not upon the sublimation of flesh into spirit, but upon God allowing Godself to be struggled with—indeed, God's giving of Godself in the struggle. The tangible corporeality of the stranger is a divine concession to Jacob: the gift of transubstantiation which makes apprehension possible. God, the Wholly Other, becomes an other, a stranger, whom Jacob is able to grip—to grab by the throat, as it were.

And yet the ineffable *mysterium* is evoked by the absurd thought that this person is also in some way God: to see the face of this person is in some way to see the Face of God (death). This hiddenness, or veiling, of the stranger prompts us to recognize how the struggle with God does not necessarily entail knowing God-in-Godself, but rather how the struggle forms an allegory of *knowing oneself before God*. As noted in our earlier discussion of the Divine Name in Exodus 3, in the ancient Near East, a name revealed the essential character of its bearer and in Jacob's case it reveals his flaw.[37] By giving his name to the stranger, Jacob would be both revealing himself and giving the other power over himself. And yet, rather than exerting absolute might over Jacob, the stranger demonstrates a different kind of authority through the gift of a new name: a name joined to the name of God (Heb. *El*) and therefore, according to Jewish tradition, a name sanctified by the mercy and power of divinity. In this sense, Jacob's identity is interrogated and revealed only for the stranger to rename him in relation to God, *Yisra'el* ("struggling with God").[38] Subsequently, the Divine Name refuses to reveal itself to desire (as the divine face does not disclose itself to Moses in Exodus 33) but instead responds in a question which asks Jacob to examine himself and preserves the *mysterium*: "Wherefore is it that thou dost ask after my name?" (Genesis 32:29).

As described above, for Hegel there is always an implicit and reciprocal risk of one's life in the contest with the other.[39] However, the allegory of Jacob's struggle with God reveals the divine grace that preserves life: the perceived threat of annihilation that is never actualized, the omnipotence that is conceded. Surely this concession of omnipotence does not extend to the threat of divine annihilation—surely, in other words, Jacob could not have *killed God*? The allegory of Jacob's mysterious struggle forms a fascinating focal point for the spiritual treatise of sixteenth-century Spanish mystic and contemporary of John of the Cross and Teresa of Jesus, Fray Juan de los Angeles (1536–1609), *Lucha espiritual y amorosa* (*The Loving and Spiritual Struggle*). Although no one can kill God (except in one's own heart, Kierkegaard tells us[40]), Fray Juan de los Angeles reads in this enigmatic contest a divine concession to the extent that God becomes vulnerable to being "wounded" by love.[41]

A further consequence of the struggle with God is that Jacob, through being subsequently reconciled to his brother Esau, is freed from the fear of the other: "I have seen thy face, as though I had seen the face of God, and thou wast pleased with me" (Genesis 33:10). As Juan de los Angeles recounts:

> And the angel said to him: *Hereafter your name shall not be Jacob* (which means fighter) *but Israel* (which means Prince of God), that you may lose your fear of Esau *for it is with God that you have been wrestling, and he who has prevailed over God shall fear no man.*[42]

The message, as Juan de los Angeles receives it in the sixteenth century, is that one who fears God should fear no other. And yet by Kierkegaard's nineteenth century, the fear of God is not regarded as a source of empowerment, or fearlessness against the other. On the contrary, Kierkegaard lives in a time when, by his own admission, the thought of God no longer evokes the archaic fear that it once did: "Christianity was originally represented (by the preachers) in the fear of God; nowadays it is represented (by the preachers) in the fear of man" (JP 4:4904 / Pap X⁵ A 40). The antagonism is reversed—echoing Proudhon's annunciation of humanity's obligation to fight back, to become the protagonist of the eternal struggle. And yet, despite this modern suppression of the fear of God, Kierkegaard insists in 1848's discourse on "The Care of Presumption" that "one cannot kill God; on the other hand, as is said, one certainly can kill the thought of Him . . . becoming oneself the master instead of the bondservant" (CD, 66–67).

Kierkegaard is writing specifically in reference to the parable of the husbandmen who plotted: "Let us kill the son, and then the vineyard is ours" (CD, 66; Matthew 21:33–46 and parallels). Nevertheless, it is possible to read the Hegelian Master-Slave dialectic between the lines: "Is not this indeed wanting to add one foot to his growth—by having the owner killed, or the thought of him, by becoming the owner oneself, becoming the master instead of the bondservant?" (CD, 67).[43] In such rebellious "presumption,"[44] as Kierkegaard reveals, one fails to identify the extent to which one "carries in his innermost being the mark that God is the strongest, the mark that he *wills* to have God against himself" (CD, 67). Hence, this presumptuous consciousness continues to define itself through the recognition of the very other it strives to deny, thereby forcing itself deeper into the very dependent structure of consciousness it hopes to free itself from: "for it certainly would be an enormous foot to add to his growth if a person directly before God were capable of denying God."[45] In this insurrection, self-derived independence is not the received blessing of a divine concession, since "no blessing accompanies stolen goods" (CD, 67). The self-abnegation of Jacob wrestling with God is nothing compared to the dependence of this presumption that *wills* to have God against him. "If the God-fearing man limps after having wrestled with God [Genesis 32:31]," Kierkegaard continues, "then truly the disbeliever is annihilated in his innermost being" (CD, 67).

Here the deicidal struggle for mastery referred to by Kierkegaard is oriented around the sort of implicit dependence that Proudhon himself identifies in the crude atheism which earns his rebuke. What actually most endangers faith for Kierkegaard is not so much the presumptuous struggle against God, but rather modernity's indifference to the radical tensions of the God-relationship. In Kierkegaard's time the *mysterium tremendum* is a *deus otiosus* already declining in the apostasy of bourgeois Christendom and the hubris of the Enlightenment's heteronomy of reason. Consequently, Levinas observes in "Enigma and Phenomenon" that the "Kierkegaardian God is revealed only to be persecuted and unrecognized, reveals himself only in the measure that he is hunted."[46] This God is the God endangered by atheism and exiled by human wisdom into appearing on the fringes of modernity only as enigma, as paradox, as a "persecuted truth."[47] Kierkegaard thus presents us with "a truth persecuted in the name of a universally evident truth, a meaning paling into meaning, a meaning thus already past and driven out."[48] The Truth of the absolute is hunted into exile by the truth of the universal, emancipated from all fear and bondage of the Lord.

In the anxious lacuna of such a divine retreat or exile, Kierkegaardian belief, as Levinas describes it, is consigned to exist as the inexpressible secret of an incommensurable subjectivity: "This incommunicable burning, this 'thorn in the flesh,' testified to subjectivity as a *tension over itself* [tension sur soi]."[49] In turn, this "thorn in the flesh" that comprises belief in a persecuted truth signifies a subjectivity that is itself exiled and persecuted by "the world" of spiritlessness. Faith discovers a melancholy solidarity with the truth of a God who is likewise manifest in suffering exile. Hence, writes Levinas: "*Belief always exists in relationship with a suffering truth* . . . the Relation with a Person who is both present and absent, with a humbled God who has suffered and died, and brought despair to those he has led to salvation."[50] However, the suffering truth does not simply endure banishment to the periphery by the universal truth of the spirit(lessness) of modernity. Rather it is a truth that has freely *chosen* to submit to crucifixion, humiliation, death. Hence the relation to this truth is an *imitatio Christi*: a following in the bloody tracks of the Savior, partaking of a degree of divinity's exile from the world. Yet this discipleship involves the anxious pursuit of an Other who eludes the consummation of the believer's understanding. Even the imitation of an inimitable divine suffering requires what Kierkegaard aptly describes in his *Journals* as "the crucifixion of one's understanding" (JP 4:4375 / Pap. X^1 A 478). It is following one who is absent—"faith simply means: What I am seeking is not here, and for that very reason I believe it" (UDVS, 218). Or as Levinas describes it: "Belief stands in the midst of this conflict between presence and absence—a conflict which remains for ever irreconcilable, an open wound, unstaunchable bleeding."[51] This is part of faith's passionate inwardness—what Levinas identifies as the inevitable "isolation of the individual relationship with the being to which, for Kierkegaard, no other kind of relationship is possible: that is to say, with God."[52] And it is this, for Levinas, which causes the passion of faith to exhibit a certain violence in the individual's severance from Others (*Autrui*) in their lonely and crucifying quest for the Wholly Other, for the elusive "crucified truth."[53]

WOUNDS FROM A BURNING ARROW

In an unsuspecting sense, Levinas is perhaps not so wrong to detect an implicit violence within Kierkegaardian subjectivity. Yet the violent severance of the suffering truth that, according to Levinas, "does not open us out to others, but to God in isolation"[54] fails to tell the whole story of Kierkegaardian inwardness. Levinas has overlooked a further form of apparent violence—a deeper source for the "thorn in the flesh" in Kierkegaard's writings. For Kierkegaard, the individual on the periphery of modernity is further isolated by the residual enmity between self and God that cannot be done away with, which gnaws like a "thorn in the flesh"—the suffering of relating to the Wholly Other. The Truth that the isolated individual struggles to sustain a relation with is also a Truth with which the individual is always in some conflict. Spirit may mean to be not of "the world," but there is no one who is yet fully transmuted into spirit. Insofar as spirit and spiritlessness are in constant internal and external antagonism, God and humanity constantly wage war against one another. As such, to be human and to be in this world means to be in conflict, not only within oneself, but also with God.

For Kierkegaard, to become spirit incurs the dreadful moment of finding oneself out of one's element in spiritlessness. As described in an article from 1855:

> Every creature feels best in its own element, can really live only there. The fish cannot live in the air, the bird cannot live in the water—and for spirit to have to live in an environment devoid of spirit means to die, agonizingly to die slowly so that death is a blessed relief. ("This Must Be Said; So Let It Be Said," 11 April 1855; LW, 78)

Evoking similar imagery, Otto writes that "man is like a fish gasping on the sand, outside the natural element in which he should function and have his being, as long as he is outside God and faith."[55] Yet Kierkegaard is emphatic that, as far as "the world" is concerned, one's most naturally accommodating element is *spiritlessness*. To become spirit does not mean to be transported to the metaphysical comfort of one's prenatal homeland, but to undergo the transmutation of spirit within the crucible of spiritlessness: "Spirit is fire," as Kierkegaard assesses in his *Journals*. "From this comes the frequent expression: As gold is purified in fire, in the same way the Christian is purified" (JP 4:4355 / Pap. XI² A 41).

In describing such suffering indicative of the God-relationship as spiritual trial (*Anfægtelse*), Kierkegaard is anxious to rehabilitate an old tension that has declined in a modern Christendom that has, according to Kierkegaard, lost sight of the infinite qualitative difference and the primal antagonism evoked within it between humanity and God. Hence Kierkegaard represents God as a Truth in exile hoping to reawaken others to the distance he senses between the modern world and God. "I am like a chaplain in a monastery, a spiritual adviser to the solitary," Kierkegaard laments in his *Journals*. "Spiritual trial [*Anfægtelse*] is literally never spoken of anymore" (JP 6:6459 / Pap. X¹ A 586).[56] No wonder Kierkegaard, in the waning light of this particular *deus otiosus*, seems anxious to rehabilitate the fear and trembling of the *mysterium tremendum* for an age already beginning to entertain rumors of the death of God. Kierkegaard strives to reinvigorate a primal struggle—but one in which God, and not the violence of atheism or the will-to-deicide, is the prime antagonist: a struggle that itself re-evokes the divine stranger who confronts us at Peni'el.

In its literal sense, the aforementioned Juan de los Angeles reads God's concession to Jacob at Peni'el as a submission that dispels fear: "But in its spiritual and mystical sense what transpires clearly to me is a struggle of a different kind, a more admirable struggle wherein man really and truly prevails over God, and man conquers God."[57] In the spiritual sense, this is a struggle of infinite qualitative difference. In adopting the allegory of Jacob's wrestling for a blessing as its motif, spiritual trial (Gn. *Anfechtung* / Dn. *Anfægtelse*) is revealed to be an assault *from God* in which God wills us to *fight back*. But it is not by atheism or epic Hegelian struggle between self and other that the authentic struggle with God is waged.[58] Instead, as Juan de los Angeles explains: "Only to love is it given to struggle with God, and God in his love wants nothing more than to be loved in return."[59] This insight is echoed by Kierkegaard's emphasis upon the divine concession of freedom and the expression of personal identity through the reciprocity of love: "God desires to have *Is*, for God desires to be loved" (JP 4:4350 / Pap. XI[1] A 487).

It is Jacob's conflict with the divine angel, de Lubac explains in *The Un-Marxian Socialist,* that typifies the human-divine encounter: "It is the condition of all greatness, and it may be the means . . . of a purer submission."[60] It is in the divine self-offering of this struggle that God submits in apparent compromise of the divine nature, as de los Angeles renders explicit: "God himself, the omnipotent, the impassible God is wounded in his heart by the gentle, blushing, loving gaze of the soul."[61] But in this war of love, this "purer submission" and this wounding are mutual; as described in John of the Cross's spiritual canticle, God's incandescent touches "like a fiery arrow strike and pierce the soul and leave it wholly cauterized with the fire of love. And these are properly called the wounds of love."[62] In Kierkegaard's writings, the notion, realized within the spiritual writings of early and medieval Christianity, that the God-relationship entails a wounding of the soul is rehabilitated in an attempt to reenergize the pathos of the struggle of love between the self and God in the malaise of modern Christendom. Essentially, the self cannot expect to sustain a relationship to one who is infinitely qualitatively different without incurring a stigmatic "thorn in the flesh."

THORNS IN THE FLESH

I know a person in Christ who fourteen years ago was caught up to the third heaven—whether in the body or out of the body I do not know; God knows. And I know that such a person—whether in the body or out of the body I do not know; God knows—was caught up into Paradise and heard things that are not to be told, that no mortal is permitted to repeat.

—*2 Corinthians 12:2–4*

if someone suddenly starts to think of the dangers of the lofty life the text speaks about, that one is overwhelmed with anxiety, just as when someone has held in his hand and played with a deadly weapon without knowing that it was deadly.

—KIERKEGAARD, *"The Thorn in the Flesh"*

The self's relation to God, as dramatically portrayed by Kierkegaard, can give the impression of such severity that the self appears fated to an ineffable thorn in the flesh that forces one "outside of the universally human" and into "the dangers of the lofty life" (JP 4:4654 / Pap X³ A 182). Though one may pray for relief from this melancholy wound, the thorn actually signifies the transforming passion of the God-relationship itself. As such, Kierkegaard concedes in his *Journals:* "If by having the thorn removed I would come to feel my communion with God less intensely, then let it remain" (JP 4:4644 / Pap X² A 246). With this sentiment, Kierkegaard replicates Luther's earlier identification of the thorn in the flesh with the authentic struggle of faith: "The tribulation of faith was that thorn which St. Paul felt, and which pierced through flesh and spirit, through soul and body."[63] As Johannes Climacus reaffirms in *Concluding Unscientific Postscript,* this thorn constitutes the mark of the God-relationship: "What sign did the Apostle have that this had happened to him? A thorn in the flesh—that is, a suffering" (CUP, 454). Here one encounters the force of Kierkegaard's idea that the God-relationship induces a deep spiritual wound for the self—the notion that entering into the service of the unconditioned implies a particular form of suffering. And yet it is also at this point that the threat of the *mysterium horrendum* becomes most acute, since it is in this dark and mystifying moment of suffering that the divine and demonic may come closest to resembling one another. As Kierkegaard writes in a rather imaginative comment in an upbuilding discourse on Paul's thorn in the flesh:

When an angel of darkness arrays himself in all his terror, convinced that if he just makes Paul look at him he will petrify him, when at the outset he jeers at Paul for not having the courage to do it, then the apostle looks at him, does not quickly shrink back in anxiety, does not strike him down in terror, does not reconnoiter with hesitant glances, but looks at him fixedly and steadfastly. The longer he looks the more clearly he perceives that it is an emissary of God who is visiting him, a friendly spirit who wishes him well. ("The Thorn in the Flesh," EUD, 342)

To become thus involved with God incorporates the danger of involving oneself with something infinitely other—with the other life. In daring to enter into the God-relationship, in standing before God, one encounters spiritual trial: "the opposition of the absolute itself in the individual's attempt to relate himself to it absolutely."[64]

In light of such spiritual suffering, Kierkegaard observes in his *Journals:* "O, so strenuous is the true God-relationship that it is always characterized by a tendency toward madness" (JP 4:4672 / Pap X^4 A 386). Plato's *Phaedrus* makes a classical affiliation between melancholy and the tendency toward frenzy and ecstasy,[65] but Paul's "thorn in the flesh" in 2 Corinthians 12 stands within a Hebraic tradition in which the spirit of prophecy (*Ruach Shtus*) shares an etymological relation with the notion of a madman (*shoteh*).[66] However, this ancient suggestion that the receiving of divine revelation may be fraught with madness confronted Kierkegaard particularly through the contemporary enigma of Danish clergyman Adolph Peter Adler's (1812–1869) claim to be the recipient of a direct revelation from Christ. Adler, apparently under the direct outpouring of the Spirit, professed to have been recipient to a "vision of light" and specific divine instruction to burn all his previous Hegelian works and receive the revealed truth about the origins of evil. On 12 June 1846 Adler published four books detailing his revelation. Kierkegaard purchased these volumes almost at once and soon found himself writing his own response: *The Book on Adler.*[67] Adler was later deposed from his Church position and finally came to renounce his claim to divine revelation, preferring instead to refer to his own works as works of "genius." But Kierkegaard continued to withhold his own manuscript on Adler, consigned among his papers and only to be published after his death. In these retained pages, he describes Adler as "a person whirled around and slung out like a warning terror . . . like the frightened bird that with wing strokes of anxiety rushes ahead of the storm that is coming" (BA, 50).

Is there something in these words that holds a clue to Kierkegaard's reluctance to publish? The possibility that Adler was insane, or "a deranged genius," had occurred to Kierkegaard, and his empathy toward any potential ordeal of public ridicule would certainly warrant his reticence. But then why write the book at all? The fact is that, as George Steiner describes, Adler had called on Kierkegaard as some kind of forerunner—to play John the Baptist to Adler's role of emissary of God. But more than that, Steiner claims, "Adler's conviction that mundane, rationalistic, officious Christianity in Denmark must be electrified into authentic crisis, was exactly Kierkegaard's. The *Magister's* readiness to suffer ridicule and ostracism on behalf of his 'absurd,' existentially enforced certitudes, must have struck a deep, unsettling chord in S.K. himself."[68] Indeed, the anxiety of Adler as "a person whirled around and slung out like a warning terror," like a bird rushing out to herald a storm is similar to a description Kierkegaard ascribed to himself in his *Journals:* "There is a bird called the storm-petrel [*Regnspaaer*—Hong and Hong translate 'rain-warner' (JP 5:5842)], and that is what I am, when in a generation storms begin to gather, individuals of my type appear" (*Journals,* ed. Dru 542 / Pap. VI A 119).

In his failure to bring the enigma of Adler into clear focus, Steiner suggests that Kierkegaard betrays his own anxieties of being the inherent focus of his so-called *Book on Adler*. In the stormy and vertiginous buffeting of Adler's soul could one read Kierkegaard, the storm-petrel, trembling before the very storm he has come to announce? Is he, beneath the façade of being a *flâneur,* a wild and frightened voice who trembles before his own call to return to God? It is interesting to note Steiner's appropriate discernment that "the image burning between the lines is that of Jacob wrestling with the Stranger."[69] For all his personal sacrifices and apostolic dread, perhaps it is Kierkegaard who is struggling, to the point of madness or annihilation, to authenticate a calling—to derive the benediction of a naming from a divine stranger; to realize his own name "divinely understood" (SUD, 34). In order to further understand just what struggles Kierkegaard believed were required by the God-relationship, it is necessary to explore the anxiety of "spiritual trial" (*Anfægtelse*) which is central to the self's becoming nothing before God, through resignation (*Gelassenheit*) to the divine will.

SPIRITUAL TRIAL AND THE ANXIETY OF THE SUBLIME

All those who have served the unconditioned have first received a blow that seemed to crush them, yet without slaying them. . . . So it was with Paul when he was thrown to the ground, so also with Luther when the lightning struck and killed his friend, so also with Pascal when the horse ran away with him.

This blow is like a sunstroke directly on the brain. It is the infinite concentrated intensively in one single blow and one single moment . . .

Moreover no man can bring himself this close to the unconditioned, he cannot do it, and no man dares venture it since this blow, this sunstroke, is like the deadliest danger, something every man must shrink from as more horrible than death . . .

— KIERKEGAARD'S *Journals*

No one, according to this entry from the *Journals* (JP 4:4903 / Pap. X⁵ A 17), can bring themselves very "close to the unconditioned" without incurring a wound in which "the infinite" is concentrated in a highly singular instant. This wound could be called a mark, or stigma, of the infinite qualitative difference;

or more exactly, a mark caused by the infinite transcending this difference in order to bring itself to bear on the finite "in one single blow and one single moment." In this sense, one might well imagine how Jacob himself carries away from the blessing an enduring wound—the shrunken sinew of his thigh (Genesis 32:32): his own reminder that serves as a "thorn in the flesh."

"As with Jacob and Paul, everyone who enters fully upon this relationship of Christian faith within the sphere of the paradoxical religiousness of Christianity must bear to some extent the marks of suffering, the *stigmata* of Christ," as H. V. Martin observes in *The Wings of Faith*. "Christian faith at its highest point involves *Anfechtung,* the trial of faith, the temptation from above."[70] This sentiment resounds throughout Kierkegaard's constant allusions to his own "thorn in the flesh": "my limitation and my cross" (JP 5:5913 / Pap VII A 126)—an evocation that Theodor Hacker discerns as ultimately relating to his comprehension of God's unconditioned will for his life.[71] In contemplating "The Unchangeableness of God," the terrifying thought inferred by Kierkegaard is that "with this immutable will you must nevertheless some time, sooner or later, come into collision . . . this immutable will, which cannot but crush you if you come into hostile collision with it" ("The Unchangeableness of God," FSE, 232). This collision is manifest in the self's inability to reconcile the human will and the divine will without the harrowing submission of the former to the latter. In *The Point of View for My Work as an Author,* Kierkegaard thus confesses his own acute anxiety over his relation to an apparently indeterminable, and yet unconditionally determined, divine destiny:

> From the very beginning I have been as if under arrest and at every moment sensed that it was not I who played the master, but that it was someone else who was the master. . . . The dialectical consists in this, that as a precautionary measure whatever extraordinariness was granted to me was granted in such a way that if I would not obey it would slay me. . . . Without God I am too strong for myself, and in perhaps the most agonizing way of all I am shattered. (PV, 74–75)

Likewise in *The Book on Adler,* Kierkegaard says of Adler himself that he "is truly shaken; he is in mortal danger. To use one of my favourite expressions, which is attributed to another author: he is out on 70,000 fathoms of water" (BA, 107–108). Adler's "confused genius," his anxiety which Steiner suggests resounds in Kierkegaard, is characterized in terms of "dizziness" (BA, 287). Adler has gazed down into the abyss of 70,000 fathoms and felt its vertigo. "Anxiety may be compared with dizziness," as pseudonym Vigilius Haufniensis concurs in *The Concept of Anxiety.* "He whose eye happens to look down into the yawning abyss becomes dizzy" (CA, 61). Or, as Kierkegaard describes it in *The Book on Adler*, "one becomes dizzy by looking down from a high tower, because the gaze plunges down and finds no boundary, no limitation. . . . What is dizzying is the expanse, the infinite, the indeterminable, and the dizziness itself is the senses' lack of restraint" (BA, 287–288). As such, dizziness is the anxious reaction to gazing into the void, or to invoke an appropriate analogy, the sublime abyss:[72] that which overwhelms and disturbs the senses which attempt to perceive it. The act of vision that causes the eye to tremble is that feeling of the sublime which is "found in a formless object," as Immanuel Kant describes in the *Critique of Judgment,* and aroused by "*boundlessness.*"[73]

One might say that Adler's God-relationship, drunk as it is on a delusion of direct revelation, has become vertiginous. The remedy for such vertigo—both physiologically and spiritually—is to seek deliverance from the infinite by attaching to the finite: "Thus when a person notices that he is becoming dizzy, he can stop it by fixing his eyes upon something particular . . . so the person who spiritually suffers from dizziness must seek to set limits for himself" (BA, 287–288).[74] As Kierkegaard recommends in *The Book on Adler,* limitation is the countermeasure for such intoxication by the infinite in which, spiritually understood, one is "going so far astray in the infinite that nothing finite can have continuance for him, [and] he can find no criterion. This kind of dizziness is most likely due to an excess of imagination" (BA, 288). And so it is that the dizziness of the "imagination" (Dn. *Fantasi*) that Adler suffers from appears conceptually close to what Anti-Climacus describes in *The Sickness unto Death* as the sort of dangerous and unsustainable "infinitizing" we discussed in the previous chapter. "The God-relationship is an infinitizing. But in fantasy this infinitizing can so sweep a man off his feet that his state is simply an intoxication" (SUD, 32). Or, as Kierkegaard warns in his *Book on Adler:* "If the imagination is permitted to run wild, then paganism's teaching about luck and fate emerges, or the unchristian doctrine of election by grace in the desperate sense" (BA, 290). In other words, fantasy run wild opens the door to the anxiety of predestination in which "it is unblessed to be excluded and cast out, unblessed to be saved in this manner" (BA, 290). In such fantasy, the anxious thought of being out over the deeps of election or damnation becomes a dreadful intoxication. Kierkegaard aptly transcribes how the disposition of a fearful anxiety, in John Milbank's words, "mutates into the state of sin: the imagining God to be terrible."[75]

This relationship to anxiety can be further elucidated by a consideration of how imagination—which Paul Ricoeur aptly calls "the crucible of every process of infinitization"[76]—can suggest the analogy of the sublime: the gaze into the abyss which overwhelms the eye. The sublime's relation to imagination is apparent in sublime anxiety, the fear of annihilation by the abyss, or by

God: what Lynn Poland suitably calls "the imagination's fantasy of injury."[77] Before the scene of the sublime—an overwhelming vision that transports one beyond oneself—there is an interplay of sensations of vertigo and narrowness. The intoxication of the sublime, overwhelming in its sheer expanse, becomes anxiously (from Lat. *angere:* "to press tightly") oppressive and even inhibitive. As Poland describes it, "sublime transport turns on an encounter with some 'opposition,' or 'difficulty'; one must first experience the limits of one's capacities, must first feel frozen in terror or astonishment, before the positive moment and movement of transport can occur."[78] Can this feeling of subjugation be equated with the sense of opposition that is inherent to spiritual trial (Gn. *Anfechtung*): the limit of the absolute forcing itself upon the individual (hence the "fantasy of injury, an imagined terror"[79])?

Yet this terror-threat of "imagining God to be terrible" is felt through the imagination, but never actualized. Kant, in his treatment of the sublime, "insists on the imagination's position of security because he wants us to see that sublimity is not in the external object, but in our relation to it."[80] Or adapting the terms of Kierkegaard's Vigilius Haufniensis as an analogy, the dizziness of anxiety "is just as much in his own eye as in the abyss, for suppose he had not looked down" (CA, 61). But *The Concept of Anxiety* does not deal explicitly with any external aesthetic encounter with the sublime. The abyss is best understood at this point as a metaphor, a fertile imaginative visualization, for anxiety.[81] Despite eliciting anxiety, the metaphorical abyss that confronts the soul is not necessarily identifiable with the (aesthetic) abyss that confronts us in the starry vault of heaven or the expanse of the ocean. In order to view such sights as sublime, Kant suggests in the *Critique of Judgment* that we suspend our scientific inquisition in deference to a purely aesthetic judgment. Hence one must not look up to the cosmos with the cartographic eye of astrology, but "must regard it, just as we see it, as a distant, all-embracing vault."[82] Likewise for the ocean to come into experience as sublime, one must not think of it in the technical terms of the oceanographer, but rather "regard it as poets do, merely by what strikes the eye—if it is at rest, as a clear mirror of water only bounded by the heaven; if it is restless, as an abyss threatening to overwhelm everything."[83] Insofar, then, as the sublime resides in the eye of the poet, might one say that it resides essentially in that Kierkegaardian sphere of the aesthetic?[84] In the religious sphere it may be more appropriate to direct ourselves toward the analogous category of the *numinous.*

As Otto wonders in *The Idea of the Holy,* might there not exist "a hidden kinship between the numinous and the sublime which is something more than mere analogy, and to which Kant's *Critique of Judgement* bears distant witness"?[85] Perhaps in the relation between the sublime and the numinous there is an overlapping of the aesthetic and the religious spheres?

After all, Otto testifies to a sense of "dizzy intoxication" that accompanies the nearly Dionysiac fascination and transport of the numen.[86] The numinous, Otto tells us, exhibits the dual elements of a *mysterium tremendum et fascinans,* and "the sublime exhibits the same peculiar dual character as the numinous; it is at once daunting, and yet again singularly attracting, in its impress upon the mind."[87] Ultimately, "'the sublime,' like 'the numinous,' is in Kantian language an idea or concept 'that cannot be unfolded' or explicated (*unauswickelbar*)."[88]

Surely the most revealing analogy resides in Kant's allusion in the *Critique of Judgment* to the sublimity of the divine. The sublime in nature, Kant maintains, initially resides in the excitation of fear. And yet one can regard something as fearful and still rise above the fear of it: "Thus the virtuous man fears God without being afraid of him."[89] In this sense, the fear of God is realized without one being overwhelmed by its horror. Whoever flees from the object in nature which incites such dread is actually incapable of forming a judgment about the sublime since, Kant argues, "it is impossible to find satisfaction in a terror that is seriously felt."[90] Hence the joy of the sublime resides in the deliverance from the perceived threat of extinction. The terror of annihilation and our comparative defenselessness, as elicited by such intimidating sights as vast overhanging rocks, brooding thunder clouds, raging volcanoes, leveling hurricanes, ungovernable oceans, and towering waterfalls all convey a sight "more attractive, the more fearful it is, provided only that we are in security."[91] And so it is that the sublime arouses in us a certain nobility by which our mind, through the judgment of reason, triumphs over nature: "we willingly call these objects sublime, because they raise the energies of the soul above their accustomed height and discover in us a faculty of resistance of a quite different kind, which gives us courage to measure ourselves against the apparent almightiness of nature."[92]

And yet, Kant concedes, this self-estimation of the sublimity of our own nature is in apparent conflict with the "subjection, abasement, and a feeling of complete powerlessness" that is an appropriate response to the representation of God "in His wrath and yet in His sublimity, in the tempest, the storm, the earthquake, etc."[93] In fact, "it would be foolish and criminal to imagine a superiority of our minds over these works of His."[94] However, Kant expresses some reticence about such "dust and ashes" self-abasement (which Otto would later extol as an authentic response to the numinous), in which he suspects a primitive tendency for implicit favor-seeking and vulgar flattery. As such, the bowing and scraping of much "prostration, adoration with bent head, with contrite, anxious demeanor and voice . . . is far from being necessarily bound up with the idea of the *sublimity* of a religion and its object."[95] Fear of the Lord God is not necessarily the beginning of wisdom, since such fear and trembling before the irresistible will and might of God does not properly place one "in the frame of mind for admiring the divine greatness. For this a mood of calm contemplation and a quite free judgement are needed."[96] Hence the Kantian insistence on the sublimity of our own nature resurfaces, albeit in the guise of moral humility:

> Only if he is conscious of an upright disposition pleasing to God do those operations of might serve to awaken in him the idea of the sublimity of this Being, for then he recognizes in himself a sublimity of disposition conformable to His will; and thus he is raised above the fear of such operations of nature, which he no longer regards as outbursts of His wrath. Even humility, in the shape of a stern judgment upon his own faults . . . is a sublime state of mind, consisting in a voluntary subjection of himself to the pain of remorse, in order that the causes of this may be removed.[97]

Moral humility, in other words, frees Kant from the fear and trembling of subjection in order to attain a sublime mind-set suitable for contemplating (aesthetically, Kierkegaard might say) the sublimity of the divine.[98] Reading Otto's *Idea of the Holy*, on the other hand, there is less of an impression of serene austerity in contemplating the sublimity of God and more emphasis upon the untranslatable infinite qualitative difference of the *mysterium tremendum*—an impassable abyss. Fear of the LORD is indeed the beginning of such wisdom.

However, a middle ground between the self-estimation of the Kantian sublime and the self-abasement of the Ottonian numinous can perhaps be found in Hegel's notion of the "negative" sublime. Commencing with Kant's prior distinction between the sublime and the beautiful, Hegel proceeds in his lectures on *Aesthetics* to name the *negative* relation of sublimity expressed in the sacred art of Hebrew poetry—expressing the nullity, dependence, subsistence of the world in contrast to the sovereignty of the creator God. Over against the divine dominion, the creature can only convey its own unworthiness and transience:

> Therefore, further, man views himself in his *unworthiness* before God; his exaltation consists in fear of the Lord, in trembling before his wrath, and we find depicted in a penetrating and affecting way grief over nullity, and the cry of the soul to God in complaint, suffering, and lament from the depths of the heart.[99]

While Hegel perceives in the Psalms such "classic examples of genuine sublimity set forth for all time,"[100] Otto discerns the analogy between the holy and the sublime to be particularly described "in an unsurpassable form in the sixth chapter of Isaiah, where there is sublimity alike in the lofty throne and the sovereign figure of God, the skirts of His raiment 'filling the temple' and the solemn majesty of the attendant angels about Him."[101] But lingering in contemplation where Otto passes swiftly on, one may discern that there is something about this vision in the temple that illuminates the numinous' decisive departure from the Kantian sublime. Otto's suggestion of Isaiah 6 as demonstrating the analogy between the holy and the sublime, once developed further, actually implies the qualitative difference inherent to an encounter with the numinous—a difference that finally sets it apart from the sublime. Isaiah's apprehension of something "other" than the sublime, something numinous, is apparent in his spontaneous response to his vision of God upon a throne. Isaiah does not join his voice to the seraphim's chorus of exaltation: "Holy, holy, holy, is the LORD of hosts" (Isaiah 6:3).[102] Instead of an ecstatic or sublime transport of the soul, Isaiah responds with the spontaneous despair of unworthiness that indicates "creature-consciousness": "Woe is me for I am undone; because I am a man of unclean lips . . . for mine eyes have seen the King, the LORD of hosts" (Isaiah 6:5). Hence one may read Isaiah's feeling as arising *between* the so-called sublimity of the sovereign figure of God and the conviction that he himself, a creature of infinite difference from God (i.e., "unclean"), gazes upon this vision—and yet is not destroyed. It is this insistence upon a radical, astonishing *difference,* rather than the sublimity of human disposition in contemplating the divine, that attests to Isaiah 6 as a distinctly *numinous* experience: one might say an unsurpassable description of the spiritual trial (Gn. *Anfechtung*) that helps to distinguish the numinous and the sublime.

While the numinous in Otto's schema is Wholly Other, the sublime as Kant maintains is as much in the imagination as dizziness, for Kierkegaard's Vigilius Haufniensis, resides within the eye. Sublimity, for Kant, resides in our mind and it is from here that contemplation of the divine takes its reference point.

> Only by supposing this idea in ourselves and in reference to it are we capable of attaining to the idea of the sublimity of that Being which produces respect in us, not merely by the might that it displays in nature, but rather by means of the faculty which resides in us of judging it fearlessly and of regarding our destination as sublime in respect of it.[103]

Yet the numinous, as discussed in chapter 4, originates in something ultimately "objective and outside the self."[104] It is this collision between self and Wholly Other that elicits a numinous dread in which the perceived threat of annihilation must have some basis in an external reality which is more than the internal "fantasy of injury." The prophet thus expresses for Otto "that feeling that man in his 'profaneness' is not *worthy* to stand in the presence of the holy one, and that his own entire personal unworthiness might defile even holiness itself."[105] Isaiah articulates something more than a loss of identity, and that is not simply the unreality of the self, but a personal conviction of oneself being but "dust and ashes." In order for this confession of creature-consciousness to occur, however, the prospect of annihilation must be held "in suspense," as it were, by the grace of God—and in this space, the self is able to confess a realization of the infinite qualitative difference between itself and the Holy. The self is ultimately not lost or annihilated, but becomes *conscious* of its own creature-feeling through its recoiling despair before the holiness that renders the threat of extinction very apparent indeed: the spiritual trial of our sense for the infinite qualitative difference. This particular tension between self and God within the spiritual trial comes into clearer focus when it is differentiated from the "imagined" oppression of the sublime and the dread induced by the immensity of existence itself. The question emerges, therefore, as to how the self survives this spiritual trial (the tension of the infinite qualitative difference) and comes to know itself *before God*.

On 12 May 1839, Kierkegaard made a vivid and unnerving confession in his *Journals* about his inner relation to existence—a bleak confession that nevertheless contains an essential glimmer of hope:

> All existence [*Tilværelsen*] makes me anxious, from the smallest fly to the mysteries of the Incarnation; the whole thing is inexplicable to me, I myself most of all; to me all existence is infected, I myself most of all. My distress is enormous, boundless; no one knows it except God in heaven, and he will not console me; no one can console me except God in heaven and he will not take compassion on me.—Young man, if you have gone astray, turn back to God, and from his upbringing you will take along with you a youthfulness strengthened for manly tasks. (JP 5:5383 / Pap. II A 420)

Kierkegaard's words of personal desolation are keenly reminiscent of the anxiety that Pascal expressed so evocatively in his posthumously published *Pensées*. Pascal speaks specifically there of a dread of the infinite rooted in "man's loneliness in the macrocosm"[106]—the felt nothingness of man before a universe that is capable of crushing him. In this sense, his oppression sometimes sounds like a kind of cosmological *Anfechtung*: he languishes in the grip of an onerous infinity. In contemplating a fathomless universe, he speaks of the space that infinitely transcends the imagination; and indeed, "it is the greatest perceptible mark of God's omnipotence that our imagination should lose itself in that thought."[107] Yet after turning man toward the immensity of the universe, Pascal declares: "I want to show him a new abyss."[108] And so Pascal redirects contemplation from the infinite to the infinitesimal: to "all the conceivable immensity of nature in this miniature atom."[109] Unlike Kant's deliberately superficial "eye of the poet" whose gaze can perceive the sublime, Pascal's melancholy meditation is consciously reflective of cosmological and scientific insights of the Enlightenment, and it is from this atomic perspective that the human body itself derives a newly discovered sublimity: "Anyone who considers himself in this way will be terrified at himself, and, seeing his mass, as given him by nature, supporting him between two abysses of infinity and nothingness, will tremble at these marvels."[110]

Pascal thus describes the anxiety of a human being suspended "between two abysses of infinity and nothingness": two perspectives which transcend the extremes of human understanding and which cause him to dread. Pascal's experience of the cosmological *tremendum,* where the "eternal silence of . . . infinite spaces fills me with dread,"[111] is reciprocated by an anthropological dread. From this perspective, the human being has become a defamiliarized *tremendum.* This feeling is perhaps closer to what Otto discusses as "the uncanny" (*das Unheimliche*) or "the monstrous" (*das Ungeheuer*), recalling Sophocles' observation in the choric song of *Antigone:* "Much there that is monstrous [*ungeheuer*]; but nought is more monstrous [*ungeheuer*] than man."[112] Sublime anxiety is hereby internalized; in Pattison's words, "it is the inconceivability of my own existence that assails me from within the very heart of that existence itself."[113]

But *Anfechtung,* spiritually understood, is more than the dread of oneself or the dread of an impersonal but sublime space that weighs upon the soul. There is a difference between an *Anfechtung* (if this is not a misapplication of the word) in which one feels the weight of boundlessness in aesthetic or cosmological senses, and the *Anfechtung* that resides in a tension between self and the Wholly Other of the God-relationship. The struggle against the cosmos, against the sublime, against existence itself, may nonetheless be a presentiment of the loving struggle with God. Hence Pascal testifies to a recognition of something within him which rationally transcends that which would extinguish him, when he declares that "even if the universe were to crush him, man would still be nobler than his slayer, because he knows that he is dying and the advantage the universe has over him. The universe knows nothing of this."[114] In this sense, as with the Kantian sublime, Pascal implies a qualitative difference between the self-aware man and the entropic universe which elicits his dread. Ironically, the sublimity *of* nature raises man *above* nature, because the sublime resides in the eye of the one who sees the world and knows the place of his own death within it. And yet the loving struggle of spiritual trial (*Anfechtung*) is marked by a more astonishing difference and a more terrible anxiety, as Isaiah 6 attests: this dread is of the Holy Other and the concomitant shadow of *consciousness of sin* that threatens one's *spiritual* existence. Yet further still, as shall be explored, spiritual trial can also denote a decisive moment in the self's becoming itself before God through the confession of sin and the acceptance of forgiveness.

HOLY HYPOCHONDRIA

a person becomes momentarily anxious and afraid of ideality and himself— and of God, who seems to be so infinitely sublime that one does not dare think of him at all. It seems as if he must become disgusted and tired of listening to one's nonsense and nauseated with one's sins.

—KIERKEGAARD'S *Journals*

"To be sure," Kierkegaard observes at one point, "the blow of the unconditioned also takes the form of sin-consciousness; there is a concentration of sin or past sins in one single blow, in one single moment, and this falls on a man's conscience" (JP 4:4903/ Pap. X⁵ A 17). When this personal consciousness of sin is lacking in an individual, then, according to Anti-Climacus in *Practice in Christianity*, "Christianity, terrifying, will rise up against him and transform itself into madness or horror until he either learns to give up Christianity or— . . . by means of the anguish of a contrite conscience, all in proportion to *his* need—[he] learns to enter into Christianity by the narrow way, through the consciousness of sin" (PC, 68). This narrow (Dn. *trang*) way is also the way of anxiety (*Angst*, deriving from the Lat. *angustiae*: "narrows").[115] Yet, in such anxiety, repentance itself is in danger of falling into an irremediable grief. "Repentance has lost its mind," as Vigilius Haufniensis describes in *The Concept of Anxiety*, "and anxiety is potentiated into repentance" (CA, 115). Repentance thus falls into despair as anxiety condemns itself: "its condemnation is certain, and the augmented judgment is that the individual shall be dragged through life to the place of execution. In other words, repentance has gone crazy" (CA, 116). Dialectically, however, just as despair may point to a rise in the consciousness of the eternal, so this madness may, Haufniensis observes, also be "the sign of a deeper nature" (CA, 116). This anxiety over sin is the kind of spiritual trial which has, lamentably—as Haufniensis regards it—been disregarded by the spiritlessness of the modern age: "In the old days, the road to perfection was narrow [*trang*] and solitary. The journey along it was always disturbed by aberrations, exposed to predatory attacks by sin, and pursued by the arrow of the past, which is as dangerous as that of the Scythian hordes" (CA, 117). As such, this madness is a kind of "holy hypochondria" (*heilige Hypochondrie*) (CA, 162*)[116] which, though it may fail in its anxiety to accurately diagnose the proportion of its guilt, at least recognizes the perilous nature of the road to perfection. Yet the self-diagnosis of a specious anxiety over sin threatens the individual with something like melancholy's capitulation into nihilism: that is, "anxiety's moment of death" (CA, 117). As such, Vigilius Haufniensis prescribes: "The only thing that is truly able to disarm the sophistry of sin is faith, courage to believe that the state itself is a new sin, courage to renounce anxiety without anxiety, which only faith can do" (CA, 117).

Such anxiety can engender the appearance of innumerable spiritual trials. Consequently, for example, Kierkegaard warns that one must be extremely careful in what is said to someone who is vulnerable—especially one as vulnerable as a child—lest a casual remark "occasion an anguished conscience in which innocent and fragile souls can easily be tempted to believe themselves guilty" (JP 1:91 / Pap. II A). Children, according to Vigilius Haufniensis's assessment, are inherently more adventurously disposed toward anxiety (CA, 42) and hence more susceptible to any anxiety that plays upon possibility, freedom, and imagination. In childish anxiety is found "the dreaming of the spirit" (CA, 42); but in such impressionable and vulnerable minds this dream may easily be transmuted into a nightmare of self-accusation. And yet it is surely not only childhood that, in the fragility of its conscience, is susceptible to that "flame of hell which ignites the tinder which is in every soul" (JP 1:91 / Pap. II A). Such an anxiety over being God-forsaken resides latently in every soul, as Kierkegaard acknowledges in his *Journals:* "Deep within every human being there still lives the anxiety over the possibility of being alone in the world, forgotten by God, overlooked among the millions and millions in this enormous household" (JP 1:100 / Pap. VIII¹ A 363).[117] It is tempting to discern a fetish for anxiety in Kierkegaard, to observe in his melancholy an inheritance of morbid religious guilt that was rendered extravagant by a strict religious upbringing.[118] Yet Kierkegaard was also emphatic that self-indictment could betray a fetishistic melancholy in which, as described in a *Christian Discourse* on Friday Communion, the heart can abase itself—and yet never enough to satisfy its impulse for self-abasement ("Discourses at the Communion on Fridays," CD, 292). He ascribed to the spirit of 1 John 3:20—"Though our heart condemn us, God is greater than our hearts"—the assurance that, although fear and trembling may be an appropriate response to holiness, pathological or melancholy self-conviction is not decisive before God. Despite his own gloomy spiritual preoccupations, and in part because of this morbid disposition, Kierkegaard stands as a striking modern exemplar within a tradition of "physicians of the soul" who variously attempted to alleviate such errors of self-mortification. As he counsels, in relation to assurance over divine forgiveness:

> whether it was a sickness of the soul that so darkened your mind every night that finally in deadly anxiety [*Dødsen Angest*], brought almost to the point of madness by the conception of God's holiness [*Forestillingen om Guds Hellighed*], you thought you had to condemn yourself; whatever it was something terrible that so weighed upon your conscience that your heart condemned itself—God is greater! (CD, 293)

Kierkegaard's warning that, through a sickness of the soul, one can be "brought almost to the point of madness by the conception of God's holiness" returns us to the theme of religious melancholy. According to Burton's *Anatomy of Melancholy*, earlier discussed, melancholic self-condemnation creates an opening in which the devil can exploit the scrupulous conscience: "The devil that then told thee it was a light sin, or no sin at all, now aggravates on the other side, and telleth thee that it is a most irremissible offence, as he did by Cain and Judas, to bring them to despair."[119] Such melancholics are transfixed by their brooding sins to the extent that, as Burton writes, "they account themselves Reprobates, quite forsaken of God, already damned, past all hope of grace, incapable of mercy, slaves of sin, and their offences so great, they cannot be forgiven."[120] To such a melancholic, God thus becomes the avenger, as David says (Lat. *ultor a tergo Deus*), or Nemesis as the poets call it.[121]

In such pathological fear of the Holy it is possible to detect echoes of a more primitive "daemonic dread," as Otto discerns in the account in Exodus 4:24 of Yahweh who, meeting Moses by the way, sought to kill him.[122] And in *Concluding Unscientific Postscript*, Johannes Climacus aptly describes spiritual trial as "a nemesis [*Anfægtelsen er Nemesis*] upon the intense moments in the absolute relation" (CUP, 459). But for Johannes, this nemesis is not only the nemesis against a melancholy consciousness of sin. For Johannes, spiritual trial (*Anfægtelse*) expresses the opposition of the absolute against the individual's attempt to relate to it absolutely: that is, the tension which is implicit in the individual's attempt to relate to one who is Wholly Other. This is the strenuously high price for asserting the God-relationship: it involves the suffering of a desire which must not succumb to the temptation of abandoning the relationship itself. It signifies a testing of the absolute relationship by the absolute itself. As such, spiritual trial is perhaps most pertinently illustrated by the tribulation of the will during Christ's agony in Gethsemane. In reference to Christ's "sorrow unto death," Otto aptly relates the "strangely parallel" and "prophetically significant" accounts of "Yahweh who waylaid

Moses by night, and of Jacob who wrestles with God."[123] Here Jacob struggled like Christ, "with the God of 'Wrath' and 'Fury,' with the *numen*, which yet is itself '*My Father.*'"[124] Both "had power with God . . . and prevailed"; or as Kierkegaard put it, were victorious in that God was victorious.

The dark nights for Jesus in Gethsemane and Jacob at Peni'el are thus connected by what Otto calls "the shuddering secret of the numen."[125] The allegory of Yisra'el suggests a mysterious *Anfechtung* (spiritual trial) that is the *angefochtene Christus* (the struggles of Christ), just as it is "Jacob wrestling with God himself."[126] In its authentic form it does not express an instance of demonic dread, because it is ultimately a struggle of love prevailing over fear. Nor is it finally a struggle to the death, since this trial seeks neither the annihilation of the self nor the death of God. These two mysterious nights of Gethsemane and Peni'el symbolize how it is Christ, as well as Jacob, who reveals what it means to struggle with God. Christ's doubts at Gethsemane, and his agonies on the cross—the *angefochtene Christus* as affirmed by Luther—also foreshadow and illuminate the *angefochtene Mensch* of the individual disciple. It is with all this in mind that a Kierkegaardian anatomy of the spiritual trial of the self before God will now be considered.

Me? or me that fought him? O which one? is it each one? That night, that year
Of now done darkness I wretch lay wrestling with (my God!) my God.
—GERARD MANLEY HOPKINS, *"Carrion Comfort"*

SIX

The Anatomy of Spiritual Trial

THE SELF BEFORE GOD: SPIRITUAL TRIAL

But this is rigorous upbringing—this going from inborn anxiety to faith. Anxiety [Angst] is the most terrible kind of spiritual trial [Anfægtelse].

—KIERKEGAARD'S *Journals*

While also evoking the *vertiginous* anxiety that is characteristic of sublime experience, spiritual trial in Luther (Gn. *Anfechtung*) and Kierkegaard (Dn. *Anfægtelse*) is most clearly defined in relation to the self's harrowing sense of paralysis or captivity *before God.* As Martin J. Heinecken describes it in *The Moment Before God,* spiritual trial

> is like the experience one has in a dream when one wants to run and yet with the utmost exertion is unable to move a muscle—this *absolute frustration.* The difference is that one is perfectly able to move about and one can do many things, and *yet there is nothing one can do before God.*[1]

By evoking the experience of spiritual trial by way of such tormenting imagery as a captive bird, a stranded fish, or an individual who is shipwrecked or adrift over 70,000 fathoms of water, Kierkegaard replicates the anxious tenor of Luther, who previously "compares the horrified conscience, which tries to flee and cannot escape, with a goose which pursued by the wolf, does not use its wings, as ordinarily, but its feet and is caught."[2]

Spiritual trial in Luther's anatomy of the self *coram Deo* came to denote "a form of temptation (*tentatio*), which takes place through an assault upon man (*impugnatio*), which is intended to put him to the test."[3] More radical than mere carnal temptation (*Versuchung*), Luther's use of spiritual trial (*Anfechtung*) denotes "tempting attacks":[4] "the trial of faith by various temptations."[5] These attacks, Tillich observes in *The Protestant Era*, engender a profound *Angst*, "a feeling of being enclosed in a narrow place from which there is no escape."[6] In *Angst* (deriving from the Lat. *angustiae:* "narrows"), the world constricts to such an extreme that in Luther's words: "There is no flight, no comfort within or without but all things accuse."[7]

Reading Kierkegaard's works, it is likewise difficult to escape the sense in which the God-relationship appears as an inescapable "death struggle" (JP 4:4725 / Pap. XI² A 67), described with such perplexing but evocative horror as "to be out on 70,000 fathoms of water and yet be joyful" (SLW, 477). The vertiginous anxiety of the formless abyss of freedom is supplanted through the God-relationship by the narrowing angst of an inescapable conflict between humanity and divinity in which the salvation of the self may appear to be impossible. As Johannes Climacus articulates in *Concluding Unscientific Postscript*, "captive in the absolute conception of God," the individual is helpless as a bird imprisoned in a cage, or like a fish thrown on shore; "lying on the ground outside its element, so, too, the religious individual is captive, because absoluteness is not directly the element of a finite existence" (CUP, 483). Reading these harrowing descriptions of Johannes Climacus's ironic, pre-Christian view of a radicalized Christianity, Daphne Hampson suggests that "it is clear that Kierkegaard was speaking of circumstances he well knew."[8] These illustrations of spiritual trial (Dn. *Anfægtelse*) in Kierkegaard evoke an experience Luther himself described as *Anfechtung* (Dn. *fægte* / Gn. *fecht* = "fight"). As Daphne Hampson explains: "*Anfechtung* (literally being fought against) is the word used within the Lutheran tradition for the sense that one is undermined/caught/pinned down when confronted by God."[9] In essence, the inescapable tension of spiritual trial is far more oppressive than the spiritual inertia described under the monastic rubric of *acedia:* while *acedia* expresses the aridity of the absence of God, spiritual trial is, recalling another of Kierkegaard's descriptions, a devastating and intensified sunstroke from the unconditioned. Or as Johannes Climacus describes it:

> The religious person has lost the relativity of immediacy, its diversion, its whiling away of time—precisely its whiling away of time. The absolute conception of God consumes him like the fire of the summer sun when it refuses to set, like the fire of the summer sun when it refuses to cease. (CUP, 485)

Kierkegaard himself conjures up the abyss to describe the perennial anxiety of the individual stranded tentatively between the inconclusive origins and ends of one's salvation: "Just as the shipwrecked person who saved himself by means of a plank and now, tossed by the waves and hovering over the abyss between life and death, strains his eyes for land, so indeed should a person be concerned about his salvation" ("We Are Closer to Salvation Now—Than When We Became Believers," CD, 220). Such anxiety over salvation is directly reminiscent of Luther—and Kierkegaard acknowledges this: "Luther says that as soon as Christ has come on board the storm immediately begins" (JP 4:4372 / Pap. X¹ A 22). Between Luther's *Anfechtung* and Kierkegaard's *Anfægtelse,* there is even a descriptive abyssal affinity: "Where Luther likens it to hanging from a cross midway between heaven and earth, Kierkegaard compares it to being suspended over a depth of 70,000 fathoms."[10]

In Luther's descriptions, both Creator and the external creation are allied in closing in upon the sinner. In terms of anxiety over sin, therefore, the alienation of the infinite difference exists between humanity and creation, not Creator and creation: "For he who is an enemy to God has the whole creation against him."[11] Through the anguished conscience, one experiences one's vulnerability, not only to the sublime magnitude of nature, but also to the more innocuous mechanisms of the universe: in the changing wind, the driven leaf, Creation rises up in animated condemnation of the sinner. "At such a rustling a leaf becomes the Wrath of God, and the whole world on which a moment before we strutted in our pride, becomes too narrow for us."[12] Luther, as Tillich explains, "experienced the anxiety of guilt and the anxiety of fate. It is the uneasy conscience which produces innumerable irrational fears in daily life. The rustling of a dry leaf horrifies him who is plagued with guilt."[13] As a harassed conscience drives him out of his mind, as it denies him any internal respite, so the world crowds him out of all external comfort. Within or without: there is no escape from this haunting, narrowing presence. "Guilt, death and the mundane press in upon man, making the world too 'narrow' for him; no longer is he alone, for now everything speaks to him—as his accuser—yet he remains in this condition alone and defenceless."[14]

This chilling vision of an inhospitable creation is a reflection of both the self's inner warfare (Gr. *psychomachia*) and its estrangement from the God whose invading and alienating gaze cannot be escaped. Unable to master the world as an object for the self, this Unhappy Consciousness now becomes the anxious object of a world that refuses to respond to its grasp. For the anxious conscience, the dread of God-forsakenness is evoked in every unforgiving tendril of a sprawling creation. Just as from the perspective of melancholy, the organic world teems with the strange dangers of mandrake and nightshade, so analogously spiritual trial causes accusation to arise from every recess and crevice of creation. "And now art thou cursed from the earth," God tells Cain, "a fugitive and a vagabond shalt thou be in the earth" (Genesis 4:11–12). Creation offers no respite from the inner bite of consciousness of sin, as Gordon Rupp writes: "the sinner is hemmed in with anxiety and fear, and his conscience is a prison to him. Cramped, cabined and confined in a kind of spiritual claustrophobia, the experience passes over into its opposite, the restless desire to flee to the ends of the earth, under the desperate certainty that there can be no escape from God."[15]

In 1840, the young Kierkegaard made a pilgrimage to the scene of the childhood transgression that his father had apparently confided to him. It is in his description of the Jutland heath—the alleged site of his father's cursing God—that one discerns an especially melancholy Lutheran climate, what might be called the very landscape of *Anfechtung* in which one cannot escape being exposed before God:

> The heath must be particularly adapted to developing vigorous spirits; here everything lies naked and unveiled before God, and here is no place for a lot of distractions, those many odd nooks and corners where the consciousness can hide, and from which earnestness often has a hard time recovering vagrant thoughts. Here consciousness must come to definite and precise conclusions about itself. Here on the heath one must truly say, "Whither shall I flee from thy presence?" [Psalm 139:7] (JP 3:2830 / Pap. III A 78)

Though there are thematic affinities between Kierkegaard's *Anfægtelse* and Luther's *Anfechtung*, however, I maintain that Kierkegaard's dialectic of *spiritual trial* not only inherits but partially divests itself of its Lutheran inheritance. In fact, Kierkegaard is not only rehabilitating the Lutheran term but critiquing, refining, and reenergizing the notion of spiritual trial for a generation that is oblivious and desensitized to its significance. Given Kierkegaard's translation of the anachronistic Lutheran idiom of spiritual trial into the modern milieu of the self before God, to what extent can Luther's *Anfechtung* be considered a medieval precursor for modern *Angst*? Or in other words, to what extent can spiritual trial be translated into a category of modern existentialism?

Paul Tillich appropriated Luther's rhetoric of spiritual trial in a 1945 essay on "The Transmoral Conscience."[16] In this essay, he describes Luther's struggles with "tempting attacks" (*Anfechtungen*) as an expression of "the state of absolute despair" of "the bad conscience."[17] Furthermore, in "The Recovery of the Prophetic Tradition" in 1950, Tillich states more explicitly that Luther "anticipates all modern Existentialism, including Pascal and Kierkegaard, when he describes the conscience as the anxiety which might be produced by the rustling of a dry leaf on a tree, or when he describes his own periods of despair which never ceased till his death. He called them 'Anfechtung,' meaning daemonic attacks in which every meaning was lost."[18]

And even in his famous 1957 study of Luther, *The Righteousness of God*, Gordon Rupp suggests that we "might call it [*Anfechtung*] an existential word since it concerns man as he grapples with himself and the universe." "But," Rupp then warns, "we must not be misled into supposing that this is mere subjectivism." The crucial factor that mitigates against reducing Lutheran *Anfechtung* to modern *Angst* resides in the self's inescapable consciousness of existing *before God:*

> The whole meaning of "Anfechtung" for Luther lies in the thought that man has his existence "Coram Deo," and that he is less the active intelligence imposing itself on the stuff of the universe around him, than the subject of an initiative and action from God who employs the whole of man's existence as a means of bringing men to awareness of their peril or need.[19]

As such, although spiritual trial denotes a struggle within the self, it is irreducibly theocentric in its orientation. Moreover, in both Luther and Kierkegaard, the anguish of spiritual trial is intensified by the feeling that the God before whom one finds oneself is dreadful to stand before, and often appears as the voyeuristic Absolute Subject before Whom one is inescapably object. In this relation, the anxious sinner, as Luther describes it, "is put to sin and shame before God":

> this shame is now a thousand times greater, that a man must blush in the presence of God. For this means that there is no corner or hole in the whole of creation into which a man might creep, not even in hell, but he must let himself be exposed to the gaze of the whole creation, and stand in the open with all his shame, as a bad conscience feels when it is really struck. . . . God takes all honour and comfort away and leaves only shame there, and this is his misery.[20]

Recalling Nietzsche, this inescapable experience of shame can translate into the experience that precedes and incites modern deicide: a desire for flight is thwarted by the inescapable omnipresence of the accusative gaze, and consequently the "object" of this gaze retaliates in a murderous act which reclaims "subjectivity." Indeed, in a sermon on Psalm 139 titled "The Escape From God," Tillich claims that the presence of God induces an anxious desire to escape the inescapable, because:

> Nobody wants to be *known*, even when he realizes that his health and salvation depend upon such a knowledge. We do not even wish to be known by ourselves. We try to hide the depths of our souls from our own eyes. We

refuse to be our own witness. How then can we stand in the mirror in which nothing can be hidden?[21]

This fear of self-disclosure before God is evident in Luther's spiritual trial no less than in Nietzsche's deicide and, as such, Tillich affirms that the "Presence of God created the same feeling in Luther as it did in Nietzsche."[22] Expanding upon Tillich's connection, it is also possible to detect an analogous feeling of oppressive divine voyeurism in what Sartre, in *Being and Nothingness,* identifies as "The Look" which induces

> shame before God; that is, the recognition of my being-as-object before a subject that can never become an object. . . . I posit my being-an-object-for-God as more real than my For-itself; I exist alienated and I cause myself to learn from outside what I must be. This is the origin of fear before God.[23]

Thus Sartre's God, as Pattison suggests, "is the one who looks at him—and, moreover, the one who looks at him when he does not want to be looked at."[24] This exemplary modern atheist, Sartre, has responded with an understandable defiance against an invasive visual interrogation, as is further elaborated in Sartre's 1964 autobiography, *Words:*

> I was busy covering up my crime when God suddenly saw me. I felt his gaze inside my head and on my hands . . . horribly visible, a living target. I was saved by indignation: I grew angry at such a crude lack of tact, and blasphemed. . . . He never looked at me again.[25]

As such, through the anxiety of the self's violation by an alien other—the anxiety for which the mere rustling of a leaf shrieks the secret of the wrath of God—we must question whether we have not slipped once again into the precarious territory of the "fantastic"? Is this Other essentially the fantasized projection of subjective anxiety and guilt? As Sartre might say to Luther, in an effort to dispel the terror induced in his tender and imbalanced conscience: "perhaps the objects of the world which I took for eyes were not eyes; perhaps it was only the wind which shook the bush behind me."[26] However, since the atheism that Sartre espouses had not yet announced itself as a live possibility, for Luther the sinner responds with a spontaneous impulse to escape confinement through flight, rather than through deicide. Furthermore, from Kierkegaard's perspective, the "terror threat" of spiritual trial may actually signify the latent authenticity of the God-relationship—a relation of fear and trembling in contradistinction to some appeasing, Feuerbachian projection with which all such terror is exorcised. Reflecting this

Kierkegaardian sentiment, Tillich also infers in his sermon on "Escape From God" that:

> It is safe to say that a man who has never tried to flee God has never experienced the God Who is really God . . . For there is no reason to flee a god who is the perfect picture of everything that is good in man. . . . Why try to escape from a reality of which we are a part?[27]

Modern atheism, as Tillich identifies it, may thus signify an aggressive existential expression of the same impulse to flee from the inescapable reality of God as is found in the late medieval and early modern idiom of spiritual trial.

Yet this begs a reevaluation of the question from the perspective of modern subjectivity: if fear and trembling signify the *only* authentic responses that the divine can evoke in a human subject, then is the self not more admirable in retaliating with "deicide" than in cultivating the self-annihilating creature-feeling that results in "spiritual trial"? Is it not ultimately inevitable that this God, appearing as some kind of invasively voyeuristic Other, should warrant the retaliation of Nietzschean rebellion? In such a heteronomy of guilt must not the slave, in order to come to know itself, legitimately rise up against its Master: as the object, approaching self-realization, reclaims its subjectivity from the Absolute Subject?

Mysterium Horrendum

Luther's impression of God as the One before Whom none can stand and Whose gaze none can escape has discernible and vivid—if not negative, visceral—elements of what Otto later identifies as the numinous. As Otto reveals: "Indeed I grew to understand the numinous and its difference from the rational in Luther's *De Servo Arbitrio* long before I identified it in the 'qādosh' of the Old Testament and in the elements of 'religious awe' in the history of religion in general."[28] However, prior to this identification of the numinous in Luther, Otto warns that Luther's alleged over-emphasis upon the non-rational element of numinous consciousness risks a dangerous privileging of God's awe-striking, non-rational character as representing, in Luther's own words, *Deus ipse, ut est in sua natura et maiestate* ("God Himself, as He is in his own nature and majesty").[29] With a similar wariness, in the first volume of his *Systematic Theology,* Tillich discerns the potentially deforming element of numinous horror implicit in Luther's notion of the "naked absolute":

> The demonic elements in Luther's doctrine of God, his occasional identification of the wrath of God with Satan, the half-divine-half-demonic picture

he gives of God's acting in nature and history—all this constitutes the greatness and the danger of Luther's understanding of the holy. The experience he describes certainly is numinous, tremendous, and fascinating, but it is not safeguarded against demonic distortion and against the resurgence of the unclean within the holy.[30]

Here Tillich identifies not simply a non-rational but indeed a "demonic" element within Luther's notion of the Holy. The apparent duality of good and evil postulated *within* the divine nature thus betrays a barely exorcised or suppressed remnant of a more primitive, satanic shadow which Otto has seen as implicit in early depictions of the wrath of God. As Otto specifies, a primal demonic element of the numinous is manifest in the "ferocity" or "wrath" of God: "It might be said that Lucifer is 'fury,' the ὀργή, hypostasized, the 'mysterium tremendum' cut loose from the other elements and intensified to *mysterium horrendum*."[31] In other words, when the negative aspects of the *mysterium tremendum* are intensified and abstracted from such elements as beauty, goodness, and forgiveness, then God mutates into the demonic: the *mysterium horrendum* which promises only annihilation to any self that stands in its presence. Is this not the Wholly Other God who confronts the self in the consciousness of sin when this consciousness is "cut loose" from the forgiveness of sins? Is the God of spiritual trial none other than the demonic *mysterium horrendum*?

In engaging this discomforting possibility from a contemporary perspective, one must initially become aware of how Luther's rhetoric of spiritual trial is haunted by the harrowing and substantial threat posed by a supernatural, satanic reality that has been lost sight of in modernity. Indeed, Luther's late-medieval mind and world "swarmed with devils and poltergeists."[32] The young man's maternally inherited superstitions rendered him susceptible to what might from a modern perspective be regarded as a vulgar belief in witchcraft and the supernatural. "Strange noises in the night, the wind in the forest, the odd behavior of a neighbor . . . all provoked the conviction that demonic forces went about the world like a roaring lion, seeking whom it might devour."[33] Luther recounts how the devil is known to "thump about and haunt houses" and even relates with some satisfaction his own composure in response to a poltergeist incident in the monastery at Wittenberg.[34] All in all it would be premature in Luther's time to retire the devil to the archives of psychology or mythology. "Luther's Devil is by no means disposed of in terms of superstition, catarrh, noises in the head and what are now fashionably described as 'poltergeist' phenomena."[35] In fact, rather than progressively overcoming medieval belief in the devil, Luther's imminent eschatological conviction and urgency can be seen to have "intensified it and lent to it additional urgency: Christ and Satan wage a cosmic war for mastery over Church and world."[36] Heiko A. Oberman even goes so far as to suggest that Luther's experience of the devil's power "affected him as intensely as Christ's."[37]

Just as Luther ascribed the negative experience of melancholy to the devil, so also does the suffering in spiritual trial conceal an apparently satanic origin. "Concealment" is certainly the most apposite term in this relation, since in the afflictions of spiritual trial Satan works in secret—in hiddenness against the individual—turning the conscience against itself. As such, when in the horror of guilt one condemns oneself in the sleepless night of damnation, it is the devil who secretly labors in the occult internal labyrinth, subtly tenderizing the vulnerable conscience. In the satanically cultivated anxiety over predestination—*tentatio de praedestinatione*—the prospect of the fiery abyss looms large and terrible for the imagination. Consequently, the task is to expose the concealed satanic engine and extricate the conscience from its mechanisms. This recognition—that the devil has deceived one into erroneous self-condemnation—allows one not only to resist Satan but also to discern the true meaning of the temptation as a trial, and the identity of the real antagonist against whom one must fight.

Luther's dramatic writings on the sources of *Anfechtung* paint a divided and potentially disturbing portrait of a Janus-faced God. While it is true that for Luther the devil is the Accuser who opposes humanity, it is also true that in spiritual trial one fights against God as well as the "ancient serpent." While it is true that Satan incites the conscience's melancholy self-condemnation, God is also hidden behind such orchestrations of the devil. As such, in his table-talk "Of the Devil and His Works," Luther reveals how God implicitly grants to the devil power over human beings in two ways: "first, over the ungodly, when he will punish them by reason of their sins; secondly, over the just and godly, when he intends to try whether they will be constant in the faith, and remain in his obedience." Ultimately, Luther asserts, the truth is that: "Without God's will and our own consent, the devil cannot hurt us."[38] In order to avoid a cosmological dualism that would undermine divine omnipotence and compromise eschatological confidence, the devil must be ultimately conceived to be under the control of—though not in a coalition with—a sovereign God. Understood from this perspective, the existence of the devil is one of constant desire to afflict the faithful—tempered only by the restraint that God places upon him for the sake of our protection. As such, God's loosening of the divine restraint upon Satan is not to be identified with explicit collaboration. "The power the devil exercises is not by God commanded," Luther explains, "but God resists him not, suffering him to make tumults, yet no longer or further than he wills, for God has set him a mark, beyond which he neither can nor dare step."[39] In the divine withdrawal which must of necessity predicate affliction, we have some sense of Luther's notion of the hiddenness of God: what Luther identified as the *Deus absconditus*. It is here, in the relation between God and the devil, that Kierkegaard clarifies a significant departure in his view of *Anfægtelse* from Luther's *Anfechtung*: namely, an emphasis upon self-responsibility which mitigates demonic elements that allegedly contaminate Luther's vision of the God of spiritual trial.

THE DEVIL AND THE DEMONIC

That Christians must suffer does not come from the devil. The suffering comes from God—and right at this point begins the most extreme spiritual strenuousness in the Christian life.

—KIERKEGAARD'S *Journals*

This emphatic assertion from his *Journals* (JP 2:1447 / Pap. XI² A 130) demonstrates how Kierkegaard situates the tension of spiritual trial irreducibly between the self and God. In this sense, Kierkegaard's dialectic of spiritual trial not only inherits aspects from, but also seeks to partially divests itself of, its Lutheran heritage. This ambivalence toward the archaic notion of *Anfechtung* is nowhere more apparent than in his indictment of Luther's belief in its satanic origins.[40] In his *Journals*, Kierkegaard accuses Luther's ascription of *Anfechtung* to Satan of being "more childish than true" (JP 4:4372 / Pap. X¹ A 22): a castigation not so much motivated by Enlightenment condescension toward medieval superstition as by Kierkegaard's desire to appropriately situate the tension of spiritual trial irreducibly between the individual and God. "No, it is spiritual trial [*Anfægtelse*] because it seems to the person himself as if the relationship were stretched too tightly," Kierkegaard continues, "as if he were venturing too boldly in literally involving himself personally with God and Christ" (JP 4:4372 / Pap. X¹ A 22). Nevertheless, despite an avowed desire to free spiritual trial from the satanic origin that Luther had ascribed to it, at this point Kierkegaard actually concurs with Luther's belief that spiritual trial is not a trial caused by worldliness, but is instead elicited and intensified by the intensity of the God-relationship. Luther's devil avenges himself upon a life that is ventured in faith. "Here," according to Oberman, "is found a radical deviation from the medieval concept of the Devil, according to which the evil one is drawn by the smell of sin, the sin of worldly concern."[41] Hence, in *Concluding Unscientific Postscript*, Johannes Climacus is consistent with Luther in describing spiritual trial as "a nemesis upon the intense moments in the absolute relation" (CUP, 459). Nevertheless, since the dialectical antagonism is not situated between God and the devil (as it ostensibly is with Luther) but between God and the individual, the Kierkegaardian nemesis of spiritual trial must be understood as explicitly divine rather than, as in Luther, apparently satanic and only indirectly of divine origin.

Essentially, Kierkegaard regards ascribing spiritual trial to Satan as essentially an omission of its most radical implications: that it is a struggle derived from above. However, Kierkegaard is cautious not to ascribe all of the antagonism of spiritual trial to God. It takes two to initiate such a struggle between spirit and spiritlessness, as Kierkegaard qualifies in his *Journals*:

> When I say that the interpretation that suffering connected with becoming a Christian comes from the devil is not a truly Christian interpretation but that suffering comes from the God-relationship itself, this must of course be understood with the addition that in one sense suffering also comes from the individual himself, from the fact that his subjectivity cannot immediately and completely surrender to God. (JP 4:4384 / Pap. XI^2 A 132)

In other words, the suffering of spiritual trial also derives from the anxious freedom of the individual who cannot unconditionally submit their self-will to the obligation of eternity. Yet, despite his more modern emphasis upon individual subjectivity and responsibility, Kierkegaard still perceives at least a partial truth in antiquated (from post-Enlightenment Christendom's stance) discussion of spiritual trial. What is lacking, however, is the (modern) emphasis upon self-responsibility:

> In older and better devotional literature we read much about thoughts which try the spirit [*anfægtende Tanker*] and cause the individual to suffer, thought described as burning arrows and ascribed to the devil. But this is not a truly Christian interpretation; such thoughts come from the individual himself, although innocently. (JP 4:4384 / Pap. XI^2 A 132)

Kierkegaard's allusion here recalls Luther, among others: "Satan ceases not to plague the Christians, and shoot at us his fiery darts."[42] However, as noted previously, within the devotional writings of John of the Cross, Teresa of Avila, and Juan de los Angeles, the flaming arrow of spiritual suffering is unleashed, not by the devil, but by *God*. And Kierkegaard introduces a third possibility. These *anfægtende Tanker* are burning arrows which may derive from the individual consciousness, rather than from the authentic God-relationship, since, for Kierkegaard, such "thoughts that try the spirit" are "related to the imagination [*Fantasi*]" (JP 4:4383 / Pap. XI^2 A 33). Consequently, these self-inflicted burning arrows may signify a fantastic form of warfare against the self (Gr. *automachia*); and as such, one must remain vigilant against being carried away or deceived by the imagination concerning spiritual trial. From this perspective, one should consider the possibility that Luther's anxiety over the "rustling leaf," which in fantasy's anxiety becomes an expression of the wrath of God, is actually an anxiety that derives from the fantasy of his individual imagination.[43]

However, while emphasizing individual responsibility, Kierkegaard's ascription of spiritual trial to human-divine rather than to satanic agency does not validate a dismissive attitude toward the power of the devil. It is a reorientation which serves another purpose: specifically an insistence on divine sovereignty.

> When I raise objection in several places to the conception which everywhere introduces the devil as the source of suffering for the Christian, it is not my intention to explain away this power. Indeed, the New Testament itself also presents Christ as having been tempted [*fristet*] by the devil.
>
> No, my aim is to block the idea so easily smuggled in, the idea that God has a cause in the human sense—and simultaneously the criterion for being a Christian is readily reduced.
>
> . . . If the situation is such that God is a Majesty who is embattled with the devil, another Majesty, and wants to have Christians for this battle in order to make use of them in this battle, it is then impossible to maintain the ideal qualifications for being a Christian. (JP 4:4384 / Pap. XI² 133)

Kierkegaard is here desperate to avoid the suggestion of any dualism that would compromise the absolute and unconditioned character of the divine. Once the devil is asserted as a cosmic protagonist with genuine potency, then God is thereby cast against as an opposite with whom demonic powers struggle for eschatological destiny. In such a cosmic dualism, the Christian becomes a mere foot soldier of God in the war against the devil. And as such, the "ideal" qualifications for being a Christian are readily reduced to a conscription into eschatological warfare. God "needs" individuals insofar as a royal figure needs good servicemen. Rather, for Kierkegaard, humanity is in need of God—a divinity who does not have "a cause in the human sense"—who is not pitched in desperate struggle with a cosmic opposite. In turn, God desires selves because, as Kierkegaard implores, God desires to be loved. Once the devil is asserted as a supernatural protagonist with genuine potency, then the radical ideal of being a Christian is compromised by the principal location of enmity between God and the devil. Instead, in the authentic fear and trembling of spiritual trial, one cannot escape the understanding that the intrinsic antagonism exists in the infinite qualitative abyss between the individual and God. "It is clear that much of what Luther explained (an explanation which actually needs its own explanation) as the work of the devil—quite as if the devil were actually able to set limits upon God—may be explained by the discrepancy between God's infinite majesty and man" (JP 4:4949 / Pap. X⁴ A 487).

THE FACE OF GOD

In his evasion of dualism, Kierkegaard could nevertheless be seen as revealing a more fundamental affinity with Luther's ideas about the origins of spiritual trial than he acknowledges. Luther's ascription of spiritual trial to the devil often implies an occult ascription to God: the God who is secretly at work, and without whose implicit permission Satan could not wreak havoc against God's servant Job.[44] "In the end, therefore, Luther saw God behind trial," as Niels Thulstrup explains. "We are directly tempted by the Devil, the world, and our own carnal selves; but it is part of God's training that we should be subject to trial, and therefore we should always be forced to prayer."[45] However, God's withdrawal and "unleashing" of Satan may imply a tacit responsibility that implicates the divine in the very administration of affliction. One apparently fights with the devil, but in fact: "Luther urges the Christian on such occasions to *fight against God himself*—a bold exhortation that suggests that God *himself* is the source of *Anfechtung*."[46] As such, Luther's demonology may obscure where his anatomy of spiritual trial is closer to Kierkegaard's own. This unveiling of the Face of God as the source of spiritual trial is the revealed secret truth of the conflict, as when Jacob realizes the stature of the one he wrestles with: he realizes the name of his assailant in the assailant's refusal to disclose that name, and so he names the place Peni'el. "Now the meaning of 'Peni'el' is 'face of God,'" as Luther himself notes:

> But "face of God" is nothing else but knowledge of God. Nobody knows God except through faith in his word. The word and promises of God declare nothing but consolation and grace in Christ; therefore, whoever believes them sees God's mercy and goodness. This amounts to knowing God properly and this makes the heart joyful and blessed, as David says in Psalm 4 [vv. 6–7]: "Raise up the light of your countenance over us thereby you bestow joy upon my heart." And Psalm 80 [v. 3] says: "O God, show us your face, then we shall be blessed."[47]

Luther's apparently ambivalent impression of God through spiritual trial divulges that "Satan was finally God's Satan, doing in a perverse way God's will. It was almost to suggest that 'Satan' was the name Luther gave to those powers and actions of God that take place outside of Christ, that God himself is divided."[48] Once again, however, although a doctrine of divine omnipotence prohibits any dualism between God and Satan, there is still an implicit dualism ostensibly residing within Godself. The apparent fluidity between the God of good and God of evil results in a disorienting identity crisis in Luther's understanding of the divine. As Craig Hinkson writes:

> the very ascription of *Anfechtung* to the devil is tantamount to an ascription to God, the devil being *God's* devil, or "mask." . . . If, in *Anfechtung, God* is our assailant, then perhaps it is not *merely* with his "mask" that we have to do; perhaps it is with God himself—i.e., the predestining God.[49]

Yet one may say that Kierkegaard's notion of *Anfægtelse* advances beyond Luther's *Anfechtung* by causing the devil's mask to slip, as it were—not solely through Enlightenment sophistication, but from a desire to expose responsibility for the antagonism of the infinite qualitative difference as irreducibly being between the individual and God.

It is essentially a characteristic part of spiritual trial that one is not immediately initiated into the "knowledge of God" until one is first confronted with the doubt (Gn. *Zweifel*) between the two (*Zwei*) "faces" of God: a doubt that threatens to intensify into despair (*Verzweiflung*). Just as Jacob questioned the identity of his mysterious assailant, so "in the absence of faith the Christian is utterly without a clue as to the true nature of the deity that assails him."[50] Humanly speaking, as Kierkegaard writes in his *Journals,* despair therefore presents itself as an understandable response in the absence of faith.

> That the unconditioned can be the divine, that what occasions so much torment and trouble can be the divine, cannot be grasped by a man before he has surrendered to it and learned from the unconditioned itself that it is the divine. If a man continues with this purely human outlook, then the unconditioned is the devil, or God is the evil, as modern French philosophy [i.e. Proudhon] maintains, God is the evil in the sense that he is guilty of all man's unhappiness; if we could only eliminate the unconditioned, knock all ideals out of our heads, everything would go well—but God makes us unhappy, he is the evil. (JP 4:4911 / Pap. XI[1] A 516)

Insofar as the God-relationship causes profound unhappiness and torment, one may feel legitimate in fleeing the unconditioned as evil. "To exist before God may seem unendurable," to recall the "fantasized" words of Anti-Climacus (SUD, 32). But the authentic nature of the unconditioned can only be learned from the unconditioned itself. According to Luther's resolution of this unendurable assault, one may flee spiritual trial; but by fleeing in faith one actually flees into the arms of God. In the anguish of spiritual trial, Luther "instructs us to cling to Christ—*fleeing*, in effect, from the God who is hidden to the God who is revealed."[51] In fact, in this regard, Luther's notion of God seems to work itself out in the fear and trembling of the dreadful dialectic between the Face of God as annihilation and the Face of God as Jesus Christ—between the *Deus absconditus* and the *Deus revelatus,* the Spirit of *mortificatio* and *illuminatio.*[52] As Luther has it in relation to the allegory of Jacob's struggle at Peniel, the Face of God—which none may see and live—becomes the "knowledge of God" which saves. As such, the doubt and despair evoked by the "mask" of God and the "averted face of God" are answered by the *facies Dei revelata* (revealed face of God) as Jesus Christ.

By being hidden "in Christ," however, one discovers more than a place of refuge from a wrathful God (or even the *mysterium horrendum*). In the passion (Lat. *passio:* "suffering") of Christ's life, one witnesses the empathic and authentic response to the trials of spirit as they were revealed in the *angefochtene Christus.* Through this divine suffering, our tribulations are sanctified by Christ's tears of blood, insofar as these tears testify to the presence of spiritual trial in a sinless humanity (though that is not to say that our own spiritual trial never relates to our sinfulness, or that Christ's tribulations were identical to ours). Nevertheless, Christ's anguish at Gethsemane (*angefochtene Christus*) transfigures the spiritual trials of humanity (*angefochtene Mensch*) through a divine solidarity and consolatory disclosure of the meaning of suffering "before God." Like humanity, Christ endured temptations from the devil; and yet, as both human and divine, he also endured the opposition of wills with the Father. "Father, let this cup pass from me," as Luther interprets in a table-talk: "Here the will was against the will, yet he turned himself presently according to his Father's will and was comforted by an angel. Christ, who in our flesh was plagued and tempted, is the best mediator and advocate with God, in our tribulation."[53]

At this point of anguish, Christ himself undergoes an apparent *psychomachia* (inner battle between "the spirit" and "the flesh"): a struggle which is resolved by a moment of *automachia* (spiritual battle against "self-will") in which he declares: "Not my will, but thy will be done!" Furthermore, Christ expresses our divine-human solidarity through the sense of desolation that accompanies his apparent God-forsakenness: the darkest hour of *Anfechtung.* Thus Luther's exposition of Christ's cry on the cross—"My God, my God, why have you forsaken me?"—"paints with terrible and sombre realism the horror of 'Anfechtung' and sets over against it the 'angefochtene Christus,' the Saviour who trod the whole grim path of 'Anfechtung' for us."[54] From the perspective of spiritual trial, therefore, it is above all Christ's expression of God-forsakenness on the cross and the reconciliation of God-forsakenness through the salvific event of the Resurrection that exposes in all its horror, but finally destroys, the infinite abyss of separation between humanity and God.

Insofar as for Luther the Face of God "becomes historically and empirically concrete in the person of Jesus Christ,"[55] there is a revelation not solely of the nature of human suffering, but also of the reconciliation of humanity with God. The *metanoia* inherent in recognizing Christ as the Face of God involves a soteriological transition from the idea of the *Deus absconditus* to the *Deus revelatus,* from wrath to mercy. Famously, for Luther, this moment is encapsulated in "the tower experience": a reference to Luther's study in the tower of the Black Cloister in Wittenberg, where Luther was wrestling with Romans 1:17: "For therein [in the Gospel] is the righteousness of God revealed from faith to faith: as it is written, The just shall live by faith." Luther received a breakthrough by which: "All at once I felt that I had been born again and entered into paradise itself through open gates." Luther realized that, rather than being a formal expression of divine punishment, "the justice of God is that by which the just person lives by a gift of God, that is by faith." Prior to this breakthrough, his anguished struggle to keep the Law of God had led to inevitable failure and resentment for the apparently damning righteousness of God (the *impossibility* of salvation). However, this spiritual trial was resolved when Luther realized that the wrath of God had, as it were, been overcome by the mercy of God within him (in Kierkegaardian terms: a triumph of divine *possibility* over human *impossibility*). "It is in the tower experience that Luther affirms that Jesus Christ is the Face of God, and this shifts his understanding from the just God who condemns to the just God who justifies."[56] However, emphasis upon the ostensibly dualistic elements of this process threatens to obscure the integrity of the Spirit at the heart of Luther's concept of God: the *Spiritus Creator* is the *one* Spirit of both *mortificatio* and *illuminatio*. What makes Luther's theology so radical, as Otto explains in *The Idea of the Holy,* is that in overcoming these "gulfs and abysses" in the understanding it is "the unapproachable which becomes approachable, the Holy One who is pure goodness . . . it is 'Majesty' which makes itself familiar and intimate."[57] Once again, in spiritual trial, the flight for Luther is one from God to God. In this sense, *Anfechtung* and the *Anfægtelse* that Kierkegaard affirms both signify a struggle against one's own perception of what it means to exist before God. Tillich describes this *metanoia* aptly in the second volume of his *Systematic Theology:*

> For those who are aware of their estrangement from God, God is the threat of ultimate destruction. His face takes on demonic traits. However, those who are reconciled to him realise that, although their experience of the wrath of God was genuine, it was not experience of a God other than the one

to whom they are reconciled. . . . He [Luther] perceives God as the God of wrath, rightly so in preliminary terms, wrongly so in ultimate terms.[58]

KIERKEGAARD'S DIALECTIC OF SPIRITUAL TRIAL

The most effective means of escaping spiritual trial [Anfægtelse] is to become spiritless, and the sooner the better.

—*The Concept of Anxiety*

Tillich's invocation of "preliminary" and "ultimate" perceptions of God's wrath in Luther sheds light on what also transpires at the heart of Kierkegaard's dialectical description of the self before God. Spiritual trial, the essential expression of this endeavor to stand before God in the face of an infinite qualitative abyss, occupies a precarious and harrowing position between motifs of life and death. According to Kierkegaard, the presence of the eternal in an individual is indicated by the willingness to freely enter into the dark tomb of their resurrection: "Just as one knows that an insect wants to become a butterfly when it begins to spin a cocoon" (JP 4:4712 / Pap. XI[1] A 377). Yet the danger is that not everyone who enters into this combustible tension between humanity and God will emerge transformed by the metamorphosis of spirit. There is a possibility that not all may move from "preliminary" wrath to "ultimate" grace. "Spirit is fire"—but there is always, Kierkegaard warns in his *Journals,* a danger in casting oneself to the flames: "not all are burned out to spirit, a few are burned out to ashes—that is, they do not become spirit in the fire" (JP 4:4355 / Pap. XI[2] A 41).

And yet Kierkegaard laments that there are few in the malaise of modernity who even venture to enter the fires of Spirit. Spiritual trial (Dn. *Anfægtelse*), as Kierkegaard warns, is vanishing in modern Christendom. The broad and blithe path of spiritlessness is sheltered from the arrows of spiritual trial. "Never involve yourself with God so long that any spiritual trial [*Anfægtelse*] has a chance to begin," Kierkegaard ironically counsels in his *Journals,* and "if you think about God once a week and bow before him the way the others do, I guarantee that you will never be subjected to spiritual trials" (JP 2:1354 / Pap. VIII[1] A 77). In fact, for Kierkegaard, Christendom's bourgeois capitulation to modernity is particularly epitomized by the decline of this particular sickness of the soul. "Because religion is not taken seriously nowadays in Christendom, there is never a hint about spiritual trials [*Anfægtelser*]. Life is just not lived religiously; this can be proved indirectly by the disappearance of spiritual trial" (JP 4:4372 / Pap. X[1] A 22). Through his counsel on the subject of spiritual trial, Kierkegaard seems determined to shock Christendom back into Christianity, while at the same time remaining anxious that Christianity not mutate into the madness or nightmare of the fantastic. Although spiritual trial is an authenticating mark of Christian inwardness, Kierkegaard warns that it is not to be forced upon oneself in the counterfeiting of Lutheran inwardness; nor should it, like melancholy, be cultivated in self-mortification or stylized despair. Spiritual trial is for the "common man," the individual, whom God will not test beyond what he can bear. Where faith is present, spiritual trial is bound to come, but each believer must discover this for oneself. One is not called to be an imitator of Luther.[59]

In empathy with the notion of *imitatio Christi* that was present in the Lutheran tradition of his time,[60] Kierkegaard's understanding of spiritual trial was determined by the *voluntary* suffering of Christ's passion. As Kierkegaard describes in his *Journals*, Christ's cry to God, "why have you forsaken me?" signifies the ultimate expression of "freedom's ultimate spiritual trial [*Anfægtelse*]" (JP 4:4611 / Pap VIII[1] A 580).[61] It is in the possibility of God-forsakenness which is conveyed by this abyssal cry that faith's anxious freedom is manifest. The call of faith is the invitation to a struggle which, following Christ, must be accepted *voluntarily* by each believer since, as Kierkegaard asserts: "When the voluntary disappears, 'spiritual trial' [*Anfægtelse*] disappears, and when spiritual trials disappear, Christianity disappears—as it has disappeared in Christendom" (JP 4:4950 / Pap. X[3] A 43).[62] As such, spiritual trial—as an expression of the infinite qualitative difference—becomes an essential mark, or stigma, of the truth of Christianity and the authenticity of the self's relation before God. However, despite Kierkegaard's often extravagant evocations, spiritual trial must be entered into voluntarily in the daily arena of the mundane; not in the cloister, the tower, or the pulpit. "If one puts on the religious for everyday use," Kierkegaard describes in his *Journals*, "the spiritual trials [*Anfægtelse*] are bound to come" (JP 4:4364 / Pap. VI A 2). Or as Johannes Climacus declares in *Concluding Unscientific Postscript*: "It is in the living-room that the battle must be fought, not imaginatively in church, with the pastor shadowboxing and the listeners looking on" (CUP, 465). As such, it is a struggle that is neither quixotic nor theatrical. Spiritual trial is not reserved for the stylized, heroic moment in which one buckles one's sword and rides out like Don Quixote; rather, as Johannes de Silentio expresses it in *Fear and Trembling*, a Knight of Faith "looks just like a tax-collector" (FT, 39).

And yet, as Kierkegaard laments, a person whose life is transfigured by faith is an all-too-hidden exception in modernity: "Spiritual trial [*Anfægtelse*] is the expression of a concentration upon Christianity as the only object. That is why most men have no spiritual trials" (JP 4:4365 / Pap. VIII[1] A 47). As Johannes Climacus explains, it is only in the attempt to relate oneself absolutely to the absolute that one "discovers the boundary, spiritual trial

[*Anfægtelse*] then becomes the expression for the boundary . . . anyone who is not very religious [and Climacus includes himself here] will not be exposed to spiritual trials either, because spiritual trial is the response to the absolute expression of the absolute relation" (CUP, 459).

Again, as Kierkegaard himself outlines in his *Journals*: "In the words of the preachers, *every* man ought to relate himself to God in *all things*, ought to refer *everything* to God" (JP 4:4372 / Pap. X¹ A 22). Yet the preacher is wrong in assuming that such a relation constitutes the resolution of spiritual trial—as if the concentration upon Christianity actually delivers one from the tension of the infinite qualitative difference. In fact, the more one refers all of life's vicissitudes in their specificity and finitude to the Infinite and the Absolute, the more one will encounter spiritual trial. It is this that Johannes Climacus calls "the response of the boundary against the finite individual": the spiritual trial which "quite rightly increases in proportion to the religiousness" of the individual (CUP, 459). In other words, as religiosity intensifies so, correspondingly, does the conflict. Kierkegaard provides an autobiographical explication of this in his *Journals*:

> Spiritual trial [*Anfægtelse*] is the divine repulsion in the *quid nimis* and can never fail to appear if one is to exist religiously, consequently as an actual, definite particular man—for example, I, Søren Aabye Kierkegaard, thirty-five years old, of slight build, master of arts, brother-in-law of businessman Lund, living on such and such a street—in short, this whole concretion of trivialities, that I dare relate myself to God, refer all the affairs of my life to him. No man has ever lived who has truly done this without discovering with horror the horror of spiritual trial, that he might be venturing too boldly, that the whole thing might really be lunacy. (JP 4:4372 / Pap. X¹ A 22)

Kierkegaard is conscious, however, that in actuality the endeavor to exist before God in all things and at all times will become too arduous: the opposition of the Absolute to the individual is altogether too intense. Ultimately, the impasse of the infinite qualitative abyss weighs too heavily upon the self, tempting it to relinquish the endeavor to become itself before God—a spiritual trial, or even an *acedia*, which Kierkegaard describes elsewhere in his *Journals* as "a disgust for the religious" (JP 4:4377 / Pap. X² A 590). The thought occurs that the whole thing might really be madness, hence the "the horror of spiritual trial." Yet this strenuous incommensurability between spirit and spiritlessness is "authentic Christian religiousness," as Kierkegaard sees it: "whether or not such a person like this is to be found, I do not know; I have never seen one" (JP 4:4372 / Pap. X¹ A 22).

Nevertheless, Kierkegaard continues in this journal entry to refer specifically to how Luther's own "Spiritedness" was authenticated by the persecution he endured at the hands of his opponents. Although there may be some implicit parallels between Luther's struggle and Kierkegaard's suffering at the hands of his contemporaries, Kierkegaard explains in another entry: "Genuinely spiritual persons are so rare that they can be handled appropriately as exceptions" (JP 4:4373 / Pap. X¹ A 452). Is Luther such an exception? His anxious conscience certainly required treatment, according to Kierkegaard's diagnosis. The scrupulous inwardness of Luther and the bourgeois complacency of the typically spiritless individual can be read as forming contrasting points for a Kierkegaardian dialectic of spiritual trial. There is "something dialectical"— and therefore in need of temperance as Kierkegaard regards it—between the unwillingness to be spirit, and the desire "to be far too much spirit" and therefore want to "love God more or differently than God will tolerate" (JP 4:4373 / Pap. X¹ A 452). Such willing to be completely spirit can either betray a "spiritual pride," or reveal one to be a "self-tormentor," or even guilty of "an over-strained dejection which actually demands too much of God and of itself" (JP 4:4373 / Pap. X¹ A 452). As such, in the perennial struggles of spiritual trial there are necessary exceptions. With the pastoral pragmatism characteristic of a monastic treatise on sicknesses of the soul, Kierkegaard writes:

> The norm, therefore, is: in a few exceptional cases recommend diversionary aids, but as a rule prescribe aids of the spirit, for men use diversionary aids all too promiscuously of their own accord. The exceptions are the sick, for whom diversionary aids are prescribed; most people are much too robust, so the operation is precisely to make them a little sick, a little weak—by prescribing that they use the aids of the spirit. (JP 4:4373 / Pap. X¹ A 452)

Here Kierkegaard provides an instance of a dialectical need for temperance between spiritual sickness and mental health. The sick soul must ground itself in diversion so as to avoid an unrealizable and presumptuous insistence upon becoming completely spirit. Similar to the description in *Concluding Unscientific Postscript*, the desire to express religiousness infinitely renders the finite incommensurable: the absolute consciousness of God consumes the individual, who is naturally unable to sustain it (CUP, 485). The desire to become spirit *absolutely* actually betrays a desire to transcend the suffering of spirit in the world of spiritlessness: an attempt to violate the infinite difference between humanity and God.

To bring the relative into relation with God may seem *impossible;* but there is yet a vital divine concession by which no one will be tested beyond what they can bear. There is, as Johannes Climacus describes, consolation in the thought that God understands the inner struggle of spiritual trial better than we who struggle. One who is in the midst of spiritual trial

> perhaps fortifies himself with the upbuilding reflection that God, who created man, certainly knows best all the numerous things that to a human being appear to be incapable of being joined together with the thought of God—all the earthly desires, all the confusion in which he can be trapped, and the necessity of diversion, of rest, as well as a night's sleep. (CUP, 489)

The absolute difference is thus expressed in humility; but not in the monastic flight from the world which, according to Johannes Climacus, betrays "an attempt at wanting to be more than a human being, an enthusiastic, perhaps pious attempt to be like God" (CUP, 492). And so, lest one dies of the spiritual trial in which one is confined by the absolute conception of God, one should permit measured distraction to come back in as a concession for the fact that no one can become spirit absolutely—a humble expression of the infinite qualitative difference in which one's humanity is "expressed most perfectly" (CUP, 412).

Nevertheless, one must not become distracted to the point of fleeing from the God-relationship itself. Kierkegaard remains clear that ultimately one must venture forth in the authentic struggle of spiritual trial. The tactic of freely choosing to confront spiritual trial is apparent in Kierkegaard's innovative differentiation of "spiritual trial" (Dn. *Anfægtelse*) from "temptation" (*Fristelse*). The qualitative difference between these concepts resides in the fact that spiritual trial originates in the God-relationship itself and so, unlike temptation, is something that should not be evaded. Temptation is rather a seduction which is conquered by distracting oneself from its allure. This relation is somewhat clearer in Walter Lowrie's 1941 translation of *For Self-Examination*, where *Fristelse* is translated as "alluring temptations" and *Anfægtelse* is rendered "deterrent temptations." One must flee what is "alluring" (*Fristelse*) and confront that which is "deterrent" (*Anfægtelse*). The temptation, which can be identified as coming from the devil, is differentiated from the spiritual trial, which Kierkegaard situates firmly in the space between the individual and God. In reference to the words of James 4:7, "Resist the devil, and he will flee from you," Kierkegaard notes in his *Journals:*

> This, then, is the tactic. Not the reverse: Flee the devil—this can be the tactic only in relation to temptation [*Fristelse*].
>
> Here we see that spiritual trial [*Anfægtelse*] lies a whole quality higher than temptation. . . . Spiritual trial can be fought only with the rashness of faith, which charges head-on. (JP 4:4378 / Pap. X A 95)

Essentially, spiritual trial occurs in opposition; and yet it is an opposition that must be confronted and not evaded: "the temptation [*Fristelse*] to sin is in accord with inclination, [the temptation] of spiritual trial [*Anfægtelse*] [is] contrary to inclination" (JP 4:4367 / Pap. VIII¹ A 93). Or, as Johannes Climacus explains in *Concluding Unscientific Postscript*, in

> the sphere of the relationship with God, it [*Anfægtelse*] is what tempta-
> tion [*Fristelse*] is in the sphere of the ethical relation. . . . In temptation, it
> is the lower that tempts; in spiritual trial it is the higher. In temptation, it is
> the lower that wants to lure the individual; in spiritual trial, it is the higher
> that, seemingly envious of the individual, wants to frighten him back. (CUP,
> 459)[63]

In other words, temptation is an enticement of inner desire that must be evaded, while spiritual trial is a confrontation that one fears but that one must, nevertheless, enter into voluntarily before God. In one sense, both partake of anxiety's ambivalent relation of desire and fear—the difference, however, is that where the religious sphere of spiritual trial is concerned this ambivalence could be best described as one of fascination and terror.[64] The essential difference can be best exemplified in the trials of Christ: the tempta-tion (*Fristelse*) of Christ in the wilderness was at the hands of the devil, and he turned away from it; the agony in the Garden was a spiritual trial (*Anfæg-telse*), which he confronted in the anguished wakefulness of prayer.[65]

Spiritual trial, as such, is usually tackled head-on through a confrontation with freedom before God. However, as in the exceptional case (and perhaps Luther was one in Kierkegaard's view) of those who become too spiritually sick in their self-torment, Kierkegaard is willing to prescribe a moderate use of diversionary tactics against the tendency toward excessive self-mor-tification.[66] As Evagrius aspired to *apatheia* (a Stoic-inflected, conscious relinquishing of mundane cares) as a means of transcending temptation, Kierkegaard also recommends the tactic of *indifference* as a possible means of confronting and overcoming the anxiety of spiritual trial:

> the most absolute indifference to them [*anfægtende Tanker*: thoughts that
> try the spirit] is itself the victory. Such thoughts want to make you anxious,
> want to worry you to the point where your spirit is so weak and cowardly
> that you imagine that you are responsible for them. . . . Once they have made
> you think this, the devil is loose. Therefore be absolutely indifferent; be more
> indifferent to them than you are to a little rumbling in your stomach. Or get
> angry, as angry as you get when someone rings your doorbell at an inoppor-
> tune time and you rush out and say: What kind of an uproar is this!—That

is, get angry just short of being afraid, for this is precisely what should be avoided.

Temptation [*Fristelse*] is best fought by running away, avoiding it. But this does not work with thoughts that try the spirit, for they pursue you. Here the tactic must be: do not get frightened, remain utterly calm, absolutely indifferent. (JP 4:4382 / Pap. XI² A 30)

This may, however, appear to be a slightly confusing prescription. How can indifference satisfy Kierkegaard's recommendation to confront spiritual trial? Is there not a contradiction between the passivity of composed indifference and retaliatory passion? However, as Louise Carroll Keeley remarks apropos this context: "Both indifference and anger can be ways to deny responsibility, to shift the focal point of responsibility away from the self to another."[67] And yet Kierkegaard affirms that one is, at least to some extent, personally responsible for (though not necessarily guilty of) spiritual trial—resulting as it does from the anxious freedom that transpires in the infinite qualitative difference. To a degree one must, as a free self, take responsibility for the conflict between self and God; but Kierkegaard is here referring to specific thoughts (fantasies) that try to make one morbidly anxious or excessively guilt-stricken. This tactic of "indifference" toward the content of spiritual trial is therefore to be distinguished from the indifference of modernity toward even entering into the crucible of spiritual trial—the indifference to which Vigilius Haufniensis's ironic evasion refers in *The Concept of Anxiety*: "The most effective means of escaping spiritual trial [*Anfægtelse*] is to become spiritless, and the sooner the better" (CA, 117).

Essentially, Kierkegaard prescribes that the avoidance of spiritual trial is indicative of spiritlessness, and therefore the struggle of spiritual trial must be confronted seriously and temperately before God, but without capitulating through excessive imagination into an irremediable guilt. It is such fear that is precisely spiritual trial's moment of death through which, figuratively speaking, the devil is loose and one is anxious to the point of imagining that one has become guilty because of it. This is described by Kierkegaard in his *Journals* as simply "the anxiety of spiritual trial [*Anfægtelse*]" (JP 4:4374 / Pap. X¹ A 477). Once perspective is lost and one becomes fantastically guilty or afraid, then one may fall into the temptation of believing that God has abandoned one, that God no longer serves as the source of *consolation* in the *desolation* of spiritual trial. This apparent God-forsakenness is what Kierkegaard ominously calls "the last spiritual trial [*Anfægtelse*]" (JP 4:4699 / Pap. X⁵ A 38).[68] And it is at this highest point of dread that, like Luther, Kierkegaard directs his gaze toward Christ's own trial.

For Kierkegaard, as for Luther: "The school of spiritual trial [*Anfægtelse*] is a frightful school" (JP 4:4376 / Pap. X² A 182).[69] This is a "school" designed by God for the spiritual upbringing, the "educational torture," of the believer. Nevertheless, Kierkegaard is keen to acknowledge the danger of spiritual trial which resides in the fact that it can be "very painful and excruciating and, in addition, dialectically complicated almost to the point of madness; if it may be thought of in this way, it is, to define it teleologically, an educational torture which, whatever else, is intended to break all self-centred wilfulness" (JP 4:4370 / Pap. IX A 333). This breaking of "self-centred wilfulness" is manifest in the self-annihilating confession:

> Before you, O God, I am nothing; do with me as you will, let me suffer all this which almost drives me to madness; you are still the one to whom wisdom and understanding belong, the loving Father. . . . If this agony collides with a passionate self-centred wilfulness which cannot become nothing before God, it must end up with the sufferer losing his mind. (JP 4:4370 / Pap. IX A 333)

As such, spiritual trial is ultimately directed toward the death of an un-reckoning self-will: not the "death of the self" that postmodern commentators have observed, but the death of *self-centeredness*. By becoming nothing *before God*, the self *voluntarily* follows Christ's surrender—"Not my will, but thy will be done!"—and becomes centered around God instead of its willing.

However, Kierkegaard is quick to observe, just as love intensified can mutate into "revulsion for the beloved," so can preoccupation with one's spiritual suffering engender a "religious spiritual trial [*Anfægtelse*], also found described by older writers, in which a disgust for the religious [i.e., *acedia*] sets in" (JP 4:4377 / Pap. X² A 590). In order to preserve oneself against the risk of *acedia* which is inherent to the "strenuous" task of "infinite transparency before God" (JP 4:4373 / Pap. X¹ A 452), the sufferer must not lose sight of the God of love lest spiritual trial drive them into the despair of God-forsakenness: spiritual trial's own moment of death. In terms categorical of spiritual trial, Kierkegaard writes: "In a moment of impatience it must seem to him as if children torturing a butterfly could not inflict worse torture than he is suffering." And this is the God one must not abandon! "One thing he must do: not despair of the possibility of salvation, not-abandon God," Kierkegaard counsels. "People talk of abandoning oneself, but this is rubbish; it is a matter of abandoning God." But this does not mean that the sufferer must deny these thoughts of God-forsakenness, as he denies himself in becoming nothing. Instead, he must acknowledge these thoughts—as Christ on the cross cried out, "Why have you forsaken me?"—in order to conquer them *before God*. Once again, Christ is the pattern. In his anguish at Gethsemane, Christ submits his will to God, but in doing so he acknowledges his own will before God: "Not my will but thy will be done!" Becoming nothing before God does not require that one *ignores* one's self-willing; rather, it requires that one must first become *conscious* of such thoughts in order to relinquish them. So Kierkegaard explains how, for the sufferer in agonizing and crucifying contradiction, "his salvation lies right here, in his acquiring the frankness to think these evil thoughts together with God before God—in order to dispose of them" (JP 4:4377 / Pap. X² A 590).

However, as Kierkegaard recognizes in relation to the figure of Job, such suffering is intensified in the paradoxical collision between the agony of suffering and the thought that God is love: the thinking of these apparently incommensurable thoughts must yet be *together,* in order to conquer them "together with God before God."

> Humanly speaking, a person who is experiencing such suffering is justified in saying: The whole thing would be far less agonizing to me if I did not have the idea of God along with it. The pain lies either in being left helpless by God, the omnipotent, who could so easily help, or in the crucifixion of one's understanding, that in spite of all this God is love and that what happens is for one's own good. (JP 4:4375 / Pap. X¹ A 478)

Indeed it requires faith to reconcile the apparently incompatible love of God with human suffering—to think this "together with God before God." However, Kierkegaard never paints an easy picture of such faith. This is a faith in the face of absurdity that Kierkegaard's pseudonymous author of *Fear and Trembling,* Johannes de Silentio, confesses is beyond him:

> I have seen the terrifying face to face . . . [but] I cannot make the movement of faith, I cannot shut my eyes and plunge confidently into the absurd; it is for me an impossibility, but I do not praise myself for that. I am convinced that God is love; for me this thought has a primal lyrical validity. When it is present to me, I am unspeakably happy; when it is absent, I long for it more vehemently than the lover for the object of his love. But I do not have faith; this courage I lack. To me God's love of God, in both the direct and the converse sense, is incommensurable with the whole of actuality. (FT, 34)

In the light of God-forsaken suffering, it may become easier to assert, as Dermot Cox does in *Man's Anger and God's Silence:* "Suffering is not the problem; God is. Without a belief in a personal God human suffering is simply a part of life, concomitant to the human condition."[70] However, the suffering of *spiritual trial* is a particular form of suffering that would not even exist were there no infinite qualitative difference—were there no idea of God! In recognition of this paradox at the heart of Job's plight, Kierkegaard acknowledges how the "real spiritual trial [*Anfægtelse*]" resides in the notion that "it is as if the God-idea itself intensified one's agony" (JP 4:4375 / Pap. X^1 A 478). Under such affliction—rather than submit to "the crucifixion of one's understanding"—it can be easier, "humanly speaking," to relieve the tension through the collapse into despair: "The alleviating aspect of despair is its unmitigated agreement that the suffering is unbearable. The strenuousness of the idea of God is to have to understand that not only is the suffering to be endured but that it is good, a gift from a God of love" (JP 4:4375 / Pap. X^1 A 478).

The dreadful paradox and "additional burden" (JP 4:4375 / Pap. X^1 A 478) of spiritual trial occurs at the moment when the suffering of the God-relationship becomes apparently unbearable, since it appears that it is the existence of God itself that causes this suffering. "God is spirit," Kierkegaard asserts elsewhere in his *Journals,* "and therefore a man (*qua* sensate being) can be involved with him only if he suffers" (JP 4:4681 / Pap. X^4 A 481). In the struggle of spiritual trial, therefore, one must through faith strive to find respite in the love of God without plunging headlong into the abyss of despair. However, for some, the infinite qualitative abyss yawns so wide that the prospect of relating to the Absolute induces nothing but the most dreadful vertigo. As Keeley describes:

At the prospect of drawing closer to God the person feels so agitated by anxiety that he is tempted to abandon his desire for a deeper relationship with God. Moreover, this anxiety is so successful in taking root that he *wants* to give up the spiritual venture and is *almost* convinced that God wants him to go back as well.[71]

But such a person must not capitulate to the desire for despair's surrender. Under such circumstances Kierkegaard advocates that one cling to God in faith, thinking these thoughts "together with God before God," no matter how dreadful this may seem, since it is *faith* that suspends offence:[72]

Does only the person who has a gracious God and Father have a God and Father? I wonder if the person who has, alas, an angry God and Father does not also have a God and Father? O, my friend, if this is your predicament, or if you have been spiritually tried [*i Anfægtelse*] in this way, continue to cling to this radical consolation; only do not let go of God, and you will find that there is help in this. The one danger is to let go of God. Even if his wrath were to hang over you all your life, this still is not nearly so dangerous.

But no doubt a man is seldom spiritually tried as this. (JP 2:1421 / Pap. X³ A 790)

While one feels the *desolatio* of God-forsakenness, one must not lose sight of the *consolatio* that, despite the *experience* of God's absence, God never abandons us. Only Christ knows what true God-forsakenness means, as Kierkegaard counsels in his discourse on "The High Priest": "surely no human being has experienced that spiritual trial [*Anfægtelse*], the spiritual trial of being abandoned by God—but he was tempted in that way" ("Three Discourses at the Communion on Fridays," WA, 121). In actuality, Kierkegaard inverts the self's conviction of its God-forsakenness; it becomes instead a question of one's forsaking God in despair. One must not let go of, abandon, or forsake God, despite the seduction of despair's apparent alleviation of the tension of the God-relation. Along these lines, Anti-Climacus, in *The Sickness unto Death*, provides an evocative description of a person who, after enduring the greatest horror, wills to collapse into such an irresolvable despair: "At this point, then, salvation is, humanly speaking, utterly impossible" (SUD, 38). But this despair over impossibility is *also* an alleviating surrender that abandons God—because, Anti-Climacus counters, "for God everything is possible!" And: "This is the battle of *faith*, battling, madly, if you will, for possibility, because possibility is the only salvation" (SUD, 38). Salvation, *humanly speaking*, is an impossibility, and despair consolidates itself by collapsing into that thought. But, in this moment of melancholy despair over salvation (*tentatio de praedestinatione*), faith has the "antidote for despair—possibility—because for God everything is possible at every moment" (SUD, 39–40). And so the only true resolution of this despair is found in the crucifying embrace of this absurdity in which faith suspends offence and self-centered willfulness, and throws itself on God.[73] As Kierkegaard affirms in his *Journals*: "O, but the height of blessedness is to agree unconditionally that God is right precisely when, humanly speaking, there seems to be a case against him" (JP 2:1421 / Pap. X³ A 790). Or in the words of Anti-Climacus, "to believe is indeed to lose the understanding in order to gain God" (SUD, 38).

The risk is, however, that the single individual's God-relationship can become diseased, and this is itself a dreadful spiritual trial (*Anfægtelse*), as Kierkegaard sees it:

This kind of spiritual trial [*Anfægtelse*] arises because the deep underlying feeling of infinite unworthiness basic to every true God-relationship becomes overpowering, is not transfigured into a greater joy in God, but oppresses one, so that a person becomes momentarily anxious and afraid of ideality and himself—and of God, who seems to be so infinitely sublime that one does not dare think of him at all. It seems as if he must become disgusted and tired of listening to one's nonsense and nauseated with one's sins. (JP 2:2008 / Pap. IX A 316)

In other words, Kierkegaard is describing the spiritual trial that emerges when God appears so sublime and Wholly Other and one becomes so essentially unworthy that one dares not even contemplate God. Yet this spiritual trial, in which one's sense of "infinite unworthiness" recommends that one abandon the thought of God, must be fought against "together with God before God" in the faith and prayer that God is love, and that therefore all things are possible.

But a person is not to give in; he is to fight against it, thank God that God has *commanded* that one *ought* to pray to him, for otherwise it is hardly possible to force one's way through the spiritual trial [*Anfægtelse*]. He is to remember that God is love, the God of patience and consolation, and that God is not one who adopts vain titles but is completely different from anything I am able to comprehend of what he says himself to be. (JP 2:2008 / Pap. IX A 316)

The emphasis here is upon God's *command* that one *ought* to pray. This sentiment recalls Luther's own words of "Comfort When Facing Grave Temptations," namely, that God "promised to hear us, yes, he commanded us to pray, for the very reason that we might know and firmly believe that our petition will be heard."[74] Here God's Wholly Otherness is encountered from the opposite side of the abyss: the God Who, in preliminary terms, seemed too "infinitely sublime" to contemplate, now appears, in ultimate terms, as the God of love; and in being revealed as love, God is "*completely different from anything I am able to comprehend of what he says himself to be*" (my emphasis). Through this *metanoia*, the Wholly Other reveals itself to be the *Holy* Other: incomprehensible not solely in the *tremendum* of infinite sublimity, but in the *mysterium* of love—the fathomless revelation of forgiveness that is itself an awe-inspiring revelation of holiness and divine possibility. "That God will forgive my sin unconditionally is the most improbable of all possibilities," as Heinecken describes in *The Moment Before God.* "Therefore, it is in the confrontation by this God, and here only that I feel the proper awe. . . . This humbles me as nothing else can. Here alone is true awe before God."[75]

In response to the *mysterium* of the impossibility of forgiveness, Anti-Climacus advocates the loving struggle of prayer. So one must fight *Anfægtelse* like Christ at Gethsemane, with the prayer that signifies faith in divine possibility over human impossibility. This prayer resists despair by the denial of self-will and submission to the divine will. The fatalist's collapse into despair is, according to Anti-Climacus, "a mute capitulation: he is unable to pray" (SUD, 40). The fatalist is unable to pray because there is for him no air of possibility in which to breathe a word; there is only despair. He has lost God and his self, but: "For prayer there must be a God, a self—and possibility—or a self and possibility in a pregnant sense, because the being of God means that everything is possible, or that everything is possible means the being of God" (SUD, 40). To pray is to break the self-enclosed silence of despair (Dn. *Indesluttehed*), to pray through despair "together with God before God," in order to struggle against human impossibility in the name of divine possibility. Christ alone has suffered "the last trial" of God-forsakenness and therefore, when in despair the self believes it is forsaken by God, one must "together with God before God" trust in the consolation that God knows what it means to be abandoned by God. "Therefore, you who are tempted," as Kierkegaard counsels in his discourse on "The High Priest," "whoever you are, do not become silent in despair, as if the temptation were suprahuman and no one could understand it" ("Three Discourses at the Communion on Fridays," WA, 121).

THE SILENT PRAYER OF UNKNOWING: *De Profundis*

Out of the depths have I cried unto thee, O LORD.

—*Psalm 130*

Through the foregoing discussion of spiritual trial it is hopefully becoming apparent that, for Kierkegaard, a leap of faith into divine *possibility* emerges as the means by which the infinite qualitative abyss is transcended. It is in this that "the deep underlying feeling of infinite unworthiness basic to every true God-relationship" is "transfigured into a greater joy in God" (JP 2:2008 / Pap. IX A 316). However, it still remains to be considered just how the infinite qualitative difference imposes itself upon the very act of speaking or praying with God. In a discourse titled "Look at the Birds of the Air; Look at the Lily in the Field," Kierkegaard asserts that "God is in heaven and the human being is on earth and therefore they can hardly converse . . . only in much fear and trembling is a human being able to speak with God, in much fear and trembling" (WA, 11). And so, just as to see God is to die: to speak is to tremble before God. In which case—is not prayer a fearful and self-annihilating task? Who could venture the prayer that might alleviate this dreadful spiritual trial? "[J]ust as anxiety makes the voice fail physically, so also much fear and trembling make speech fall into silence" (WA, 11). So, in the end, is prayer also defeated by the chasmic distance, the infinite sublimity, of the One to whom it would speak?

Or in the act of becoming nothing before God (resignation), toward which spiritual trial ultimately directs the self, does silence actually signify the humble form that prayer must initially take? For Kierkegaard, "just as the fear of God is the beginning of wisdom [Proverbs 9:10], so silence is the beginning of the fear of God" (WA, 11). And so in praying one falls silent because there is nothing that one can say—a freely chosen silence of self-abnegation that is qualitatively different from the imposed silence of despair.[76] Instead, one listens and learns that, far from being irremediably and oppressively infinitely sublime, God is "*completely different from anything I am able to comprehend of what he says himself to be.*" And this silence of faith's prayer is a silence of unknowing in which the self esteems its capacities as nothing before God; the prayer of silence which, by renouncing the despair of human impossibility, marks the beginning of faith in divine *possibility.*

From the perspective of human impossibility, it remains continually tempting to speak to God in despair over salvation, as if one understood sin's chasmic difference—and consequently God's holiness—better even than God in heaven. But this despair once again asserts a chasmic distance between self and God. As Anti-Climacus puts it in *The Sickness unto Death*:

When the sinner despairs of the forgiveness of sins, it is almost as if he walked right up to God and said, "No, there is no forgiveness of sins, it is impossible," and it looks like close combat. Yet to be able to do this and for it to be heard, a person must become qualitatively distanced from God, and in order to fight *cominus* [in close combat] he must be *eminus* [at a distance] . . . In order that the "No," which in a way wants to grapple with God, can be heard, a person must get as far away from God as possible. The most offensive forwardness is at the greatest distance. (SUD, 114)

If this offensive and combative speech is contrasted with the surrendering intimacy of prayer, it is discovered that, unlike the despair which wants to grapple with God but only does so by becoming qualitatively distanced, prayer is actually a silent waiting upon God: an unknowing expression of self-surrender through faith. "And so it is; to pray is not to listen to oneself speak but is to become silent and to remain silent, to wait until the one praying hears God" ("Look at the Birds of the Air; Look at the Lily in the Field," WA, 12).

Prayer signifies an act of silence: an act which breaks the silence of despair in the face of human impossibility; and at the same time also a silence which listens to God at the moment when despair would pronounce its offence. The silence of prayer for Kierkegaard fulfils what Henri de Lubac looks for in "a purer submission." It does not struggle at a distance with God in its despairing defiance, but rather it transcends, as it were, the infinite distance by its submission to faith:

> prayer is the weapon not of one who attacks another or of one who defends himself but of one who yields . . . when there is no praying, God is in heaven and man is on earth, and consequently the distance is too great; but when there is praying, they are indeed too close to each other, then there is no inbetween that can be marked out as the battleground. ("One Who Prays Aright Struggles in Prayer and is Victorious—in that God is Victorious," EUD, 383)[77]

Prayer is thus the leap of faith into the silence of unknowing: the self-surrendering intimacy that overcomes the infinite abyss of offence that has served as the battlefield between God and humanity. "[T]ogether with God before God" (JP 4:4377 / Pap. X^2 A 590), prayer realizes the human-divine struggle which is the cessation of all struggles against God. "How numerous the struggles are, how varied the struggle in which the one who prays tries himself *with* God (since someone who tries himself *against* God does not struggle in prayer)" (EUD, 387). Prayer is thus the struggle of faith in which the abyss (Dn. *Afgrund*) of despair is overcome by the Holy ground (*grund*) on which one becomes a self, in self-surrender and silence, intimately *before God*. It is thus by the self-surrender of human impossibility's despair that one discovers the ground of *divine possibility* in which one may receive the gift of the self before God. It is to a concluding explication of the Kierkegaardian transition from despair—through self-surrender—to the self before God that the penultimate chapter now turns.

So the struggle goes; the struggler contends with God in prayer, or he struggles
with himself and in his prayer calls on God for help against himself.
—*Eighteen Upbuilding Discourses*

SEVEN

The Gaze of the Abyss

The previous chapter concluded with the notion that the self-surrender of spiritual trial—as expressed by the silent prayer of faith in divine possibility—opens the wounded self to the possibility of becoming itself before God: a relation that, as this chapter will elaborate, transcends and transfigures the infinite qualitative difference to the point of proposing a heterogeneous "resemblance" between the struggling self and the Holy Other. However, in this chapter, consideration will also be given to how this transition is traumatized by freedom's inviolable possibility of "offence" toward the forgiveness of sins: this is the ultimate expression of human freedom, which constitutes the grief of God as well as the despair of the self.

"TO SEE GOD IS TO DIE": THE OPTICAL MOTIF

one must never avoid questions, as one must not turn one's gaze away
from the abyss.
    —ELIE WIESEL, *Four Hasidic Masters and Their Struggle against Melancholy*

On 30 July 1849, Kierkegaard published his most explicit work on the self before God, *The Sickness unto Death,* under the exalted pseudonym Anti-Climacus. In parallel to this important volume, Kierkegaard published "Three Discourses at the Communion on Fridays" (14 November 1849) under his own name.[1] The three discourses contained therein are comprised of "The High Priest," on Hebrews 4:15 (which was considered in the previous chapter in relation to God-forsakenness); "The Tax Collector," on Luke 18:13; and "The Woman Who Was a Sinner," on Luke 7:37ff. The latter two are both considered in this chapter in relation to repentance before God. But all three discourses reprise many of the central themes of *The Sickness unto Death* from a more explicitly pastoral perspective: the consciousness of sin, forgiveness, and the individual before God. As preparation for the act of communion, these three discourses engage with the dilemma of the individual's sense of unworthiness, as sinner, to enter into intimate presence with God (i.e., forgiveness)—a dilemma that is given more formalized expression in *The Sickness unto Death*'s consideration of the centrality of sin (despair) and forgiveness to the self's endeavor to become itself before God. Contained within Kierkegaard's discourse on "The Tax Collector," in particular, is the impression of *distance* between the individual and God that is postulated by the consciousness of sin—a distance that *The Sickness unto Death* expresses by way of Kierkegaard's category of the "infinite qualitative difference."

As the previous chapter concluded, however, the distance between the self and God is one which can be transcended by the intimacy derived by the self-surrender of prayer. And yet, as Kierkegaard's discourse on "The Tax Collector" elucidates, the attitude of prayer is itself determined by a dreadful and humble recognition of the distance between the one who prays and the Holy One. In prayer, one stands "before God"—but also at a distance, as Kierkegaard expounds in this discourse on Luke 18:13: "And the tax collector stood far off and would not even lift up his eyes to heaven, but beat his breast and said: God, be merciful to me, a sinner!" "The tax collector *stood far off*," Kierkegaard emphasizes. But this gesture enunciates an apparently paradoxical element to the attitude of prayer. "What does that mean? It means to stand by yourself, alone with yourself before God—then you are far off, far away from people, and far away from God, with whom you are still alone" ("The Tax Collector," WA, 128).[2]

And yet, as remarked at the end of the last chapter, has Kierkegaard not declared in an upbuilding discourse on prayer that there is no distance between prayer and God (EUD, 383)? The tax collector is alone before God and still, Kierkegaard concedes, a distance exists between them: a distance between the self and the Holy that is postulated by the consciousness of sin. "What is further away from guilt and sin than God's holiness—and then, oneself a sinner, to be alone with this holiness: is this not being infinitely far off!" ("The Tax Collector," WA, 129). According to this discourse on "The Tax Collector," the thought of God's holiness coming into agonizing contrast with the consciousness of sin postulates an infinite distance between the sinner and the Holy One. In visual terms, the gaze of the sinner becomes lost in this infinite distance between the Holy and the unholy, as if, analogously, the sinner were gazing into the darkness of the abyss. The amorphous gloom of the abyss is seen by the gaze; but it is essentially an *excess of nothingness* for it. There is nothing on which the eye can rest, and so the gaze is unable to ground itself in the abyss, in which it encounters the vertigo of the infinite.

In this distance, the consciousness of sin asserts, not the hidden Face of God, but the dizzily averted gaze of the sinner:

And he would not even lift up his eyes to heaven; that is, he cast his eyes down. Well, no wonder! Even physically there is something in the infinite that overwhelms a person since there is nothing on which he can fix his eyes [recalling the sublime]. This effect is called dizziness; then one must shut one's eyes. And the one who, alone with his guilt and his sin, knows that if he opens his eyes he will see God's holiness [*Hellighed*] and nothing else, that one surely learns to cast his eyes down; or he perhaps looked up and saw God's holiness—and cast his eyes down. He looked down, saw his wretchedness; and more heavily than sleep weighs on the eyelids of the exhausted, more heavily than the sleep of death, the conception of God's holiness weighed his eyes down; like one exhausted, indeed, like one dying, he was unable to lift up his eyes. ("The Tax Collector," WA, 130)

Alone with his guilt and sin, the abyssal distance between the sinner and the Holy seems to bespeak such an incommensurability that the gaze must contend only with this prospect: to see God is to die. Once again, this *mysterium tremendum,* this visual expression of the sublime burden of holiness, forcing itself upon the eyes of the sinner, is arrayed in all its fearfulness in Kierkegaard's parallel discourse on "The Woman Who Was a Sinner." The infinite induces dizziness, but here the disclosure of holiness threatens to annihilate the sinner through illumination:

For example, when one is a sinner, man or woman, to come near to the Holy One [*den Hellige*], to become disclosed before him, that is, in the light of holiness. Ah, the night does not flee more terror-stricken before the day, which wants to annihilate it, and if there are ghosts, an apparition is not more anxiously startled when day is dawning than the sinner who shrinks from the holiness that, like the day, discloses everything. ("The Woman Who Was a Sinner," WA, 137)

However, through the course of this beautiful allegory, Kierkegaard relates how the woman who was a sinner became able, through her loving contrition, to anoint the feet of the Holy One with her tears: "her many sins are forgiven her, because she loved much" (Luke 7:47). By the same sentiment, Kierkegaard also describes how the humility of "The Tax Collector"—the humble gaze that dares not look upon holiness—is, ironically, the gaze that is enabled to behold the Holy One. "He cast his eyes down, but the downcast gaze *sees*

God, and the downcast gaze is the *uplifting* of the heart" ("The Tax Collector," WA, 132). Analogous to the notion that the prayer of faith is one of silence, so the gaze of faith is one with eyes closed—a gaze which, as Kierkegaard describes it, "humanly speaking, is blind," in contrast to the presumptuous clear-sightedness of reason (WA, 132). In this discourse, Kierkegaard illustrates this contrast by explaining that it is not the tax collector but the presumptuous Pharisee (who like Moses presumes to look upon God) who is in the end not permitted to see God. Contrary to his pious expectations, it is the Pharisee and not the tax collector who, owing to his presumption against the infinite difference between sin and divinity, finds that his gaze is occluded by the forbidding nemesis of holiness: "the Pharisee, who began by proudly lifting up his eyes to heaven, him God opposes, and God's opposition is an annihilating pressing down" (WA, 132). As such, it is by humility that prayer acknowledges and expresses the infinite qualitative difference between self and God (it does so even by virtue of approaching God in the downcast and silent attitude of prayer, and not face-to-face as one speaks to the other). And yet the irony of the self's humble relation "before God" is that by standing far off, by casting one's gaze downward, one is actually enabled to stand before God with an uplifted head. Face-to-face, as one speaks to a friend (Exodus 33:11), one is able to behold the face of the One "whom none may see and live."

Figuratively speaking, therefore, it could be claimed that it is in response to the downcast gaze that the Holy One refrains from annihilating the one who is unholy, or infinitely different. The moment of death for the gaze is thus the point at which the Holy appears so infinitely incommensurable to the sinful self that it cannot accept the possibility of beholding the Face of God (forgiveness). This moment of death recalls Kierkegaard's essential "SUBDIVISIO," with which this work began: "If the DIVISIO [namely the infinite, radical, qualitative difference] is everything, then God is so infinitely sublime [*uendelig ophøiet*] that there is no intrinsic or actual relationship between God and the individual human being" (JP 2:1383 / Pap. X¹ A 59). By virtue of its fixation upon the infinite sublimity of the divine and the infinite sinfulness of its own self, the gaze becomes engulfed and overwhelmed by the infinite qualitative abyss that it beholds. Even the angels cover their eyes before the sublimity of God (Isaiah 6); again, no one can see God and live. This dictum is a difficult one to forget, and thus signifies the divine vanishing point for the *mysterium tremendum et fascinans* and the infinite qualitative difference. As such, can no eye, without averting or covering its gaze, ever truly come to behold the Holy One face-to-face?

Reviewing the present work up to this point, it becomes apparent that, from the beginning, an intrinsic optical motif has arisen as the principal means for expressing the struggle of the self before God. Despite Kierkegaard's above notion that the downcast gaze is enabled to behold God, the visual motif has constituted, for the most part, an overwhelmingly negative expression of the prospect of existing before God. Struggling with the nocturnal shapes of anxiety, melancholy, despair, and spiritual trial, it is tempting to derive the impression that the gaze of God is such that, in Luther's words, "there is no corner or hole in the whole of creation into which a man might creep, not even in hell, but he must let himself be exposed to the gaze of the whole creation." Once again—"to see God is to die"; or else, according to Nietzsche's inversion: "The god who saw everything, *even man*—this god had to die!" This is, in optical terms, the either/or of the self's struggle for recognition. Reprising such motifs, it is clear that such visualizations tend to evoke only the maddening horror of the *mysterium horrendum*. "That a sparrow can live is comprehensible," as Anti-Climacus himself acknowledges; "it does not know that it exists before God. But to know that one exists before God, and then not instantly go mad or sink into nothingness!" (SUD, 32).

And yet, as well as capturing the abyssal anxiety of the endeavor to stand before the Wholly Other, the notion of the optical emerges as the motif that aptly expresses the dialectic of the self becoming itself before God through the consciousness of sin and forgiveness. According to what Kierkegaard calls "the *autopsy* of faith" (from Gr. *autopsia:* "a seeing with one's own eyes"), one can only truly come to know oneself before "the mirror of the Word. . . . To stand before the mirror means to stand before God" (JP 4:3902 / Pap. X⁴ A 412). It is only *post mortem* that an autopsy can be performed, and so it is that one must die to oneself—die to one's own "reflection"—in order to perform the autopsy of faith. "It is well known that men are afraid to see themselves physically, that superstition thought that to see oneself was an omen of death," Kierkegaard explains in his *Journals*. "And so it is spiritually: to see yourself is to die, to die to all illusions and all hypocrisy—it takes great courage to dare look at yourself—something which can only take place in the mirror of the Word" (JP 4:3902 / Pap. X⁴ A 412).

Despite the preliminary dread at the prospect for which "to see God is to die," Kierkegaard ultimately evokes a vision of death to self, a death to sin and impossibility, by which the self is given the possibility of becoming truly itself, of standing before the gaze of God without being reduced to the madness or nothingness of despair. In this vision of the self before God, there is a *gaze of faith* that sees God without suffering annihilation—and its enigma resides in a humble *unwillingness to gaze* presumptuously upon God's holiness. The irony of the tax collector is that by casting his eyes down, he sees God; by "standing far off" he stands *before God*. The irony of faith's humility is that the downcast gaze (the consciousness of sin) is lifted up (the divine possibility of forgiveness) to behold God. But still, one might finally question whether this Kierkegaardian vision of the self before God can be described as anything other than a continual guarding-against the annihilation and despair that constitute a persistent threat to the self's existence. How, in other words, can the self direct its gaze, without despair, *into* and finally *beyond* the abyss?

"Faith is," according to Anti-Climacus, "that the self in being itself and in willing to be itself rests transparently in God" (SUD, 82). Here is the optical crux of the matter. Faith is related to clear-sightedness: the transparency that is aptly described by C. Stephen Evans as being "willing to stand before God and open myself to his gaze."[3] But will opening oneself to the gaze of God not induce some form of madness or annihilation, as Anti-Climacus describes in the extreme terms of the "fantasized religious person" (SUD, 32)? As will be explored through the remainder of this chapter, the resolution of this dilemma depends upon how the self is willing to perceive the abyss. The possibility of becoming a self before God is ascertained in relation to the twin aspects of the infinite qualitative abyss. First, it is a question of how the self perceives its own *sinfulness*—the consciousness of sin, despair over sin, and sense of the infinite chasmic abyss. But second, the possibility of the self before God is determined by how the self sees itself in relation to the *forgiveness* of sins—the reparation of the infinite chasmic abyss. In optical terms, it is the perspective with which the abyss is gazed upon that is decisive for the possibility of how the self stands before God. In other words, the infinite qualitative difference is sin, and sin is despair; so one might say that despair is the gaze of the abyss, or the gaze into the abyss—for, according to Vigilius Haufniensis's much noted observation, it is as much in the eye as in the abyss (CA, 61). As will be examined below, the nature of the self's despair before God can, therefore, be read in terms of how the self gazes into, and is in turn penetrated by, the infinite qualitative abyss of sin and forgiveness.

"BEFORE GOD": OPTICAL ILLUSIONS

As the above reference to Anti-Climacus's "fantasized religious person" testifies, once the prospect of beholding or being beheld by God is being considered, then the question of the role of imagination (Dn. *Fantasi*) for selfhood is destined to reemerge. However, while imagination has in such an instance become *fantastic,* imagination itself retains a critical existential role in subjectivity's devotion to a life-transforming relation—though it is not without the dangerous extremities of scrupulosity or madness. Kierkegaard's *Journals* illustrate this through an enchanting parable on the eye of imagination. This entry from 1844 tells of a man who, spying a drowning animal through his field glasses, wades decisively into the water to its rescue. Upon discovering that he has rescued something "no bigger than a lady bug" he is subjected to the derision of the onlooking crowd and subsequently arrested for his behavior. "The error," Kierkegaard explains, "does not lie in their [the crowd's] not being able to understand his compassion (there is no question of this at all) but in their inability to perceive that a trifling little thing, through the power of a man's imagination etc., can come to occupy him *absolutely*" (JP 2:1827 / Pap. V A 24).

The lesson of an "absolute relation" is clear (though living "before God" is hardly such a "trifling little thing"): one's devotion to that which is seemingly absurd will predictably elicit the derision of the crowd. As acknowledged previously, Kierkegaard's decisive existential category "before God" inevitably evokes the Lutheran notion of existing *coram Deo* (as distinct from *coram hominibus:* "before humanity"). In relation to Kierkegaard's parable on the eye of the imagination, the individual may be incomprehensible *coram hominibus*, before the crowd; but he is understood before God better even than he can understand himself (and as for Luther, the unbeliever is righteous *coram hominibus* whereas the believer is righteous *coram Deo*).[4]

For Luther, the meaning of the Latin *coram Deo* followed the sense of the Greek *prosopon* and, more importantly, also the Hebrew *panîm*, in denoting both before the "face" of God, and also in the "presence" of God. Kierkegaard's Danish word *for* ("before"), as Eller notes, "can mean 'for the sake of' as well as 'in the sight of,' and undoubtedly both meanings were part of S.K.'s intention."[5] When it comes to standing before God—or as Anti-Climacus formulates it, "*with the conception of God*" (*Forestillingen om Gud*) (SUD, 77)—M. Jamie Ferreira moreover suggests that "the Danish word *Forestilling* resonates with nuances of imaginative activity."[6] While the English word "conception" generally has "connotations of abstraction associated with the notions of thought or idea or concept," Ferreira maintains that the Danish word *Forestilling* "calls to mind a very concrete apprehension, and the imaginative engagement appropriate to a performance or introduction."[7]

But Ferreira is not claiming that imagination functions "freely," via Romanticism's valorization of productive imagination and reverie. Rather, "in my *Forestilling* of God, I am thereby placed before God; in a presentation of God, I am confronted by God."[8] This sense of performance, introduction, or presentation is also implicit in Kierkegaard's analogy of the actor in a theater for whom God is "the critical spectator": "he is, if I may put it this way, the actor, who in the true sense is acting before God" ("On the Occasion of a Confession," UDVS, 125). In the act of confession which commits the self to transparency before God, one is no longer to be concerned with "the crowd" as spectator of the absolute relation. Moreover, as George Pattison points out:

this is not so much a matter of direct experience (as if we might, one day, *feel* the eyes of God boring through us), but of a critical self-relation in which we actively adopt and take upon ourselves a certain understanding of life, a matter of actively and deliberately sustaining a certain kind of awareness, of learning to take note of how our thoughts might be bearing witness against us.[9]

It is, crucially, the subject's free choice to see itself in this way.[10]

And further, Pattison elsewhere suggests that the Kierkegaardian concept of "before God" might be read as a Kantian "regulative concept" (a concept that does not constitute the possibility of its object for theoretical reason but indicates a condition for *how* practical reason should guide life), rather than a constitutive or experientialist foundation upon which metaphysical and ontological claims can be established.[11] The implication for such a reading would be that "although believers are to understand their lives 'as if' lived 'before God' they are not obliged to make any claims as to the actual existence or non-existence of God."[12] From this perspective, the phrase "before God" signifies an anthropocentric attitude of faith that nevertheless lacks theoretical "proof" of its *telos*.

However, while this may be amenable to a post-ontotheological attitude, this potentially non-realist reading of "the self before God" raises questions about the objective reality of a God who is known as Wholly Other. What would this mean for the infinite qualitative difference and the reality of sin and forgiveness by a Holy Other on which the present work insists? Is the notion "before God" here vulnerable to the claim that "God is not something external. Hence, to stand alone before the face of God is not to stand before something external"?[13] Jerome I. Gellman supports this particular claim by reference to Anti-Climacus's assertion in *The Sickness unto Death*: "God is not some externality in the sense that a policeman is" (SUD, 80). However, Gellman draws insufficient attention to Anti-Climacus's contextual discussion of the consciousness of sin: "The error [of older dogmatics] consisted in considering God as some externality and in seeming to assume that only occasionally did one sin against God. But God is not some externality in the sense that a policeman is" (SUD, 80). In other words, God should not be conceived as the judicial externality that one can elude or avoid, nor as the omnipresent voyeur who sees the sinner from his heavenly window. "With his glance," Kierkegaard explains in *Works of Love*, God "guides the whole world and educates these countless human beings. For what is conscience? In the conscience it is God who looks upon a human being so that the human being now must look to him in all things" (WL, 346). Conscience is thus comparable to the gaze which *reciprocates,* which does not capture the self in the voyeurism of the subject/object split. "Conscience" is therefore not a scrupulous tendency to anguish of mind and morbid obsession with intro-spection. Rather, conscience means a relational "with-knowing" (from the Lat. *con-scientia*)—in this instance, it is knowing-in-relation to God. God is in our hearts, one might say, and therefore "every sin is before God, or, more correctly, what really makes human guilt into sin is that the guilty one has the consciousness of existing before God" (SUD, 80)—and again, this "before" does not connote externality. But the glance of God does not forbid the gaze of the sinner; instead the gaze of God actually encourages the human being to look to God in reciprocity. The conscience is thereby grounded in the gaze of God which asks the individual to look back to God: to meet the eyes of God, as it were, without self-annihilation or the madness of self-accusation, in the ethical responsibility of becoming a self before God. Hence one may, follow-ing the example of the tax collector, "stand far off" with downcast gaze—beholding the infinite difference in humility—and yet still stand *before God*.

"BEFORE GOD": THE GAZE OF DESPAIR

Alas, it is terrible to see a person rushing headlong to his own downfall; it is terrible to see him dancing on the edge of the abyss without suspecting it; but this clarity about himself and his own downfall is even more terrible.
—*Upbuilding Discourses in Various Spirits*

While the notion of freedom resides at the heart of existing "before God," it is a freedom that discovers itself in "looking to God in all things." As this work has explored, there are discernible differentiations in Kierkegaard's writ-ings between what could be called authentic and inauthentic "conceptions" (Dn. *Forestellingen*) of God—the numinous Wholly Other, and the manner in which the "infinite qualitative difference" between humanity and God is perceived are decisive in this differentiation. In addition to the deluded intox-ication of "the fantasized religious person," which has been much observed up to this point, Anti-Climacus also remarks on what he deems to be "poet-existence": an existence that is guilty of "the sin of poeticizing instead of being, of relating to the good and the true through the imagination instead of being that—that is existentially striving to be that" (SUD, 77).[14] Such a per-son is characterized by the tendency "to poeticize God as somewhat different from what God is, a bit more like the fond father who indulges his child's every wish far too much" (SUD, 78).

Nevertheless, some conception of God is present for poet-existence, albeit one that fails to fully grasp the pathos of the infinite qualitative difference. As such, the poeticized self is also in some measure "before God." Onto-logically speaking, every creature exists as wholly visible to the gaze of God;

but "becoming a self before God" involves an existential decision regarding how God is conceived or, more aptly, *how God is received*. For the self to truly become the self it is destined to become in all its fullness, God is not to be imagined as merely the indulgent father, or the occasionally externalized policeman, since, as Anti-Climacus affirms in *The Sickness unto Death,* "the greater the conception of God, the more self there is; the more self, the greater conception of God" (SUD, 80). Authentic selfhood is therefore only realizable in proportion to the greatness of the conception of God to which the self is willing to open itself. As such, the self before God is qualitatively contrasted with what Luther would identify as the individual *coram hominibus,* and what Anti-Climacus analogously calls "the human self, or the self whose criterion is man" (SUD, 79). According to Anti-Climacus's formulation, any self comes to know itself in relation to that which it stands *before:* "A cattleman who (if this were possible) is a self directly before his cattle is a very low self, and, similarly, a master who is a self directly before his slaves is actually no self—for in both cases a criterion is lacking" (SUD, 79).

This latter illustration clearly touches on Hegel's dialectic of *Herrschaft und Knechtschaft* (Lordship and Bondage) and its depiction of the mutual struggle for self-recognition.[15] It also points toward Anti-Climacus's anatomization of atheistic self-mastery: "In Despair to will to Be Oneself: Defiance." However, in Anti-Climacus's examination of this form of despair, it is not so much in relation to the other that the self struggles to become itself; instead it is decisively over *itself* that it wishes to become the master. In the despair to will to be oneself, the self defiantly wills to be "the infinite self":

> the most abstract form, the most abstract possibility of the self . . . severing the self from any relation to a power that has established it, or severing it from the idea that there is such an idea. With the help of this infinite form, the self in despair wants to be master of itself or to create itself . . . in order to fashion out of it a self such as he wants, produced with the help of the infinite form of the negative self—and in this way he wills to be himself. (SUD, 68)

While the terminology recalls Hegel, such a willfully Promethean self is not only formulated in defiance of an establishing power such as God,[16] but also in defiance of any equal relation to the human other by which it may be defined. This self wills to become itself *ex nihilo:* starting "not at and with the beginning, but 'in the beginning'" (SUD, 68). This self, "satisfied with paying attention to itself" (SUD, 69), forsakes the gazes of the human and divine others in deference to a reflected introversion of narcissistic self-regard. This self seeks to transmute itself into a higher form of itself through the creative act of self-reflection. As such, this formulation of despair can be read as an anatomization of the decomposition of the modern self and its ill-fated struggle for self-creating self-authentication:

> The self is its own master, absolutely its own master; and precisely this is the despair, but also what it regards as its pleasure and its delight. On closer examination, however, it is easy to see that this absolute ruler is a king without a country, actually ruling over nothing; his position, his sovereignty, is subordinate to the dialectic that rebellion is legitimate at any moment. (SUD, 69)

This diagnosis of self-consciousness determined through the mastery of the self by the infinite self could again sound rather Hegelian—except that in the severance of this self from the other, the relational dialectic is actually internalized. In an upbuilding discourse, Kierkegaard specifies that "despair" (*Fortvivlelse*) may actually signify "double-mindedness" (*Tvesindethed*) since "everyone in despair has two wills, one that he futilely wants to follow entirely, and one that he futilely wants to get rid of entirely" (UDVS, 30). Echoing this notion of internal schism, Anti-Climacus diagnoses how, in the realization that the master is "a king without a country," it becomes inevitable that the slave—the self that the infinite self believes it has mastered—will reappear in the failure of the self to actualize the self that it imagines. In the failure to create itself *for itself,* the finite self ("a self acted upon") inevitably undermines the ambition and sovereignty of the infinite self ("the acting self")—an unsustainable sovereignty which is "subordinate to the dialectic that rebellion is legitimate at any moment." The self, willing in despair to be itself, transpires as an impenetrable and ungovernable abyss—a "self" as boundless and unfathomable as the ocean.

> Consequently, the self in despair is always building only castles in the air, is only shadowboxing . . . in the final analysis, what it understands by itself is a riddle; in the very moment when it seems that the self is closest to having the building completed, it can arbitrarily dissolve the whole thing into nothing. (SUD, 69–70)

This self-examination, which fails to fathom what Kant appropriately identifies as "the scarcely penetrable abysses of the human heart,"[17] is built upon what transpires as an optical illusion of self-mastery. It cannot reconcile itself as its own master since it is essentially master over nothingness—an abyss. And so it is in the failure of self-mastery that this irresolvable abyss of inner despair itself becomes the master. The despairing "person is freely in the power of an alien force, is freely or in freedom slaving under it, or he is freely-unfreely in his own power," as Kierkegaard sketches in the final draft of *The*

Sickness unto Death. "If one calls the alien force the master, then the person in despair is free in self-inflicted slavery for this master . . . he consequently slaves for himself, is his own slave" (Pap. VIII² B 170:6). The internalized dialectic of master (acting self) and slave (acted-upon self) has created a self that is estranged from itself—and from its own freedom—through its defiant but futile efforts at self-authentication. This dialectic is actually further redolent of Hegel's diagnosis of the Unhappy Consciousness: "the duplication which formerly was divided between two individuals, the lord and the bondsman, is now lodged in one . . . the *Unhappy Consciousness* is the consciousness of self as a dual-natured, merely contradictory being."[18]

Such alienated "unhappiness" is derived from the self's undermining of itself—or, more specifically, the inversion of the mastery of the infinite creating self over the finite created self. The acting self thus becomes the acted-upon self, as Anti-Climacus observes; and this inversion can be traced psychologically to an inherent defect within the self:

Perhaps such an imaginatively constructing self, which in despair wills to be itself, encounters some difficulty or other while provisionally orienting itself to its concrete self, something the Christian would call a cross, a basic defect, whatever it may be. The negative self, the infinite form of the self, will perhaps reject this completely, pretend that it does not exist, will have nothing to do with it. But it does not succeed; its proficiency in imaginary constructing does not stretch that far, and not even its proficiency in abstracting does. In a Promethean way, the infinite, negative self feels itself nailed to this servitude. Consequently, it is a self acted upon. (SUD, 70)

And so the infinite creating self is internally undermined by a fatal flaw from which it is unable to abstract itself. It becomes no longer the master but the slave to this flaw—a flaw which itself comes to signify the inability of the self to create itself. It is this flaw which undermines the narcissistic effort to fashion, or transmute, the self into whatever the infinite self imagines it to be. "What, then, are the manifestations of this despair that is: in despair to will to be oneself?" (SUD, 70).

Such a despairing person, transfixed by this defect, is ultimately "unwilling to hope in the possibility that an earthly need, a temporal cross, can come to an end":

He has convinced himself that this thorn in the flesh gnaws so deeply that he cannot abstract himself from it (whether this is actually the case or his passion makes it so to him), and therefore he might as well accept it forever, so to speak. He is offended by it, or, more correctly, he takes it as an occasion to be offended at all existence . . . in spite of or in defiance of all existence, he wills to be himself with it, takes it along, almost flouting his agony. Hope in the possibility of help, especially by virtue of the absurd, that for God everything is possible—no, that he does not want. . . . Rather than to seek help, he prefers, if necessary, to be himself with all the agonies of hell. (SUD, 70–71)

And so it is that a thorn in the flesh may be taken as the occasion for a further, more conscious form of defiance: *offence*. Rather than accept divine help, he is so enmeshed in his despair to will to be oneself, so mesmerized by the morbid narcissism of his gazing into this thorn in the flesh,[19] that he cannot endure the "giving up being himself" involved in submitting to "the 'Helper' for whom all things are possible" (SUD, 71). As such, he now feels that he is only authentically himself insofar as he is fixated upon his defect. It is this thorn in the flesh that has become the secret transforming principle of his narcissistic self-transmutation; this defect, which refused to conform the concrete self to the creative vision of the infinite self, now becomes the melancholy object of his infinite passion. It is by this cross alone that he now wills to be himself. It becomes, as it were, the mark of his authenticity and he has become "demonic" in his devotion to it.

> So now he makes precisely this torment the object of all his passion, and finally it becomes a demonic rage. By now, even if God in heaven and all the angels offered to help him out of it—no, he does not want that, now it is too late . . . now he would rather rage against everything and be the wronged victim of the whole world and of all life. . . . This eventually becomes such a fixation that for an extremely strange reason he is afraid of eternity,[20] afraid that it will separate him from his, demonically understood, infinite superiority over other men, his justification, demonically understood, for being what he is.—Himself is what he wills to be. He began with the infinite abstraction of the self, and now he has finally become so concrete that it would be impossible to become eternal in that sense; nevertheless, he wills in despair to be himself. (SUD, 72)

It would not be exact to say that this self is seeking to become a self before God, in the true sense of the term; but neither can it be said that this self ignores the power that has established it. In willing to be itself, this self has closed itself off from the other; in this sense it has demonically closed itself off from the possibility of salvation. But the flaw, by which he becomes what he wills, is also demonically directed against the possibility of God. And so he wages war on God with a demonic enmity that surpasses mere defiance.

not even in defiance does it want to tear itself loose from the power that established it, but for spite wants to force itself upon it, to obtrude defiantly upon it, wants to adhere to it out of malice. . . . Rebelling against all existence, it feels that it has obtained evidence against it, against its goodness. The person in despair believes that he himself is the evidence, and that is what he wants to be, and therefore he wants to be himself, himself in his torment, in order to protest against all existence with this torment. (SUD, 73–74)

Like Prometheus chained to his rock at the edge of the world, raging against Zeus from the periphery of existence, this self attaches itself defiantly to the injustice of his bonds. He gnaws at his chains and bears them heavily.[21] According to Greek myth, the griffon daily devours the liver of Prometheus, only for him to endure the agony of its nightly re-growth and re-consumption. The tenacious life of his sickness is endlessly unto death; his melancholy—which appropriately, according to classical physiology, is secreted from the liver as black bile—is eternally devoured and then renewed. The insurrection of the self in-despair-willing-to-be-itself derives its demonic vitality from taking itself to be an icon for the injustice of the Creator. "Figuratively speaking," Anti-Climacus describes this as analogous to an error that has slipped into an author's writing and

became conscious of itself as an error . . . and now this error wants to mutiny against the author, out of hatred toward him, forbidding him to correct it and in maniacal defiance saying to him: No, I refuse to be erased; I will stand as a witness against you, a witness that you are a second-rate author. (SUD, 74)

Anti-Climacus later aptly observes that the demonic self is similar to the alcoholic "who keeps himself in a perpetual state of intoxication out of fear of stopping" (SUD, 108). In his intoxicated rage he is able to maintain himself by an "internal consistency" (SUD, 108): a solidifying of the self through the demonic coherence of identity. As such, he may believe that there is authenticity in his refusal to let his flaw "be erased" and in his defiant rejection of salvation. It is here that he believes that he has found a way to become himself. "Only in the continuance of sin is he himself, only in that does he live and have an impression of himself" (SUD, 108).

However, Anti-Climacus suggests that through witnessing the decomposition of the self through its inherent defect, and through his demonic acknowledgment of sin, this defiant self may be seen to have actually taken a step toward the eternal in order to become itself. But the problem that prevents him from accepting the help of the eternal is the fact that, in this willing despair, he has actually closed himself off to the other—"severing the self from any relation to a power that has established it, or severing it from the idea that there is such an idea" (SUD, 68)—or else he relates to it only through the negativity of demonic insurrection. But this demonic rage is also a malignant severance from repentance, for repentance would mean that the self has contradicted itself, has literally turned away from itself and from its bondage to the Promethean rock of torment. "Sin itself is severance from the good," as Anti-Climacus warns, "but despair over sin is the second severance" (SUD, 109).

THE SECOND SEVERANCE: *Abyssus Abyssum Invocat*

And the abyss calls for another abyss.
    —ELIE WIESEL, *Four Hasidic Masters and Their Struggle Against Melancholy*

If sin forms the infinite chasmic abyss that separates the self from God, then despair over sin is, venturing a potentially mystifying image, a second and even more fatal abyss. Yet, whereas the consciousness of sin is revealed by God, this second fracture is a supplementary abyss that the self has willed of itself by despairing over this revelation. It is a second, obscuring abyss that is born from *despairing* over the revealed abyss of sin. Hence, this abyss forms a dreadful obstacle on the path to self-knowledge which the consciousness of sin has initiated, since it is an abyss—an impasse on the way to self-knowledge— that is willed by the self for itself. Sin, according to Anti-Climacus, "may be termed the break with the good"; *despair over sin* is the break "with repentance" (SUD, 109). As such, the pattern of demonic self-willing is as follows:

> despair over one's sin indicates that sin has become or wants to be internally consistent. It wants nothing to do with the good . . . it closes itself up within itself, indeed, locks itself inside one more inclosure, and protects itself against every attack or pursuit of the good by despairing over sin. It is aware of having burned the bridge behind it and of thereby being inaccessible to the good and of the good being inaccessible to it, so that if in a weak moment it should itself will the good, that would still be impossible. (SUD, 109)

Here the self imprisons itself in an abyss of its own willing: a prison constructed from the belief that forgiveness and reconciliation with the divine— the next stage on the way to self-knowledge—are *impossible*. Impossibility is therefore a self-willed, second severance from the infinite abyss of the consciousness of sin. This intensified second severance "squeezes the uttermost demonic powers out of sin" by fortifying itself against forgiveness, by considering all "repentance and grace not only as empty and meaningless but also as its enemy, as something against which a defense must be made most of all" (SUD, 109). And so, burning the bridge across the abyss behind it, it bids farewell to penitence and—like the melancholy figure of the Wandering Jew—throws itself into a hopeless but tenacious exile.

"Nevertheless," Anti-Climacus asserts, "despair over sin is conscious particularly of its own emptiness, that it has nothing on which to live, not even an idea of its own self" (SUD, 110). Hence it must maintain itself, like the decadent, through continual intoxication. The despair over one's sin, in its demonic vitality, can thus be considered a form of the state of being: "in despair to will to be oneself." But this is a self which, in its desire to be internally consistent, loses all relation to the *possibility* of grace and therefore to its true self as known before God (SUD, 110). Such despair, Anti-Climacus acknowledges, may resemble a melancholy brooding over sin. It may even suggest the melancholy sensitivity toward sin, that "deep nature" of the *homo religiosus* who, with scrupulous self-indictment, despairs that "I will never forgive myself" (SUD, 111). Such self-condemnation may apparently conceal a troubled soul that is captured in the melancholy narrowness (Dn. *trængsel*) of the consciousness of sin, but it belies an implicit hubris toward one's very guilt: a confidence in the omniscient potency of self-indictment and consequently of self-forgiveness. This is a deceptively hubristic piety by which "the wrath within you wanted, as it were, to come to the aid of divine wrath so that the punishment might consume you" (EUD, 47). This presumptuous melancholy may betray an implicit form of self-denunciation which is in reality a grasp at mastery over oneself.

In a portrayal that is reminiscent of the Hegelian terminology of *The Sickness unto Death,* Dietrich Bonhoeffer's *Act and Being* aptly describes this self-mastery in terms of the conscience "in Adam" when, "under the Atlas-burden of a world's creator, in the cold silence of his eternal solitude, man begins to fear himself, to shudder in alarm":

> Thereupon, exalting himself to be his own final judge, he proceeds to his own indictment—which is couched in the language of conscience. . . . The conscience and remorse of man in Adam are his final grasp at himself, the final confirmation and justification of his self-lordly, self-masterly attitude. Man makes himself the defendant and exhorts himself upward to his better self. But the cry of conscience serves only to dissemble the mute loneliness of his desolate isolation [analogous to what Kierkegaard identifies as *Indesluttehed:* the "inclosing reserve"], it sounds without echo into the world that is governed and constructed by the self. . . . Conscience can torture, can drive to despair, but is unable of itself to kill man, because indeed it is his final grasp at himself.[22]

This internalized gaze of the conscience "in Adam" is oriented inwardly, in contrast to what Anti-Climacus describes as the conscience "before God" in which God "looks upon a human being so that the human being now must look to him in all things" (WL, 346). In despairing over sin, such a self is still captured in the internalized Hegelian master-slave dialectic of the will to be oneself. One may say, as in Anti-Climacus's portrayal, "I can never forgive myself"; but one may be "even more deceptive" in alleging that "God can never forgive him for it. Alas, this is just a subterfuge" (SUD, 112). In both positions hubristic desire for self-indictment becomes evident. It is the error of believing that the self can itself decide what sin is and decide the extent of the *possible* reach of forgiveness. The flaw is in conflating what one can forgive oneself with what God can forgive one: that is, the omission of the infinite qualitative *difference* between human and divine forgiveness. This introspective grasp at the self is a denial of the "offensive" truth that one "has to learn what sin is by a revelation from God" (SUD, 95).[23] It is thus a concealed form of presumptuous self-willing to prescribe the possible parameters of divine forgiveness and to assert that one is beyond the reach of salvation. It is the *contritio activa* of self-willing, rather than the *contritio passiva* in which faith encounters Christ in the consciousness of sin. While such despair may have the appearance of deep penitence, in reality, Anti-Climacus writes, "this kind of talk is exactly the opposite of the brokenhearted contrition that prays to God to forgive" (SUD, 111). The heart condemns itself—but God is greater than our hearts. And it is the broken heart—the broken self—that opens its gaze to the Holy Other for forgiveness.

And yet the encounter with the prospect of salvation "in Christ"—"a self directly before Christ" (SUD, 113), where the prospect of forgiveness is more explicit—is not immunized against its own forms of despair. According to Anti-Climacus, "the intensification of the consciousness of the self is the knowledge of Christ, a self directly before Christ." As such, a "self directly before Christ is a self intensified by the inordinate concession from God, intensified by the inordinate accent that falls upon it because God allowed himself to be born, become man, suffer and die also for the sake of this self." Furthermore, therefore, "the greater the conception of Christ, the more self." However, "the more self there is, the more intense is sin" (SUD, 113–114). Specifically, the intensified possibility before Christ is identified as "despair of the forgiveness of sins." In the context of this discussion, it may manifest itself as a form of "in despair to will to be oneself—a sinner—in such a way that there is no forgiveness" (SUD, 113). This takes the form of a refusal of the divine offer of reconciliation—to regard it through human eyes as nothing but *impossible*. Recalling the earlier discussion in the previous chapter: "When the sinner despairs of the forgiveness of sins, it is almost as if he walked right up to God and said, 'No, there is no forgiveness of sins, it is impossible,' and it looks like close combat" (SUD, 114). But the self in despair has become distanced from the God against whom it wishes to struggle: "the most offensive forwardness towards God is at the greatest distance" (SUD, 114). This despair is, once again, an expression of the most profound enmity between the self and God; and yet this enmity conceals the implicit dependence of the self upon God which is asserted by way of contradiction. Through this insurrection, one becomes presumptuously and dialectically "self-important by being the opposition" (SUD, 115).

In its still more intensified form, such despair becomes the "sin of dismissing Christianity *modo ponendo* [positively], of declaring it to be untruth." This Anti-Climacus equates with the unforgivable sin, the sin against the Holy Spirit (cf. Matthew 12:31–32): "Here the self is at the highest intensity of despair; it not only discards Christianity totally but makes it out to be a lie and untruth" (SUD, 125).[24] This sin against the Holy Spirit, Kierkegaard suggests in his *Journals,* may be the pride that cannot forgive itself, the hubris that believes that its own sin has exhausted the possibilities of divine mercy.[25] While the despair of the forgiveness of sins may desperately deny the possibility of redemption due to an apparently melancholy conviction of one's wretchedness, in actuality:

[this] intensification is an ascent from the defensive to the offensive. . . .
Despair of the forgiveness of sins is a definite position over against an offer of God's mercy; sin is not solely retreat, not merely defensive action. But the sin of renouncing Christianity as untruth and a lie is offensive war. (SUD, 125)

At its root is a form of "offence" toward the claim to forgive sins, an offence toward the truth of the infinite qualitative difference that "there is one way in which man could never in all eternity come to be like God: in forgiving sins" (SUD, 122). It is here that offence mounts its offensive.

THE DIALECTIC OF OFFENCE: "AN INVENTION OF A MAD GOD"

The heart of this offence—which in bitter enmity declares the forgiveness of sins to be impossible or Christianity to be untruth—is identified by Anti-Climacus as "sin against the Holy Spirit . . . *the positive form of being offended"* (SUD, 125; my emphasis). Earlier in *The Sickness unto Death,* Anti-Climacus states that the imperative qualification "before God" contains "Christianity's crucial criterion: *the absurd, the paradox, the possibility of offence"* (SUD, 83). Despite the *apparent* offence evoked by the infinite qualitative abyss, what is *truly* found to be most offensive about Christianity, Anti-Climacus argues, is not eventually its rigorous assertion of alterity, but the realization that ironically "it is too high. . . . Because it wants to make man into something so extraordinary that he cannot grasp the thought" (SUD, 83). The real offence resides in the utter absurdity of God's revelation that every individual human being, regardless of status, race, gender, profession, etc., freely "exists before God, may speak with God any time he wants to, assured of being heard by him—in short this person is invited to live on the most intimate terms with God!" (SUD, 85). Taken at face value, "then Christianity—if we call paganism's fiction of the gods human madness—is an invention of a mad god" (SUD, 126). But more than that, Christianity teaches that this "mad god" has been born into the world, suffered and died, become the persecuted truth, and all for the sake of every single individual. "Truly, if there is anything to lose one's mind over, this is it!" (SUD, 85).

Yet for this reconciliation to become realized the infinite chasmic abyss of sin must be overcome—an absurdity and an impossibility! But just how can the infinite qualitative distance between self and Wholly Other, the abyss which Kierkegaard's writings strain with such intensity to evoke, finally be overcome? It has been noted how the so-called death of God ensues when the aggressive "servile subject tries to master the terror that absolute *alterity* provokes by negating the wholly other."[26] But the terror of absolute *alterity* is always negated in the repudiation of God as Wholly Other, the denial of the infinite qualitative abyss between humanity and divinity. In one important way, as it happens, Christianity is itself inherently "guilty" of bringing humanity and the Wholly Other into closer intimacy than either speculative Hegelianism or Feuerbachian anthropology dared. Indeed, as Anti-Climacus asserts: "No teaching on earth has ever really brought God and man so close together as Christianity, nor can any do so, for only God himself can do that, and any human fabrication remains just a dream, a precarious delusion" (SUD, 117).[27]

Here is the final, decisive discovery in our anatomy of the abyss. Kierkegaard's writings express their own vitriolic offence toward any blurring of humanity and divinity that denies the infinite qualitative difference; and yet the (typically Kierkegaardian) irony is that the Christianity one finds in these writings is one which itself teaches that *God has actually defied that very distance*. This *divine defiance of the abyss* is identified as being an offence to reason in the highest degree: an offence that is at the dialectical heart of the struggle for faith. The essence of the Kierkegaardian offence toward Feuerbach, Hegel, paganism, Christendom, etc., is an offence directed toward every *human denial* of the infinite difference. In the face of such human denials or omissions, the abyss of sin and human-divine *alterity* requires strident assertion. And yet, on the other hand, the offence toward Christianity is ironically also an offence toward God's transcendence of the infinite difference through the impossible possibility of the forgiveness of sins. Paganism is offensive because it represents a human failure to recognize the abyss and therefore an implicit denial of it. Christianity is offensive, initially because it directs the gaze despairingly toward the abyss; but latterly, and more decisively, it is offensive because it is the Wholly Other who actually transcends the abyss of otherness. The offence is first that God is Wholly Other; but second, that one may live in paradoxical intimacy before the Holy Other.

And still, it must be observed, Christianity perpetually protects itself against any merging between humanity and God—"the most dreadful of all blasphemies" (SUD, 117)—by virtue of the irrevocable *possibility* of offence itself. "The existence of an infinite qualitative difference between God and man constitutes the possibility of offence, which cannot be removed" (SUD, 127). The possibility of offence—"the guarantee whereby God protects himself against man's coming too close" (SUD, 125)—is therefore the reminder that God has accomplished the impossible, something which requires the consent, not of human comprehension, but the consent of the free will to that which is revealed by God (SUD, 95). As such, as long as there is freedom in life there remains the anxious possibility that the abyss may induce offence—namely, despair—whether at the depth and breadth of the abyss or at the Holy One's claim to have crossed it. Hence the claim to reconcile the abyss may elicit a despairing offence more violent than the assertion of the infinite qualitative difference itself. The *possibility* of offence may thus be understood as an undeniable expression of human-divine *alterity*. For one who is captivated by the despair of the abyss of sin, the prospective intimacy of God as Holy Other may actually incite greater enmity and estrangement than the alienation of seeing God as Wholly Other. Indeed, such offence at the idea that the abyss has been crossed may indicate that one at least holds some sense of the breadth of the abyss: it takes "singular spiritlessness not to be offended at the very idea that sin can be forgiven" (SUD, 116). Therefore, it is possible that "despair over sin is dialectically understood as pointing toward faith"—something that is "implied in despair's also being the first element in faith" (SUD, 116*). That is to say that, humanly speaking, a genuine conception of the immensity of the abyss may legitimately cause one to think that the claim to transcend the distance is absurd, an offence to reason. Human comprehension cannot transcend this inexorable distance: "As sinner, man is separated from God by the most chasmic qualitative abyss. In turn, of course, God is separated from man by the same chasmic abyss when he forgives sins" (SUD, 122). Here is the heart and soul of a Kierkegaardian sense of God as Wholly Other. And here is one of Kierkegaard's most significant and surprising contributions to the notion of human-divine *alterity:* the sense in which the infinite qualitative abyss is itself the grief of God as well as humanity.

Precisely this is Christ's grief, that "he cannot do otherwise" . . . *What a rare act of love, what unfathomable grief of love, that even God cannot remove the possibility that this act of love reverses itself for a person and becomes the most extreme misery—something that in another sense God does not want to do, cannot want to do.*

—*The Sickness unto Death*

Decisively, it is Christ who, according to Johannes Climacus in *Philosophical Fragments,* suffers from "bearing the possibility of the offence of the human race when out of love [he] became its savior!" (PF, 32). It is the God-man whose unrequited love for humanity suffers at the offence of human reason. As Johannes Climacus illustrates through a familiar biblical motif: "There was a people who had a good understanding of the divine; this people believed that to see the god was death.—Who grasps the contradiction of this sorrow: not to disclose itself is the death of love; to disclose itself is the death of the beloved" (PF, 30). And so God, becoming human in disclosure to the beloved's gaze, elicits the sorrowful possibility of offence. To see God is to die; and yet, God becomes a servant—"look, behold the man! [John 19:5]" (PF, 33)—and this look of offence becomes God's own death at the hands of the beloved. This paradox is a terrifying *mysterium* to the understanding, *tremendum* to a degree potentially more dreadful than the numinous: "for it is indeed less terrifying to fall upon one's face while the mountains tremble at the god's voice [Exodus 19:16–19] than to sit with him as his equal, and yet the god's concern is precisely to sit this way" (PF, 34–35).

The incongruity of the God-man draws attention to itself as a contradiction, an offence. *Ecce homo!* Once again, by the element of *fascinans* it draws the gaze to itself; but a gaze which, encountering a divine mirror, is reflected back to interrogate the self—since it is the human self and not the "unfathomable grief" of God that we ultimately know how to speak of. As Anti-Climacus describes the *fascinans* evoked by the God-man's contradiction in *Practice in Christianity:*

There is something that makes it impossible not to look—and look, as one is looking one sees as in a mirror, one comes to see oneself, or he who is the sign of contradiction looks straight into one's heart while one is staring into that contradiction. A contradiction placed squarely in front of a person—if one can get him to look at it—is a mirror; as he is forming a judgment, what dwells within him must be disclosed. (PC, 126–127)

And so the decisive question for the self before God is whether this sign of contradiction—which, like the abyss, one cannot resist gazing into though it also gazes back—induces the either/or of despair or faith: as Anti-Climacus formulates it in *The Sickness unto Death,* "either you shall be offended or you shall believe" (SUD, 122). This either/or demand must be answered by each "single individual" to whom it is addressed in the God-given gift of freedom.[28] As such, "the possibility of offence," as Kierkegaard himself asserts, "unconditionally makes a person first of all and qualitatively an 'individual'" (Pap. X^5 B 208). It is not humanity in the abstract, or the speculative idea of the human, but each *single individual* who must gaze into the contradiction since each individual must confront for themselves the im/possibility of the forgiveness of their own sins as evoked by the infinite qualitative abyss. Thus Anti-Climacus can also claim: "The category of sin is the category of individuality" (SUD, 119).

The divine concession of the free single individual—who carries the inalienable possibility of offence, of despairing over the abyss—gives rise to the anxious possibility of atheism as *inherent* within the struggle for faith. It is *always* conceivable that the gaze of the contradiction who "looks straight into one's heart"—evoking the abyss of sin—will become a gaze that one strives to escape or deny, as one may wish to flee in terror from one's own reflection, "an omen of death" (JP 3:3902 / Pap. X^4 A 412) for the self. This desire to escape asserts a desire for severance between the sinner and the consuming consciousness of sin. Kierkegaard illustrates this perfectly in his discourse on the dictum, "Love Shall Hide a Multitude of Sins":

Would that there were a border, however narrow, if it still makes a separation between me and my sin! Would that on the other side of a chasmic abyss there were a spot, however little, where I can stand, while the consciousness of my sin must remain on this side. Would that there were a forgiveness, a forgiveness that does not increase my sense of guilt but truly takes the guilt from me, also the consciousness of it. Would that there were oblivion. ("Two Discourses at the Communion on Fridays," WA, 184)

The agony of incommensurability is that it is *before God* that one becomes aware that sin cannot stand before holiness. The tension of this difference is asserted as one is disclosed as a sinner before God, and Anti-Climacus describes this by way of analogy in *The Sickness unto Death:*

the opposites are kept together in a double sense: they are held together (*continentur*), they are not allowed to go away from each other, but by being held together in this way the differences show up all the more sharply, just as when two colors are held together, *opposita juxta se posita magis illucesunt* [the opposites appear more clearly by juxtaposition]. (SUD, 121–122)

Once one is before God, then, recalling the spirit of Lutheran spiritual trial (*Anfechtung*), one flees but cannot escape the opposition that exposes the crushing contrast of infinity upon the finite. And yet, if one is willing to become conscious of oneself as a sinner then, according to Anti-Climacus in *Practice in Christianity,* God will not aggravate the tender conscience— "he will not break the bruised reed even more"—but rather will "raise you up when you accept him; he will not identify you by contrast, by placing you apart from himself so that your sin becomes even more terrible" (PC, 20). As such, the self's acceptance of forgiveness negates the crushing juxtaposition of the infinite difference. Perhaps it would be best to say that salvation signifies an end to the infinite abyssal severance or harrowing *distinction* between the self and God. At the same time, *difference* (the *mysterium*) is perpetually maintained—a difference which is itself asserted in the act of forgiveness. It is through forgiveness that the notion of contrast or opposition is overcome. Instead of the conscience restlessly fleeing in search of a hiding place from the light of guilt, it listens to the call of Christ: "Come unto me!" Through this call, God "will grant you a hiding place with himself, and hidden in him he will hide your sins" (PC, 20).

As such, the gaze of God that discloses the eye of the beholder to itself is finally a gaze that neither interrogates sin with voyeuristic relish, nor annihilates that which it looks upon. It is the gaze of one who has freely chosen to sit as one's equal. It is a gaze that Pattison has rightly referred to as "the look of love"[29]—a look one might contrast to the crucifying look of offence with which the self beholds the God-man after the *Ecce homo!* It is with this look of love, rather than the harrowing gaze of justice, that God beholds sinners. Evoking the visual motif of spiritual trial, Kierkegaard illustrates this contrast in his discourse "But One Who Is Forgiven Little Loves Little":

> Justice looks judgingly at a person, and the sinner cannot endure its gaze; but love, when it looks at him—yes, even if he avoids its gaze, looks down, he nevertheless does perceive that it is looking at him, because love penetrates far more inwardly into life, deep inside life, in there whence life emanates, than justice does, which repellingly establishes a chasmic abyss between the

sinner and itself, whereas love is on his side, does not accuse, does not judge, but pardons and forgives. . . . Whither shall I flee from justice? If I take the wings of the morning and fly to the nearest sea, it is there. *And if I hide myself in the abyss, it is there, and thus it is everywhere* [Psalm 139:7–12; my emphasis]. Yet, no, there is one place to which I can flee—to love. ("But One Who Is Forgiven Little Loves Little," WA, 172)

The penitent must therefore "stop staring at his guilt"—which, recalling Vigilius Haufniensis's analogy in *The Concept of Anxiety,* has the dangerous allure of the serpent's glance. In order to free himself from this fascination with guilt, the penitent must "shut his eyes" and "open the eyes of faith so that he sees purity where he saw guilt and sin!" ("Love Shall Hide the Multitude of Sins," WA, 185). The penitent then ceases to flee from himself—"the futile attempt that only leads more deeply to despair or madness"—and flees instead to Christ who will "shield me from the eyes of justice" (WA, 187).

Following the Lutheran dialectic of spiritual trial (*Anfechtung*), the penitent flees from the wrath of heaven and into the merciful arms of Christ. Once hidden in Christ, the eyes of divine justice do not see sin. But this is not the mercy of God deceptively blinding the eyes of God's justice—this would constitute another source of "offence." It is more a problem of the self's own anxious gaze of guilt which, due to offence, will not see sin through the eyes of faith as forgiven. Justice "repellingly establishes a chasmic abyss" into which one cannot lose oneself ("Would that there were oblivion!") since "if I hide myself in the abyss, it is there"; but "love is on his side"—on the sinner's side of the abyss, metaphorically speaking. It is also from the inner eyes of guilt, temptation, and self-accusation that the believer is hidden in God. Once again, Vigilius Haufniensis's *The Concept of Anxiety* remarks the insidious and anxious gaze of one who is "a divine prosecutor . . . in relation to himself," one for whom guilt has "the fascinating power of the serpent's glance" (CA, 103). Indeed, as Kierkegaard explains in a discourse on Christ's dictum, "No Man Can Serve Two Masters," it is the devil's glance in temptation—"this glittering gaze that looks as if it could penetrate earth and sea and the most hidden secrets of the heart" ("No Man Can Serve Two Masters," WA, 33)—from which the believer is hidden in God. "He is sharp-sighted, the evil one whose snare is called temptation and whose prey is called the human soul." And yet, such "temptation does not actually come from him" (WA, 33). It comes from the "ambivalence" of the human subject—conceptually related to what Haufniensis describes as the ambivalence of the fearful desire of the gaze of anxiety—on which the glittering gaze catches. "But the person who by unconditional obedience [i.e., without ambivalence] hides in God is unconditionally secure; from his secure hiding place he can see the devil, but the devil cannot see him" (WA, 33). Retaining the optical motif, Kierkegaard explains in his *Journals:* "That a person wants to sit and brood and stare at his sin and is unwilling to have faith that it is forgiven" signifies faithlessness, "a minimizing of what Christ has done" (JP 4:4036 / Pap. X² A 477). Thus the (omniscient) inward gaze of melancholy reveals our great tragedy of despair to be "that we have no real conception of what sin is in God's eyes" (JP 4:4026 / Pap. X² A 400).

THE EYES OF FAITH

In 1847's *Works of Love,* Kierkegaard describes how the precarious life of sin is a life which "hovers over the abyss [*Afgrund*] and therefore has no foothold" (WL, 276). Analogously, Anti-Climacus thus warns in 1850's *Practice in Christianity* how the gravitation of sin "leads downward so easily . . . as easily as when the horse, completely relieved of pulling, cannot, not even with all its strength, stop the wagon, which now runs it into the abyss [*Dyb*]." In these parallel illustrations of sin's grasp upon the individual, both of the spatial aspects of the abyss are evoked: it is groundless (*Afgrund*) and a deep (*Dyb*). Thus, reliant solely upon oneself, one cannot extract oneself from the formless deeps of the abyss. But, Anti-Climacus counsels, one must ensure that one does "not despair over every relapse" (PC, 19). When anatomized solely from the perspective of guilt, the abyss is fathomed without relation to that which lies beyond its shores. The anatomization of the distance and depth of sin—something that surpasses human understanding—cannot be grasped by introspection but only by divine revelation, since, as is echoed in *The Sickness unto Death,* "that is what you know least of all, how far from perfect you are and what sin is" (SUD, 96). As with the consciousness of sin, so must the consciousness of forgiveness be received in relation to God.

An apposite illustration of this relational understanding can be found in one of Luther's tactics for coping with the trial of spirit. Rebuffing the assaults upon his conscience wrought by the devil's manipulation of scripture, Luther found deliverance, not through his own knowledge, but through appealing to what he aptly called the "alien word," which, as Rupp explains, "is the Gospel, which is not 'my own,' but which I must hear spoken 'to me' . . . a Christian can only be promised absolution, the Word of forgiveness, 'from outside.'"[30] This "alien word" is the *mysterium* of forgiveness that offers reconciliation over alienation. As humanity can never fathom the true breadth and depth of sin, so humanity, as Anti-Climacus asserts, can never know what it is for God to forgive sins. Sin is "that which man cannot think as a divine thought."[31] Within this abyss lies the *metanoia* that Kierkegaard describes as the "crucifixion of one's understanding" (JP 4:4375 / Pap. X¹ A 478). Through this *metanoia,* "the abyss" comes to also express the fathomless plenitude of the divine work of forgiveness. An illustration for this sense of *mysterium* can be gleaned from Otto's observation that when the Psalmist "gazes down into the immeasurable, yawning Depth of the divine Wisdom, dizziness comes upon him."[32] Here is the true vertigo of the abyss: the fathomless and inexhaustible depths of divine grace.

Here the conclusion to our anatomy of the abyss returns to its beginning: an assertion of an infinite qualitative difference between humanity and God—between knowledge of self and knowledge of God; only now, the emphasis is upon the infinite qualitative difference of *forgiveness,* rather than sin. As Anti-Climacus asserts in *The Sickness unto Death,* the infinite difference between divinity and humanity is irreducibly "maintained as it is in the paradox and faith, so that God and man do not, even more dreadfully than ever in paganism, do not merge in some way, *philosophice, poetice,* etc., into one—in the system" (SUD, 99). However, with the gift of forgiveness, this "gulf of qualitative difference between God and man" (SUD, 99) becomes transfigured—via the *metanoia* of self-understanding before God—into an abyss (or *mysterium*) that is free from the "moment of death" that is contained within melancholy, anxiety, and despair over sin. When faith is present, the abyssal consciousness of sin is transformed into a gulf between human and divine forgiveness, between human *impossibility* and divine *possibility.* As the consciousness of sin cannot be truly grasped by the self without the relational consciousness of forgiveness before God, so the abyss of sin cannot be anatomized without this gulf between the human impossibility and divine possibility of forgiveness. *The true meaning of the infinite qualitative difference is the infinite quality of mercy.*

"Blessed is the one who is not offended," therefore, since the infinite qualitative difference of divine forgiveness is the *mysterium,* made *tremendum et fascinans* by the Holy Other which arouses a fear and fascination expressed most authentically by humanity through worship of God: "The person who does not take offence *worships* in faith. But to worship, which is the expression of faith, is to express that the infinite, chasmic, qualitative abyss between them is confirmed. For in faith the possibility of offence is again the dialectical factor" (SUD, 129).

At this point, Anti-Climacus's words return us to the aphorism of Johannes Climacus with which the first chapter of this work began: "Precisely because there is the absolute difference between God and man, man expresses himself most perfectly when he absolutely expresses the difference" (CUP, 412). However, as Anti-Climacus underlines above, the true meaning of the infinite qualitative difference is finally expressed through acceptance of the forgiveness of sins, rather than through the consciousness of sin: through worship rather than despair. But—and here is the reminder of our inalienable and anxious freedom—the *possibility* of offence can never be removed, just as a thorn in the flesh remains as the self's enduring stigma of the infinite qualitative difference between itself and God. As such, by maintaining this persistent risk of offence, the gulf of forgiveness may itself become known as a possible moment of death for the self before God. The anxious possibility of freedom's offence ensures that the abyss can always gape wide and dark for the gaze which, in the self's darkest hour of spiritual trial, dares not or cannot look upon God. By despairing over the possibility of forgiveness, one may easily become, as Kierkegaard describes in a student sermon in 1842, "crushed by the thought that you were a nothing and your soul lost in infinite space" (JP 4:3915 / Pap. III C 1). To one who is lost in this nothingness, it may appear that God has become nothing but the abyss itself—the infinitely forbidding difference between humanity and its salvation in divinity; the holy abyss that overwhelms the eye with dizziness.

But God—the Wholly Other—is not *ultimately* another name for the abyss. Through the acceptance of forgiveness, God also becomes known as the Holy Other who bestrides the abyss through the gracious act of salvation. In this thought of forgiveness resides what Kierkegaard describes in his *Journals* as "confidence before God," the confidence of faith in spite of the fathomlessness of the abyss:

> It sometimes happens that our eyes turn toward heaven, and we are astonished at the infinite distance, and the eye cannot find a resting place between heaven and earth—but when the eye of the soul seeks God and we feel the infinite distance, then it is a matter of confidence—but here we have a mediator. (JP 2:1200 / Pap. II A 326)

Echoing this motif, Kierkegaard explains in *Works of Love* how in the God-relationship one discovers "a holding-on place in existence, for God has hold of it." God has hold of the self even in the abyss, and thus the act of standing fast before God relieves "the dizziness which is the beginning of mutiny" (WL, 122). By faith's self-surrendering of its own despair, the self realizes that God has hold of it and therefore chooses to follow the pattern of the loving struggle of Jacob over the futile rage of Prometheus against his bonds. Here, as Anti-Climacus describes in *Practice in Christianity*, the self responds to the call of Christ which is given to those "whose residence has been assigned among the grave": that is, to the one who is "not buried, yet dead . . . belonging neither to life nor to death . . . you, too, come here, here is rest, and here is life!" (PC, 18).

It is in worship rather than offence, therefore, that the self discovers the assured ground on which it stands before God—the Holy Other: and God's *alterity* is affirmed in the very act of worship (SUD, 129). The *possibility* of offence can never be removed: it is a mark of the God-given openness of human freedom and source of the unfathomable grief of divine love. But worship expresses faith's overcoming, or suspension, of offence: the self-denying suspension of despair against the apparent *impossibility* of divine forgiveness. By choosing to suspend offence against that which "humanly speaking" is *impossible,* faith transfigures "the deep underlying feeling of infinite unworthiness basic to every true God-relationship . . . into a greater joy in God" (JP 2:2008 / Pap. IX A 316), and thus rejoices—worships—in the grace of the infinite qualitative difference (for the difference is also a gift of grace, an impossible possibility of forgiveness and self-becoming). And as worshipper—as a self who is capable of loving God in return—one becomes oneself by suspending offence against human impossibility and becoming nothing before God. And yet here once more is the (characteristically Kierkegaardian) irony of the "self before God": while rejoicing in the infinite difference, Kierkegaard also claims that "worship is what makes the human being resemble God. . . . The human being and God do not resemble each other directly but inversely; only when God has infinitely become the eternal and omnipresent object of worship and the human being always a worshipper, only then do they resemble each other" (UDVS, 193).

The notion of human-divine resemblance is further explored in Kierkegaard's upbuilding discourse on prayer, with which the previous chapter concluded. As acknowledged in both the previous chapter and in this chapter, the struggle of prayer is actually a humble expression of the infinite qualitative difference in which the human and the divine are brought into intimate relationship: "when there is praying, they are indeed too close to each other, then there is no inbetween that can be marked out as the battleground" ("One Who Prays Aright Struggles in Prayer and is Victorious—in that God is Victorious," EUD, 383). As this discourse proceeds, Kierkegaard explains how one who struggles in prayer comes "face-to-face" with God; but in order to "reflect the image of God," the struggler "must become nothing" before God:

> Whom should the struggler desire to resemble other than God? But if he himself is something or wants to be something, this something is sufficient to hinder the resemblance. Only when he himself becomes nothing, only then can God illuminate [*gjennemlyse*] him so that he resembles God. No matter how great he imagines his self to be, he is unable to manifest himself in God's likeness; God can imprint himself in him only when he himself has become nothing. When the ocean is exerting all its power, that is precisely the time when it cannot reflect the image of heaven, and even the slightest motion blurs the image; but when it becomes still and deep [*dybt*], then the

image of heaven sinks into its nothingness. ("One Who Prays Aright Struggles in Prayer and is Victorious—in that God is Victorious," EUD, 399)

As such, it is only by suspending offence, by becoming nothing before God, that one comes to "reflect the image of God" (EUD, 400). The imagery Kierkegaard employs at this point is at once elegant, mysterious, and illuminating: it is only when the ocean is at its stillest that it reflects the heavens; when it rages, this image is distorted or obliterated. Even at moments when the ocean merely ripples, the light of the sun may glitter on its surface but not sink into its depths. But all along, the sky and the sea remain *different*—elementally different—even though the *image* of heaven may be reflected deep within the stillness of the ocean.

This resemblance is a question of *heterogeneous* reflection and illumination. In terms of the gaze, the self before God becomes reflected back to itself through the gaze of the Holy Other. It comes to see itself reflected in the divine "mirror of the Word" (JP 4:3902 / Pap. X⁴ A 412), through the eyes of God as forgiven, as a creature who is able to stand before God. And more than that—before God, "the self rests transparently [*gjennemsigtigt*] in the power that established it" (SUD, 14). Once the self has thus opened itself to the divine gaze, the divine will "illuminate [*gjennemlyse*] him so that he resembles God" ("One Who Prays Aright Struggles in Prayer and is Victorious—in that God is Victorious," EUD, 399). As such, the self comes to see itself as a creature that is able to "reflect the image of God," as the ocean reflects the heavens from which it nonetheless remains different. In conclusion, the self's journey to this reflection before the "mirror of the Word" is not one of self-willing, but rather one of the free surrender of its will-to-offence. By surrendering its despair before God, the self becomes open to forgiveness: the gift from the divine which is the impossible possibility of coming to know oneself as one is known by God. Through this gift, the self realizes the real meaning of the infinite qualitative difference as the *mysterium* of divine forgiveness rather than the abyss of despair. Through this gift of forgiveness, the self also realizes that the infinite qualitative difference is actually the divine gift of human freedom. This freedom is the freedom formed by the divine withdrawal that creates a space in which the self can become itself before God.

But the shadow of this gift is the possibility of offence that cannot be removed, and with it the unfathomable possibility of divine grief. As such, this infinite qualitative difference between self and God retains a *mysterium tremendum et fascinans* between the human and the divine that continually endures and that remains as a *possible* source of human offence. Therefore, as Kierkegaard asserts in the above discourse on prayer, the struggling believer must realize that one may not always receive the desired "explanation [*Forklaring*] from God" for all things; but one is instead "transfigured [*forklaret*] in God, and his transfiguration [*Forklarelse*] is this: to reflect the image of God" ("One Who Prays Aright Struggles in Prayer and is Victorious—in that God is Victorious," EUD, 400). But many questions may remain lost in the abyss between the human and the divine, since the self before God is finally more a matter of "transfiguration" (*Forklarelse*) than "explanation" (*Forklaring*). In this abyss, the *possibility* of offence resides alongside the *mysterium* of forgiveness. By suspending offence and accepting an "impossible" forgiveness, however, the self freely opens itself to a transfiguration of the infinite qualitative abyss and of its own self *before God*. In this it seeks not only to become the self that each individual is destined to become, but also to express the image of God in creation—to help bring closer to consummation God's desire to behold God.

EIGHT

Conclusions

The (Im)possible and the (Un)forgivable

In this concluding chapter, the ultimate meaning of the infinite qualitative difference as forgiveness is employed as a lens through which to view the relation between our being forgiven by God and the *possibility* of our forgiving "the other." In this exploration, the key notion of the "impossible possibility" of divine forgiveness is read as a model for the "suspension" of offence by which the self remains open to the possibility of forgiving "the unforgivable." This finally gives rise to the more expansive question of what it might mean for the self to express faith by "forgiving God."

THE OTHER BEFORE GOD

What has been portrayed in this anatomy of the Kierkegaardian abyss may for some resemble the lonely heroism of the self struggling to know itself before God, in the face of modernity's disdain for the infinite qualitative difference between the human and the divine: "Christian heroism—a rarity, to be sure—to venture wholly to become oneself, an individual human being, this specific human being, alone before God" (SUD, 5). For many, however, Kierkegaard's depiction of the self before God irrevocably places the individual upon a precipice, trembling over a holy abyss, necessarily forsaking every creaturely "other" in its anguished struggle to relate to a Wholly Other. "We, ourselves wandering on the narrow ridge, must not shrink from the sight of the jutting rock on which he stands over the abyss; nor may we step on it," Martin Buber famously warns. "We have much to learn from him, but not the final lesson."[1] This "final lesson" that Buber alludes to is apparently undermined by the conspicuous absence of "the other" in Kierkegaard's writings. Kierkegaardian inwardness, in this inscription, is consigned to serving as a relic of modern melancholy, the fading silhouette of an overly individualized "self" whose contours, in the vague light of post/modernity, have become increasingly uncertain.

It is, so Charles Taylor exhorts, by way of the "ethic of authenticity" that humanity responds to the sense of loss which features in our characteristic "malaises of modernity."[2] But in the indeterminate agitation of the *postmodern*, what becomes of that passionate modern search for "authenticity" which, according to Jacob Golomb, begins with a confession from Kierkegaard and threatens to shipwreck on the shoals of deconstruction?[3] Hopefully it has become apparent that the present work sees the common depiction of Kierkegaardian subjectivity as an icon of a definitively modern inwardness as an increasingly dubious fallacy. What is becoming clearer is that Kierkegaard can be read as transcribing the actual *iconoclasm* of modern selfhood, in order to raise up from its ashes a self becoming itself in the openness of relating to God. To exist *before God* actually requires "immense passivity, vulnerability and wounded openness" which, as George Pattison rightly observes, "calls for an orientation of the self that is quite alien to the mainstream of Western philosophical thought about the self and is certainly in profound tension with the post-Enlightenment pursuit of autonomy."[4] And neither does this "wounded openness" hermetically seal itself off from the human other—despite the apparent primacy of the self *before God*. At this point I wish to assert that, while the relation between self and human others has not been the primary focus of the present work, a concern with the "self before God" implies a vision of the human-divine relation that *begins with* deeming *all individuals* to be irreducibly equal before God: a valuation which, aspiring to see the human other through the eyes of God, is the starting point for a recognition of the divinely given *alterity* of every human other.

As such, the principal scope of the present work could be aptly summarized by the words of C. Stephen Evans: "God is not the only 'other' to which selves can relate and thereby become selves, though God remains the crucial 'other' for selfhood in the highest sense."[5] As Kierkegaard describes the human struggle for self-recognition in *Works of Love*: "The desire is to exist in the eyes of the mighty"—but it is precisely through the eyes of God that one learns that "the relationship between man and man ought and dare never to be one in which the one worships and the other is worshipped" (WL, 128). The notion of the self before God thus calls for all others to be equally valued as inviolably free individuals before God: a freedom and individuality which no human possesses the inherent right to violate. Living "before God" is, accordingly, "the source and origin of all individuality," and to believe in one's "authentic individuality" means concomitantly to

> believe in the individuality of every other person; for individuality is not mine but is God's gift by which he gives me being and gives being to all, gives being to everything. It is simply the inexhaustible swell of goodness in the

goodness of God that he, the *almighty,* nevertheless gives in such a way that the receiver obtains individuality, that He who created out of nothing nevertheless creates individuality, so that creation over against him shall not be nothing, although it is taken from nothing and is nothing and yet becomes individuality. (WL, 253)

If the omnipotent God, who created *ex nihilo,* can allow a human being to become something "over against him," then by what power and right does a human being prevent any other from becoming something? By asserting that selfhood is a gift of God, one is asserting that no one has the entitlement to desecrate that sacred gift in any other. And so "before God" one speaks not simply of the *alterity* of "the other," but of the open relation to "the neighbor" who is as much a recipient of the divine gift as one is oneself: "The concept of *neighbour* means a duplicating of one's own self. *Neighbour* is what philosophers would call the *other,* by which the selfishness in self-love is to be tested" (WL, 37).

As such, in this last chapter I move to a brief but expansive consideration of how the role of forgiveness in the relation between self-God-other can be elucidated with reference to the infinite qualitative difference between the human and the divine: specifically, the infinite qualitative difference between human and divine *forgiveness* which this present work has detected at the heart of the self's relation to God. This chapter will thus explore the significance of (im)possibility and the "infinite qualitative difference" for human and divine forgiveness; and finally for faith's suspension of offence and the difficult notion of faith as an expression of "forgiving God."

INFINITE DIFFERENCE: SIN AND FORGIVENESS

In a journal entry dated 20 July 1848, Kierkegaard noted an aspiration to write a new book with the provisional title: "The Radical Cure or The Forgiveness of Sins and the Atonement." The apparent motivation for this work would be to satisfy Kierkegaard's avowal that "now the doctrine of the forgiveness of sins must come forth in earnest" (JP 6:6210 / Pap. IX A 176). However, before this work could come to fruition, Kierkegaard proposes that it "may be best to write a smaller book prior to this one," for which he suggests the title: "Blessed is he who is not offended in me." This title eventually emerges as the motif for No. II of 1850's *Practice in Christianity,* written by Anti-Climacus and edited by Kierkegaard himself. This proved to be the last of the pseudonymous monographs published during Kierkegaard's lifetime. "The Radical Cure or The Forgiveness of Sins and the Atonement" was never to be published in its proposed form. And yet this is not testament to a failure on Kierkegaard's part to fulfill his private intent to have "the doctrine of the forgiveness of sins . . . come forth in earnest." When, in *Practice in Christianity*, Anti-Climacus declares "blessed is the one who is not offended but believes in the forgiveness of sins" (PC, 75), he recognizes and advances an anxious relation between forgiveness and offence, previously articulated in *The Sickness unto Death*, which represents one of the most profound and psychologically evocative contributions to the theology of forgiveness in modern Christian thought.

As has been explored throughout the present work, in *The Sickness unto Death* Kierkegaard develops an anatomy of despair in which the self before God is traumatized by the will's struggle between acceptance of and resistance to the forgiveness of sins. The self becomes itself *before God* in relation to the individual's faith in the divine *possibility* of the forgiveness of its sins. As examined in the last chapter, integral to this notion of the self before God is the either/or of *faith* or *offence*: a dilemma that is further articulated in terms of the perceived *possibility/impossibility* of the forgiveness of sins by God. Offence and the divine/human (im)possibility of forgiveness are themselves decisive expressions of the infinite qualitative difference between humanity and divinity: the chasmic abyss that opens up between a self and the God before whom it must become itself. Expanding upon this perspective, I shall explore the potential significance of a Kierkegaardian insistence upon an infinite qualitative difference between human and divine forgiveness for the questions of the (im)possibility of human forgiveness, the unforgivable, and what it might mean to "suspend" offence and "forgive God."

There is one passage from Anti-Climacus's section on "The Sin of Despairing of the Forgiveness of Sins (Offense)" at the end of *The Sickness unto Death*—a section emphasized previously in the present work—that stands above all others as a decisive affirmation of the infinite qualitative difference between sin and forgiveness. Immediately preceding the passage in question, Anti-Climacus asserts: "Sin is the one and only predication about a human being that in no way, either *via negationis* [by denial] or *via eminentiæ* [by idealization], can be stated of God" (SUD, 122).[6] From this point Anti-Climacus proceeds with one of the most revealing formulations of the infinite qualitative difference in Kierkegaard's authorship:

> As sinner, man is separated from God by the most chasmic qualitative abyss. In turn, of course, God is separated from man by the same chasmic qualitative abyss when he forgives sins. If by some kind of reverse adjustment the divine could be shifted over to the human, there is one way in which man could never in all eternity come to be like God: in forgiving sins. (SUD, 122)

Anti-Climacus's sublime qualification of the infinite qualitative difference does at least two things. First, as has been maintained throughout the present work, it suggests a theologically nuanced angle for gazing into the chasmic abyss: one that perceives the ineffable otherness of God, not simply via the alienation of sin, but rather via the impossible *mysterium* of divine forgiveness.

Second, however, while this emphasis gestures toward mitigating some of the despair that often attends the infinite qualitative abyss in Kierkegaard's writings, the infinite qualitative difference between human and divine forgiveness of sins appears at first glance to disrupt a more relational view of human-divine forgiveness as it was outlined in 1847's *Works of Love*. In the conclusion to *Works of Love*, Kierkegaard recognizes the Christian imperative: "Forgive, and you also will be forgiven" (Matthew 6:12, 14–15). He writes of this: "Christianity's view is: forgiveness is forgiveness; your forgiveness is your forgiveness; your forgiveness of another is your own forgiveness; the forgiveness you give is the forgiveness you receive, not the reverse, that the forgiveness you receive is the forgiveness you give" (WL, 380). Kierkegaard challenges the notion that one could receive forgiveness from God and yet never give forgiveness to one's neighbor: "God forgives you neither more nor less nor otherwise than as you forgive those who have sinned against you" (WL, 380). Here Kierkegaard accepts a primitive resemblance between human and divine forgiveness which, at first glance, sits awkwardly with Anti-Climacus's emphasis upon their absolute difference: "there is not a more exact agreement between the sky above and its reflection in the sea, which is just as deep as the distance is high, than there is between forgiveness and forgiving" (WL, 380).

The employment of this metaphor of the sky reflected in the sea in *Works of Love* echoes Kierkegaard's use of the same imagery in the 1844 discourse considered at the end of our last chapter, "One Who Prays Aright Struggles in Prayer and is Victorious—in that God is Victorious" (EUD, 399). In that instance, "reflection" was seen to express the resemblance between the believer and God: a reflection of the image of God in which the elemental difference between self/God or ocean/heaven is retained. In *Works of Love*, the metaphor rather evokes a resemblance between forgiveness received and forgiveness given that seems to weaken Anti-Climacus's assertion of an infinite qualitative difference between human and divine forgiveness of sins. However, there is something here other than an apparent incongruity between Kierkegaard and his pseudonym, Anti-Climacus. Anti-Climacus, for his part, is evidently asserting that humanity can never, ontologically one might say, forgive itself for the sins that God has forgiven us; while Kierkegaard, in *Works of Love*, is implying that there is an inexorable reciprocity between our forgiveness by God and our forgiveness of our neighbor.

It would be contradictory of the "extraordinary" Christian Anti-Climacus to assert that, because God's forgiveness reveals an infinite qualitative difference from human forgiveness, the believer is thereby released from the Christian obligation: "Forgive, and you also will be forgiven." Anti-Climacus is not making this claim here. Rather, the forgiveness that Kierkegaard writes of in *Works of Love* is the forgiveness of the other in reciprocity, or harmonious agreement, with God's forgiveness of the self. What Anti-Climacus is eliciting in *The Sickness unto Death* is the chasmic qualitative abyss between God's forgiveness of the self and the self's judgments upon its own potential forgiveness. Throughout his anatomy of despair, Anti-Climacus exposes the futility of the self's attempts to grasp itself through a defective reflection on its own sinfulness and its own "possibility" of salvation: "that is what you know least of all, how far from perfect you are and what sin is" (SUD, 96).

In this sense, Anti-Climacus's insistence on the otherness of God's forgiveness can be read as potentially delivering the self from a pathologically anxious self-scrutiny. While the consciousness of sin is an essential companion on the path to faith, morbidly gazing at one's own sin will more likely lead to pathological despair over/of the forgiveness of sins, than to faith. Kierkegaard, in *Works of Love,* reminds the reader that, especially where forgiveness is concerned, our duty is not to obsess with our forgiveness of our own sins, but to be concerned with our forgiveness of others (WL, 381). The mysterious relationship between human and divine forgiveness—a relationship that is only expressed by faith—is encapsulated by Kierkegaard in an apparently paradoxical journal entry from 1854: "To forgive sins is divine not only in the sense that no one is able to do it except God, but it is also divine in another sense so that we must say that no one can do it without God" (JP 2:1224 / Pap. XI^2 A 3).

The apparent paradox is such that only with God can one forgive, and yet it is in forgiving the other that one receives forgiveness oneself. We are called to be in agreement with divine forgiveness—just as the ocean reflects the sky, even though the ocean and the sky are elementally different from one another and this difference is a precondition for any "reflection" whatever. "Of course we are called to forgive each other," Paul Sponheim writes, "but God's forgiveness is of a wholly other order."[7] But in what sense is this divine forgiveness "wholly other"? And how then is human forgiveness to "reflect" divine forgiveness? "How different is the divine from the human!" Kierkegaard continues in the above-quoted 1854 journal entry: "The only kind of forgiveness which can be sustained at all [between humans] is a mutual repaying" (JP 2:1224 / Pap. XI^2 A 3). As such, this *compensatory* view of human forgiveness places it within the traditional economy of the gift: the economy of exchange whereby the giving of a gift implicitly places the receiver in debt to the giver. Human forgiveness thereby comes to be oriented around the reparation of debt, obligation, and implicit power. The divine gift of forgiveness, however, is something "impossible" that can never be reciprocated, or repaid, and which by its very nature does not place us in the thrall of an irresolvable debt. "It is the Deity's joy to forgive sins," Kierkegaard declares, "just as God is almighty in creating out of nothing, so he is almighty in—uncreating something, for to forget, almightily to forget, is indeed to uncreate something" (JP 2:1224 / Pap. XI² A 3).

Here Kierkegaard reaffirms one of his stranger perspectives on divine forgiveness: the notion of "uncreating," or the "forgetting" of sins. In "Love Hides a Multitude of Sins," in the second series of *Works of Love,* Kierkegaard writes impressionistically of God forgetting, as well as forgiving sins. God's forgetting of sins, figuratively speaking, reflects the way in which forgiven sins are not held over the head of the one who is forgiven like an (un-repayable) debt. Human forgiveness is typified by the ethos that says (despite our truism to the contrary) "Forgive, but *do not* forget!"—a watchword in which debt and possible future reparation are implicitly retained. But forgiveness, Kierkegaard declares, must be an expression of love: "By *forgiveness* love hides a multitude of sins . . . forgiveness takes the forgiven sin away" (WL, 294).

Of course, at the heart of the self before God resides the abiding consciousness of forgiveness. Forgiveness, the mystery of the atonement by which the infinite qualitative difference is transfigured, is never to be forgotten. But what is to be remembered is the forgiveness itself; the sin itself is no longer memorialized, for otherwise how could there be assurance that it is forgiven? The endless melancholy recollection of sin—remembering that true consciousness of sin can only be received from God—has a tendency toward self-mortification that delivers itself over to despair. Kierkegaard himself knew this better than most. As such, it becomes crucial to emphasize the potency of love's forgiveness over the nothingness of past sins:

> Forgetting, when God does it in relation to sin, is the opposite of creating, since to create is to bring forth from nothing, and to forget is to take back into nothing. What is hidden from my eyes, that I have never seen; but what is hidden behind my back, that I have seen. The one who loves forgives in this way: he forgives, he forgets, he blots out the sin, in love he turns toward the one he forgives; but when he turns toward him, he of course cannot see what is lying behind his back. (WL, 296)

What this rather curious anthropomorphism hopes for is an expression, in figurative terms, of an essentially pastoral consolation that not only are sins forgiven; they are no longer seen when God looks at the believer. What is seen is one who is irrevocably forgiven—not one who will one day, one way or another, be held accountable for the very gift of forgiveness by which their sins were forgiven. And as God "forgets" sins, as it were, so it is the duty of the believer to strive to *accept* that sins have been forgiven and have become as nothing before the eyes of God. As Kierkegaard writes in his *Journals:* "A man rests in the forgiveness of sins when the thought of God does not remind him of the sin but that it is forgiven, when the past is not a memory of how much he trespassed but of how much he has been forgiven" (JP 2:1209 / Pap. VIII¹ A 230).

This memory of how much has been forgiven, this forgetting of sin is, however, difficult for many to accept—something that Kierkegaard was only too aware of, and that he strove to realize in himself. As such, he explores the psychology of the forgiveness of sins and bears witness to the "impossibility" and "offence" that dictate the self's responses to divine grace. Evidently offence also resides at the heart of human efforts to forgive one another— even though between self and other there is not the same infinite qualitative difference of sin and forgiveness as there is between self and God. It is this difference which, from the human perspective, renders divine forgiveness offensive, ineffable, paradoxical, and above all *impossible.*

"IT IS IMPOSSIBLE!"

In a discourse contained in *Christian Discourses* titled "The Joy of It: That Hardship Does Not Take Away But Procures Hope," Kierkegaard laments that the phrase "It is impossible!" is hardly ever said in relation to the forgiveness of sins: "Scarcely anyone turns away offended and says, 'It is impossible'; even less does anyone say it in wonder." Nor does anyone utter these words from a desire to believe what they dare not believe. Even less are these words said by "one whose repentance is mitigated into a quiet sorrow that in turn is transfigured into a blessed joy, the one who therefore, expressing his unspeakable gratitude to God, refreshes his soul by repeating, 'It is impossible!'" But the mystery of faith in the forgiveness of sins—the transfiguration of despair into blessed joy—also finds wondrous expression in these words. "Oh, blessed refreshment, that the one who was brought close to despair because it was impossible now believes it, blessedly believes it, but in his soul's wonder continues to say, 'It is impossible!'" (CD, 107. Cf. JP 2:1202 / Pap. III C 16).

It is this simple phrase which expresses the inexpressible: the impossible divine possibility of the forgiveness of sins. But just how do these words become a confession of blessedness rather than a gasp of despair? "The eternal consolation in the doctrine of the forgiveness of sins," Kierkegaard suggests, "is this: You shall believe it." And in like manner, "when the anxious conscience begins with heavy thoughts [i.e., guilt over sin], and it is as if they could never in all eternity be forgotten, then comes this: You shall forget"

(JP 2:1217 / Pap. IX A 177). This acceptance of forgiveness as the triumph of divine possibility over human impossibility is contingent upon the either/or of offence or faith, as Anti-Climacus expresses it: "either you shall be offended or you shall believe" (SUD, 122). Arguably, it is through the "suspension" of despair, or offence, against the impossibility of divine forgiveness that faith is able to respond to the words: "You shall believe." However, this apparently imperative command is predicated upon an ineluctable freedom that is bestowed on human life by the infinite qualitative difference itself. "The existence of an infinite qualitative difference between God and man constitutes the possibility of offence, which cannot be removed" (SUD, 127). The possibility of offence—"the guarantee whereby God protects himself against man's coming too close" (SUD, 125)—is therefore a reminder that God has accomplished the impossible: an absolute gift that requires the consent, not of human comprehension, but of the free will (SUD, 95).

Therefore, as considered earlier in the present work, faith possesses the "antidote for despair—possibility—because for God everything is possible at every moment" (SUD, 39–40). As such, the only true resolution of despair is found in the embrace of this absurdity in which faith "suspends"[8] offence and throws itself on God. However, the *impossible* divine gift of forgiveness is offered *under the possibility* that it may be refused: this is the indefinite "possibility of offence, which cannot be removed." It is freedom's possibility of offence—the rejection of forgiveness—that constitutes the "unfathomable grief of love, that even God cannot remove the possibility that this act of love reverses itself for a person and becomes the most extreme misery" (SUD, 126). It is at this moment that Kierkegaard glimpses the sense in which the infinite qualitative abyss is itself the grief of God as well as humanity. But this possibility of offence is the constitutive risk of the divine gift of human freedom.

From a certain perspective, therefore, might it be said that the acceptance of divine forgiveness implies the free will's "suspension" of offence: the suspension of despair over the impossible, the suspension of judgment against ourselves and even against God? And with the sense of suspended judgment, is there not also some figurative sense of reciprocal "forgiveness" between self and God? Through faith the believer is required to forgive oneself—but might there also be a sense, "humanly speaking," in which faith also suspends the judgment of offence and "forgives" God?

THE (IM)POSSIBLE AND THE (UN)FORGIVABLE

Offence at the divine claim to forgive sins is interwoven with the self's will to become its own judge; the "I" wants to believe itself to be a *better judge* of its own guilt and forgiveness than is God. In short, "I" assert myself as the judge of what is *(im)possible*—even for God. As Hugh Pyper has explored in his insightful and evocative essay, "Forgiving the Unforgivable: Kierkegaard, Derrida and the Scandal of Forgiveness," there is an intriguing coincidence at this point between a Kierkegaardian view of forgiveness and Jacques Derrida's more recent reflections on "forgiving the unforgivable." In "Le Siècle et le Pardon,"[9] Derrida responds to Vladimir Jankélévitch's uncompromising writings on the "unforgivable" in relation to the Holocaust. "Forgiveness is impossible. . . . Forgiveness," writes Jankélévitch, "died in the death camps."[10] The persecuting other must remain unforgivable for the sake of the dead victims who are not present to grant their own forgiveness. Jankélévitch thus capitulates before an "uncrossable barrier"[11]—an abyss between the forgivable and the unforgivable (in Kierkegaardian terms it might also be called the possible and the impossible) which cannot be reconciled or overcome. Derrida counters Jankélévitch with the claim that "forgiveness forgives only the unforgivable." As Pyper describes it:

> To forgive what is forgivable is, after all, tautologous. The very act of deciding that a given situation is forgivable is tantamount to forgiving it. It is only when faced with the unforgivable that the work of forgiveness becomes appropriate or required. Indeed, it is the existence of the unforgivable which is the condition for forgiveness.[12]

Or, in Kierkegaardian terms, it is because despair can lament of forgiveness, "It is impossible!" that faith in the forgiveness of sins may respond with blessed joy, "It is impossible!" The impossible possibility of forgiveness arises from the abyss of despair itself because faith believes that "with God all things are possible."[13]

As has been asserted previously, it is God who, by the gift of human freedom, allows for the *possibility* of offence against all claims to forgive sins—even the forgiveness of those who are unforgivable, "humanly speaking." This freedom is, as Pyper explains, the outcome of God's love—a divine love that is impossible (or offensive) to espouse, since it "leads to his [i.e., God's] acceptance of those we cannot accept, his acceptance of those we cannot forgive, and most pertinently, his forgiveness of us." By allowing freedom—and therefore offence, despair, and freedom's most horrific expressions—God has to be "forgiven" for his love, namely, the divine possibility of forgiveness that is offered to *all*. "The subjective motion of accepting the forgiveness of sins is to forgive God his temerity, his weakness, and his harshness for loving us."[14] By "forgiving" God, as it were, faith breaks with a presumptuous despair that cries to God, "No—there is no forgiveness of sins, it is impossible!" Faith, by suspending offence, "forgives" God for the possibility of forgiving that which the self saw as *impossible* for forgiveness.

In part, this notion of "forgiving" the divine takes its cue from Derrida's own response to the question: "Can you forgive God?" Derrida replies that "we are constantly trying to judge God," especially in light of the atrocities of the Holocaust. Even the perpetual "movement to evaluate God ethically, trying to understand the will and the strategies and designs of God is a way of judging him."[15] This would also hold true of the despairing self who seeks to judge God relative to the limits of forgiveness, rather than *rejoicing in the blessing of the impossible*. As such, Derrida identifies "the believers" as "those who think that they do not have the right to judge, that a priori they forgive God for whatever he does." However, in a rather Kierkegaardian tone, Derrida balances this observation with the tension that the "people who have faith in God . . . are also people who are constantly tempted not to forgive God, tempted to accuse or denounce God. That is part of the risk of faith. I am sure that we are constantly struggling with the temptation to judge God, constantly."[16] As such, the life of faith is lived under the persistent temptation to judge God—in despair and offence, to declare "It is impossible!"—as Abraham was tempted to judge God during the *Akedah* (binding of Isaac), after hearing the command: "Take now thy son, thine only son Isaac, whom thou lovest, and get thee into the land of Moriah; and offer him there for a burnt offering upon one of the mountains which I will tell thee of" (Genesis 22:2).

As claimed in *Fear and Trembling*, to receive Isaac back from death in fulfillment of the divine promise was an absurd, *impossible* proposition. And yet—Abraham suspended the offence of the ethical (the temptation to judge God) and resolutely moved by faith into the absurd.[17] The Knight of Faith believes "by virtue of the absurd, by virtue of the fact that for God all things are possible" (FT, 46). In this sense, Abraham suspends the ethical, thereby suspending the will-to-offence that judges God. By stilling the offence in his heart, Abraham's faith might thus be construed as a form of forgiving God, humanly speaking, for the paradoxical command to sacrifice Isaac.

Whether Isaac himself can forgive God is another, more expansive question which requires more space than the present work can devote to it. But an acknowledgment of its relevance marks how there may be moments when suspending the offence of the ethical actually gives birth to further potentially offensive implications. Yet Abraham suspends his offence, due to faith in the "impossible" belief that "God himself will provide a lamb for the burnt offering." Without these words, Abraham is lost (FT, 116). Crucially, however, just as the acceptance of forgiveness never forgets that despair has lamented the impossible, so Abraham passionately acknowledges "the impossibility with his whole heart and soul." At the same moment as he "believes the absurd," Abraham dares to "look the impossibility in the eye" (FT, 47). As such, in Kierkegaardian terms, the divine gift of freedom ensures that one is never truly free from the struggle against despair: the constant temptation of offence—the possibility that God "cannot"—will not remove. And it is this possibility which forms not just the despair of humanity, but the unfathomable grief of divine love.

In conclusion, whether or not such faith is possible must, following the hermeneutical spirit in Kierkegaard, remain open to the free decision of the individual reader. However, Kierkegaard recommends that, in struggling against the "impossible" abyss of despair, one should struggle through prayer to think such dark thoughts "together with God before God" (JP 4:4377 / Pap. X² A 590). In the much-cited discourse "One Who Prays Aright Struggles in Prayer and is Victorious—in that God is Victorious," Kierkegaard further elaborates how through the intimacy of prayer one seeks the self-surrender by which the divine light will "illuminate [*gjennemlyse*] him so that he resembles God" (EUD, 399). As noted previously, this resemblance is likened to the heavens being reflected in the depths of a very calm ocean. To recapitulate further, Kierkegaard duplicates this metaphor in *Works of Love* with reference to the resemblance between the forgiveness received from God and the forgiving which we ought to give to one another.[18] Integrating these two instances of the metaphor of how the sky is reflected in the sea, I suggest that it is by forgiving the other that the self aspires to reflect divine forgiveness and the image of God. As the present work has maintained, the infinite qualitative difference is in part expressed by the realization that the self is unable to forgive itself ("that is what you know least of all, how far from perfect you are and what sin is") (SUD, 96). However, the fuller expression of this infinite qualitative difference is discovered in faith's rejoicing in the thought that "It is impossible!" It is perhaps by taking the impossible possibility of God's forgiveness of us as a model for our forgiveness of one another that one may learn what it means to suspend offence (while remaining conscious of its possibility) in order to make room for the possibility of forgiveness. In seeking to reflect divine forgiveness in our relation to others, we may come closer to resembling the image of God, allowing the light of heaven to penetrate ever further into the inner abyss of selfhood.

NOTES

PREFACE

1. Barth, "Kierkegaard and the Theologians," 64.

2. P. T. Forsyth, preface to *The Work of Christ*, xxxii. The first part of Forsyth's description forms the title for H. V. Martin's *Kierkegaard: The Melancholy Dane*.

3. Cf. Blake's *Marriage of Heaven and Hell*, ca. 1790–1793.

4. ". . . separating us in such a way that the passage femininely belongs to the pseudonymous author, the responsibility civilly to me" ("A First and Last Explanation," CUP, 627). And: "I am impersonally or personally in the third person a *souffleur* [prompter] who has poetically produced the *authors*, whose *prefaces* in turn are their productions, as their names are also. Thus in the pseudonymous books there is not a single word by me. I have no opinion about them except as third party, no knowledge of their meaning except as a reader, not the remotest private relation to them, since it is impossible to have that to a doubly reflected communication" ("A First and Last Explanation," CUP, 625–626). At this point, in February 1846, it appears that Kierkegaard intends to "take leave of the pseudonymous authors with doubtful good wishes for their future fate" ("A First and Last Explanation," CUP, 629). However, this came to mark the end of the so-called "first authorship." After becoming embroiled in a literary dispute with the satirical paper *The Corsair* between 1845 and 1846, Kierkegaard began to reawaken as an author. Between 1846 and 1848, he published short discourses and *Works of Love* without the aid of pseudonyms. Following Kierkegaard's personal spiritual awakening in 1848, the so-called "second authorship" was initiated. During this period of prodigious productivity (1848–1851), Kierkegaard employed new pseudonyms predominantly as a means of effacing his own authority with regards to the ideal of authentic Christianity.

5. Roger Poole's *Kierkegaard: The Indirect Communication* is perhaps the most notable monographic reading along these lines. In riposte to what he sees as the mainline trajectory of univocal readings of Kierkegaard's pseudonymous works from the 1840s, Poole seeks to elicit "some openness to reading Kierkegaard as a philosopher who uses all the major tools of deconstructive theory long before they were given a local habitation and a name by Derrida" (p. 7).

6. See Hinkson, "Luther and Kierkegaard: Theologians of the Cross," 28.

7. Dooley, *The Politics of Exodus: Søren Kierkegaard's Ethics of Responsibility*, xv.

8. Ferreira, *Love's Grateful Striving: A Commentary on Kierkegaard's Works of Love*, 11.

9. I have explored this relation further elsewhere, particularly as it pertains to the notion of *Anfechtung*, in Podmore, "The Lightning and the Earthquake: Kierkegaard on the *Anfechtung* of Luther."

10. *Anfægtelse* is a Danish cognate for the German *Anfechtung*, both of which center etymologically around the notion of "fight" (Dn. *fægte* / Gn. *fecht*): as in to be fought against by, and to fight back against, God. As such, I would prefer to translate these words as something like "spiritual struggle" rather than the conventional "spiritual trial" implemented by the Hong and Hong translations of Kierkegaard's works. However, for consistency I have chosen to follow the Hongs' convention of rendering *Anfægtelse* as "spiritual trial," periodically retaining Kierkegaard's original Danish or Luther's German in parentheses, as a reminder. Nonetheless, *Anfægtelse* and *Anfechtung* are difficult to translate into English and, as a result, this important but under-examined category often passes unrecognized for what it is. "Spiritual trial" rightly evokes the tension of "spirit" that is inherent to Kierkegaard's notion of *Anfægtelse*, but the crucial etymological root of "fight" is lost in the phrase. A more expansive definition of these terms will emerge over the course of this work, but for now the following must suffice: as Niels Thulstrup warns, the "different meanings in which SK uses the word trial [*Anfægtelse*] show the difficulties of formulating a definition in which due concern can be paid to both the contents of the term and its range" ("Trial, Test, Tribulation, Temptation," 116. See this work for a concise exploration of the uses of the term in Kierkegaard's corpus.) Specifically, it is Kierkegaard's fertile use of the word as appropriate to the God-relationship that is of most concern for us: "trial as a threat against Christian faith . . . often close to: offence" (ibid., 115). These understandings "point in one specific direction, namely towards the original, etymological, and figurative sense of the word: attack, offensive struggle—and the difficulties which man enters in the state of trial" (ibid., 116–117).

11. In chapter 2, "The Consciousness of Sin / Faith and Forgiveness," of her excellent recent book *Living Christianly: Kierkegaard's Dialectic of Christian Existence*, Sylvia Walsh also identifies and explicates the "central dialectical relationship in Christian existence . . . between sin and faith, or more precisely, between the consciousness of sin and the forgiveness of sin in faith" within "the second period [1847–1851] of Kierkegaard's authorship" (p. 17). On the other hand, my work examines this particular dialectic relative to the category of the infinite qualitative difference as it appears throughout Kierkegaard's authorship with reference to despair, anxiety, melancholy, and spiritual trial, and in relation to a more expansive range of themes and thinkers in Western theology and philosophy.

12. Anxiety, melancholy, and despair are identified by Vincent McCarthy as the three phenomenological "moods" in Kierkegaard's thought (see his *Phenomenology of Moods in Kierkegaard*). To this trinity of interrelated and frequently overlapping moods, I would add Kierkegaard's notion of "spiritual trial" (*Anfægtelse*) which is an "essential expression" of both the infinite qualitative difference and the self's relation to God, and, as such, is deeply intertwined with the three "moods" that McCarthy focuses on. It is, furthermore, an element of the relation "before God," and thus analogous to Luther's earlier notion of "spiritual trial" (*Anfechtung*) as evoked by existing *coram Deo*.

13. At this time, Kierkegaard considered publishing *The Sickness unto Death*

under his own name—in one volume along with manuscripts that later became part of *Practice in Christianity, The Point of View, Armed Neutrality,* and *Two Minor Ethical-Religious Essays*—in order to then "make a clean break" (JP 6:6517 / Pap. X² A 147) and pursue the possibility of becoming a rural pastor. Kierkegaard ultimately came to understand this way of life to be unrealizable for himself. He published *The Sickness unto Death,* after much agonizing about the "ideality" of the work and the humble actuality of his own life, under the new pseudonym "Anti-Climacus": a pseudonym who marked a "halt" and a qualitative change in his authorship as a whole (JP 6:6454 / Pap. X¹ A 557). See further the Hongs' historical introduction to *The Sickness unto Death,* and Perkins's introduction to the *International Kierkegaard Commentary. Volume 20: Practice in Christianity,* ed. Robert L. Perkins.

14. See, for example, Anti-Climacus's reference to the similarity of the "relation between ignorance and despair" and "the relation between ignorance and anxiety" in Vigilius Haufniensis's *The Concept of Anxiety* (SUD, 44).

15. "The person who is not before God is not himself either, which one can be only by being in the one who is in and for himself. If one is oneself by being in the one who is in and for himself, one can be in others or before others, but one cannot be oneself merely by being before others" ("The Care of Lowliness," CD, 40).

16. As such, David Kangas suggests that although Kierkegaard's category of the "before God" establishes God as "the *before whom* of existence itself," it also "by itself . . . leaves unclarified how Kierkegaard conceives God more precisely and whether or not—and here is the onto-theological question par excellence—God fulfils the role of a unifying, *grounding ground* in his thought" (*Kierkegaard's Instant,* 6).

17. "The term 'ontotheology' was first used by Kant in reference to the metaphysical deduction of God's existence with no appeal to experience. It has come into common parlance, however, through the work of Martin Heidegger, for whom the entire history of Western metaphysics, from Plato to Nietzsche, can be called 'ontotheology,' the mark of which is an inability to think the conditions of its own possibility" (Rubenstein, "Unknow Thyself: Apophaticism, Deconstruction, and Theology After Ontotheology," 389). And: "In recent years . . . the word's sense has been expanded by both Heidegger and Derrida so that it now includes the metaphysics Kant called into question and aspects of the critical philosophy itself" (Hart, *The Trespass of the Sign,* 75).

1. INTRODUCTION

1. See also Hoberman, "Kierkegaard on Vertigo," 185, where he explores how the metaphor of vertigo is employed throughout Kierkegaard's writings "as a phenomenological rendering of several kinds of psychological (and, ultimately, religious) disorientation. What is more, it has analogues within the conceptual repertory of the authorship and is thereby conjoined by Kierkegaard with ideas that are of central importance to his thinking, such as freedom, guilt, anxiety, possibility, ambiguity, faith, and the limits of reason."

2. One may also speak of the conjoined adjective *afgrundsdyb,* "abysmal."

3. Kierkegaard applies this phrase to Adler (as discussed below, in chapter 5): "He truly is shaken; he is in mortal danger . . . he is out over 70,000 fathoms of water." By contrast, Bishop Mynster "has never been out on 70,000 fathoms of water and learned out there; he has always clung to the established order and now has completely coalesced with it" (JP 5:5961 / Pap. VIII¹ A 221).

4. For example, the phrase "absolute [*absolut*] difference" is mostly confined to the writings of Johannes Climacus, while the rest of the authorship tends to favor a variation upon an "eternal" (*evig*) or "infinite" (*uendelig*) difference.

5. See the discussion of the sublime in chapter 5, below.

6. Nietzsche, *Beyond Good and Evil,* 89.

7. Nietzsche, *The Portable Nietzsche,* 126.

8. Hoberman, "Kierkegaard on Vertigo," 202.

9. *Mysterium horrendum* is the term Rudolf Otto used to describe the demonic or negative element of the *mysterium tremendum* when "cut loose from the other elements and intensified" (*Idea of the Holy,* 110 n. 2). I discuss this further in chapter 6, below.

2. THE INNER ABYSS

1. Gouwens, *Kierkegaard as Religious Thinker,* 10.

2. Ferguson, *The Science of Pleasure,* 209.

3. Pattison, *Agnosis: Theology in the Void,* 54.

4. Nishitani, *The Self-Overcoming of Nihilism,* 7.

5. Ibid., 7.

6. Søe, "Anthropology," 28.

7. Hegel, *Phenomenology of Spirit,* 180, 111.

8. Raschke, "The Deconstruction of God," 20.

9. Tillich, *The Courage To Be,* 131.

10. Taylor, *Sources of the Self,* 178.

11. Camus, *The Myth of Sisyphus,* 24. Note also the echoes of Augustine's *Confessions* IV.4: "I had become a hard riddle to myself."

12. Cf. Plato, *Republic* X, 609d: "Do injustice and other forms of evil by their persistent presence in it [the soul] destroy and weaken it, till they finally kill it and sever it from the body?"

13. I am therefore reading parts I and II of *The Sickness Unto Death* as coherent, though this is a matter of some contention. See Grøn, "The Relation Between Part One and Part Two of *The Sickness Unto Death,*" 35–50; see also Deede, "The Infinite Qualitative Difference: Sin, the Self, and Revelation in the Thought of Søren Kierkegaard," 25–48.

14. The "Greek fire" refers to a material, used by the ancient Greek navy, that was combustible underwater (JP 4, 660 n. 306).

15. "Indeed, *The Sickness unto Death,* as well as the entire earlier pseudonymous literature of Kierkegaard, can be seen as an 'anatomy' of self-deception, as an escape from the self, a denial of the self" (Gouwens, *Kierkegaard as Religious Thinker,* 38).

16. Foucault, *The Order of Things,* xxiii.

17. "The Greeks were notoriously capable of formulating the injunction '*gnōthi seauton*'—'know thyself'—but they didn't normally speak of the human agent as '*ho autos,*' or use the term in a context which we would translate with the indefinite article" (Taylor, *Sources of the Self,* 113).

18. Thus David Willows: "the Spirit of Socrates, with all its quest for divine knowledge via introspection, hovers over much of modernity with relentless optimism about the capacity of the human mind" (*Divine Knowledge,* 34).

19. "But 'master of oneself' is an absurd phrase. For if you're master *of* yourself you're presumably also subject *to* yourself, and so *both* master *and* subject. For there is only one person throughout" (Plato, *Republic*, 430e).

20. Taylor, *Sources of the Self*, 120.

21. Willows, *Divine Knowledge*, 5.

22. Taylor, *Sources of the Self*, 131.

23. Taylor, *Erring: A Postmodern A/Theology*, 35.

24. Sorabji, *Emotion and Peace of Mind: From Stoic Agitation to Christian Temptation*, 252.

25. See *Enneads* IV 8, 1, 1–11. St. Ambrose of Milan (339–397), whose sermons aided Augustine the months preceding his conversion, wrote a sermon "On Isaac or the Soul" comparing this experience of Plotinus to Paul's ecstatic experience alluded to in 2 Corinthians 12:1–4. See Hadot, *Plotinus or The Simplicity of Vision*, 25 n. 5.

26. Taylor, *Sources of the Self*, 134.

27. Turner, *The Darkness of God: Negativity in Christian Mysticism*, 56.

28. Ibid., 61.

29. Lyotard, *The Confession of Augustine*, 49.

30. Taylor, *Sources of the Self*, 156.

31. Ibid., 158.

32. Cupitt, *The Time Being*, 1.

33. Ibid., 22–24.

34. Ibid., 26.

35. Lyotard, *The Postmodern Condition*, 15.

36. Tillich, *The Courage To Be*, 124.

37. See Corngold, *The Fate of the Self: German Writers and French Theory*, 3.

38. Taylor, *Sources of the Self*, 184.

39. Corngold, *The Fate of the Self*, 8.

40. The Sphinx in Greek mythology being the creature who terrorized the city of Thebes by posing riddles and killing all who were unable to solve them. The riddle that Oedipus famously solved was: "A being with four feet has two feet and three feet, and only one voice; but its feet vary, and when it has most it is weakest." Oedipus solved the riddle by identifying this being as "Man," who crawls on all fours as an infant, then stands on his own two feet, and finally supports himself with a staff at old age. Upon hearing Oedipus's answer the Sphinx killed itself. In other words, the Sphinx poses the murderous riddle, the answer to which is "Man." It is only when the riddle is solved that the question destroys itself and the one who answers is emancipated from the question.

41. Despland, "On Not Solving Riddles Alone," 150–151.

42. Hegel, "The Religions of Transition b. The Egyptian Religion," in *Lectures On the Philosophy of Religion*, 639.

43. Hegel, *Aesthetics*, 361.

44. Despland, "On Not Solving Riddles Alone," 152.

45. Bonhoeffer, *Act and Being*, 98.

46. Corngold, *The Fate of the Self*, 8.

47. Beabout, "Existential Despair in Kierkegaard," 174.

48. Ibid., 168.

49. "The possibility of dizziness lies in the synthesis of the psychical and the

physical as a relation (but not as a relation that relates itself to itself, which is a quali-fication of spirit)" (Pap. VIII² 170:7; deleted from final draft).

50. Rubenstein, "Unknow Thyself," 393.

51. Harper, *The Seventh Solitude*, 4.

52. Taylor, *Deconstructing Theology*, 89.

53. Friedman, *Problematic Rebel*, 456.

54. Marion, *God Without Being*, 54.

55. Cf. Pseudo-Dionysius's plea "to honour in respectful silence the hidden things which are beyond me" (*The Celestial Hierarchy* XV, 9).

56. Marion, *God Without Being*, 54.

57. Ibid., 107.

58. Ibid., 15.

59. Ibid., 35.

60. Ibid., 29.

61. ". . . the 'death of God' presupposes a concept equivalent to that which it appre-hends under the name of 'God'" (ibid., 29).

62. Rubenstein, "Unknow Thyself," 410.

63. Harr, "Nietzsche and the Metamorphosis of the Divine," 160.

64. Nietzsche, *The Portable Nietzsche*, 378–379.

65. Harr, "Nietzsche and the Metamorphosis of the Divine," 162.

66. Nietzsche, *The Portable Nietzsche*, 379.

67. Harr, "Nietzsche and the Metamorphosis of the Divine," 163.

68. Camus, *The Myth of Sisyphus*, 53.

69. Tillich, *The Courage To Be*, 178–179.

70. Ibid., 180.

71. MacIntyre and Ricoeur, *The Religious Significance of Atheism*, 68.

72. Westphal, *Overcoming Onto-Theology*, 257.

73. MacIntyre and Ricoeur, *The Religious Significance of Atheism*, 68.

74. Westphal, *Suspicion and Faith*, 10.

75. Ibid., 284.

76. Jüngel, *God as the Mystery of the World*, 205.

77. Ibid., 205.

78. Ibid., 48.

79. Altizer, "The Beginning and Ending of Revelation," 76.

80. Ibid., 77.

81. Taylor, *Erring*, 37. Taylor does to an extent qualify: "It would be a mistake, however, to hear these words merely as the representation of simple equality-with-self. . . . When God is understood as the absolutely self-identical, which in-itself is complex, He is grasped as substance. Substance (*substantia: sub*, under + *stare*, to stand) is traditionally associated with the Greek *ousia* or essence" (loc. cit.).

82. Jäger, "The Living God and the Endangered Reality of Life," 245.

83. Tracy, "Response to Adriaan Peperzak on Transcendence," 195.

84. Marion, *God Without Being*, 73.

85. Kearney, *The God Who May Be*, 22.

86. See Greisch, "Divine Selfhood and the Postmodern Subject," 251.

87. Kearney, *The God Who May Be*, 22. It should also be noted that the ancient Hebrew language does not possess a typical past, present, or future tense. Instead, it

has an imperfective aspect and perfective aspect as indicators of time, with no actual determined time.

88. Ibid., 1.

89. Marion, *God Without Being*, 45.

90. Ibid., 46.

91. Ibid., 46.

92. Hegel, *Phenomenology of Spirit*, 454–455. Kierkegaard may have been acquainted with the phrase from his own Lutheran tradition. The familiar Lutheran hymn declares the death of God with a sense of eventual triumph: "O great distress! / God himself lies dead. / On the cross he died, / and by doing so he has won for us the realm of heaven" (Johannes Rist, 1641).

93. Hegel, *Faith and Knowledge*, 190.

94. Hegel, *Phenomenology of Spirit*, 470–471.

95. Schöndorf, "The Othering (Becoming Other) and Reconciliation of God in Hegel's *Phenomenology of Spirit*," 395.

96. "Like Hegel's unhappy consciousness, Kierkegaard sees the absolute difference—the unbridgeable gulf—between man's particular, individual consciousness and the Absolute" (Rozema, "Hegel and Kierkegaard On Conceiving the Absolute," 215).

97. From this perspective, Kierkegaard and Hegel represent inversions of one another: "What Hegel regards as self-realization Kierkegaard sees as self-alienation, and what Hegel interprets as self-estrangement is for Kierkegaard self-fulfilment. Conversely, what Kierkegaard views as authentic selfhood Hegel believes to be inauthentic selfhood, and what Kierkegaard sees as inauthenticity is for Hegel authenticity" (Taylor, *Journeys to Selfhood: Hegel and Kierkegaard*, 14).

98. See Stewart, *Kierkegaard's Relation to Hegel Reconsidered*, 341–355. Stewart's book identifies Kierkegaard's polemic as directed at contemporary Danish Hegelians more than at Hegel himself.

99. Ultimately the difference is that Kierkegaard's interest concerns the individual life of faith: "In Hegel the death of God is understood not only in the context of religious piety, as it had been earlier, but in the context of a philosophy of history. . . . The religious intensity is transformed by Hegel into a moment of world history as the point at which spirit is estranged from itself" (Scharlemann, *Theology at the End of the Century*, 5).

100. Schöndorf, "The Othering (Becoming Other) and Reconciliation of God in Hegel's *Phenomenology of Spirit*," 400.

101. Cf. Lessing, "On the Proof of Spirit and of Power"; and for an excellent discussion of this debate concerning Christianity and historical truth, see Rae, *Kierkegaard's Vision of the Incarnation: By Faith Transformed*, 80–85.

102. Cited in Jüngel, *God as the Mystery of the World*, 76.

103. Feuerbach, *The Essence of Christianity*, xvi.

104. See Stewart, *Kierkegaard's Relation to Hegel Reconsidered*, 62, 140.

105. Arbaugh, "Kierkegaard and Feuerbach," 8–9; and see JP 1:546 / Pap. XI^1 A 70; JP 3:3530 / Pap. X^5 A 62.

106. Feuerbach, *The Essence of Christianity*, xvi.

107. Arbaugh, "Kierkegaard and Feuerbach," 9.

108. "Consciousness of God is self-consciousness, knowledge of God is self-knowledge" (Feuerbach, *The Essence of Christianity*, 12).

109. Arbaugh, "Kierkegaard and Feuerbach," 9.

110. H. Richard Niebuhr's foreword to Feuerbach, *The Essence of Christianity*, vii.

111. Ibid., *The Essence of Christianity*, viii.

112. Barth, "An Introductory Essay" to *The Essence of Christianity*, x.

113. Ibid., xix. Charles Taylor also relates how the particularly "Protestant culture of introspection becomes secularized as a form of confessional autobiography," which in turn contributes to the formation of the secular modern novel (*Sources of the Self*, 184).

114. "Protestantism has lived with the crisis longest and most intensely, lived with it, that is, as an internal rather than an external cataclysm. This is because Protestant thought has always been particularly open to the spirit of modernity" (Berger, *A Rumour of Angels*, 22).

115. Barth, "A Thank You and a Bow: Kierkegaard's Reveille," 4.

116. See, e.g., Barth, *The Epistle to the Romans*, 116, 497–499.

117. "It is precisely we who proclaim the right of the individual, the eternal worth of each single one (Kierkegaard!), by announcing that his soul is lost before God and, in him, is dissolved—and saved" (ibid., 116).

118. Ibid., 10.

119. Ibid., 98.

120. Barth, "A Thank You and a Bow: Kierkegaard's Reveille," 6.

121. Ibid., 6.

122. Ibid., 7.

123. Barth, "Kierkegaard and the Theologians," 64.

124. Søe, "Karl Barth," 225.

125. Barth, "A Thank You and a Bow: Kierkegaard's Reveille," 6.

126. Pattison, *Kierkegaard, Religion and the Nineteenth-Century Crisis of Culture*, 177. However, Pattison asks the question: "Is the nineteenth century's ignoring of Kierkegaard perhaps yet another of the many myths that have bedevilled the reception of Kierkegaard?" (p. 178). Habib Malik's ranging work, *Receiving Søren Kierkegaard: The Early Impact and Transmission of His Thought*, also provides an important corrective to this impression.

127. Pattison, *Kierkegaard, Religion and the Nineteenth-Century Crisis of Culture*, 177.

128. Cox, *The Secular City*, 262.

129. Taylor, *Erring*, 6.

130. Crites, *In the Twilight of Christendom: Hegel vs. Kierkegaard on Faith and History*, 56.

131. "The major responsibility for this new atheism is for SK in the Hegellian philosophy, and the radical symptom was above all Feuerbach" (Fabro, "Atheism," 271).

132. Vahanian, *The Death of God*, 230–231.

133. Ibid., 210.

134. Ibid., 210.

135. Altizer, "Theology and the Death of God," 102–103.

136. Ibid., 104.

137. MacIntyre and Ricoeur, *The Religious Significance of Atheism*, 15.

138. Cox, *The Secular City*, 104.

139. Cupitt, *Taking Leave of God*, 8.

140. Sartre, "Kierkegaard: The Singular Universal," 75.

141. Ibid., 77.

142. Friedman, *Problematic Rebel*, 457.

143. Buber, "The Question to the Single One," 41.

144. Ibid., 39.

145. See chapter 6, below.

146. Levinas, "Enigma and Phenomena," 71.

147. Merold Westphal aptly calls this divine paradox "the transparent shadow that shows itself while remaining invisible" (*Levinas and Kierkegaard in Dialogue*, 35).

148. Agacinski, *Aparté: Conceptions and Deaths of Søren Kierkegaard*, 92. However, as Merold Westphal also observes, "Abraham is alone only to secular or pantheistic eyes for which the only actual Other is a human person. But Abraham is alone—before God. *Coram Deo* means that the knight of faith is never alone" (*Levinas and Kierkegaard in Dialogue*, 105).

149. Derrida, *The Gift of Death*, 79. See also Llewelyn, *Margins of Religion: Between Kierkegaard and Derrida*, 34–35, 67–68, 240–241.

150. Derrida, *The Gift of Death*, 57–58.

151. Ibid., 53.

152. Ibid., 53.

153. Ibid., 56.

154. See also ibid., 6 and 27.

155. Otto, *The Idea of the Holy*, 26.

156. Derrida, *The Gift of Death*, 57.

157. Ibid., 68–69.

158. Ibid., 70.

159. Ibid., 68.

160. Ibid., 78.

161. Caputo, "Instants and Singularities: Dealing Death in Kierkegaard and Derrida," 222.

162. Caputo, "God is Wholly Other—Almost: 'Différance' and the Hyperbolic Alterity of God," 191.

163. Ibid., 191.

164. "On this account the Wholly Other will not manage to be the highest name of God, a divine hypernym. Instead, in an unholy reversal, *God* will be but one possible name for the Wholly Other" (ibid., 191).

165. Westphal, "Faith as the Overcoming of Ontological Xenophobia," 161.

166. Ibid., 164.

167. Agacinski, *Aparté*, 84.

168. "In paganism God was regarded as the unknown [*det Ubekjendte*]" (JP 2:1351 / Pap. VIII¹ A 30).

169. Buber, *I and Thou*, 167.

170. Heinecken, *The Moment Before God*, 116.

171. Ibid., 107.

172. Otto, *The Idea of the Holy*, 26.

173. See also Raphael, *Rudolf Otto and the Concept of Holiness*, 26 and 37.

174. See further the discussion of "inverse resemblance" between self and God in chapter 7, below.

175. As David Law points out: "Kierkegaard rejects the idea of mystic union. There is no idea in Kierkegaard's works of the individual being absorbed into the Godhead . . . for Kierkegaard God is and will always remain beyond our grasp" (*Kierkegaard as Negative Theologian,* 214). For this reason, Law claims that Kierkegaard can be understood as a negative theologian who is actually "*more apophatic* than the negative theologians" (ibid., 34).

3. THE ABYSS OF MELANCHOLY

In this work I have chosen to translate both Danish terms *Tungsind* and *Melancholi* with the English word "melancholy" rather than, as in the Hong translations, "depression." This is due to my belief that Kierkegaard's writings on the subject stand within a philosophical, theological, and literary tradition that regards melancholy as a mood or philosophical attitude toward existence, self, and God which is not necessarily to be conflated with the more strictly clinical designation, "depression," in contemporary English.

1. Melancholy's classical genealogy derives from the physiological influences of Pythagorean pathology, according to which melancholy derived from an excess of "black bile" (possibly secreted by the liver) which, due to a resulting physiological imbalance, gave rise to a psychological condition of depression, dejection, or pensiveness. Ideally, harmonious levels of "black bile" were maintained in biological and psychological equilibrium with the three other bodily fluids: yellow bile, blood, and phlegm. Both physical and mental health was classically conceived in terms of the balance and composure of the four bodily fluids—a balance that was rudimentary to the medical theory of the second-century Greek anatomist Galen. According to the influential physiology of Galen's *Prognosis,* the four bodily fluids (yellow bile, blood, phlegm, and black bile) corresponded to the four elements (fire, earth, water, air) and the four Hippocratic qualities (hot, cold, moist, dry). (See Perkins, *The Suffering Self: Pain and Narrative Representation in the Early Christian Era,* 152.) Under this schematism, illness "was conceived as the excess of one humour (*chymoi:* juice or flavour) over the others" (Ferguson, *Melancholy and the Critique of Modernity,* 7). It was Galen's direction toward the possibility of knowing the interior of the body—the mental self as well as the physical self—that "helped set the course for an inner-directed, reflexive 'self'" (Perkins, *The Suffering Self,* 150). As such, it begins to become apparent how the diagnosis of melancholy plays a significant role in the historical turn toward introspection, and thus in the formulation of a modern subjectivity which derives in part from the earlier enquiries of classical biology and philosophy. Abstracted from Hippocratic medical theory, however, modern melancholy has become increasingly remote from its elemental associations with "earth" and physiological origins in "black bile." In modern attempts to define melancholy, Ferguson writes, "two apparently unconnected formulations have become canonical; melancholy is both 'sorrow without cause' and 'loss of being'" (*Melancholy and the Critique of Modernity,* xvi). See Ferguson's book for a useful outline of the genealogy of melancholy in Western thought.

2. Foucault, *The Order of Things,* 387.

3. Ferguson, *Melancholy and the Critique of Modernity,* 30.

4. Erikson, *Young Man Luther,* 37.

5. See, e.g., Fenger, *Kierkegaard, The Myths and Their Origins,* 62–80.

6. See Garff, *Søren Kierkegaard: A Biography*, 458–461.

7. As alleged in Magnussen's *Søren Kierkegaard set udefra* (*Søren Kierkegaard Seen from Outside*) and *Det saerlige Kors* (*The Special Cross*), published together in 1942. Although he was certainly "round-shouldered," it is hard to see how Kierkegaard could have kept such a deformed hunchback a *secret* when his enemies were so keen to satirize his spindly legs and uneven trousers; see Croxhall, *Kierkegaard Commentary*, xvi n. 2. For a concise overview of scholarly commentaries on the secret etymology of Kierkegaard's "thorn in the flesh," see also "Appendix: The Problem of Kierkegaard's Melancholy" in Grimsley, *Søren Kierkegaard and French Literature: Eight Comparative Studies*.

8. It is important to note that while Kierkegaard uses "despair," the diagnosis is closer at this point in his authorship to a more general "melancholy" than what he later formulates as "despair": "It is not yet the formulation of an exact theological concept, which was to emerge later on when he began distinguishing between dread [anxiety] and desperation [despair], but only the 'nuclear embryo'—as it were—from which these notions derive" (Fabro, "Desperation," 132). See also Aquinas, *Summa Theologiæ*, on the question of whether *acedia* gives rise to despair (*desperatio*). Aquinas replies: "Because acedia is a kind of sadness having this depressive effect upon the spirit (*acedia est tristitia quædam dejectiva spiritus*), it gives rise to despair." On the relation between Aquinas's *desperatio* and "despair" in *The Sickness unto Death*, see Theunissen, *Kierkegaard's Concept of Despair*, 92–104. Theunissen suggests: "The context in which the reduction of Thomas Aquinas is embedded anticipates so much of *The Sickness unto Death* that its independence from Aquinas hardly seems credible. Thomas Aquinas especially prepares the interpretation of despair as sin" (p. 93). Nevertheless: "By contrasting despair with hope, Aquinas excludes the opportunity seized by Kierkegaard to put despair into an opposition to faith" (p. 94). In fact, Aquinas asserts that "despair can be found without lack of faith [*desperatio sine infidelitate*]." See also Hojnowski, "Autonomy, Authenticity, and the Flight from God: The Phenomena of Despair and Defiance in the Writings of Søren Kierkegaard and Thomas Aquinas," 73–75.

9. A similar portrait is fictionalized under "Quiet Despair" in 1845's *Stages On Life's Way*, 199–200: "Poor child, you are in a quiet despair. . . . And the father believed that he was responsible for his son's melancholy, and the son believed that it was he who caused his father's sorrow—but never a word was exchanged about this" (p. 200).

10. "Classically it is defined as 'spiritual sloth,' but probably the nearest current synonym is the colloquialism 'fed-upness'" (Dicken, *The Crucible of Love*, 251).

11. Ferguson, *Melancholy and the Critique of Modernity*, 10.

12. Dicken, *The Crucible of Love*, 251.

13. Lake, *Clinical Theology: A Theological and Psychiatric Basis to Clinical Pastoral Care*, 111. See chapter 2, "The Understanding of Depressed, Melancholy or Accidious Persons."

14. John of the Cross, *The Dark Night of the Soul*, bk. I, chap. iv, 6, 20.

15. "When melancholy is the occasion of these visitations of Satan, men in general cannot be delivered from them till their bodily health is improved, unless the dark night has overtaken the soul, gradually freeing it from all trouble" (ibid., bk. I, chap. iv, 6, 20–21). There is an important distinction between the "dark nights" and

melancholia, as Denys Turner explains: "for the one, melancholia, he assumes to have a physiological cause, the other, the spiritual condition, is brought about by God—or rather inevitably by the closeness of God to the soul" (*The Darkness of God*, 235). See also ibid., chapter 10: "John of the Cross: The Dark Nights and Depression."

16. John of the Cross, *The Dark Night of the Soul*, bk. I, chap. vii, 2, 31.

17. See Raposa, *Boredom and the Religious Imagination*, 12. While Aquinas later reinvigorated *acedia* as "sorrow for the divine good," Raposa identifies John Cassian (ca. 360–435) as largely responsible for the more superficial rendering of Evagrius's initial teachings. As such, physical remedies (such as ascribed to Father Seraphim) became dominant forms of spiritual counsel. See also ibid., 22–23.

18. Lake, *Clinical Theology*, 103–104.

19. Ibid., 104.

20. See Sorabji, *Emotion and Peace of Mind*, 362.

21. Ibid., 369.

22. See ibid., 370.

23. Burton, *The Anatomy of Melancholy*, 244.

24. Lepenies, *Melancholy and Society*, 88.

25. Shakespeare, *Kierkegaard, Language and the Reality of God*, 86.

26. Raposa, *Boredom and the Religious Imagination*, 12.

27. Aristotle, *Problems* XXX.1: "Why is it that all those who are outstanding in philosophy, poetry or the arts are melancholic?"

28. Screech, *Montaigne and Melancholy*, 23.

29. Baudelaire, *Les Fleurs Du Mal et Oeuvres Choises*, 192.

30. Ferguson, *Melancholy and the Critique of Modernity*, 25.

31. Burton, *The Anatomy of Melancholy*, 246.

32. Baudelaire, *Les Fleurs Du Mal et Oeuvres Choises*, 84. The translation of *ennui*, as Raposa suggests, is best understood as a "boredom tinged with deep melancholy" (*Boredom and the Religious Imagination*, 13).

33. Allen, *Three Outsiders: Pascal, Kierkegaard, Simone Weil*, 65.

34. As Jean-Luc Marion describes it: "Under the black sun of vanity, nothing matters . . . interest itself in no way interests man; he no longer feels interested in interest, since vanity renders indifferent every difference peculiar to the world and internal to it" (*God Without Being*, 123).

35. Raposa, *Boredom and the Religious Imagination*, 2.

36. McCarthy, *The Phenomenology of Moods in Kierkegaard*, 53.

37. Ibid., 56.

38. Taylor, *Journeys to Selfhood: Hegel and Kierkegaard*, 240 n. 110.

39. McCarthy, "Kierkegaard's Religious Psychology," 254.

40. Taylor, *Journeys to Selfhood: Hegel and Kierkegaard*, 240.

41. McCarthy, "Kierkegaard's Religious Psychology," 254.

42. Khan, "Melancholy, Irony, and Kierkegaard," 68.

43. "*Tungsind* is aligned with the constant longing to eternalize, or freeze, a peak sensual experience, whereas *Melancholi* is in conformity with irony from a personal standpoint. They are essentially two different conditions of melancholy" (Khan, "Melancholy, Irony, and Kierkegaard," 78).

44. Ibid., 80.

45. McCarthy, "Kierkegaard's Religious Psychology," 254.

46. Khan, "Melancholy, Irony, and Kierkegaard," 75.

47. McCarthy, "'Melancholy' and 'Religious Melancholy' in Kierkegaard," 162.

48. Croxhall, *Kierkegaard Commentary*, xv n. 2. Also cited in Grimsley, *Søren Kierkegaard and French Literature*, 166 n. 2.

49. A. S. Aldworth and W. S. Ferrie translate as "heavy-hearted or light-hearted" (*Gospel of Sufferings*, 45).

50. "Depression is the hidden face of Narcissus, the face that is to bear him away into death, but of which he is unaware while he admires himself in a mirage" (Kristeva, *Black Sun: Depression and Melancholia*, 5).

51. A also says in "Diapsalmata": "My melancholy is the most faithful mistress I have known—no wonder, then, that I return the love" (E/O I, 20).

52. Grimsley, *Søren Kierkegaard and French Literature*, 45.

53. B precedes this statement with a refutation of the material nature of melancholy: "for you scarcely assume, as do many physicians that melancholy inheres in the physical, and, strangely enough, physicians nevertheless are unable to eliminate it."

54. In his influential 1917 essay "Mourning and Melancholia," Freud makes the connection between depression or melancholia and the unconscious state of mourning over a lost object. In melancholia, the ego undergoes a narcissistic identification of itself with the lost object, internalizing its loss and thereby diminishing itself. The depressed person is able to direct their aggression toward the lost object only by vilifying their own ego. Hatred toward the internalized lost object is manifest in aggression toward, and a sadistic negation of, the self. It is this *self*-denigration that ultimately distinguishes melancholia from customary grief or mourning. In the usual processes of grief and mourning, Freud maintains, the person does not seek to incorporate the deceased into the ego, so much as come to terms with the reality of a life lived in severance from the lost other. Here mourning is possible beyond the self-mortification of melancholia.

55. Ferguson, *Melancholy and the Critique of Modernity*, 26–27.

56. McCarthy, "Kierkegaard's Religious Psychology," 238.

57. See Hollywood, "Acute Melancholia," 4.

58. Burton, *The Anatomy of Melancholy*, 315.

59. Augustine, *Confessions*, I.5.

60. In *Philosophical Fragments*, Johannes Climacus reiterates an analogous tension by way of the story of a king (the god) who wishes to experience true love (redemption) with a lowly maiden (humanity). Such a possibility is fraught with the hiddenness of the divine: "There was a people who had a good understanding of the divine; this people believed that to see the god was death.—Who grasps the contradiction of this sorrow: not to disclose itself is the death of love; to disclose itself is the death of the beloved" (PF, 30). Given the fatal consequences of a theophany for the human soul, a love-relationship is only possible through a gracious divine descent to the lowliness of the maiden. The incognito presence of the god thereby becomes a divine concession of the lover to the beloved, "for he did not want his own glorification but the girl's" (PF, 29).

61. Augustine, *Confessions*, I.3.

62. Ibid., 137.

63. McCarthy, "Kierkegaard's Religious Psychology," 257. Cf. David Gouwens's description of melancholy as "the unutterable sadness that arises as a person becomes aware of his or her need for the 'eternal'" (*Kierkegaard as Religious Thinker*, 80).

64. McCarthy, "'Melancholy' and 'Religious Melancholy' in Kierkegaard," 162.

65. McCarthy, "Kierkegaard's Religious Psychology," 238.

66. Maio, *St. John of the Cross: The Imagery of Eros*, 10.

67. John of the Cross, "Living Flame of Love," in *The Complete Works of Saint John of the Cross*, vol. 3, 23.

68. ". . . thou must ever hold Him as hidden, and serve Him after a hidden manner, as One that is hidden" ("Spiritual Canticle," ibid., vol. 2, 200).

69. Ibid., vol. 2, 31.

70. Maio, *St. John of the Cross: The Imagery of Eros*, 227.

71. John of the Cross, *The Dark Night of the Soul*, bk. I, chap. vii, 2, 31.

72. Dicken, *The Crucible of Love*, 427.

73. John of the Cross, *The Dark Night of the Soul*, bk. I, chap. v, 24. I have further explored the analogous relation between weaning and the absence of God in John of the Cross and Kierkegaard in Podmore, "The Dark Night of Suffering and the Darkness of God: God-forsakenness or Forsaking God in *Gospel of Sufferings*," 229–256.

74. Turner, *The Darkness of God*, 47.

75. Ibid., 17–18.

4. THE MELANCHOLY THEOPHANY

1. "No one has enunciated more definitively than this master-thinker that God transcends all reason, in the sense that He is beyond the powers of our conceiving, not merely beyond the powers of comprehension" (Otto, *The Idea of the Holy*, 98).

2. Ibid., 31.

3. Ibid., 13.

4. Ibid., 29.

5. Otto, *The Kingdom of God and the Son of Man*, 40.

6. Otto, "The Prophet's Experience of God," in *Religious Essays*, 32.

7. Ibid., 32.

8. Rieger, *God and the Excluded*, 43.

9. Gooch, *The Numinous and Modernity*, 2.

10. Philip Almond, citing Paul Seifert's *Die Religions philosophie bei Rudolf Otto*, suggests this. See Almond, *Rudolf Otto*, 68.

11. Almond, *Rudolf Otto*, 68.

12. Westphal, *God, Guilt, and Death*, 38. Elsewhere Westphal suggests that, in relation to Otto's terminology, "Abraham's faith [in *Fear and Trembling*] is an encounter with the *mysterium tremendum*. As *mysterium*, God escapes our conceptual grasp, to be sure, but in a particular direction signified by the qualifier, *tremendum*" (*Transcendence and Self-Transcendence*, 204).

13. Almond, *Rudolf Otto*, 154 n. 39.

14. Gooch, *The Numinous and Modernity*, 136. In a letter to Jakob Wilhelm Hauer dated 20 May 1928, Otto also dismisses Heidegger's existentialist philosophy after reading *Sein und Zeit* as "a kind of mental illness (*Geisteskrankheit*)." Cited in ibid., 211 n. 42.

Melissa Raphael notes that "the assimilation of the Ottonian concept of holiness into existentialist philosophies is foreign to Otto's thought. At the end of his life, Otto utterly derided the equation of the 'Holy' and 'Being.' He did not consider 'being' holy in itself" (*Rudolf Otto and the Concept of Holiness*, 83).

15. "Sittengesetz und Gotteswille," cited in Gooch, *The Numinous and Modernity*, 136.

16. Bultmann, who had been a friend of Otto's at Breslau, wrote in a letter to Barth how "Otto and I grew so far apart that our students, too, were aware of the antithesis between his work and mine" (cit. Lattke, "Rudolf Bultmann on Rudolf Otto," 353).

17. Poland, "The Idea of the Holy and the History of the Sublime," 184.

18. "Obituary for Rudolf Otto," *The Friend* (19 March 1937), 258; cited in Almond, *Rudolf Otto*, 4.

19. "The holy God of Scripture is certainly not 'the holy' of R. Otto, that numinous element which, in its aspect as *tremendum*, is in itself and as such the divine" (Barth, *Church Dogmatics* II.1, 360). And: "Whatever 'the holy' of Rudolf Otto may be, it certainly cannot be understood as the Word of God, for it is the numinous and the numinous is the irrational, and the irrational can no longer be differentiated from an absolutized natural force" (ibid., I.1, 135).

20. Otto, *The Idea of the Holy*, 29.

21. Gooch, *The Numinous and Modernity*, 24.

22. Ibid., 187. Gooch bases this assessment on Otto's manuscript "Fortsetzung," an apparent continuation of his 1927 lectures on *Glaubenslehre*.

23. The phrase is from Poland, "The Idea of the Holy and the History of the Sublime," 185.

24. Gooch, *The Numinous and Modernity*, 213.

25. Otto, *The Philosophy of Religion*, 124–125.

26. Ibid., 124–125.

27. Westphal, "Faith as the Overcoming Ontological Xenophobia," 156.

28. Berger, *A Rumour of Angels*, 13.

29. Cited in Gooch, *The Numinous and Modernity*, 133.

30. Ibid., 133.

31. Ibid., 134–135.

32. Ibid., 215.

33. See, for example, Donald Capps's examination of Otto as a victim of "religious melancholia" in his 1997 study in the psychology of religion, *Men, Religion, and Melancholia*.

34. Gooch, *The Numinous and Modernity*, 215.

35. Ibid., 215–216.

36. Minney, "The Development of Otto's Thought 1889–1917: From *Luther's View of the Holy Spirit* to *The Holy*," 511.

37. Gregory D. Alles therefore sees Otto's self-appointed task as "a development of a science of religion as an apologetics of religion" which "made it possible for Otto partially to realize his childhood aspirations: to immunize religion . . . against the septic investigations of history and the natural sciences" ("Toward a Genealogy of the Holy: Rudolf Otto and the Apologetics of Religion," 338).

38. Similarly L. Philip Barnes regards Otto's assessment of religious experience as non-conceptual, in distinction to conceptual, knowledge as a defensive strategy, "an apologetic device to safeguard the autonomy of religion and protect religious truth claims from rational criticism" ("Rudolf Otto and the Limits of Religious Description," 222).

39. Cited in Gooch, *The Numinous and Modernity*, 116.

40. Otto, *The Idea of the Holy*, 68.

41. Hegel, *Lectures on the Philosophy of Religion*, 747.

42. Gooch, *The Numinous and Modernity*, 117.

43. Cited in ibid., 116.

44. Ibid., 117.

45. Ibid., 116.

46. Berger, *A Rumour of Angels*, 24.

47. Ibid., 68. Furthermore, Harvey Cox in *The Secular City* diagnoses: "Both philosophical existentialism and Paul Tillich's theology are expressions of the mourning period which began with the death of the God of metaphysical theism and Western Christian civilization, but the wake is now over. That is why existentialist theologies and philosophies do not partake of the spirit of the emerging age but symbolize rather the passing of the old" (p. 93).

48. Altizer, *The Gospel of Christian Atheism*, 87. Altizer elsewhere treats "The Otherness of God as an Image of Satan"; see his chapter in *The Otherness of God*, 206–215.

49. For example, the vocabulary of the numinous has been appropriated into the lexicons of psychology, aesthetics, literature, etc., without recourse to the realist divine ontology upon which Otto establishes his idea of the Holy.

50. Otto, *The Idea of the Holy*, 11.

51. Campbell, "Lecture XVIII: The Objective Validity of Religion," in *On Selfhood and Godhood*, 377. Campbell's example is the possibility of the experience of *mysterium tremendum* being simulated in a dream (p. 376).

52. Berger, *A Rumour of Angels*, 14.

53. "The difficulty may be framed as follows. If the numinous is truly other, how can we tell that the source of this experience is divine? We have no standard in thought or experience to tell us whether the numinous arises from natural or supernatural sources" (Ware, "Rudolf Otto's *Idea of the Holy*: A Reappraisal," 52). Lorne Dawson also contests Otto's inference of an objective numinous reality from a numinous experience: "Otto unacceptably seeks to secure tautologically the foundational character of a root religious feeling through assuming that the unusual character of the object inferred from the feeling is synonymous with its supernatural status." Instead, the sensation is derivable from a "something natural (though unusual)" ("Otto and Freud on the Uncanny and Beyond," 289).

54. Alles, "Toward a Genealogy of the Holy: Rudolf Otto and the Apologetics of Religion," 325.

55. Otto, *The Idea of the Holy*, 8.

56. According to Melissa Raphael, for example, Otto does not sufficiently appreciate the extent to which his "androcentric—indeed monosexual—structure of numinous experience" is predicated upon patriarchal religious norms ("Feminism, Constructivism and Numinous Experience," 519).

57. *The Tremendum*, 18–19. Cohen's reading of the *tremendum* is itself co-habitant with the notion that "we of the modern age are no longer able to deal with the Holy, cannot perceive it, or authenticate its presence, but contrary and fractious, regard ourselves as alone and autonomous in the universe. . . . Is it not the case that in such a civilization all that was once permitted to the infinite power of God and denied to the finite and constrained power of men is now denied to the forgotten God and given over to the potency of infinitized man?" (p. 18).

58. Ibid., 108–109.

59. Ibid., 19.

60. Levinas, *Totality and Infinity*, 199.

61. Stoker, *Is the Quest for Meaning the Quest for God?* 85.

62. Raphael, *Rudolf Otto and the Concept of Holiness*, 207.

63. Otto, *The Idea of the Holy*, 92.

64. Ibid., 40.

65. Ibid., 40.

66. Raphael, *Rudolf Otto and the Concept of Holiness*, 92.

67. Otto, *The Idea of the Holy*, 13.

68. Altizer, *The Gospel of Christian Atheism*, 127.

69. "Specially noticeable is the *emāt* of Yahweh ('fear of God'), which Yahweh can pour forth, dispatching almost like a daemon, and which seizes upon a man with paralysing effect" (Otto, *The Idea of the Holy*, 14).

70. Raphael, *Rudolf Otto and the Concept of Holiness*, 78.

71. Derrida, *The Gift of Death*, 95–98.

72. Ibid., 91.

73. Ibid., 108.

74. Levinas, *Totality and Infinity*, 215.

75. Ibid., 77.

76. In reference to the pagan notion of divine madness see Plato's *Phaedrus*, chap. 22. Here Johannes Climacus emphasizes the negative aspects of religious existence in order to reenergize an existential tension which is lost sight of in modern bourgeois Christendom. "Like Rudolf Otto, he finds the *mysterium* to be *tremendum* (terrifying, repelling) before it is *fascinans* (attractive, reassuring)" (Westphal, *Becoming a Self: A Reading of Kierkegaard's Concluding Unscientific Postscript*, 163).

77. "The fantastic [*Phantastiske*], of course, is most closely related to the imagina-tion [*Phantasie*], but the imagination in turn is related to feeling, knowing, and will-ing; therefore a person can have imaginary feeling, knowing, and willing" (SUD, 30). However, the Danish word Anti-Climacus uses for "imagination" (*Phantasi*) connotes some different nuances from the English word "fantasy," which resounds with more immediately negative suggestions of reverie or delusion. See Ferreira, "Imagination and the Despair of Sin," 16–34.

78. Anti-Climacus considers that "Infinitude's Despair is to Lack Finitude," by which the human wills itself to be infinite without the limit of the finite, or the con-crete. "When feeling or knowing or willing has become fantastic," the self loses itself in abstraction or fantasy (SUD, 30–32).

79. Feuerbach, *The Essence of Christianity*, 127.

80. "Not only is the saying of Luther that the natural man cannot fear God per-fectly correct from the stand-point of psychology, but we ought to go further and add that the natural man is quite unable to shudder (*graven*) or feel horror in the real sense of the word" (Otto, *The Idea of the Holy*, 15).

81. Ibid., 17. Cf. Isaiah 6:3: "And one called to another and said: 'Holy, holy, holy is the Lord of hosts; the whole earth is full of his glory.'" This theophany is discussed in further detail in chapter 5, below.

82. "The whole initiative in the birth of faith is attributable to divine action only" (Otto, "The Christian Idea of 'Lostness' Compared with Moral Depravity," in *Religious Essays*, 21).

83. Otto, *The Idea of the Holy*, 18. This inevitably evokes the death of Uzzah from putting forth his hand to steady the Ark of the Covenant (2 Samuel 6:6–7).

84. This paradoxical self-affirmation in the face of the fear of annihilation finds an illustrative philosophical analogy in the rhetoric of the Kantian sublime. See chapter 5, below.

85. Wessel Stoker intriguingly relates this passage to Levinas's notion of the independence of the created from the Creator—itself related to the doctrine of *tzimtzum* (divine "contraction") in Lurianic Kabbalah. See Stoker, *Is the Quest for Meaning the Quest for God?* 186.

86. "On the subjective side, it is an awareness of the nothingness of the self over against that by which it is confronted in the numinous experience. This nothingness is both ontological and valuational. . . . Concomitant with these feelings of ontological and valuational nothingness, the *numen* is objectively and immediately apprehended as *mysterium*" (Almond, *Rudolf Otto*, 67–68).

87. "The human personality is not a source of wonder or religious exhilaration to Otto" (Raphael, *Rudolf Otto and the Concept of Holiness*, 89).

88. Ibid., 10. "But this 'creature-feeling' itself is only the negative aspect of some positive recognition of the 'numen' as actually present in experience and borrows specific quality from that" (Bennett, "Religion and the Idea of the Holy," 461).

89. "But religion does not fully express itself even in this; there is yet another note that sounds still deeper and is the keynote of the triad. 'Let a man examine himself.' . . . For this is the most real characteristic of religion; it seeks depth in things, reaches out towards what is concealed, uncomprehended, and mysterious. It is more than humility; it is piety. And piety is experience of mystery" (Otto, *Naturalism and Religion*, 39–40).

90. "And this forms the numinous raw material for the feeling of religious humility" (Otto, *The Idea of the Holy*, 20).

91. Ibid., 21.

92. Ibid., 10.

93. "The point from which speculation starts is not a 'consciousness of absolute dependence'—of myself as result and effect of a divine cause—for that would in point of fact lead to insistence upon the reality of the self; it starts from a consciousness of the absolute superiority or supremacy of a power other than myself, and it only falls back upon ontological terms to achieve its end—terms generally borrowed from natural science—that the element of the 'tremendum,' originally apprehended as 'plenitude of power' becomes transmuted into 'plenitude of being'" (ibid., 22).

94. "The Unchangeableness of God," in FSE, 233. "This thought is terrifying, all fear and trembling" (FSE, 231).

95. Derrida, *The Gift of Death*, 56–57.

5. THE ALLEGORY OF YISRA'EL

1. Handelman, "'Torments of an Ancient Word': Edmond Jabès and the Rabbinic Tradition," 57.

2. Lang, "Writing-the-Holocaust: Jabès and the Measure of History," 201.

3. Furthermore, for example, the notion of "the breaking of the vessels" involved in the act of creation, according to Lurianic Kabbalah, can be seen as "a Kabbalistic metaphor for the Jewish experience of being out of place and homeless at a particularly

dark hour in Israel's history" (Rubenstein and Roth, *Approaches to Auschwitz: The Legacy of the Holocaust*, 326).

4. Pattison, *Kierkegaard, Religion and the Nineteenth-Century Crisis of Culture*, 76. See also the outline in Pattison's "'Cosmopolitan Faces': The Presence of the Wandering Jew in *From the Papers of One Still Living*," 109–130.

5. Cited in Pattison, *Kierkegaard, Religion and the Nineteenth-Century Crisis of Culture*, 84.

6. Praz, *The Romantic Agony*, 136.

7. Pattison, "'Cosmopolitan Faces,'" 129–130.

8. "In *Either/Or* this figure [the Wandering Jew] is presented as the unhappiest of all persons because he could not die; consequently he is doomed to endless wandering about the earth in search of a grave of rest and peace" (Walsh, "Patterns for Living Poetically," 288).

9. See further David Kangas's explication in *Kierkegaard's Instant*, 47–56.

10. Whereas for Hegel Judaism is the alienated religion of the Unhappy Consciousness and therefore inferior to the classicism of ancient Greece, for Kierkegaard's Vigilius Haufniensis "Judaism lies in anxiety" and it is "precisely by the anxiety of guilt that Judaism is further advanced than Greek culture" (CA, 103).

11. Taylor, "Journeys to Moriah: Hegel vs. Kierkegaard," 307. According to Sylviane Agacinski, "Hegel and Johannes [de Silentio] actually see Abraham in the same way: he is the figure of the stranger, but this figure is necessarily valorized by them in inverse proportion to each other" (*Aparté*, 94). Judith Butler also compares the "trembling" of Abraham with that of Hegel's bondsman in the *Phenomenology of Spirit*: "How far is the bondsman's trembling at the sight of his own freedom from Abraham's anxiety in the face of his own potential act?" ("Kierkegaard's Speculative Despair," 383).

12. Otto, on the other hand, discerns in the Abrahamic creature-consciousness—"I which am but dust and ashes"—something more than Hegel's abashed and alienated consciousness; instead he sees a consciousness that is profoundly "far more than, and something other than, *merely* a feeling of dependence [Cf. Schleiermacher]" (*The Idea of the Holy*, 10).

13. "To say that Abraham is sublime is to say that he has become a stranger to us. We tremble before the man of faith just as he trembled before his God" (Agacinski, "We Are Not Sublime: Love and Sacrifice, Abraham and Ourselves," 44).

14. Hegel, "The Spirit of Christianity and its Fate, i. The Spirit of Judaism," in *Early Theological Writings*, 187. Despite the apparent resemblance, Mark Taylor draws attention to the fact that Hegel's early theological writings were only published in the twentieth century, thus making any direct influence of Hegel's consideration of Abraham on Kierkegaard improbable. See Taylor, "Journeys to Moriah," 306.

15. Hegel, *Early Theological Writings*, 186. Mark Taylor notes that "Hegel's entire philosophical system is unified by a consistent dialectical progression that seeks to sublate the inauthentic form of selfhood expressed in the life of Abraham" ("Journeys to Moriah," 306). However, it should be noted that Hegel's assessment of an alienated Abraham is later contrasted by the consideration of Abraham's infinite trust/faith in God; see "The Religion of Sublimity (Jewish Religion)," in *Lectures On The Philosophy of Religion*, vol. 2, 424n. Hegel here refers to a community-affirming trust arising from a positive fear: "It is this trust, this faith of Abraham's, that causes the history of this people to carry on" (ibid., 446).

16. Hegel, *Early Theological Writings*, 187.

17. Taylor, "Journeys to Moriah," 310.

18. Butler, "Kierkegaard's Speculative Despair," 383.

19. Hyppolite, *Studies on Marx and Hegel*, 172.

20. See Plato, *Phaedrus* 22 and 37.

21. Hegel, *Early Theological Writings*, 187.

22. Cited in Rupp, *The Righteousness of God*, 112. Luther also discusses *Anfechtung* (spiritual trial, struggle with God) in an exposition of Abraham's near-sacrifice of Isaac.

23. Derrida, *The Gift of Death*, 57.

24. Cited in de Lubac, *The Un-Marxian Socialist*, 179.

25. I have explored this contrast further in Podmore, "Struggling with God: Kierkegaard/Proudhon," 90–103.

26. See Barthes, "Wrestling with the Angel: Textual Analysis of Genesis 32:23–33," 84–95. Writes Valentine Cunningham: "Because of Barthes, Wrestling Jacob has become a main icon of poststructuralist critique, the text of his story one of the most versatile and necessary of critical sites" ("Roland Barthes (1915–1980): Introduction," 74).

27. Cited in Handelman, "'Torments of an Ancient World': Edmond Jabès and the Rabbinic Tradition," 56.

28. Hegel, *Phenomenology of Spirit*, 113.

29. Levinas, "Existence and Ethics," 30.

30. Jean Hyppolite has commented that "God is the master and man is the slave. A form of alienation that reduces man to an existential nothingness results in a humiliation of man which, as Feuerbach noted, might have serious moral consequences" (*Studies on Marx and Hegel*, 133). Among others, Henri de Lubac has suggested that the insurrection of the unhappy "slave" consciousness can be read as symbolizing the insurrection of an aggressive will-to-deicide in atheist humanism by which God appears as "an antagonist, the enemy of his dignity" (*The Drama of Atheist Humanism*, 23).

31. Hegel, *Phenomenology of Spirit*, 111.

32. Ibid., 112.

33. Derrida, *The Gift of Death*, 28.

34. Hegel, *Phenomenology of Spirit*, 113–114.

35. Ibid., 117.

36. Ibid., 117–118 (Proverbs 1:7 and 9:10; Psalm 111:10).

37. The name "Jacob" can also be etymologically related to "deception"—in reference to Jacob's supplanting of his brother Esau in order to gain the blessing of their father Isaac (Genesis 27:36).

38. To see God is to die, but, paradoxically, as Elliot Wolfson maintains, "one would do well to consider the etymology of the word 'Israel' as 'one who sees God'" (*Through a Speculum That Shines*, 50).

39. Hegel, *Phenomenology of Spirit*, 113.

40. Cf. Kierkegaard, "The Care of Presumption" (CD, 66).

41. Dedication of Juan de los Angeles, *The Loving Struggle between God and the Soul*, xviii.

42. Ibid., 16.

43. See also WL, 119: "men find this bondservice to be a burdensome imposition and are more or less openly intent upon deposing God in order to enthrone man."

44. In willing to be the master, "presumption" is related to "in despair to will to be oneself (defiance)." See below, chapter 7 under the section head, "Before God: The Gaze of Despair."

45. ". . . or if it should even be the case that it is God who is in need of human beings, perhaps as the wisdom of this age has understood it (if it is at all understandable) in order to understand Himself" (CD, 67).

46. Levinas, "Enigma and Phenomenon," 71.

47. Ibid., 71. And Levinas elsewhere writes of "the idea of a truth that manifests itself in its humility, like the still small voice in the biblical expression—the idea of a persecuted truth" ("A Man-God?" 55). He also employs the phrase "persecuted truth" in his consideration of Kierkegaard in "Existenz und Ethik" (see "Existence and Ethics," 26–38). On the contrast between absolute difference in Kierkegaard and Levinas, see also Weston, "Kierkegaard, Levinas, and 'Absolute Alterity,'" 153–168.

48. Levinas, "Enigma and Phenomenon," 71.

49. Levinas, "Existence and Ethics," 27.

50. Ibid., 29.

51. Ibid., 29.

52. Ibid., 29.

53. Ibid., 30.

54. Ibid., 30.

55. Otto, *Religious Essays*, 19.

56. Likewise in *Concluding Unscientific Postscript*, Johannes Climacus iterates how one never hears "spiritual trial" mentioned, except when it is conflated with mere "temptation" (*Fristelse*) (CUP, 458). Louise Carroll Keeley writes: "Not speaking about it intensified the aloneness of the experience. Save for the experienced guides of the older devotional literature, one rarely met with any assistance" ("Spiritual Trial in the Thought of Kierkegaard," 313).

57. Juan de los Angeles, *The Loving Struggle between God and the Soul*, 17.

58. Indeed, Kierkegaard notes the irony that "the tendon which God touched in wrestling with Jacob is generally called '*tendo Achillis*' by physicians [though the sciatic nerve may be more accurate], and thus it bears the name of paganism's most powerful and valiant hero; [but] paganism never came in such close contact with the divine that its physical strength suffered under it, and yet it must be said that Jacob was far more powerful" (JP 3:3060 / Pap. II A 545).

59. Juan de los Angeles, *The Loving Struggle between God and the Soul*, 17.

60. de Lubac, *The Un-Marxian Socialist*, 275.

61. Juan de los Angeles, *The Loving Struggle between God and the Soul*, 28–29.

62. John of the Cross, "Spiritual Canticle," in *The Complete Works of Saint John of the Cross*, vol. 2, 35.

63. Luther, *The Table Talk of Martin Luther*, DCXLIV, 273.

64. Smith, "The Dialectic of Selfhood in the Works of Søren Kierkegaard," 69.

65. Plato, *Phaedrus* 244d.

66. "As the Talmud puts it: 'Who is deemed a *shoteh*? One who goes out alone at night; who sleeps in the cemetery; who tears their clothes.' Later the Talmud adds: 'One who destroys all that is given to them'" (Cooper, "The Cracked Crucible: Judaism and Mental Health," 67). Cooper also points out that "the storyteller chooses a word for Saul's 'raving' [in 1 Samuel] which is the same word used in different biblical contexts for 'prophesying'" (ibid., 66).

67. See Steiner, "The Wound of Negativity," 109.

68. Ibid., 109.

69. Ibid., 110.

70. Martin, *The Wings of Faith*, 101.

71. See Haecker, *Kierkegaard The Cripple*, 43–44.

72. See Milbank, "The Sublime in Kierkegaard," where he explores the link, itself pre-Kierkegaardian, "between the psychology of anxiety and the aesthetics of sublimity. The mediating term between the two is 'suspense.' The sublime sensation arises before an abyss, a gulf, an ultimate edge, an interval without apparent end; before this suspension we must remain, temporarily, 'in suspense,' and so (ontologically) 'anxious'" (p. 153 n. 38).

73. Kant, *Critique of Judgment*, 82. George Pattison also notes "the strong conceptual analogies between Kantian sublimity and Kierkegaardian anxiety" ("Sublimity and the Experience of Freedom in Kierkegaard," 189). While acknowledging that Kierkegaard does not derive a concept of "the sublime" (whether referring to *det Sublime* or *Ophøietheden*), Pattison also considers "Kierkegaardian sublimity" under what he calls "the anxious sublime" ("Kierkegaard and the Sublime," 245–275). Elsewhere Pattison also explains how the concept of anxiety "clearly occupies the same logical space as the concept of the sublime, situated at the very point of balance between nature and freedom, between unconscious absorption in the world and the free self-affirmation of the self that, in concern, has become responsible to and for itself" (*Kierkegaard's Upbuilding Discourses*, 87).

74. See also CA, 61.

75. Pattison, "The Sublime in Kierkegaard," 142.

76. Ricoeur, "Kierkegaard and Evil," 56.

77. Poland, "The Idea of the Holy and the History of the Sublime," 181.

78. Ibid., 178.

79. Ibid., 180.

80. Ibid., 180.

81. Throughout his authorship, Kierkegaard constantly evokes sublime imagery of the ocean or the storm. However, as Pattison explores, "Kierkegaard's aim in drawing upon such imagery is not simply to invoke a sublime aesthetic—although I would argue that it is central to his method that he exploits the sublime resonances stirred by his imagery. For sea, storm and tempest are only symbols of what is really dangerous: the inner dissolution of the self into the changeableness of life in time or its destruction at the hands of its own raging impatience. The real conflict is within" (*Kierkegaard's Upbuilding Discourses*, 89).

82. Kant, *Critique of Judgment*, 110.

83. Ibid., 111.

84. Pattison also wishes "to speak of 'the anxious sublime,' in an attempt to locate an impulse towards the religious within the aesthetic that is none the less appropriately experienced and interpreted as aesthetic" ("Kierkegaard and the Sublime," 248). Kierkegaard, moreover, describes modern understanding of the sublime as an "aesthetic accountancy" for transcendence: ". . . we are unable to form properly for ourselves an idea of God's sublimity. We always bog down in our aesthetic quantifying—the amazing, the tremendous, the very influential etc" (JP 1:981 / Pap. X^2 A 178). Nonetheless, the sublime has been discerned as central to the poetic style of

Kierkegaard's *Fear and Trembling*. As Bo Kampmann Walther describes it, the book is "a texture that weaves together all of the Longinian sources of sublimity—writing of great matters: *exclamatio, isocolon, apostrophe, ellipsis, adynaton, hypotoposis, evidentia, prosopopeia, asyndeton,* various forms of *transgressio,* all are but a few examples of an epideictic eloquence to which Kierkegaard attentively responded" ("Web of Shudders: Sublimity in Søren Kierkegaard's *Fear and Trembling,*" 766). Johannes de Silentio also writes of Abraham's endeavor to "express the sublime [*det Sublime*] in the pedestrian."

85. Otto, *The Idea of the Holy,* 65. Just as for Otto the Sphinx at Gizeh set the sublime "throbbing in the soul almost like a mechanical reflex" (p. 68), so Kant also recounts how the pyramids of Egypt arouse the sense of the sublime. See Kant's *Observations on the Feeling of the Beautiful and Sublime,* 49; and *Critique of Judgment,* 90.

86. Otto, *The Idea of the Holy,* 30.

87. Ibid., 43.

88. Ibid., 42. However, while it may be understandable to explain God's "transcendence" *analogously* by God's "sublimity," Otto warns that this should not be taken *literally.* Religious feelings are ultimately unidentifiable with aesthetic feelings, even "the sublime" (p. 42 n. 1).

89. Kant, *Critique of Judgment,* 100.

90. Ibid., 100.

91. Ibid., 100.

92. Ibid., 100–101.

93. Ibid., 103.

94. Ibid., 103.

95. Ibid., 103.

96. Ibid., 103.

97. Ibid., 103.

98. Effectively, Kant's moral sublime constituted "the interiorization of absolute immensity" by which, as Sylviane Agacinski argues, "the fear was exorcized: the absolute was no longer external" ("We Are Not Sublime: Love and Sacrifice, Abraham and Ourselves," 136).

99. Hegel, *Aesthetics,* 376.

100. Ibid., 375.

101. Otto, *The Idea of the Holy,* 65. Otto Kaiser further observes the mysteriously evocative picture that Isaiah paints, in the midst of which "Yahweh is enthroned in sublime majesty and power, on his raised throne" (*Isaiah 1–12: A Commentary,* 76).

102. Furthermore, as Kaiser observes, even the Seraphim cover their eyes because they cannot behold the face of God: "The attitude of the angelic beings emphasizes the infinite distance between God and every creature, and recalls the holiness of God to Isaiah" (*Isaiah 1–12: A Commentary,* 76). Kaiser further invokes Ottonian terms by asserting that the "Holy One is the wholly other, whom man cannot reach by himself, who remains far away and terrible, unless each man turns to him in his free grace, which cannot be forced and cannot be merited" (ibid., 77).

103. Kant, *Critique of Judgment,* 104.

104. Otto, *The Idea of the Holy,* 11.

105. Ibid., 56.

106. Harper, *The Seventh Solitude,* 27.

107. Pascal, *Pensées*, 89.

108. Ibid., 89.

109. Ibid., 90.

110. Ibid., 90.

111. Ibid., 95.

112. Otto, *The Idea of the Holy*, 40. The resemblance between the monstrous and the sublime is apparent in Otto's observation that the celebrated Goethe employs *ungeheuer* to denote "what is too vast for our faculty of space-perception, such as the immeasurable vault of the night sky" (p. 41).

113. Pattison, "Sublimity and the Experience of Freedom in Kierkegaard," 195.

114. Pascal, *Pensées*, 95. Hence Pattison writes: "When I judge a storm to be sublime, I am able to do so because I recognize, with Pascal, that even if it should destroy me physically, there is that in me which is of another order than mere physical force and which enables me to confront even actual danger as 'marvellous! Sublime!'" ("Kierkegaard and the Sublime," 253).

115. As Tillich observes in his *Systematic Theology*, vol. 2, 39.

Similarly in Danish, *Angst* associates with *trang* ("narrow") and *trængsel* ("narrowness" or "tribulation," also suggesting "crowd"). See "Not That the Way is Narrow [*trang*], But That Narrowness [*trængsel*] is the Way" (*Gospel of Sufferings*, 97). Kierkegaard writes: "That we find the way narrow [*trang*], that tribulation [*trængsel*] then is an encountering of opposition, it is an obstacle on the way; there is something to win through, but then the way does lead to bliss" (ibid., 107). And the Danish of 1 Thessalonians 3:3 reads: "We are appointed to tribulations [*trængsler*]." However, as noted previously, *Angst* in the Kierkegaardian corpus also has a strongly vertiginous connotation.

116. Vigilius Haufniensis quotes this phrase from the radical counter-Enlightenment figure Johann Georg Hamann.

117. As John of the Cross analogously describes this sense of "desolation": ". . . the greatest affliction of the sorrowful soul in this state is the thought that God has abandoned it, of which it has no doubt; that He has cast it away into the darkness as an abominable thing" (*The Dark Night of the Soul*, 89).

118. H. V. Martin makes such an observation in *Kierkegaard: The Melancholy Dane*, 16.

119. Burton, *The Anatomy of Melancholy*, 401.

120. Ibid., 410.

121. Ibid., 402–403. Burton even goes so far as to identify God as a cause of melancholy, "for the punishment of sin, and satisfaction of his justice, many examples and testimonies of holy Scriptures make evident unto us. . . . He brought down their heart with heaviness. He stroke them with madness, blindness and astonishment of heart" (p. 156).

122. Otto, *The Idea of the Holy*, 74.

123. Ibid., 88. The 1929 edition of *Das Heilige* contains an extensive citation from F. W. Robertson ("Ten Sermons, III: Jacob's wrestling, point II: The revelation of Mystery") that strongly evokes a sense of the *mysterium tremendum*: "God is approached more nearly in that which is indefinite, than that which is definite and distinct. He is felt in awe, and wonder and worship rather than in clear conception. There is a sense in which darkness has more of God than light has. He dwells in thick darkness.

Moments of tender, vague mystery often bring distinctly the feeling of His presence. When day breaks and distinctness comes, the Divine has evaporated from the soul like morning dew . . . Yes, in solitary, silent, vague darkness, the Awful One is near. . . . That night, in that strange scene He impressed on Jacob's soul a religious awe, which he was hereafter to develop" (cit. *Das Heilige*, 238–239).

124. Otto, *The Idea of the Holy*, 88.

125. Ibid., 88.

126. Heinecken, *The Moment Before God*, 320.

6. THE ANATOMY OF SPIRITUAL TRIAL

1. Heinecken, *The Moment Before God*, 320.

2. Tillich, *The Protestant Era*, 163.

3. McGrath, *Luther's Theology of the Cross*, 170.

4. Tillich, *The Protestant Era*, 162.

5. Rupp, *The Righteousness of God*, 235.

6. Tillich, *The Protestant Era*, 162.

7. Cited in Rupp, *The Righteousness of God*, 109.

8. Hampson, *Christian Contradictions: The Structures of Lutheran and Catholic Thought*, 256.

9. Hampson, *Christian Contradictions*, 31.

10. Hinkson, "Luther and Kierkegaard: Theologians of the Cross," 41.

11. Cited in Rupp, *The Righteousness of God*, 108.

12. Cited in ibid., 109. Leviticus 26:36 reads: "And upon them that are left alive of you I will send a faintness into their hearts in the lands of their enemies; and the sound of a shaken leaf shall chase them; and they shall flee, as fleeing from a sword; and they shall fall when none pursueth."

13. Tillich, *The Courage To Be*, 163.

14. Bonhoeffer, *Act and Being*, 167–168.

15. Rupp, *The Righteousness of God*, 109.

16. This essay appeared in *Crozer Quarterly* XXII, no. 4, and subsequently reappeared in 1948 in James Luther Adams's collected translation of several of Tillich's essays, *The Protestant Era*.

17. Tillich, "The Transmoral Conscience," in *The Protestant Era*, 145–146.

18. Tillich, "The Recovery of the Prophetic Tradition," in *Theological Writings*, vol. 6, 340.

19. Rupp, *The Righteousness of God*, 106.

20. Cited in ibid., 108.

21. Tillich, "The Escape From God," in *The Shaking of the Foundations*, 43–44.

22. Ibid., 44.

23. Sartre, *Being and Nothingness*, 290.

24. Pattison, *Kierkegaard's Upbuilding Discourses*, 107.

25. Sartre, *Words*, 70–71.

26. Sartre, *Being and Nothingness*, 276.

27. Tillich, *The Shaking of the Foundations*, 42.

28. Otto, *The Idea of the Holy*, 103.

29. ". . . an assumption which would be in fact a dangerous and erroneous one; for

no distinction of the non-rational and the rational aspects of God should imply that the latter is less essential than the former" (ibid., 102).

30. Tillich, *Systematic Theology*, vol. 1, 241.

31. Otto, *The Idea of the Holy*, 110 n. 2.

32. Marius, *Martin Luther: The Christian Between God and Death*, 27.

33. Ibid., 27.

34. See Oberman, *Luther*, 105.

35. Rupp, *The Righteousness of God*, 347.

36. Oberman, *Luther: Man between God and the Devil*, 104.

37. Ibid., 155.

38. Luther, "Of the Devil and His Works," in *The Table Talk of Martin Luther*, 265.

39. Ibid., 263–264.

40. See also Podmore, "The Lightning and the Earthquake: Kierkegaard on the *Anfechtung* of Luther," 562–578.

41. Oberman, *Luther*, 106.

42. Luther, *The Table Talk of Martin Luther*, 262.

43. However, Luther seems to have been aware of the embellishing tendencies of one's anxious imagination. As such, for example: "Luther favors occasionally partaking of the Eucharist without confession, 'that a man may learn to trust in the mercy of God' rather than in his own diligence. This is not despising the sacrament or tempting God, if it is done to 'accustom a troubled conscience to trust God and not to tremble at the rustling of every falling leaf'" (McNeill, *A History of the Cure of Souls*, 167).

44. Kierkegaard seems aware of the ultimate governance of God over the devil in Luther when he cites approvingly: "In one of Luther's table-talks he tells how he acts when the devil tempts [*anfægter*] him during the night. He says to him: My good Satan, you must really let me have peace now, for you know it is God's will that man shall work by day and sleep by night" (JP 3:2526 / Pap. X³ A 335).

45. "In the petition, 'Lead us not into temptation' we pray that God, without removing the trial, will give us strength to resist it" (Thulstrup, "Trial, Test, Tribulation, Temptation," 107).

46. Hinkson, "Kierkegaard's Theology: Cross and Grace. The Lutheran and Idealistic Traditions in His Thought," 36–37.

47. Luther, "Sermons II," in *Luther's Works*, vol. 52, 129–130.

48. Marius, *Martin Luther*, 78.

49. Hinkson, "Kierkegaard's Theology: Cross and Grace," 38.

50. Ibid., 38.

51. Ibid., 37.

52. "The Creator Spirit comes to mortify, to convict of sin before God. Thus, like the human spirit, it begins in conflict and works through transformation into a new creation. . . . Mortification—to convict of sin—sounds dark and oppressive, but as an act of the Creator Spirit, it is intended to be just the opposite" (Loder, *The Logic of the Spirit*, 110).

53. Luther, "Of Temptation and Tribulation," in *The Table Talk of Martin Luther*, 274.

54. Rupp, *The Righteousness of God*, 238.

55. Loder, *The Logic of the Spirit*, 119.

56. Ibid., 242.

57. Otto, *The Idea of the Holy*, 103.

58. Tillich, *Systematic Theology*, vol. 2, 89.

59. Kierkegaard "asserts that Luther's personal trial was not the normal one, but something peculiar, for which reason it is also wrong to consider, with 'Protestantism,' Luther as the typical Christian living in mortal dread and trial" (Thulstrup, "Trial, Test, Tribulation, Temptation," 117).

Note, however, that Luther himself appears to appreciate the relativity of *Anfechtung*: "God can make a wisp of straw as heavy as a hundred hundred-weight of corn, so do not despise those who have only small temptations."

60. See Hannay, *Kierkegaard: A Biography*, 394–395 and 484 n. 26. Included among the most notable examples of this theological heritage are the full Danish translation of Thomas à Kempis's *De imitatione Christi* in the same year that Kierkegaard wrote *Practice In Christianity*, Johann Arndt (1555–1621), and H. A. Brorson (1694–1764), lines from whose hymn adorn Kierkegaard's memorial. See also Bukdahl, *Søren Kierkegaard and The Common Man*, 130.

61. This entry is a continuation of 4610 with double cross-hatching over it. Elsewhere, Kierkegaard is cautious to qualify that, as only human, one cannot comprehend Christ's own cry of divinity abandoned by divinity; a point he iterates in *Gospel of Sufferings*.

62. According to Hinkson, "it is Luther's presumed failure to have recognised the voluntary nature of Christian suffering which earns S.K.'s sharpest rebuke" ("Kierkegaard's Theology: Cross and Grace," 77–78).

63. Insofar as it entices us to fall away from the ethical, temptation "is in continuity with the individual's ethical character, whereas spiritual trial lacks continuity and is a mark of the resistance offered by the absolute as it lays down the limit" (Thulstrup, *Commentary on Kierkegaard's Concluding Unscientific Postscript*, 349).

64. In these terms, the *fascinans* would relate to the individual's longing for the God-relationship; while the *tremendum* would be an expression of the infinite qualitative abyss between humanity and divinity that incites the individual to shrink in fear before the (Wholly Other) will of God.

65. I have further examined this relation between temptation (Dn. *Fristelse*) and spiritual trial (*Anfægtelse*) through a Kierkegaardian reading of Nikos Kazantzakis's novel *The Last Temptation* in Podmore, "Crucified by God: Kazantzakis and The Last Anfechtung of Christ," 419–435.

66. However, for many sufferers submission is the only recourse. The attempt to flee from trying thoughts in anxiety only serves to exacerbate further anxiety: "In anxiety he flees from them in every way; he perhaps strains to the point of despair all his powers of ingenuity and concentration in order to avoid not only them but even the remotest contact with anything that could be related to them. It does not help; the anxiety becomes even greater. Neither does the usual advice help—to forget, to escape, for that is just what he is doing, but it merely nourishes the anxiety" (JP 4:4370 / Pap. IX A 333).

67. Keeley, "Spiritual Trial in the Thought of Kierkegaard," 322.

68. Rupp identifies six waves of attack in Luther's notion of spiritual trial (*Anfechtung*): "In the first wave the soul experiences its nakedness and shame before creation. In the second wave, all creation appears to condemn. In the third wave, scripture is brought to condemn. In the fourth wave, the Gospel adds to the terror of the Law. In

the fifth wave, the soul turns from Christ. Finally, the soul believes it is predestined to damnation (God-forsaken)" (*The Righteousness of God*, 238–239).

69. Also, "God is the Teacher" in the "school of sufferings" ("That the School of Sufferings Fits us For Eternity," *Gospel of Sufferings*, 57). Luther compares spiritual trial to a father thrashing a child. As Hinkson writes, "*Anfechtung*, then, is an expression of fatherly discipline; it is the 'school' through which God puts his children in order that they may come to know themselves, and him" ("Kierkegaard's Theology: Cross and Grace," 38).

70. Cox, *Man's Anger and God's Silence: The Book of Job*, 11.

71. Keeley, "Spiritual Trial in the Thought of Kierkegaard," 316.

72. By this notion of "suspension" I mean to express that it is by a free decision of the will that faith trusts that God is love—accepting that this possibility exceeds human understanding. However, the offence against suffering is held in anxious "suspension" since the divine gift of freedom entails the inexorable *possibility* of offence "which cannot be removed." This notion of faith as a teleological suspension of offence is explored further in relation to the im/possibility of forgiveness in chapters 7 and 8, below.

73. Theunissen aptly calls this moment the "leap into the abyss of the idea that everything is possible for God [which] appears as the only way out of a situation in which nothing is possible for the person anymore" (*Kierkegaard's Concept of Despair*, 86–87).

74. Luther, "Comfort When Facing Grave Temptations," in *Luther's Works*, vol. 42, 186.

75. Heinecken, *The Moment Before God*, 149.

76. See Rocca, "Søren Kierkegaard on Silence," 80.

77. ". . . if a person yields himself completely in prayer, he does not struggle" ("One Who Prays Aright Struggles in Prayer and is Victorious—in that God is Victorious," EUD, 383). And: "The more one comes to realize the difficulty of prayer, the more one realizes that in a sense the only real prayer is that one might be enabled to pray; then prayer becomes a silent surrendering of everything to God" (in LeFevre, *The Prayers of Kierkegaard*, 202).

7. THE GAZE OF THE ABYSS

1. This volume is collected in the Hong and Hong edition in a volume titled *Without Authority*: the title derives from Kierkegaard's repeated insistence that he is an author of discourses "without authority," rather than a teacher or preacher of sermons.

2. As Kierkegaard acknowledges, this discourse is "related to the last pseudonym, Anti-Climacus" (JP 6:6515 / Pap X 2 A 126) or "parallel to Anti-Climacus" (JP 6:6519 / Pap X 2 A 148).

3. Evans, *Søren Kierkegaard's Christian Psychology*, 59.

4. See McGrath, *Iustitia Dei: A History of the Christian Doctrine of Justification*, 199.

5. Eller, *Kierkegaard and Radical Discipleship*, 109.

6. Ferreira, "Imagination and the Despair of Sin," 24.

7. Ibid., 24.

8. Ibid., 25.

9. Pattison, *Kierkegaard's Upbuilding Discourses,* 96.

10. Ibid., 95.

11. Pattison, "'Before God' as a Regulative Concept," 70–84.

12. Ibid., 72.

13. Gellman, *Abraham! Abraham! Kierkegaard and the Hasidim on the Binding of Isaac,* 37. And see Gellman's equally fascinating *The Fear, the Trembling, and the Fire: Kierkegaard and the Hasidic Masters on the Binding of Isaac,* 14.

14. Kierkegaard identifies himself with "the religious poet" to whom Anti-Climacus refers (see JP 6:6437 / Pap. X¹ A 525). Cf. Podmore, "Kierkegaard as Physician of the Soul: On Self-Forgiveness and Despair."

15. "The [Hegelian] notion of recognition is the key to interpreting what Kierkegaard means by the levels of consciousness before God" (Stewart, "Kierkegaard's Phenomenology of Despair in *The Sickness unto Death,*" 131). Cf. Stewart, *Kierkegaard's Relation to Hegel Reconsidered,* 585.

16. In this sense, "defiance" conceptually parallels "The Anxiety of Presumption" in Kierkegaard's *Christian Discourses.* See above chapter 5, under the section head "The Primal Enmity." Theunissen specifies that "the despair of defiance is heir to [Aquinas's] *praesumptio*" (*Kierkegaard's Concept of Despair,* 96), and Anti-Climacus discerns a Faustian genre of defiance rooted in the hubristic will to be oneself as found in the sin of *superbia* (pride or excessive self-esteem). As such, "Kierkegaard goes beyond Aquinas primarily by expanding the concept of despair, which was restricted to *desperatio,* to *praesumptio.* Seen against the backdrop of the Medieval conception, the innovation of his projection is that he discovers an independent form of despair in *praesumptio.* . . . Indeed, a *praesumptio* identified as despair can no longer be the one that Aquinas thought of" (ibid., 95).

17. Kant, *The Metaphysics of Ethics,* 248.

18. Hegel, *Phenomenology of Spirit,* 126. Though finally omitted, Kierkegaard had drafted in *The Sickness unto Death* (SUD, 37): "Both forms [i.e., 'desiring/craving' and 'the melancholy-imaginary'] are forms of an unhappy consciousness" (Pap. VIII² B 150:8). Daniel Berthold-Bond is also keen to point out that "in an important sense, Hegel also sees 'unhappy consciousness,' or 'soul in despair,' as the disunity of the self *before God*" ("Lunar Musings? An Investigation of Hegel's and Kierkegaard's Portraits of Despair," 41).

19. Note that while the phrase "thorn in the flesh" is applied elsewhere to describe an authentic mark of the God-relationship, of spiritual trial (*Anfægtelse*), here its dramatic use is ironic, pointing to the constant danger of fantastic or melancholy embellishment in one's self-diagnosis.

20. Vigilius Haufniensis describes this "Anxiety of Sin" in *The Concept of Anxiety* as a form of "Anxiety about the good (the demonic)" (CA, 118–136).

21. Though in reference to *Christian* suffering, Kierkegaard elsewhere warns: "To bite at the chain is to bear it heavily, to scorn the chain is also to bear it heavily" (UDVS, 242). Once again there is no suffering, "Christian" or "demonic," that is entirely immune to the risk of the fetishism of melancholy.

22. Bonhoeffer, *Act and Being,* 157–158.

23. "The possibility of offense lies in this: there must be a revelation from God to teach man what sin is and how deeply it is rooted" (SUD, 96).

24. As Cornelio Fabro observes, "the principle that desperation [despair] is a 'duplicate sin,' the radical sin, also called the sin against the Holy Spirit, is well known in Christian Spirituality and could have been located by Kierkegaard in, among others, the work of St. Johannes Climacus" ("The Problem of Desperation and Christian Spirituality in Kierkegaard," 64)—namely, the sixth-century monk at Mount Sinai and author of *The Ladder of Divine Ascent,* a mystical/ascetic text describing the soul's ascent to *theosis* or "union with God." His resemblance to Kierkegaard's pseudonym Johannes Climacus is oblique at best. See also Aquinas: "It would seem that presumption, which is a sin against the Holy Spirit, is a case of relying, not upon God, but upon one's own power"; and yet, "presumption as an unwarranted dependence upon God is a worse sin than the presumption which involves reliance upon personal resources. To rely upon the divine power for something ill-befitting God is, in effect, to belittle that power and is obviously a more serious sin than to exaggerate one's own power" (*Summa Theologiæ,* 2a2æ: 21, 1).

25. "Perhaps the sin against the Holy Spirit was rather the pride with which he would not forgive himself. There is also a severity in condemning oneself and not wanting to hear about grace which is nothing but sin" (JP 4:4029 / Pap. X² A 429). As Hugh Pyper writes: "The unforgivable sin, then, is not to forgive oneself, or not to acknowledge that one is forgiven: the two come to the same thing in Kierkegaard's eyes" ("Forgiving the Unforgivable: Kierkegaard, Derrida and the Scandal of Forgiveness," 11).

26. Taylor, *Erring,* 24.

27. See also *Philosophical Fragments,* 36: "Presumably it could occur to a human being to poeticize himself in the likeness of the god or the god in the likeness of himself, but not to poeticize that the god poeticized himself in the likeness of a human being, for if the god gave no indication, how could it occur to a man that the blessed god could need him?"

28. ". . . it is not that man on his own initiative chooses to be *den Enkelte* in order to address God; rather, God first has addressed man as *den Enkelte,* and man must then get into that role if he is to hear and respond. *Den Enkelte* is first of all the character of God's address and only then the nature of man's response" (Eller, *Kierkegaard and Radical Discipleship,* 110–111).

29. "The look of love with which Christ transforms our penitent love for him into an eternal image of forgiveness, is God's own look of love" (Pattison, "Looks of Love: The Seducer and the Christ"). I must acknowledge my particular gratitude to Prof. Pattison for providing me with a copy of his paper which, though also concerned with the counterpoint of "the spectacular city," deals with many of the same instances of "the gaze" in Kierkegaard's writings as are dealt with in this chapter.

30. Rupp, *The Righteousness of God,* 226.

31. Darío González, "Sin, Absolute Difference," 374.

32. Otto, *The Idea of the Holy,* 186.

8. CONCLUSIONS

1. Buber, "The Question to the Single One," 42.

2. Taylor, *The Ethics of Authenticity,* 1.

3. "The search for authenticity in modern Western thought begins with the

desperate journal entry, dated 1 August, 1835, of a 22-year-old Dane: 'the thing is to find a truth, which is true *for me,* to find the idea for which I can live and die'" (Golomb, *In Search of Authenticity,* 33). And later: "There is today a grave danger that we are facing the death of authenticity. Poststructuralist thought and other currently fashionable streams of what is usually called 'postmodernism' attempt to dissolve the subjective pathos of authenticity which lies at the heart of existentialist concern" (ibid., 203–204).

4. Pattison, "'Before God' as a Regulative Concept," 84.

5. Evans, "Who Is the Other in *The Sickness unto Death*? God and Human Relations in the Constitution of the Self," 8.

6. "To say of God (in the same sense as saying that he is not finite and consequently, *via negationis,* that he is infinite) that he is not a sinner is blasphemy" (SUD, 122).

7. Sponheim, "Is Forgiveness Enough? A Kierkegaardian Response," 322.

8. To reiterate, I am using the notion of "suspension" to express that it is by a free decision of the will that self-willing denies itself through faith's trust in the divine possibility of forgiveness. However, the offence against forgiveness is not overcome once and for all, but is held in anxious "suspense," since the divine gift of freedom entails the constant *possibility* of offence "which cannot be removed," and of which the self remains ever conscious.

9. Translated as "To Forgive: The Unforgivable and the Imprescriptible."

10. Derrida, "To Forgive," 27.

11. Ibid., 40.

12. Pyper, "Forgiving the Unforgivable," 8. See also p. 13: "Only because there is unforgivable sin is forgiveness meaningful, as only a God who does not forgive can forgive."

13. As such, Pyper explains: "The denial of possibility is the unforgivable. All sin is sin against the Holy Spirit, because all sin is a failure, in one way or another, to love in the light of the incomprehensible fact that 'with God all things are possible'" (ibid., 12).

14. Ibid., 19.

15. Derrida, "On Forgiveness: A Roundtable Discussion with Jacques Derrida," 61.

16. Ibid., 61.

17. ". . . he who expected the impossible became the greatest of all" (FT, 16).

18. ". . . there is not a more exact agreement between the sky above and its reflection in the sea, which is just as deep as the distance is high, than there is between forgiveness and forgiving" (WL, 380).

BIBLIOGRAPHY

SØREN KIERKEGAARD'S WORKS IN DANISH

Søren Kierkegaards Skrifter. Copenhagen: G. E. C. Gads Forlag, 1997–2007.

SØREN KIERKEGAARD'S WORKS IN ENGLISH

Armed Neutrality and An Open Letter. Ed. and trans. Howard V. Hong and Edna H. Hong. Bloomington: Indiana University Press, 1968.

The Book on Adler. Ed. and trans. Howard V. Hong and Edna H. Hong. Bloomington: Indiana University Press, 1998.

Christian Discourses, The Crisis and a Crisis in the Life of an Actress. Ed. and trans. Howard V. Hong and Edna H. Hong. Bloomington: Indiana University Press, 1997.

The Concept of Anxiety. Ed. and trans. Reidar Thomte, in collaboration with Albert B. Anderson. Princeton: Princeton University Press, 1980.

The Concept of Irony: With Constant Reference to Socrates. Ed. and trans. Howard V. Hong and Edna H. Hong. Bloomington: Indiana University Press, 1989.

Concluding Unscientific Postscript to Philosophical Fragments. Ed. and trans. Howard V. Hong and Edna H. Hong. Bloomington: Indiana University Press, 1992.

Eighteen Upbuilding Discourses. Ed. and trans. Howard V. Hong and Edna H. Hong. Princeton: Princeton University Press, 1990.

Either/Or: A Fragment of Life. Part I. Ed. and trans. Howard V. Hong and Edna H. Hong. Princeton: Princeton University Press, 1987.

Either/Or: A Fragment of Life. Part II. Ed. and trans. Howard V. Hong and Edna H. Hong. Princeton: Princeton University Press, 1987.

Fear and Trembling. Repetition. Ed. and trans. Howard V. Hong and Edna H. Hong. Princeton: Princeton University Press, 1983.

For Self-Examination. Judge For Yourself! Ed. and trans. Howard V. Hong and Edna H. Hong. Princeton: Princeton University Press, 1990.

Gospel of Sufferings. Trans. A. S. Aldsworth and W. S. Ferrie. Cambridge: James Clarke & Co., 1982.

Journals and Papers, 7 vols. Ed. and trans. Howard V. Hong and Edna H. Hong. Bloomington: Indiana University Press, 1967–1978.

The Journals of Søren Kierkegaard—A Selection. Ed. and trans. Alexander Dru. London and New York: Oxford University Press, 1951.

The Moment and Late Writings. Ed. and trans. Howard V. Hong and Edna H. Hong. Princeton: Princeton University Press, 1998.

Philosophical Fragments. Ed. and trans. Howard V. Hong and Edna H. Hong. Princeton: Princeton University Press, 1985.

The Point of View For My Work as an Author. Ed. and trans. Howard V. Hong and Edna H. Hong. Princeton: Princeton University Press, 1998.

Practice in Christianity. Ed. and trans. Howard V. Hong and Edna H. Hong. Princeton: Princeton University Press, 1991.

The Sickness unto Death. Ed. and trans. Howard V. Hong and Edna H. Hong. Princeton: Princeton University Press, 1983.

Stages on Life's Way. Ed. and trans. Howard V. Hong and Edna H. Hong. Princeton: Princeton University Press, 1988.

Two Ages: The Age of Revolution and The Present Age (A Literary Review). Ed. and trans. Howard V. Hong and Edna H. Hong. Princeton: Princeton University Press, 1978.

Upbuilding Discourses in Various Spirits. Ed. trans. Howard V. Hong and Edna H. Hong. Princeton: Princeton University Press, 1993.

Without Authority. Ed. and trans. Howard V. Hong and Edna H. Hong. Princeton: Princeton University Press, 1995.

Works of Love. Ed. and trans. Howard V. Hong and Edna H. Hong. Princeton: Princeton University Press, 1995.

SECONDARY WORKS ON KIERKEGAARD

Agacinski, Sylviane. *Aparté: Conceptions and Deaths of Søren Kierkegaard.* Trans. Kevin Newmark. Tallahasee: Florida State University Press, 1988.

———. "We are Not Sublime: Love and Sacrifice, Abraham and Ourselves." In *Kierkegaard: A Critical Reader,* ed. Jonathan Rée and Jane Chamberlain. Oxford: Blackwell, 1997.

Allen, Diogenes. *Three Outsiders: Pascal, Kierkegaard, Simone Weil.* Cambridge, Mass.: Cowley, 1983.

Arbaugh, George E. "Kierkegaard and Feuerbach." In *Kierkegaardiana XI,* ed. Niels Thulstrup. Copenhagen: C. A. Reitzels Boghandel, 1980.

Beabout, Gregory R. "Existential Despair in Kierkegaard." *Philosophy and Theology* (Winter 1992): 167–174.

———. *Freedom and Its Misuses: Kierkegaard on Anxiety and Despair.* Milwaukee: Marquette University Press, 1996.

Berthold-Bond, Daniel. "Lunar Musings? An Investigation of Hegel and Kierkegaard's Portraits of Despair." *Religious Studies* 34 (1998): 33–59.

Buber, Martin. "The Question to the Single One." In *Søren Kierkegaard: Critical Assessments of Leading Philosophers. Volume III. Philosophy of Religion: Kierkegaard Contra Contemporary Christendom,* ed. Daniel W. Conway with K. E. Gover. London: Routledge, 2002.

Bukdahl, Jørgen. *Søren Kierkegaard and The Common Man.* Ed. and trans. Bruce H. Kirmmse. Grand Rapids, Mich.: William B. Eerdmans, 2001.

Butler, Judith. "Kierkegaard's Speculative Despair." In *The Age of German Idealism,* ed. Robert C. Solomon and Kathleen M. Higgins. London: Routledge, 1993.

Caputo, John D. "Instants and Singularities: Dealing Death in Kierkegaard and Derrida." In *Kierkegaard in Post/Modernity,* ed. Martin J. Matuštík and Merold Westphal. Bloomington: Indiana University Press, 1995.

Crites, Stephen. *In the Twilight of Christendom: Hegel vs. Kierkegaard on Faith and History.* Chambersburg, Penn.: American Academy of Religion, 1972.

Croxhall, T. H. *Kierkegaard Commentary.* London: Nisbet, 1956.

Deede, Kristen K. "The Infinite Qualitative Difference: Sin, the Self, and Revelation in the Thought of Søren Kierkegaard." *International Journal for Philosophy of Religion* 53, no. 1 (February 2003): 25–48.

Dietrichson, Paul. "Kierkegaard's Concept of the Self." *Inquiry* 8, no. 1 (1965): 1–32.

Dooley, Mark. *The Politics of Exodus: Søren Kierkegaard and the Ethics of Responsibility.* New York: Fordham University Press, 2001.

Dupré, Louis. "The Constitution of the Self in Kierkegaard's Philosophy." *International Philosophical Quarterly* 3 (1963): 506–526.

———. "Of Time and Eternity in Kierkegaard's Concept of Anxiety." *Faith and Philosophy* 1, no. 2 (1984): 160–176.

Eller, Vernard. *Kierkegaard and Radical Discipleship: A New Perspective.* Princeton: Princeton University Press, 1968.

Evans, C. Stephen. *Søren Kierkegaard's Christian Psychology: Insight for Counselling and Pastoral Care.* Vancouver, B.C.: Regent College, 1990.

———. "Who Is the Other in *Sickness unto Death*? God and Human Relations in the Constitution of the Self." In *Kierkegaard Studies Yearbook 1997,* ed. Niels Jørgen Cappelørn and Hermann Deuser. Berlin: Walter de Gruyter, 1997.

Fabro, Cornelio. "Atheism." In *Bibliotheca Kierkegaardina. Vol. 5: Theological Concepts in Kierkegaard,* ed. Niels Thusltrup and Marie Mikulová Thulstrup. Copenhagen: C. A. Reitzels Boghandel, 1980.

———. "Desperation." In *Bibliotheca Kierkegaardiana. Vol. 7: Kierkegaard and Human Values,* ed. Niels Thusltrup and M. Mikulvá Thulstrup. Copenhagen: C. A. Reitzels Boghandel, 1980.

———. "The Problem of Desperation and Christian Spirituality in Kierkegaard." In *Kierkegaardiana IV,* ed. Niels Thulstrup. Copenhagen: Munksgaard, 1962.

Fenger, Henning. *Kierkegaard, The Myths and Their Origins: Studies in the Kierkegaardian Papers and Letters.* Trans. George C. Schoolfield. New Haven and London: Yale University Press, 1980.

Ferguson, Harvie. *Melancholy and the Critique of Modernity: Søren Kierkegaard's Religious Psychology.* London: Routledge, 1995.

Ferreira, M. Jamie. "Imagination and the Despair of Sin." In *Kierkegaard Studies Yearbook 1997,* ed. Niels Jørgen Cappelørn and Hermann Deuser. Berlin: Walter de Gruyter, 1997.

———. *Transforming Vision: Imagination and Will in Kierkegaardian Faith.* Oxford: Clarendon Press, 1991.

Florin, Frits. "Was Kierkegaard Inspired by Medieval Mysticism?" In *Kierkegaardiana* 22, ed. Dario González, et al. Copenhagen: C. A. Reitzels Forlag, 2002.

Garff, Joakim. *Søren Kierkegaard: A Biography.* Trans. Bruce H. Kirmmse. Princeton and Oxford: Princeton University Press, 2005.

Gellman, Jerome I. *Abraham! Abraham! Kierkegaard and the Hasidim on the Binding of Isaac.* Aldershot: Ashgate, 2003.

———. *The Fear, the Trembling, and the Fire: Kierkegaard and the Hasidic Masters on the Binding of Isaac.* New York and London: University Press of America, 1994.

González, Darío. "Sin, Absolute Difference." In *Kierkegaard Studies Yearbook 2003,* ed. Niels Jørgen Cappelørn, Hermann Deuser, and Jon Stewart. Berlin: Walter de Gruyter, 2003.

Gouwens, David J. *Kierkegaard as Religious Thinker.* Cambridge: Cambridge University Press, 1996.

Grimsley, Ronald. *Søren Kierkegaard and French Literature: Eight Comparative Studies.* Cardiff: University of Wales Press, 1966.

Grøn, Arne. "The Relation Between Part One and Part Two of *The Sickness Unto Death.*" In *Kierkegaard Studies Yearbook 1997,* ed. Niels Jørgen Cappelørn and Hermann Deuser. Berlin: Walter de Gruyter, 2007.

Haecker, Theodor. *Kierkegaard the Cripple.* Trans. C. Van O. Bruyn. London: Harvill Press, 1948.

Hamilton, Kenneth. *The Promise of Kierkegaard.* Philadelphia: J. B. Lippincott Co., 1969.

Hannay, Alastair. *Kierkegaard: A Biography.* Cambridge: Cambridge University Press, 2001.

Harper, Ralph. *The Seventh Solitude: Metaphysical Homelessness in Kierkegaard, Dostoevsky and Nietzsche.* Baltimore: Johns Hopkins University Press, 1967.

Hinkson, Craig. "Kierkegaard's Theology: Cross and Grace. The Lutheran and Idealistic Traditions in His Thought." PhD diss., University of Chicago, 1993.

———. "Luther and Kierkegaard: Theologians of the Cross." *International Journal of Systematic Theology* 3, no. 1 (March 2001): 27–45.

Hoberman, John H. "Kierkegaard on Vertigo." In *International Kierkegaard Commentary. Volume 19: The Sickness unto Death,* ed. Robert L. Perkins. Macon, Ga.: Mercer University Press, 1987.

Hojnowski, Peter Edward. "Autonomy, Authenticity and the Flight from God: The Phenomena of Despair and Defiance in the Writings of Søren Kierkegaard and Thomas Aquinas." PhD diss., Fordham University, 1993.

Huntington, Patricia J. "Heidegger's Reading of Kierkegaard Revisited: From Ontological Abstraction to Ethical Concretion." In *Kierkegaard in Post/Modernity,* ed. Martin J. Matuštík and Merold Westphal. Bloomington: Indiana University Press, 1995.

Kangas, David J. *Kierkegaard's Instant: On Beginnings.* Bloomington: Indiana University Press, 2007.

Keeley, Louise Carroll. "Spiritual Trial in the Thought of Kierkegaard." In *International Kierkegaard Commentary: Concluding Unscientific Postscript to "Philosophical Fragments,"* ed. Robert L. Perkins. Macon, Ga.: Mercer University Press, 1997.

Khan, Abrahim H. "Melancholy, Irony, and Kierkegaard." *International Journal for Philosophy of Religion* 17 (1985): 67–85.

———. *Salighed as Happiness? Kierkegaard on the Concept Salighed.* The Kierkegaard Monograph Series, ed. Alastair McKinnon. Waterloo, Ontario: Wilford Laurier University Press, 1985.

Kirmmse, Bruce H. *Encounters With Kierkegaard: A Life as Seen by His*

Contemporaries. Trans. Bruce H. Kirmmse and Virginia R. Laursen. Princeton: Princeton University Press, 1996.

Kroenker, Ernest B. "Søren Kierkegaard on Luther." In *Interpreters of Luther: Essays in Honor of William Pauck,* ed. Jaroslav Pelikan. Philadelphia: Fortress Press, 1968.

Law, David R. *Kierkegaard as Negative Theologian.* Oxford: Clarendon Press, 1993.

LeFevre, Perry, ed. *The Prayers of Kierkegaard.* Chicago: University of Chicago Press, 1956.

Levinas, Emmanuel. "Existence and Ethics." In *Kierkegaard: A Critical Reader,* ed. J. Reé and J. Chamberlain. Oxford: Basil Blackwell, 1998.

Llewelyn, John. *Margins of Religion: Between Kierkegaard and Derrida.* Bloomington: Indiana University Press, 2009.

Magnussen, Rikard. *Søren Kierkegaard set udefra* and *Det saerlige Kors,* 2 vols. Copenhagen: Munksgaard, 1942.

Malik, Habib. *Receiving Søren Kierkegaard: The Early Impact and Transmission of His Thought.* Washington, D.C.: Catholic University of America Press, 1997.

Martin, H. V. *Kierkegaard: The Melancholy Dane.* London: Epworth Press, 1950.

———. *The Wings of Faith: A Consideration of the Nature and Meaning of Christian Faith in the Light of the Work of Søren Kierkegaard.* London: Lutterworth Press, 1950.

Manheimer, Bruce. *Kierkegaard As Educator.* Berkeley and London: University of California Press, 1977.

McBride, William L. "Sartre's Debt to Kierkegaard: A Partial Reckoning." In *Kierkegaard in Post/Modernity,* ed. Martin J. Matuštík and Merold Westphal. Bloomington: Indiana University Press, 1995.

McCarthy, Vincent A. "Kierkegaard's Religious Psychology." In *Kierkegaard's Truth: The Disclosure of the Self,* ed. Joseph H. Smith. New Haven: Yale University Press, 1981.

———. "'Melancholy' and 'Religious Melancholy' in Kierkegaard." In *Kierkegaardiana X,* ed. Niels Thusltrup. Copenhagen: C. A. Reitzels Boghandel, 1977.

———. *The Phenomenology of Moods in Kierkegaard.* The Hague: Martinus Nijhoff, 1978.

Milbank, John. "The Sublime in Kierkegaard." In *Post-Secular Philosophy,* ed. Philip Blond. London: Routledge, 1998.

Murphy, Nancey, and James Wm. McClendon, Jr. "Distinguishing Modern and Postmodern Theologies." *Modern Theology* 5, no. 3 (April 1989): 191–214.

Newmark, Kevin. "Between Hegel and Kierkegaard: The Space of Translation." In *Modern Critical Views: Søren Kierkegaard,* ed. Harold Bloom. New York: Chelsea House Publishers, 1989.

Nordentoft, Kresten. *Kierkegaard's Psychology.* Trans. Bruce H. Kirmmse. Pittsburgh: Duquesne University Press, 1978.

Pattison, George. "'Before God' as a Regulative Concept." In *Kierkegaard Studies Yearbook 1997,* ed. Niels Jørgen Cappelørn and Hermann Deuser. Berlin: Walter de Gruyter, 1997.

———. "'Cosmopolitan Faces': The Presence of the Wandering Jew in *From the Papers of One Still Living.*" In *International Kierkegaard Commentary. Volume 1: Early Polemical Writings,* ed. Robert L. Perkins. Macon, Ga.: Mercer University Press, 1999.

———. *Kierkegaard: The Aesthetic and the Religious.* London: SCM Press, 1999.

———. "Kierkegaard and the Sublime." In *Kierkegaard Studies Yearbook 1998,* ed. Niels Jørgen Cappelørn and Hermann Deuser. Berlin: Walter de Gruyter, 1998.

———. *Kierkegaard, Religion and the Nineteenth-Century Crisis of Culture.* Cambridge: Cambridge University Press, 2002.

———. *Kierkegaard's Upbuilding Discourses: Philosophy, Theology, Literature.* London: Routledge, 2002.

———. "Looks of Love: The Seducer and the Christ." Paper presented in 2004 at The Annual Conference of the Søren Kierkegaard Society of the United Kingdom: "Kierkegaardian Images of Christ." University of Manchester, 8 May 2004.

———. "Sublimity and the Experience of Freedom in Kierkegaard." In *Kierkegaard and Freedom,* ed. James Giles. Houndsmill: Palgrave, 2000.

Pedersen, Jørgen. "Augustine and Augustinianism." In *A Kierkegaard Critique,* ed. Howard A. Johnson and Niels Thulstrup. New York: Harper & Bros., 1962.

Perkins, Robert L. "Introduction." In *International Kierkegaard Commentary. Volume 20: Practice in Christianity,* ed. Robert L. Perkins. Macon, Ga.: Mercer University Press, 2004.

Podmore, Simon D. "Crucified by God: Kazantzakis and The Last *Anfechtung* of Christ." *Literature and Theology* 22, no. 4 (December 2008): 419–435.

———. "The Dark Night of Suffering and the Darkness of God: God-forsakenness or Forsaking God in *Gospel of Sufferings.*" In *International Kierkegaard Commentary: Upbuilding Discourses in Various Spirits,* ed. Robert L. Perkins. Macon, Ga.: Mercer University Press, 2005.

———. "Kierkegaard as Physician of the Soul: On Self-Forgiveness and Despair." *Journal of Psychology & Theology* 37, no. 3 (Fall 2009): 174–185.

———. "The Lightning and the Earthquake: Kierkegaard on the *Anfechtung* of Luther." *Heythrop Journal* 48 (2006): 562–578.

———. "Struggling with God: Kierkegaard/Proudhon." In *Acta Kierkegaardiana. Vol. II: Kierkegaard and Great Philosophers,* ed. C. Diatka and R. Králik. Mexico City and Barcelona: Sociedad Iberoamericana de Estudios Kierkegaardianos, University of Barcelona, Kierkegaard Society in Slovakia, 2007.

Poole, Roger. *Kierkegaard: The Indirect Communication.* Charlottesville: University Press of Virginia, 1993.

Prenter, Regin. "Luther and Lutheranism." In *Bibliotheca Kierkegaardina. Vol. 6: Kierkegaard and Great Traditions,* ed. Niels Thulstrup and Marie Mikulová Thulstrup. Copenhagen: C. A. Reitzels Boghandel, 1981.

Pyper, Hugh S. "Forgiving the Unforgivable: Kierkegaard, Derrida and the Scandal of Forgiveness." In *Kierkegaardiana 22,* ed. Dario González, et al. Copenhagen: C. A. Reitzels Forlag, 2002.

Quinn, Philip L. "Does Anxiety Explain Original Sin?" *Nous* 24 (1990): 227–244.

Rae, Murray. *Kierkegaard's Vision of the Incarnation: By Faith Transformed.* Oxford: Clarendon Press, 1997.

Ricoeur, Paul. "Kierkegaard and Evil." In *Modern Critical Views: Søren Kierkegaard,* ed. Harold Bloom. New York: Chelsea House Publishers, 1989.

Rocca, Ettore. "Søren Kierkegaard on Silence." In *Anthropology and Authority: Essays on Søren Kierkegaard,* ed. Poul Houe, Gordon D. Marino, and Sven Hakon Rossel. Amsterdam: Rodolphi, 2000.

Rose, Tim. *Kierkegaard's Christocentric Theology*. Aldershot: Ashgate, 2001.

Rozema, David L. "Hegel and Kierkegaard On Conceiving the Absolute." *History of Philosophy Quarterly* 9, no. 2 (April 1992): 207–225.

Sagi, Avi. *Kierkegaard, Religion, and Existence: The Voyage of the Self*, trans. Batya Stein. Amsterdam: Rodopi, 2000.

Sartre, Jean-Paul. "Kierkegaard: The Singular Universal." In *Modern Critical Views: Søren Kierkegaard*, ed. Harold Bloom. New York: Chelsea House Publishers, 1989.

Shakespeare, Steven. *Kierkegaard, Language and the Reality of God*. Aldershot: Ashgate, 2001.

Sløk, Johannes. "Kiekegaard and Luther." Trans. A. Roussing. In *A Kierkegaard Critique*, ed. Howard A. Johnson and Niels Thulstrup. New York: Harper & Bros., 1962.

Smith, Joel Robert. "The Dialectic of Selfhood in the Works of Søren Kierkegaard." PhD diss., Vanderbilt University, 1977.

Søe, N. H. "Anthropology." In *Bibliotheca Kierkegaardiana. Vol. 7: Kierkegaard and Human Values*, ed. Niels Thusltrup and M. Mikulvá Thulstrup. Copenhagen: C. A. Reitzels Boghandel, 1980.

———. "Karl Barth." In *Bibliotheca Kierkegaardiana. Vol. 8: The Legacy and Interpretation of Kierkegaard*, ed. Niels Thusltrup and M. Mikulvá Thulstrup. Copenhagen: C. A. Reitzels Boghandel, 1981.

Sponheim, Paul. *Kierkegaard on Christ and Christian Coherence*. New York: Harper & Row, 1968.

———. "Is Forgiveness Enough? A Kierkegaardian Response." *Word and World* 16, no. 3 (Summer 1996): 320–327.

Steiner, George. "The Wound of Negativity." In *Kierkegaard: A Critical Reader*, ed. J. Reé and J. Chamberlain. Oxford: Basil Blackwell, 1998.

Stewart, Jon. "Kierkegaard's Phenomenology of Despair in *The Sickness unto Death*." In *Kierkegaard Studies Yearbook 1997*, ed. Niels Jørgen Cappelørn and Hermann Deuser. Berlin: Walter de Gruyter, 1997.

———. *Kierkegaard's Relation to Hegel Reconsidered*. Cambridge: Cambridge University Press, 2003.

Taylor, Mark C. "Journeys to Moriah: Hegel vs. Kierkegaard." *Harvard Theological Review* 70 (July 1977): 305–326

———. *Journeys to Selfhood: Hegel and Kierkegaard*. Berkeley: University of California Press, 1980.

Theunissen, Michael. *Kierkegaard's Concept of Despair*. Trans. Barbara Harshav and Helmut Illbruck. Princeton: Princeton University Press, 2005.

Thulstrup, Marie Mikulová. "Studies of Pietists, Mystics, and Church Fathers." In *Bibliotheca Kierkegaardina. Vol. 1: Kierkegaard's View of Christianity*, ed. Niels Thulstrup and Marie Mikulová Thulstrup. Copenhagen: C. A. Reitzels Boghandel, 1978.

Thulstrup, Niels. *Commentary on Kierkegaard's Concluding Unscientific Postscript*. Trans. Robert J. Widenmann. Princeton: Princeton University Press, 1984.

———. "Theological and Philosophical Studies." In *Bibliotheca Kierkegaardina. Vol. 1: Kierkegaard's View of Christianity*, ed. Niels Thulstrup and Marie Mikulová Thulstrup. Copenhagen: C. A. Reitzels Boghandel, 1978.

———. "Trial, Test, Tribulation, Temptation." In *Bibliotheca Kierkegaardina. Vol. 16: Some of Kierkegaard's Main Categories*, ed. Niels Thulstrup and Marie Mikulová Thulstrup. Copenhagen: C. A. Reitzels Forlay, 1988.

Walsh, Sylvia. *Living Christianly: Kierkegaard's Dialectic of Christian Existence.* University Park: Pennsylvania State University Press, 2005.

———. "Patterns for Living Poetically." In *Søren Kierkegaard: Critical Assessments of Leading Philosophers. Volume I,* ed. Daniel W. Conway with K. E. Gover. London: Routledge, 2002.

Weston, Michael. "Kierkegaard, Levinas, and 'Absolute Alterity.'" In *Kierkegaard and Levinas: Ethics, Politics, and Religion,* ed. J. Aaron Simmons and David Wood. Bloomington: Indiana University Press, 2008.

Westphal, Merold. *Becoming a Self: A Reading of Kierkegaard's Concluding Unscientific Postscript.* West Lafayette, Ind.: Purdue University Press, 1996.

———. *Levinas and Kierkegaard in Dialogue.* Bloomington: Indiana University Press, 2008.

———. *Transcendence and Self-Transcendence: On God and the Soul.* Bloomington: Indiana University Press, 2004.

Willows, David. *Divine Knowledge: A Kierkegaardian Perspective on Christian Education.* Aldershot: Ashgate, 2001.

Wilson, Colin. *Religion and the Rebel.* Cambridge, Mass.: Riverside Press, 1957.

GENERAL

Alles, Gregory D. "Toward a Genealogy of the Holy: Rudolf Otto and the Apologetics of Religion." *Journal of the American Academy of Religion* 69, no. 2 (June 2001): 323–342.

Almond, Philip C. *Rudolf Otto: An Introduction to His Philosophical Theology.* Chapel Hill: University of North Carolina Press, 1984.

Altizer, Thomas J. J. "The Beginning and Ending of Revelation." In *Theology at the End of the Century: A Dialogue on the Postmodern,* ed. Robert P. Scharlemann. Charlottesville: University Press of Virginia, 1990.

———. *The Gospel of Christian Atheism.* Philadelphia: Westminster Press, 1966.

———. "The Otherness of God as an Image of Satan." In *The Otherness of God,* ed. Orrin F. Summerell. Charlottesville: University Press of Virginia, 1998.

Altizer, Thomas J. J., and William Hamilton. *Radical Theology and the Death of God.* Harmondsworth: Penguin, 1968.

Aquinas, Thomas. *Summa Theologiæ. Vol. 23: Hope (2a2æ. 17–22),* trans. W. J. Hill. Cambridge: Blackfriars, 1966.

Augustine. *Confessions.* Trans. Albert C. Outler. Nashville: Thomas Nelson, 1999.

Barnes, L. Philip. "Rudolf Otto and the Limits of Religious Description." *Religious Studies* 30 (1994): 219–230.

Barth, Karl. *Church Dogmatics. Volume II: The Doctrine of God.* Ed. G. W. Bromily and T. F. Torrance, trans. T. H. L. Parker, W. B. Johnston, Harold Knight, and J. L. M. Haire. Edinburgh: T. & T. Clark, 1957.

———. *The Epistle to the Romans.* Trans. from 6th edition by Edwyn C. Hoskyns. Oxford and New York: Oxford University Press, 1933.

———. "An Introductory Essay." In Ludwig Feuerbach, *The Essence of Christianity,* trans. George Elliot. New York and London: Harper & Row, 1957.

———. "Kierkegaard and the Theologians." *Canadian Journal of Theology* 13 (1967): 64–65.

————. "A Thank You and a Bow: Kierkegaard's Reveille." *Canadian Journal of Theology* 11, no. 1 (1965): 3–7.

Barthes, Roland. "Wrestling with the Angel: Textual Analysis of Genesis 32:23–33." In *The Postmodern God: A Theological Reader*, ed. Graham Ward. Oxford: Blackwell, 1997.

Baudelaire, Charles. *Les Fleur du Mal et Oeuvres Choises*. New York: Dover, 1963.

Bennett, Charles A. "Religion and the Idea of the Holy." *The Journal of Philosophy* 23, no. 17 (Aug. 1926): 460–469.

Berger, Peter L. *A Rumour of Angels: Modern Society and the Rediscovery of the Supernatural*. London: Penguin, 1970.

Bonhoeffer, Dietrich. *Act and Being*. Trans. Bernard Noble. London: Collins, 1962.

Buber, Martin. *I and Thou*. Trans. Ronald Gregor Smith. Edinburgh: T. & T. Clark, 1958.

Burton, Robert. *The Anatomy of Melancholy*. New York: The New York Review of Books, 2001.

Campbell, C. A. *On Selfhood and Godhood*. London: George Allen & Unwin / New York: The MacMillan Co., 1957.

Camus, Albert. *The Myth of Sisyphus*. Trans. Justin O'Brian. Harmondsworth: Penguin, 1975.

Caputo, John D. "God is Wholly Other—Almost: Différance and the Hyperbolic Alterity of God." In *The Otherness of God*, ed. Orrin F. Summerell. Charlottesville: University Press of Virginia, 1998.

Capps, Donald. *Men, Religion, and Melancholia: James, Otto, Jung, and Erikson*. New Haven: Yale University Press, 1997.

Cavaliero, Glen. *The Supernatural and English Fiction*. Oxford and New York: Oxford University Press, 1995.

Chalier, Catherine. "The Philosophy of Emmanuel Levinas and the Hebraic Tradition." In *Ethics as First Philosophy: The Significance of Emmanuel Levinas for Philosophy*, ed. Adriaan T. Peperzak. New York: Routledge, 1995.

Cohen, Arthur. *The Tremendum: A Theological Interpretation of the Holocaust*. New York: Crossroad, 1981.

Cohn-Sherbok, Dan. *God and the Holocaust*. Leominster: Gracewing, 1996.

Cooper, Howard. "The Cracked Crucible: Judaism and Mental Health." In *Psychiatry and Religion: Context, Consensus and Controversies*, ed. Dinesh Bhugra. London: Routledge, 1997.

Corngold, Stanley. *The Fate of the Self: German Writers and French Theory*. New York: Columbia University Press, 1986.

Cox, Dermot. *Man's Anger and God's Silence: The Book of Job*. Middlegreen: St. Paul Publications, 1990.

Cox, Harvey. *The Secular City: Secularization and Urbanization in Theological Perspective*. Harmondsworth: Penguin, 1968.

Cunningham, Valentine. "Roland Barthes (1915–1980): Introduction." In *The Postmodern God: A Theological Reader*, ed. Graham Ward. Oxford: Blackwell, 1997.

Cupitt, Don. *Taking Leave of God*. London: SCM Press, 1980.

————. *The Time Being*. London: SCM Press, 1992.

Dawson, Lorne. "Otto and Freud on the Uncanny and Beyond." *Journal of the American Academy of Religion* 57, no. 2 (1989): 283–311.

Derrida, Jacques. *The Gift of Death*. Trans. David Wills. Chicago: University of Chicago Press, 1996.

———. "On Forgiveness: A Roundtable Discussion with Jacques Derrida." In *Questioning God*, ed. John D. Caputo, Mark Dooley, and Michael Scanlon. Bloomington: Indiana University Press, 2001.

———. "To Forgive: The Unforgivable and the Imprescriptible." In *Questioning God*, ed. John D. Caputo, Mark Dooley, and Michael Scanlon. Bloomington: Indiana University Press, 2001.

Despland, Michel. "On Not Solving Riddles Alone." In *Derrida and Negative Theology*, ed. Harold Coward and Toby Foshay. Albany: State University of New York, 1992.

Dicken, E. W. Trueman. *The Crucible of Love: A Study of the Mysticism of St. Teresa of Jesus and St. John of the Cross*. London: Darton, Longman & Todd, 1963.

Erikson, Erik H. *Young Man Luther: A Study in Psychoanalysis and History*. New York and London: W. W. Norton & Co., 1993.

Fabro, Cornelio. *God in Exile: Modern Atheism—A Study of the Internal Dynamic of Modern Atheism, from Its Roots in the Cartesian 'Cogito' to the Present Day*. Ed. and trans. Arthur Gibson. New York: Newman Press, 1968.

Ferguson, Harvie. *The Science of Pleasure: Cosmos and Psyche in the Bourgeois World View*. London: Routledge, 1990.

Feuerbach, Ludwig. *The Essence of Christianity*. Trans. George Elliot. New York: Prometheus Books, 1989.

Forsyth, P. T. *The Work of Christ*. Blackwood, Australia: New Creation Publications, 1994.

Foucault, Michel. *The Archaeology of Knowledge*. Trans. A. M. Sheridan Smith. London: Tavistock Publications, 1972.

———. *The Order of Things: An Archaeology of the Human Sciences*. London: Tavistock Publications, 1970.

Friedman, Maurice. *Problematic Rebel: Melville, Dostoievsky, Kafka, Camus*. Chicago: University of Chicago Press, 1970.

Frost, Christopher J. *Religious Melancholy or Psychological Depression?* New York: University Press of America, 1985.

Golomb, Jacob. *In Search of Authenticity: From Kierkegaard to Camus*. London: Routledge, 1995.

Gooch, Todd A. *The Numinous and Modernity: An Interpretation of Rudolf Otto's Philosophy of Religion*. Berlin: Walter de Gruyter, 2000.

Greisch, Jean. "Divine Selfhood and the Postmodern Subject." In *Questioning God*, ed. John D. Caputo, Mark Dooley, and Michael Scanlon. Bloomington: Indiana University Press, 2001.

Hadot, Pierre. *Plotinus or The Simplicity of Vision*. Trans. Michael Chase. Chicago: University of Chicago Press, 1998.

Hampson, Daphne. *Christian Contradictions: The Structures of Lutheran and Catholic Thought*. Cambridge: Cambridge University Press, 2001.

Handelman, Susan. "'Torments of an Ancient World': Edmond Jabès and the Rabbinic Tradition." In *The Sin of the Book: Edmond Jabès*, ed. Eric Gould. Lincoln: University of Nebraska Press, 1985.

Harr, Michel. "Nietzsche and the Metamorphosis of the Divine." In *Post-Secular Philosophy*, ed. Philip Blond. London: Routledge, 1998.

Hart, Kevin. *The Trespass of the Sign: Deconstruction, Theology and Philosophy*. Cambridge: Cambridge University Press, 1989.

Hegel, G. W. F. *Aesthetics: Lectures On Fine Art. Volume I*. Trans. T. M. Knox. Oxford: Clarendon Press, 1975.

———. *The Christian Religion*. Trans. Peter C. Hodgson. Missoula, Mont.: Scholars Press, 1979.

———. *Early Theological Writings*. Trans. T. M. Knox. Chicago: University of Chicago Press, 1948.

———. *Faith and Knowledge*. Trans. Walter Cerf and H. S. Harris. Albany: State University of New York Press, 1977.

———. *Lectures On the Philosophy of Religion. Volume 2: Determinate Religion*. Ed. Peter C. Hodgson, trans. R. F. Brown, P. C. Hodgson, J. M. Stewart, and H. S. Harris. Berkeley and London: University of California Press, 1987.

———. *Phenomenology of Spirit*. Trans. A. V. Miller. Oxford: Oxford University Press, 1977.

Heinecken, Martin J. *The Moment Before God*. Philadelphia: Muhlenberg Press, 1956.

Hollywood, Amy. "Acute Melancholia." *Harvard Theological Review* 99, no. 4 (2006): 381–406.

Howard-Snyder, Daniel, and Moser, Paul K., eds. *Divine Hiddenness: New Essays*. Cambridge: Cambridge University Press, 2002.

Hyppolite, Jean. *Studies on Marx and Hegel*. Ed. and trans. John O'Neill. New York and London: Harper & Row, 1973.

Ignatius of Loyola. *The Spiritual Exercises of Saint Ignatius of Loyola*. Trans. W. H. Longridge. London: Robert Scott, 1919.

Jäger, Alfred. "The Living God and the Endangered Reality of Life." In *The Otherness of God*, ed. Orrin F. Summerell. Charlottesville: University Press of Virginia, 1998.

John of the Cross. *The Complete Works of Saint John of the Cross: Doctor of the Church*, 3 vols. Ed. and trans. E. Allison Peers. London: Burns, Oates & Washbourne, 1934–1935.

———. *The Dark Night of the Soul*. Trans. B. Zimmerman. Cambridge: James Clarke & Co., 1973.

Juan de los Angeles. *The Loving Struggle between God and the Soul*. Trans. Eladia Gómez-Posthill. London: Saint Austin Press, 2001.

Jüngel, Eberhard. *Death: The Riddle and the Mystery*. Edinburgh: Saint Andrews Press, 1975.

———. *God as the Mystery of the World: On the Foundation of the Theology of the Crucified One in the Dispute Between Theism and Atheism*. Trans. Darrell L. Guder. Edinburgh: T. & T. Clark, 1983.

Kaiser, Otto. *Isaiah 1–12: A Commentary*. Trans. R. A. Wilson. London: SCM Press, 1972.

Kant, Immanuel. *Critique of Judgment*. Trans. J. H. Bernard. New York: Hafner Publishing Co., 1966.

———. *The Metaphysics of Ethics*. Edinburgh: T. & T. Clark, 1869.

———. *Observations on the Feeling of the Beautiful and Sublime*. Trans. John T. Goldthwait. Chicago: University of Chicago Press, 1960.

Kearney, Richard. *The God Who May Be: A Hermeneutics of Religion*. Bloomington: Indiana University Press, 2001.

Kristeva, Julia. *Black Sun: Depression and Melancholia.* Trans. Leon S. Roudiaz. New York: Columbia University Press, 1989.

Lake, Frank. *Clinical Theology: A Theological and Psychiatric Basis to Clinical Pastoral Care.* London: Darton, Longman & Todd, 1966.

Lang, Berel. "Writing-the-Holocaust: Jabès and the Measure of History." In *The Sin of the Book: Edmond Jabès,* ed. Eric Gould. Lincoln: University of Nebraska Press, 1985.

Lattke, Michael. "Rudolf Bultmann on Rudolf Otto." *Harvard Theological Review* 78 (1985): 353–360.

Lepenies, Wolf. *Melancholy and Society.* Trans. Jeremy Gaines and Doris Jones. Cambridge, Mass.: Harvard University Press, 1992.

Lessing, G. E. "On the Proof of Spirit and of Power." In *Lessing's Theological Writings,* trans. Henry Chadwick. London: Adam & Charles Black, 1956.

Levinas, Emmanuel. "A Man-God?" In *entre nous: Thinking-of-the-Other,* trans. Michael B. Smith and Barbara Harshav. New York: Columbia University Press, 1998.

———. "Enigma and Phenomenon." In *Basic Philosophical Writings,* ed. Adriaan T. Peperzak, Simon Critchley, and Robert Bernasconi. Bloomington: Indiana University Press, 1996.

———. *Totality and Infinity: An Essay on Exteriority.* Trans. Alphonso Lingis. Pittsburgh: Duquesne University Press, 1969.

Loder, James E. *The Logic of the Spirit: Human Development in Theological Perspective.* San Francisco: Jossye-Bass, 1998.

de Lubac, Henri. *The Drama of Atheist Humanism.* Trans. Anne Englund Nash, Edith M. Riley, and Mark Sebanc. San Francisco: Ignatius Press, 1995.

———. *The Un-Marxian Socialist: A Study of Proudhon.* Trans. R. E. Scantlebury. London: Sheed & Ward, 1948.

Luther, Martin. "Devotional Writings I." In *Luther's Works,* vol. 42, ed. Martin O. Dietrich. Philadelphia: Fortress Press, 1969.

———. "Sermons I." In *Luther's Works,* vol. 51, ed. John W. Doberstein. Philadelphia: Muhlenberg Press, 1959.

———. "Sermons II." In *Luther's Works,* vol. 52, ed. Hans J. Hillerbrand. Philadelphia: Fortress Press, 1974.

———. *The Table Talk of Martin Luther.* Ed. and trans. William Hazlitt. London: H. G. Bohn, 1857.

Lyotard, Jean-François. *The Confession of Augustine.* Trans. Richard Beardsworth. Stanford, Calif.: Stanford University Press, 2000.

———. *The Postmodern Condition: A Report on Knowledge.* Trans. Geoff Bennington and Brian Massumi. Manchester: Manchester University Press, 1997.

———. *Postmodern Fables.* Trans. Georges Van Den Abbeele. Minneapolis: University of Minnesota Press, 1993.

MacIntyre, Alasdair, and Paul Ricoeur. *The Religious Significance of Atheism.* New York: Columbia University Press, 1969.

Maio, Eugene A. *St. John of the Cross: The Imagery of Eros.* Madrid: Playor, S. A., 1973.

Marion, Jean-Luc. *God Without Being: Hors Texte.* Trans. Thomas H. Carlson. Chicago: University of Chicago Press, 1991.

Marius, Richard. *Martin Luther: The Christian Between God and Death.* Cambridge, Mass.: Belknap Press of Harvard University Press, 1999.

McGrath, Alister E. *Iustitia Dei: A History of the Christian Doctrine of Justification.* Cambridge: Cambridge University Press, 1998.

———. *Luther's Theology of the Cross.* Oxford: Blackwell, 1990.

McNeill, John T. *A History of the Cure of Souls.* London: SCM Press, 1952.

Minney, Robert. "The Development of Otto's Thought 1889–1917: From *Luther's View of the Holy Spirit* to *The Holy.*" *Religious Studies* 26 (1990): 505–524.

Moltmann, Jürgen. *The Crucified God: The Cross of Christ as the Foundation and Criticism of Christian Theology.* London: SCM Press, 1974.

Nayani, Tony, and Bhugra, Dinesh. "Guilt, Religion and Ritual." In *Psychiatry and Religion: Context, Consensus and Controversies,* ed. Dinesh Bhugra. London: Routledge, 1997.

Niebuhr, H. Richard. "Foreword." In Ludwig Feuerbach, *The Essence of Christianity,* trans. George Elliot. New York and London: Harper & Row, 1957.

Niebuhr, Reinhold. *The Nature and Destiny of Man: A Christian Interpretation. Volume I: Human Nature.* London: Nisbet & Co. Ltd., 1941.

Nietzsche, Friedrich. *Beyond Good and Evil: Prelude to a Philosophy of the Future.* Trans. Walter Kaufman. New York: Random House, 1966.

———. *The Portable Nietzsche.* Ed. and trans. Walter Kaufman. New York: Penguin, 1976.

Nishitani, Keiji. *The Self-Overcoming of Nihilism.* Trans. Graham Parkes with Setsuko Aihara. Albany: State University of New York, 1990.

Oberman, Heiko A. *Luther: Man between God and the Devil.* Trans. Eileen Walliser-Schwarzbart. New York and London: Doubleday, 1992.

Otto, Rudolf. *Das Heilige: über das Irrationale in der Idee des Göttlichen und sein Verhältnis zum Rationalen.* Gotha: Leopold Klotz Verlag, 1929.

———. *The Idea of the Holy: An Inquiry Into the Non-Rational in the Idea of the Divine and its Relation to the Rational.* Trans. John W. Harvey. London: Oxford University Press, 1924.

———. "Introduction." In Friedrich Schleiermacher, *On Religion: Speeches to Its Cultured Despisers,* trans. Salvator Attanasio. New York: Harper & Row, 1958.

———. *The Kingdom of God and the Son of Man: A Study in the History of Religion.* Trans. Floyd V. Filson and Bertram Lee Woolf. Grand Rapids, Mich.: Zondervan Publishing House, 1938.

———. *Naturalism and Religion.* Ed. W. D. Morrison, trans. J. Arthur Thomson and Margaret R. Thomson. London: Williams & Norgate / New York: G. P. Putnam's Sons, 1913.

———. *The Philosophy of Religion: Based on Kant and Fries.* Trans. E. B. Dicker. London: Williams & Norgate, 1931.

———. *Religious Essays: A Supplement to "The Idea of the Holy."* Trans. Brian Lunn. London and New York: Oxford University Press, 1937.

Pascal, Blaise. *Pensées.* Trans. A. J. Krailsheimer. Harmondsworth: Penguin, 1966.

Pattison, George. *Agnosis: Theology in the Void.* Basingstoke: Macmillan Press, 1996.

Pensy, Max. *Melancholy Dialectics: Walter Benjamin and the Play of Mourning.* Amherst: University of Massachusetts Press, 1993.

Perkins, Judith. *The Suffering Self: Pain and Narrative Representation in the Early Christian Era.* London: Routledge, 1995.

Plato. *The Republic.* Trans. Desmond Lee. Harmondsworth: Penguin, 1973.

Plotinus. *Collected Writings of Plotinus.* Trans. Thomas Taylor. Somerset: The Prometheus Trust, 1994.

Poland, Lynn. "The Idea of the Holy and the History of the Sublime." *Journal of Religion* 72 (1992): 175–197.

Praz, Mario. *The Romantic Agony.* Trans. Angus Davidson. London: Oxford University Press, 1960.

Pseudo-Dionysius. *The Complete Works.* Trans. Colm Luibheid. New York: Paulist Press, 1987.

Raphael, Melissa. "Feminism, Constructivism and Numinous Experience." *Religious Studies* 39 (1994): 511–526.

———. *Rudolf Otto and the Concept of Holiness.* Oxford: Clarendon Press, 1997.

Raposa, Michael L. *Boredom and the Religious Imagination.* Charlottesville: University Press of Virginia, 1999.

Raschke, Carl A. "The Deconstruction of God." In *Deconstruction and Theology,* ed. Thomas J. J. Altizer, Max A. Myers, Carl A. Raschke, Robert P. Sharlemann, Mark C. Taylor, and Charles E. Winquist. New York: Crossroad, 1982.

Rieger, Joerg. *God and the Excluded: Visions and Blind Spots in Contemporary Theology.* Minneapolis: Fortress Press, 2001.

Rubenstein, Mary-Jane. "Unknow Thyself: Apophaticism, Deconstruction, and Theology After Ontotheology." *Modern Theology* 19, no. 3 (July 2003): 387–417.

Rubenstein, Richard L., and John K. Roth. *Approaches to Auschwitz: The Legacy of the Holocaust.* London: SCM Press, 1987.

Rupp, Gordon. *The Righteousness of God: Luther Studies.* London: Hodder & Stoughton, 1953.

Sartre, Jean-Paul. *Being and Nothingness: An Essay on Phenomenological Ontology.* Trans. Hazel E. Barnes. London: Routledge, 1969.

———. *Words.* Trans. Irene Clephane. London: Hamish Hamilton, 1964.

Scharlemann, Robert P. "The Being of God When God Is Not Being God: Deconstructing the History of Theism." In *Deconstruction and Theology,* ed. Thomas J. J. Altizer, Max A. Myers, Carl A. Raschke, Robert P. Scharlemann, Mark C. Taylor, and Charles E. Winquist. New York: Crossroad, 1982.

Scharlemann, Robert P., ed. *Theology at the End of the Century: A Dialogue on the Postmodern.* Charlottesville: University Press of Virginia, 1990.

Schöndorf, Harold. "The Othering (Becoming Other) and Reconciliation of God in Hegel's *Phenomenology of Spirit.*" In *The Phenomenology of Spirit Reader: Critical and Interpretive Essays,* ed. Jon Stewart. Albany: State University of New York Press, 1998.

Screech, M. A. *Montaigne and Melancholy: The Wisdom of the Essays.* London: Gerald Duckworth & Co. Ltd., 1983.

Shrag, Calvin O. *The Self After Postmodernity.* New Haven: Yale University Press, 1997.

Sontag, Frederick. *The God of Evil: An Argument from the Existence of the Devil.* New York and London: Harper & Row, 1970.

Sorabji, Richard. *Emotion and Peace of Mind: From Stoic Agitation to Christian Temptation.* Oxford: Oxford University Press, 2000.

Stoker, Wessel. *Is the Quest for Meaning the Quest for God? The Religious Ascription of Meaning in Relation to the Secular Ascription of Meaning.* Trans. Lucy Jansen-Hofland and Henry Jansen. Amsterdam and Atlanta: Rodopi B. V., 1996.

Taylor, Charles. *The Ethics of Authenticity.* Cambridge, Mass.: Harvard University Press, 1991.

——. *Sources of the Self: The Making of the Modern Identity.* Cambridge: Cambridge University Press, 1989.

Taylor, Mark C. *Deconstructing Theology.* New York: Crossroad / Chicago: Scholar's Press, 1982.

——. *Erring: A Postmodern A/Theology.* Chicago: University of Chicago Press, 1984.

Thorson, James A. "Religion and Anxiety: Which Anxiety? Which Religion?" In *Handbook of Religion and Mental Health,* ed. Harold G. Koening. London and San Diego: Academic Press, 1998.

Tillich, Paul. *The Courage To Be.* London: Nisbet & Co., 1952.

——. *The Protestant Era.* Trans. James Luther Adams. London: Nisbet & Co., 1951.

——. "The Recovery of the Prophetic Tradition." In *Theological Writings. Volume 6,* ed. Gert Hummel. Berlin and New York: De Gruyter / Berlin: Evangelisches Verlagswerk, 1992.

——. *The Shaking of the Foundations.* New York: Charles Scribner's Sons, 1952.

——. *Systematic Theology,* vols. 1–3. Hertfordshire: James Nisbet & Co., 1968.

Tracy, David. "Response to Adriaan Peperzak on Transcendence." In *Ethics as First Philosophy: The Significance of Emmanuel Levinas for Philosophy,* ed. Adriaan T. Peperzak. New York: Routledge, 1995.

Turner, Denys. *The Darkness of God: Negativity in Christian Mysticism.* Cambridge: Cambridge University Press, 1995.

Vahanian, Gabriel. *The Death of God: The Culture of Our Post-Christian Era.* New York: Georges Braziller, 1961.

Vawter, Bruce. *Job and Jonah: Questioning the Hidden God.* New York: Paulist Press, 1983.

Walther, Bo Kampmann. "Web of Shudders: Sublimity in Søren Kierkegaard's *Fear and Trembling.*" *Modern Language Notes* 112, no. 5: *Comparative Literature Issue* (Dec. 1997): 753–785.

Ward, Graham, ed. *The Postmodern God: A Theological Reader.* Oxford: Blackwell, 1997.

Ware, Owen. "Rudolf Otto's *Idea of the Holy:* A Reappraisal." *Heythrop Journal* 48, no. 1 (2007): 48–60.

Weil, Simone. *Gravity and Grace.* London: Routledge, 1963.

Westphal, Merold. "Faith as the Overcoming of Ontological Xenophobia." In *The Otherness of God,* ed. Orrin F. Summerell. Charlottesville: University Press of Virginia, 1998.

——. *God, Guilt, and Death: An Existential Phenomenology of Religion.* Bloomington: Indiana University Press, 1984.

——. *Overcoming Onto-Theology: Toward a Postmodern Christian Faith.* New York: Fordham University Press, 2001.

——. *Suspicion and Faith: The Religious Uses of Modern Atheism.* Grand Rapids, Mich.: Williams B. Eerdmans, 1993.

Wettstein, Howard. "Doctrine." *Faith and Philosophy* 14, no. 4 (Oct. 1997): 423–443.

Wiesel, Elie. *Four Hasidic Masters and Their Struggle Against Melancholy.* Notre Dame, Ind.: University of Notre Dame Press, 1978.

Wolfson, Elliot. *Through a Speculum That Shines.* Princeton: Princeton University Press, 1997.

18, 23, 24, 25, 26–28, 31–42, 78, 92,
100, 103, 169, 198n61, 199nn92,99,
208n47; of despair, 8, 23; *deus otiosus,* xxii, 91, 101; as enemy, 39, 62,
102–104; existence and essence of, 28;
face of, xxii, 49, 64–67, 68, 100, 132,
157; hiddenness of, xiii, 66–67, 80, 88,
128–129; Gift of Godself, xxiii, 30, 99;
God-in-Godself, xiii, xx, xxi, xxii, 28,
49, 99, 126, 198n81; God-relationship,
xxiii, 41, 58, 84, 88, 103, 105–106,
109, 115, 121, 125, 129, 130, 133, 140,
145–148, 178, 194n10, 219n64, 221n19;
goodness of, 86; grief of, 42, 170–180,
189; holiness of, xvi, 118, 149, 152–154,
207n19, 215n102; the Holy Other, xv,
xviii, xix, 9, 48–49, 86, 116, 170, 177;
as idol, 25–31; image of (*also* resemblance), xxiv, 178–180, 185–186, 192;
love of, xxiii, 64–67, 85, 86, 100, 104,
139, 144–145, 147, 170–180, 190; name
of (*'ehyeh asher 'ehyeh*), 28–31, 44,
70, 99–100; objective reality of, xxi;
omnipotence of, 85–86, 88, 100, 115,
131, 187; otherness of, xvi, xxi, 32, 35,
38, 42; *posteriora dei,* 65, 67, 68; as
projection, 26; proof of the existence
of, 63; rebellion against, 26–27, 149,
168, 169, 212n30; silence of, 25, 43,
96; sublimity of, 8, 40, 48, 83, 147,
154, 214n84, 215n88; unconditioned,
the, 107, 116, 133; union with, 86,
222n24; Unmoved Mover, 28; will of,
107–108, 112, 128, 134–136, 218n44,
219n64. *See also* alterity; before God;
forgiveness (*also* forgiveness of sins);
gaze, the; Holy, the (*also* the Holy
One); impossibility; unknown, the;
Wholly Other
the god, as absolutely different, 4, 7, 171,
205n60, 222n27; as the unknown, 7,
46, 48, 85, 201n168
God-forsakenness, 32, 90, 91, 117, 122,
134, 137, 142–148, 206n73, 220n68; of
Christ, xxiii, 134, 137, 142–148; forsaking God, 91, 146
Gooch, Todd, 73

grace, 8, 40, 100, 114, 132, 136, 165, 166,
176, 178, 188, 215n102
Gregory the Great, Pope, 54
guilt, 6, 7, 26–27, 117–118, 122, 125–126,
128, 142, 152, 153, 159, 166, 172–175,
188, 189, 211n10; and innocence, 27,
117, 130

Hampson, Daphne, 121
Hegel, G. W. F., 12, 16, 20, 31, 77,
92–96, 98–100, 112, 160–162,
199nn96,97,98,99, 211nn10,11,12,14,15;
Hegelianism, xx, 169
Heinecken, Martin J., 48
Holocaust, 79–80, 190–191, 211n3
Holy, the (*also* the Holy One), 1, 40, 42,
48–49, 67, 71, 72, 74, 75, 80, 84, 118,
127, 135, 150, 152–154, 170
hope, 63, 162–163, 203n8

imagination, 57, 77, 109–111, 114–115,
117, 128, 130–131, 156–159, 209n77,
218n43; fantasy (*also* the fantastic),
xxiii, 8, 27, 63, 83–84, 130–131, 156–157,
209nn77,78; idol of, 25; intoxication,
8, 81–84, 109–111, 159, 164, 166
impossibility, xxiii, 121, 131, 135, 139, 144,
146, 148–150, 155, 163, 165, 167–171,
176–181, 184–185, 187, 188–192; divine
possibility, xxiii, 30–31, 40, 61, 135,
146–149, 170, 172, 176–181, 184–185,
187, 188–192. *See also* forgiveness
(*also* forgiveness of sins); possibility
inclosing reserve (*also* Indesluttethed),
xviii, 6, 7, 166. *See also* despair
infinite qualitative difference (*also* absolute difference), xi–xxiv, 1–9, 31–42,
44, 47, 48, 49, 51, 62, 64, 65, 66, 68,
70, 72, 73, 76, 84, 94, 97, 99, 103, 107,
112, 122, 133, 137–140, 142, 145, 148,
151, 159, 177–179, 194nn11,12, 196n4,
199n96, 213n47; as forgiveness, xii,
xxii, 7, 72, 158, 167–170, 173, 176, 179,
181–192; as sin, xii, 4, 6, 48–49, 72,
149, 152, 154, 156, 158, 173
irony, 19, 154, 155, 169, 178, 204n43
Isaac, 41, 191, 197n25, 212nn22,37

SIMON D. PODMORE is Gordon Milburn Junior Research Fellow at Trinity College and British Academy Postdoctoral Fellow in the Faculty of Theology, University of Oxford. He holds a doctorate in systematic theology from King's College, University of London, and has published in *Literature and Theology, Journal of Psychology & Theology, International Kierkegaard Commentary,* and elsewhere. He is also the Secretary of The Søren Kierkegaard Society of the United Kingdom.

CPSIA information can be obtained at www.ICGtesting.com
Printed in the USA
LVOW041335231212

312943LV00003B/7/P